THE LOST LEGIONS OF
FROMELLES

The mysteries behind one of the most
devastating battles of the Great War

PETER BARTON

Translations from the original German
by Michael Forsyth

Constable • London

For Hester, Stanley, Victor and Kitty

CONSTABLE

First published by Allen & Unwin, Australia, 2014

This paperback edition published in Great Britain in 2014 by Constable

3 5 7 9 10 8 6 4 2

A CIP catalogue record for this book
is available from the British Library.

ISBN 978-1-47211-712-0 (Trade paperback)

Typeset in 11/15pt Minion by Midland Typesetters, Australia
Printed and bound in Great Britain by
CPI Group (UK) Ltd, Croydon CR0 4YY

Constable
is an imprint of
Little, Brown Book Group
Carmelite House
50 Victoria Embankment
London EC4Y 0DZ

An Hachette UK Company
www.hachette.co.uk

www.littlebrown.co.uk

CONTENTS

—➤●◀—

LIST OF MAPS

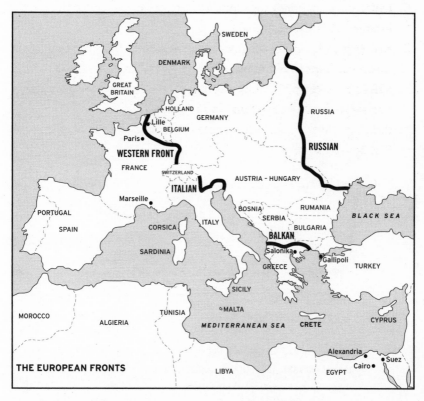

Map 1: Theatres of war in Western Europe and the Middle East

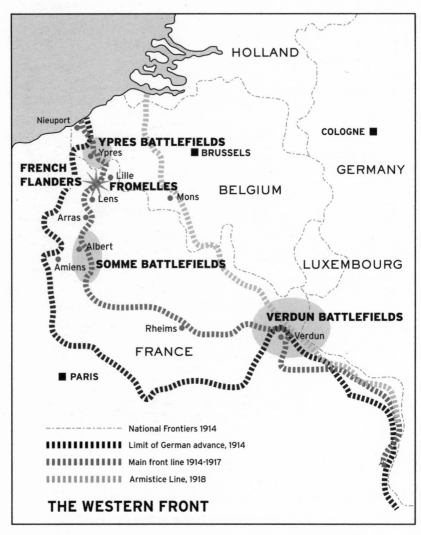

Map 2: The Western Front showing the major battlegrounds. Fromelles is in French Flanders.

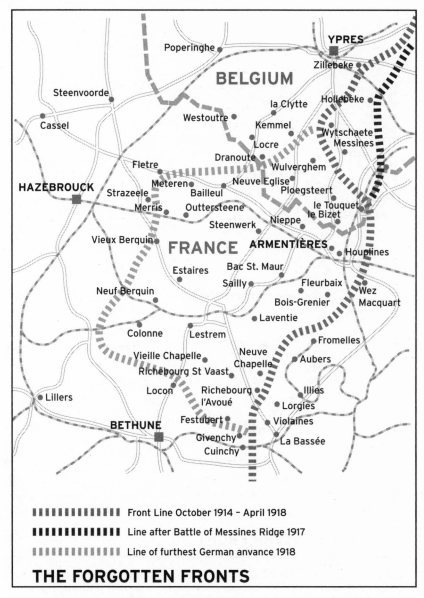

THE FORGOTTEN FRONTS

Map 3: The towns and villages of French Flanders, and the positioning of the front line between September 1914 and November 1918.

PREFACE

On the way back we spent some time in the old No Man's Land of four years duration, round about Fauquissart and Aubers. It was a morbid but intensely interesting occupation tracing the various battles amongst the hundreds of skulls, bones and remains scattered thickly about. The progress of our successive attacks could be clearly seen from the types of equipment on the skeletons; soft caps denoting 1914 and early 1915, then respirators, then steel helmets marking attacks in 1916. Also Australian slouch hats, used in the costly and abortive attack in 1916. There were many of these poor remains all along the German wire.

Major Phillip Harold Pilditch, Royal Field Artillery,
The War Diary of an Artillery Officer, 1914–1918

It was on Thursday 30 July 1914 that warning telegrams from London arrived in Melbourne and Wellington: a European war against Germany and Austria–Hungary appeared unavoidable; Britain was mobilising. Three days later Australia followed suit, placing her forces on a war footing and activating coastal defences. By the evening of 6 August Australia and New Zealand had both offered an Expeditionary Force. Having converged upon King George Sound at Albany, Western Australia, on 1 November

1914 the initial convoy of twenty-eight troop ships set sail, striking out towards the first military action of the recently federated Common-wealths. The ripples from their bow waves still lap upon the shores of Australasia. Their final destination was not to be, as all on board expected and probably desired—France—but the Gallipoli Peninsula, a Turkish battleground on the very seam of Europe and Asia. There they would for eight months struggle alongside French, British and Indian allies in a calamitous campaign that achieved no strategic benefit for either the Empire or the Entente.

Meanwhile, on the Western Front, Britain, India, Canada and France were suffering a chain of revelatory malfunctions. After Gallipoli, the men of the Australian Imperial Force (AIF) reorganised, reinforced and recon-ditioned in Egypt, and prepared themselves for their opening engagement in France, an assault that began at 6.00 p.m. on 19 July 1916 near the small village of Fromelles. Although the Somme, Arras, Passchendaele and the great and crucial clashes of 1918 were still part of an unimaginable future, the subsequent fourteen hours of vicious combat were to prove the most cata-strophic of the one thousand days of Anzac presence on the Western Front.

And so from the vast and distant universe that was Australia, with all its air, light and prosperity, the Diggers were flung into the foul gutter of Flanders, again to struggle alongside the British Tommies. Life in the trenches was a strange blend of boredom, dread, uncertainty, discomfort, hard labour, violence and sudden death that demanded a peculiar forti-tude to endure with sanity intact. Hope seldom entered the equation. Men were by necessity fatalistic, and yet supported by a tide of intimate and deeply cherished comradeship that the presence of mutual mortal danger engendered and cultivated—'mateship', in the Australian vernacular. It was the first time that most of the middle- and upper-class soldiers had been pressed into close living proximity with workers and labourers. The enforced intimacy generated degrees of understanding that had never before existed, or indeed been able to exist; it was an understanding that frequently led to profound respect. Partly in this manner, the Great War began to change the social structures of a score of nations.

In 1919, for both Australian and Briton, there was a harsh homecoming. The war had almost bankrupted that seemingly invulnerable edifice, the British Empire. Civilian life was altered, and work hard to find. The personal legacy of the war was profound. For legions of men the mental and physical consequences of the conflict would remain all their lives. In the Britain of the 1960s there were still hospital wards filled with uncured and incurable victims. The last of them, Private David Ireland of the Black Watch, died in Scotland in 2001; he had been in psychiatric care since 1924—seventy-seven years.

As ever, for such is human nature, in all the belligerent nations buoyancy and optimism returned. The cadence of 'normal' life resumed, and with it came the sense of a more certain future. For many families, however, a particular form of nightmare persisted. Every theatre of conflict concealed a multi-national 'lost' army. Along the thin ribbon of Europe that had so recently been the Western Front, in 1919 there still lay unfound the remains of half a million soldiers. No family ever surrendered the hope that one day the body of their man, their boy, their child, would be recovered and given a grave, a grave that might be visited. And yet after the Armistice of November 1918 the search for the missing was officially drawn to a close within thirty-six months, far sooner than most had anticipated. It was a decision that brought anguish, anger and misery, leaving a void in the lives and hearts of millions. The Fromelles Project, which began in 2006 with the scrutiny of a piece of French pastureland and ended in 2010 with the exhumation and reburial in a new cemetery of the 250 soldiers found there, has shown that that void endures until through knowledge generations long dislocated are reconnected with the true legacy of war: irreplaceable human loss. That recognition frequently seeds the demand to know and understand, but like the poppy, conditions must be perfect before germination can occur. Above all, the ground in which that seed lies must be regularly disturbed.

In the case of Fromelles and Pheasant Wood, the disturbance was created by a Melbourne teacher by the name of Lambis Englezos. Since he began his extraordinary campaign at the end of the 20th century, many people, even those unrelated by blood ties, have formed a close personal and emotional relationship with Fromelles, and especially the men who for over ninety years lay in the oak-shaded graves bordering what the Bavarians once called *Fasanen-Wäldchen* (Pheasant Wood).

I have been associated with the project since 2003, being part of the team that carried out the non-invasive geophysical study in 2006, and present at the haunting discovery of the remains themselves in 2007. At the same time I was exploring a mountain of Australian, British, but primarily Bavarian, records that described in extraordinary detail the events that had led to the deaths of the very men whose remains I was to gaze upon. The combination had a profound effect, upon myself, upon the team, and upon everyone who came into contact with the site and the story.

It is not unusual for First World War historians who spend as much time working on the battlefields as in their office, to uncover human remains—such adventitious finds are almost unavoidable: it had happened to me on several occasions. Fromelles, however, was atypical: here, long before the archaeological trowels appeared, we were actively seeking not just evidence of burial, but the names of the dead. There was thus a unique practical and emotional dynamic in play, and as a result the challenge for all who became involved in the project was simple: the work must be worthy of the sacrifice.

In forensic archaeology and anthropology one sees, feels and smells things that cannot be expressed by the written word. When the Pheasant Wood graves were finally opened in the spring of 2007, the events of 19/20 July 1916 lay before our eyes and beneath our fingers. Each night during the dig images loitered in the mind, and a distinctive scent lingered in the nostrils. They still do. Archival research thus assumed an importance far greater than the customary sifting, selection and translation of dusty papers to produce a report, colourise the pages of a book or enhance the frames of a film. These documents told us why those men came to be there, who killed whom, where and how they met their end, who they were and where they came from.

Even to the untrained eye, it was plain to see that many of those young men had experienced the very essence of warfare. They had not died 'impersonally' by shell, mortar or gas, but in close face-to-face, hand-to-hand combat. There was nothing glorious about the prospect. The graves were shabby and undignified, the sights cruel, and the scene as a whole profoundly unheroic. Indeed, few Diggers or Tommies who attacked at Fromelles in July 1916 were granted the opportunity to be heroic. Many had never before been in action, and some would never actually see a German, let alone have the opportunity of killing one.

At the end of the proving process, when all the graves had been scruti-nised, conditions assessed and numbers calculated, came the most difficult task of all: the protection and re-interment of the remains before full recovery the following year. To an archaeologist, exposing one's 'treasure' and then covering it up again is deeply counter-intuitive; in this case it was surprisingly disturbing. The men were ultimately to be buried three times: by the Bavarians in 1916, by the Glasgow team in 2007, and by the Commonwealth War Graves Commission in 2010.

But the story is actually greater than this, for the men who lay for ninety-five years in the pits before Pheasant Wood had legions of antecedents. For almost two years before July 1916 others occupied the same trenches, carried out the same tasks, felt the same emotions, and lived and died in similar fashion. A thousand or more who had earlier shared the same fate still lie nearby—somewhere as yet unfound. The circumstances of their deaths in 1914 and 1915 are integral to the disaster of 1916. This volume must there-fore begin at the beginning, at the moment war first arrived in Fromelles.

In historical research there are three classes of source material: primary, secondary and finding aids. A primary source is evidence that offers an intimate view of an event, often from an eyewitness. It can take the form of a diary, an interview, letters, minutes, official records gathered at the time, photographs and film. Secondary sources are one step removed: interpret-ations by a third party, i.e. material produced after an event, usually (but not always) by someone who was not a witness. Examples include books, magazine and newspaper articles, unit histories and biographies. The third category is the 'finding aid': documents compiled by librarians, curators or archivists containing information about the nature and scale of an indi-vidual record or a collection. Often appended with notes, they are used by researchers to determine whether data may be relevant to their work.

Although several published works on the 1916 battle existed prior to the commencement of the Fromelles Project, each employing a wide-ranging selection of Anglo–Australian primary sources, no author had elected to investigate the corresponding German accounts. Given that the battle was a fourteen-hour encounter with such catastrophic and far-reaching results, this is a peculiar exclusion, because so much uniquely valuable informa-tion was to be gained by gathering comprehensive comparative versions of events from both sides of No Man's Land; indeed, it is essential, for the most intriguing and indeed mysterious part of the battle was fought within Bavarian territory. In many Great War titles the German narrative is sometimes so superficial as to make the enemy practically invisible. Probably the best-known Fromelles publication, Robin Corfield's extraordinary but disorderly and frequently confusing 500-page *Don't Forget Me, Cobber*, relied for its 'enemy view' upon Bavarian regimental histories and propagandised newspaper reports—secondary sources. As we shall see, the latter—a fascinating animal—may be analysed. It is an enthralling exercise. As for the former, they should certainly not be regarded as inaccurate; indeed, in my opinion some of the most important books to appear in recent years are by Jack Sheldon and Ralph J. Whitehead. They concern themselves solely with the German narrative, but base their work primarily on published accounts: regimental histories. By reason of their necessarily abbreviated nature, however, such histories are treacherously incomplete, and in a detailed scrutiny cannot sufficiently nourish the historian's needs. They also require corroboration. For example, Dr Fridolin Solleder's *Vier Jahre Westfront: Geschichte des Regiments List R.I.R. 16* (Adolf Hitler's unit) appears an impressive tome, yet its several hundred pages represent only a fraction of the primary sources upon which the book was based. In *Through German Eyes: The British on the Somme 1916*, Christopher Duffy examines Bavarian primary source intelligence documents, touching briefly upon Fromelles; he reveals the wider potential. So too does Dr Robert Foley's work on the evolution of tactics. As far as I know, however, this is the first time a 'complete' action has been comparatively evaluated through the primary sources of both belligerents.

The work from which most publications take their initial lead is Volume III of Charles Bean's *Official History of Australia in the War of 1914–1918* (*OHA*), and Bean's extensive collection of wartime diaries, folders and notebooks in the Australian War Memorial (AWM), Canberra (all available online). As a result of Bean's familiarity with the 'nursery' sectors of French Flanders and the men who commanded the neophyte Anzac units, there were few who knew better than he how calamitous an opening for the Australian forces Fromelles—and indeed certain other preceding but ostensibly lesser events—had been. Yet in their official works, both Bean and his British counterpart, Wilfrid Miles—author of the corresponding volume of the 'British Official History' (entitled *History of the Great War Based on Official Documents*) covering the era during which Fromelles was fought—must have continually posed questions that only primary German sources could answer. Many of them were never answered, which leaves a truncated narrative lacking certain essential contexts, especially in relation to 'failed' enterprises.

When it comes to writing of such things, the bitter pill of defeat requires a variety of sweetening agents, which often take the form of drawn-out descriptions, justifications and rationalisations: the printed politics of disappointment. It is a fact that the reporting of failure (when it is reported as such) always commands many more column inches than success; it is also a fact that although they are by no means alone, many narrators and writers of popular First World War Australian military histories possess a certain reputation for embellishment, a propensity that Charles Bean called 'romancing'. Research has revealed that Bean himself was not averse to bending or even ignoring unpalatable facts; indeed, it was part of the war reporter's work, and of course his copy was subject to the censor's hovering red pencil. But there is rather more to the story than this. During the war Bean was a co-creator of an Australian national narrative and new individualism: the Anzac legend. With it came a heavy responsibility.

For its era, however, and indeed in comparison with British accounts, it must be said that the *OHA* is remarkably comprehensive, sensitive and splendidly personal: there is little talk of 'other ranks' in Bean. But it is nevertheless not as three-dimensional and candid as many might believe. The author was hamstrung by a shortage of time (the *OHA* appeared in 1929 whereas Wilfrid Miles' volume was published in 1938), but most importantly by his inability to *personally* scrutinise the full range of German primary source documents relating to the early period of Australian presence on the Western Front. Despite a 119-page chapter containing detail to the level of individuals, and many a reference to German records, we now know there are gaps in Bean's narrative, which he had neither the material, the time, nor in several cases the inclination, to fill. There is evidence of intentional omission of key facts.

The *OHA* was of course produced primarily for Australians, and therefore had to relate the Australian tale. On the surface it is a splendid strategic, tactical and personal appreciation of events, all expertly condensed and combined. Within, one finds accounts of inferior leadership, shabby planning and misguided tactics; of appalling communication and questionable decisions and actions at all levels; of unnecessary loss and wanton cruelty. But there is much more to this story than the faults that derived solely from the Allied camp. What is missing from Bean's work is an adequate comparative version of events as experienced by the enemy. It has become clear that without the Bavarian accounts it is impossible to generate an accurate narrative of the catastrophe of 19 July 1916, or indeed valid perceptions of the period of Digger occupation of French Flanders.

The German Army of the First World War was not a single entity. On the unification of the country in January 1871, the formation of the Army of the Realm (*Deutsches Reichsheer*) brought a diverse collection of smaller States under the command of four kingdoms: Bavaria, Prussia, Saxony and Württemberg. Each kingdom subsequently formed a dedicated army commanded by its respective king. Prussia became the national nucleus, with Kaiser Wilhelm II as commander-in-chief, and the nation's capital, Berlin, forming the seat of the 'Great Headquarters', the *Oberste Heeresleitung* (OHL). In 1914, although unified under the Kaiser, each kingdom still had its own war ministry to which all military records found their way. Rather than being assembled primarily in one location therefore, as is the case, for example, with the AWM in Canberra or National Archives in London, German documents were stored in several separate and distinct regional repositories.

It is a popular misconception that Second World War bombing destroyed the majority of German First World War records. This is true (and only in part) of Prussian and Saxon archives, whose collections were seriously damaged as a result of Allied air raids on Potsdam and Dresden in 1945. In the Fromelles and Aubers sectors, from March 1915 until September 1916 the adversary was Bavarian, and its army, war ministry and military archive—the *Kriegsarchiv*—were based in Bavaria's State capital, Munich.

Although the buildings carry the scars of Second World War bombing, they and their contents survived. The collection is believed to be the most complete of any of its kind in Germany. For day-to-day detail on actions, prisoners, wounded and dead—and of course burials—in relation to the Bavarian military of the First World War, it is therefore the principal font of information.

The records of the Cabinet Office (CAB 45) in the National Archives at Kew in London show that Charles Bean received German material for his *OHA* via the offices of Captain J.J.W. Herbertson, an English officer who for some years after the war served as political officer for the Inter-Allied Rhineland High Commission based in Koblenz. It was one of Herbertson's duties to take Bean's questionnaires and pass them to a German colleague by the name of Stenger. The records suggest that *Archivrat* Stenger was a well-educated man and an accomplished speaker, translator and writer of English. The Federal Archive at Potsdam in which he worked had been set up in 1919 as a result of a suite of stipulations within the Versailles Treaty that required the dissolution of certain martial institutions. The storage of military records was the subject of one such clause, and as a result during Bean's period of writing in the 1920s all war-associated documents were gathered from the archives of the various German kingdoms and concentrated in Potsdam.

For more than a decade after 1918 the archive was a hive of activity, for official, regimental and divisional historians from every German kingdom were obliged to utilise the facility when compiling their own post-war histories—over a thousand of them. Stenger may have assisted his own countrymen in their tasks, but he clearly also carried out research for foreign historians, scrutinising original war diaries and supplying typed copies for Herbertson and others to translate, or indeed doing the work himself. Although we do not learn why, Bean's papers reveal that he preferred Stenger's translations to Herbertson's. Probably because of the sheer scale of the wider commission and the associated time constraints, Bean's questions relating to the Fromelles action were simple, defined and—given the outcome and symbolism of the action—surprisingly few.

Stenger appeared to be under no obligation to deliver a specific quantity of detail in his answers.

The most important aspect of this research period from the point of view of our present appreciation of the final published *OHA* narrative, is that at no time does Stenger appear to stray beyond boundaries: he provides circumscribed answers to circumscribed questions. Nevertheless, it is enough to distinguish where Bean came upon instances when he had to make a delicate choice: what to include and exclude. In having no direct access to many interrelated enemy documents, and such meagre opportunities for wider selection of material or lateral research, he may have been unaware of the monumental scope of German wartime record-keeping. For example, there is no indication that he ever saw more than a small percentage of the extraordinary and revelatory array of maps, plans, drawings and photographs that so extensively illuminate not only the unfolding of the fourteen hours of the Fromelles battle but also the events before and especially after the battle, including the order for the digging of graves at Pheasant Wood.

At the time of writing, the relevant German unit histories were largely extant and available. German material quoted in both the *OHA* and its British counterpart derives, primarily, although certainly (and importantly) not entirely, from *post-war* accounts as opposed to those produced at the time of the action. This is a most significant aspect because the two sources, even if written by one and the same person (which was sometimes the case), are found to differ greatly in scale and thus content, tone and style. German primary source operational documents are matter-of-fact, extraordinarily comprehensive and often brutal in their candour, sometimes to the point of self-incrimination. They are also self-deprecating, self-critical and profoundly incisive in analysis, which is exactly what is required if one wishes to properly scrutinise an incident and improve the performance of a unit that is standing stolidly and deliberately on the defence, which at the time of Fromelles is exactly what the Germans were doing in French Flanders. They show not just a willingness to learn from mistakes, but almost a paranoid preoccupation in doing so. Where credit is seen to be due, German chroniclers seldom fail to praise their enemy, for they too were a key source of inspiration and education. Bean took careful note of this aspect.

There therefore exists between primary and secondary sources a fundamental distinction in approach, ambience and content. By their very nature, unit histories are able to utilise only a fraction of the mountain range of data upon which they are based. Most importantly, they lack the enlightening minute day-to-day details, the authors being constrained by the requirement to produce a readable narrative. Primary source war diaries and reports were subject to no such limitations.

But there is more. Being the 'victors', British, Australian and other Entente chroniclers were free to be as pompous and smug as they wished, and to resume the long-established tone of superiority employed by the administrators of a vast and powerful empire. Some British and Australian unit histories may indeed be sober and serious, but others to their detriment take advantage of the climate of victory to produce a narrative that is almost painfully jingoistic. One finds scorn and derision born from triumphal hindsight; indeed, certain volumes could readily be employed to produce dictionaries of heroic adjectives.

Although none are as uncluttered by class-consciousness as Bean's socially balanced history, nevertheless his work too remains chauvinistic. The Anzac legend—or myth as it is today often termed—gets in the way. As a Briton, I have no right to comment on what the term means to Australians, the reasons for its seeding, and why it has been so carefully nurtured ever since; in the context of this study, it is not its existence that matters, but the events that contributed to its creation and obligatory subsequent nurture.

Having made the transition from journalist to historian, in the preface to Volume I of the *OHA* Charles Bean opened a window upon his perspectives:

> *In his search for rigid accuracy the writer was guided by one deliberate and settled principle. The more he saw and knew of the men and officers of the Australian Imperial Force the more fully did the writer become convinced that the only memorial which could be worthy of them was the bare and uncoloured story of their part in the war. From the moment when, early in the war, he realised this, his duty became*

strangely simple—to record the plain and absolute truth so far as it was within his limited power to compass it. To the men and officers of the Australian Forces, both those who live and those who fell, whose comradeship is his proudest and dearest memory, he dedicates this effort to produce a history in which he has striven to attain a truthfulness worthy of them and their nation.

These words confirm that the *OHA* was more than simply a history, it was a textual shrine. The work thus demanded great care in its construction— what should or could be included or excluded? Without an accurate and balanced reporting of events, readers' perceptions are automatically defective. Official and unit histories—including the *OHA*—do not offer this balance. They were not designed to do so, for at times fidelity and duty to one's countrymen and their sacrifice outweighed absolute truthfulness. The result is history written from the inside looking in.

The works of Bean's German counterparts suffer from a similar disease, but one contracted from a different host: the sense of betrayal and bitterness that characterised the close of hostilities, combined with a national humiliation carefully engineered by the Allies to compound the sensation of dishonour to its limit. This potent blend sometimes led to the use of language so belligerent that it degrades the value of the account as an historical document.

Continuing this theme, in recent years there has been debate as to which official history, Australian or British, is 'more truthful'. This is both an academic and an unanswerable question. In 2003, Donald Rumsfeld, then United States Secretary of Defense, probably encapsulated the problem in his celebrated and indeed remarkable statement: 'there are known knowns; there are things we know we know. We also know that there are known unknowns; that is to say, we know there are some things that we do not know. But there are also unknown unknowns—the ones we don't know we don't know.'

The passage makes complete sense, and its message may be applied to any action anywhere in the world during any *period* in military history, including the 1916, 1915 and 1914 actions at Fromelles and the way they have since been recounted.

One wonders how Bean's account of Fromelles might have looked had the full Bavarian resource been available to him. We shall never know, but it may well have remained exactly as it is. The existence of anomalies, especially inconvenient ones, does not guarantee that they will be laid out before the reader; certainly, if one finds a collection of inconsistencies relating to an action of only fourteen hours, one may assume there will be many more in a war lasting four years. During the ten years of research for the Fromelles Project and this book, I was reminded time and again of the critical necessity to preserve a vigorous scepticism, for many long-established perceptions were assaulted by alternative—and of course equally valid—German appreciations.

I have not offered orders of battle, artillery arrangements, detail of lines of communication, etc., simply because there is too great a wider story to tell. They can be found online, in Bean's *OHA*, and in other titles such as *Don't Forget Me, Cobber*, Paul Cobb's *Fromelles 1916*, Roger Lee's *The Battle of Fromelles: 1916*, Patrick Lindsay's *Fromelles*, and Captain A.D. Ellis' *The Story of the Fifth Australian Division*, all of which I recommend be consulted in conjunction with this volume, for each adds valuable material for combination and contrast. Likewise, because it would occupy so much space, a full set of footnotes and references have been omitted from this volume; they will follow in another format elsewhere. A basic source list and bibliography has been included.

It has been my primary intention to recount the story—the surprising story—of the spring and summer of 1916 as painstakingly recorded by the troops occupying the eastern side of No Man's Land: the 6th Bavarian Reserve Infantry Division and their parent unit *Armee-Oberkommando 6*— the true perpetrators of the catastrophe that was Fromelles, and to amalgamate it with key aspects of the Anglo–Australian narrative. To do this, except on a few comparative occasions, I have eschewed flawed post-war narratives in favour of the much more edifying and extensive primary contemporary Bavarian documents upon which they were based.

Integral to the Fromelles story, within this narrative there also lies an account of the work of the Red Cross, the remarkable band of ferociously neutral humanitarians with apparently infinite patience and sensitivity who carried news both good and ill from the trenches and shell-holes of France and Flanders to doorsteps across the globe. There is a section on the interrogations of Anglo–Australian prisoners of war immediately after the battle, and their transformation into propaganda. To complete the circle there is an account of my own involvement with the admirable group whose resolve eventually obliged the authorities to investigate the Pheasant Wood graves, followed by an analysis of how those graves may have been overlooked in the post-war years.

My last word at this early stage is cautionary. Even when the contents of this volume are amalgamated with all other writings on Fromelles, the product will still remain merely a partial narrative. Curiosity and the desire for knowledge is an eternal process. In military history one discovery regularly propagates another, which means there will always be fresh accounts—and therefore fresh perspectives.

Peter Barton
August, 2013

INTRODUCTION

—◦◦◦—

*By about 8.30 p.m. the whole trench was back in our hands with the
exception of a 50-metre stretch astride the Rouges Bancs–Tommybrücke
road, where the enemy held out doggedly until 3.00 a.m. when 4/RIR16
(Divisional Reserve, Oberleutnant Gebhard) stormed their position and
forced them into submission. On the left flank of the area under attack,
where the British had broken in to Sector f in the morning, the trench was
recaptured by 6 p.m. Here, without external support, the trench garrison
drove in from left and right and trapped the British in a pincer movement;
no prisoners were taken.*

Report dated 29 May 1915 on an action at Fromelles by the
6th Bavarian Reserve Infantry Division

The area referred to here as being 'astride the Rouges Bancs–Tommybrücke
road' was the scene of a slaughter of British soldiers during the action
known as the Battle of Aubers Ridge, 9 May 1915. That ground is today
partly occupied by a memorial park within which lie the tumbled concrete
remnants of the old German front-line defences and a larger-than-life
bronze representation of an Australian soldier carrying a wounded comrade
from the field of battle.

Neither the park nor the sculpture, however, were designed to commemorate the 1915 action, but one that was fought at the same location more than a year later: the encounter of 19/20 July 1916 known to the Australian nation as the Battle of Fromelles. The neatly kept patch of lawns and paths is the Australian Memorial Park, and the statue is the celebrated 'Cobbers Memorial'.

Some 300 metres away, to the north-west and located in the old No Man's Land, lies the VC Corner Cemetery and Memorial. Within its walls lie the remains of 410 unidentifiable soldiers. The cemetery's name has its origin in a yet earlier British enterprise: what one might call the 'first' battle of Fromelles, which took place at the birth of trench warfare, in December 1914. After the war, during the period of official recovery between 1918 and 1921, the bodies of soldiers who died in all three actions were gathered from the fields and reburied. In preparation for the VC Corner Cemetery, however, each body was carefully identified by nationality and equally carefully separated to make certain that *only* Australians were interred there. Engraved upon a screen at the cemetery's rear are the names of 1300 missing Diggers—men with no known grave. The battlefield upon which the cemetery and screen were established has since become *their* battlefield—an Australian battlefield. To learn the names of missing British soldiers who died there between August 1914 and November 1918 one must visit the Loos or Ploegsteert Memorials, each more than 20 kilometres from the site.

At neither the memorial park nor the cemetery is there reference to any pre- or post-July 1916 actions, nor indeed mention of the endeavours of any nation but Australia. These omissions mean that few Australian visitors are aware of the many other events that took place precisely where they stand—and the numerous chilling similarities between each one. If they were, their appreciation and understanding of what happened to their forefathers in July 1916, and indeed *why* it happened, would be greatly enhanced.

The three major encounters at Fromelles—those of December 1914, May 1915 and July 1916—were fought in exactly the same sector and upon exactly the same ground. The latter two actions unfolded in almost the same way, and on each occasion the final German *coup de grâce* took place at precisely the same location, astride the Rouges Bancs road and within the boundaries of today's Australian Memorial Park. Even more uncannily, the number of missing as a result of the British attack in 1915 is almost identical to the Australian figure for July 1916: approximately 1300 men. The most important factor of all, however, is how the lessons learned in 1915 influenced the catastrophe of the following summer.

At present the history of the Fromelles sector is at best truncated, at worst hidden completely. The danger of obscuring the wider context of conflict in favour of a single fourteen-hour event is a real one. No battle-field that witnessed four years of positional warfare should be seen as frozen in time.

In 1914 French, Indian and British troops fought side by side here, stemming the German advance during the Battle of Armentières, and thus playing their part in the creation of the impasse that was fully established during that December. There then followed the earliest set-piece encounters of the period, plus an extraordinary and well-documented Christmas Truce. The 9 May 1915 battle provided a bloody and bizarre rehearsal for 19 July 1916. In late September 1915, a string of diversionary assaults were launched at nearby Bois-Grenier, Neuve Chapelle and Givenchy to assist the grand but disastrous British push at Loos, itself designed to support an even grander but equally ill-fated French offensive in Champagne. These assaults offered more valuable learning opportunities for the Germans.

The last Allied blood to be shed at Fromelles was that of the 47th (London) Division, when they finally liberated the village in October 1918. But before that the sector had been occupied by Portuguese troops and consumed by the colossal German spring offensive known as Georgette, a firestorm that came perilously close to concluding the war in favour of the Central Powers. In other words, from the first moment of fighting in September 1914 to the day when the guns at last fell silent, there was sniping, shelling, gassing, tunnelling, aerial combat, patrols, raids, a host of associated nearby actions, and of course the three key closely related encounters of 1914, 1915 and 1916. Amalgamation of casualties sustained in this sector throughout the war makes it one of the most bloody stretches of battlefield on the entire Western Front. There is therefore a wider and greater tale to be told, a tale that complements 19 July 1916 by adding not only colour but essential perspective to an action that—solely because of the Fromelles Project—has now become one of the highest-profile episodes of the Great War.

PART I

CAUSES AND EFFECTS

Chapter 1

STRANGE MEETING

⸺⸺⸺

It was on Wednesday 3 September 2003 that I first met Lambis Englezos. Having delivered a lecture on First World War tunnelling at the Australasian Institute of Mining and Metallurgy in Melbourne, I was drawn into an unexpected and somewhat one-sided conversation about Pheasant Wood and the missing Diggers of Fromelles. Englezos, a Melbourne teacher, had been invited to the event by his colleague Ward Selby, a member of the Institute and regular visitor to the battlefields. Englezos' absolute conviction was that the bodies of many missing Australian soldiers still lay in a set of mass graves dug by the Germans after the battle. Ignoring the theme of the day, Englezos relentlessly outlined his theory to me. He had exchanged letters, emails and telephone calls with the Office of Australian War Graves (OAWG) and the Minister for Veterans' Affairs, but every plea for an investigation had met with a bluntly negative response. He said that on 22 July the matter had been raised in the Australian parliament by a member of the opposition, and that the press were becoming more interested by the day. His frustration at the official stonewalling permeated every syllable of the diatribe. He wanted to prove the graves' existence—what could I do to help?

That the Fromelles sector had seen its share of carnage was common historical knowledge; likewise that there remained throughout that region of French Flanders an incalculable number of unfound British, French, Indian, German, Portuguese, Canadian and Australian dead. During many years of research, archaeology and exploration on the Western Front, I had personally stumbled upon the remains of several soldiers, but these discoveries, like most others, were accidental: fragments of bone or uniform revealed by the plough or during ditching, which upon closer scrutiny turned out to be more than just fragments. Although there are numerous instances of nocturnal scavengers knowingly rifling bodies for buttons, badges and personal effects, illegally exposed by metal detection, human remains are typically found by chance, generally during agricultural or engineering works. In 2003 I was aware of no circumstance on any battlefield where a *deliberate* search had ever been officially sanctioned. It was an intriguing case, and Englezos' passion and determination were clear; Selby added some compelling and carefully selected words to the argument. I was keen to know more.

It was not the first time I had been presented with such a case, although never one on such a potentially large scale. There exist protocols. For an historian, the correct approach is to adopt a resolutely sceptical stance until one is able after research to transform a theory from possibility to probability and final certainty. This is especially so where war dead are concerned. Because the action of 19 July 1916 had been an Anglo–Australian enterprise, incurring heavy casualties for both nations, I was there and then able to offer Englezos an avenue of potential assistance: to bring the matter to the attention of the British All-Party Parliamentary War Graves and Battlefield Heritage Group (now the All-Party Parliamentary War Heritage Group) in the House of Lords. However, first there was a need to review the historical data. I therefore offered my support, but with one important precondition: the production of credible documentary evidence to support the theory.

Information began to arrive. Selby identified the location where it was claimed the bodies had originally been buried, and found a German map that revealed the site to be adjacent to what the Germans called

Fasanen-Wäldchen (Pheasant Wood) or sometimes simply *Fasanenwald* (the '*chen*' suffix merely emphasises the fact that it was a small wood, or what Charles Bean later called a 'copse'). I was quickly able to establish by means of Google Earth that this small stand of trees, now mature, still occupied a similar footprint to the wood of 1916. At the same time Englezos had been making enquiries with local enthusiasts in Fromelles, and with the village mayor. Did anyone know of graves being present? Who were the landowners? Were there any signs of pits in the landscape? How might one go about exploring such a site? The questions drew a uniformly negative response: there was nothing to see on the ground, nobody was aware of anything relating to graves, and permission for a speculative search would be more than difficult to obtain.

However, there was one exception. In an article entitled 'Lest We Overlook 250 of our Fallen', published in *The Australian* newspaper on 18 July 2003, Martial Delebarre, the president of the local historical group known at that time as the ASBF (*Association pour le Souvenir de la Bataille de Fromelles en* 1916), spoke about 'lost graves'. Reporter Jonathan King wrote that Lambis Englezos had 'teamed up with local historian Martial Delebarre, who grew up on a farm nearby'. The mass grave of Australians was 'common knowledge', M. Delebarre was quoted as saying. 'We have always known Australians were lying in this farmer's field but nobody has ever believed us, especially the Government of Australia who have been coming here since 1919.'

In historical research local information is often found to be very valuable; but not in this case, because no one appeared to support the statement and no documentary evidence was produced, not even by M. Delebarre. It appeared merely to be hearsay. To be even mildly persuasive against the resistance of officialdom, a good deal more confirming data, especially contemporary German reports and eyewitness accounts, would be required.

Having established that on 19 July 1916 the German unit facing Allied attacks was the 6th Bavarian Reserve Infantry Division, my specific and often-repeated recommendation was that Englezos, Selby and their colleagues find a way to scrutinise the war diaries of the division, its two brigades and four regiments and all the relevant associated units. There was little point in investing energy in dissecting British or Australian archives

because the records of burial, if they existed, could *only* have been generated
by those responsible: the Bavarians. Contemporary British and Australian
accounts might contain data indicating that the military of the time were
aware of features believed to be graves, such as maps carrying annotations
or symbols, but that is as far as Allied intelligence sources were able to
go, for the interpretation of landscape features within hostile territory was
made primarily through the study of aerial photographs, and was therefore
a question of educated guesswork. By mid-1916, on both sides of No Man's
Land a huge variety of fieldworks existed in the advanced 'fighting zone' at
Fromelles, the quantity increasing enormously during the eighteen months
following the battle. British trench maps of the era therefore contain hosts
of identified, unidentified and indeed unidentifiable features—that was the
nature of the war.

Apart from formally established cemeteries, gravesites containing the
bodies of enemy troops were seldom marked as such, not least because
the trade of war is in lives and one's existence as a soldier consisted mainly
in finding more effective ways of taking life. A cemetery was a cemetery, a
grave was a grave, and on the Western Front both were ubiquitous. They
held no tactical significance unless other military features were present,
and in the case of war dead that was more than rare because no one wished
to disturb a recently established burial ground (potentially containing one's
comrades) by associating it with a feature that would draw enemy fire. This
does not, however, hold true in relation to civilian cemeteries. The critical
information about the alleged burials at Pheasant Wood—if indeed it
had ever been recorded and still existed—was therefore likely to reside in
the place where the Bavarian military archives were held: the capital of the
Bavarian State, Munich.

Given the paucity of documentary evidence at this time, it was unsurprising that Australian politicians, historians and officials poured cold
water (and sometimes considerable buckets of invective) on the Englezos
theory. It was not the previous *existence* of graves that they found
troublesome—although for a long time a number of historians stead-
fastly refused to believe this too, even when presented with evidence—but
the implausibility of graves containing large numbers of Allied soldiers
still being occupied almost a century later. Given that dedicated specialist

units had combed the Western Front battlegrounds for three years after the Armistice, it seemed most unlikely that *documented* mass graves—for it soon become apparent that the British and Australian military authorities had been made aware of the burials at the site soon after they had taken place (and on several later occasions)—could have been overlooked.

The natural starting point for this kind of research is the Commonwealth War Graves Commission (CWGC). The CWGC archive at Maidenhead, Berkshire, UK, had no record of post-war recoveries being made near Pheasant Wood; nor did the OAWG. However, the key documents—the huge database of 'burial returns', which is effectively a diary listing the location that individual bodies were recovered, when, by whom, whether they were identifiable, and where they were reburied—were for this sector known to be substantial but incomplete. It could therefore not be safely concluded through the study of these documents that the remains had *not* been found and dealt with. It was later to become apparent that—like the Bavarian and indeed many relevant Australian records—how, when and by whom the post-war examination and reclamation of the Fromelles battlefields had taken place was itself relatively unresearched.

Englezos' team embarked upon the search for German evidence, at the same time using the mission's emotive character to retain keen media attention, and all the while doggedly knocking on doors in every relevant corridor of power in Australia. The response remained negative, but the matter was never allowed to disappear over the official horizon. It remained eminently newsworthy.

With the help of Tasmanian politician Harry Quick, Englezos obtained a list of military archives from the German defence attaché in Canberra, while Selby asked his brother-in-law Mr Walter Dumps—a Bavarian himself—to undertake the written enquiries. Selby, whose grandfather had fought at Fromelles in July 1916 and survived, had visited the battlefield in April 2002. By chance, Englezos, an enthusiast since the late 1980s and founding member of the Friends of 15th Brigade, an association that celebrated the endeavours of the unit that suffered severe casualties at Fromelles, was present at the same time. Their meeting proved momentous, for it was then that a notable anomaly was discussed: the number of Australian dead accounted for after the battle did not equal the sum of those with identified graves, with names on Memorials to the Missing and beneath 'Known unto God' headstones.

Mr Dumps received his first response in July 2004; it directed him to the Bavarian military archive in Munich. In August a letter was received from Dr A. Fuchs, the archive's director, stating that the digging of mass graves at *Fasanen-Wäldchen* was indeed recorded in the 1923 regimental history of the 21st Bavarian Reserve Infantry Regiment (RIR 21), one of four regiments that constituted the 6th Bavarian Reserve Infantry Division (6 BRD) and the unit that faced the brunt of the Australian assault on 19 July 1916. Its author, *Generalmajor* Julius Ritter von Braun, commanded the regiment at the time of the action; as a participant, his narrative carried considerable persuasive weight. Dr Fuchs quoted the key passage:

Great care was taken over the recovery and formal identification of the fallen and the collection of their personal belongings by officers and the company sergeant majors. The big cemetery at Beaucamps had to be substantially extended once again. For the enemy dead, mass graves were dug behind the Fasanen-Wäldchen. Work also had to be begun on filling in two saps which had been dug by the enemy from his lines to ours during the night of 19/20.7 and were now full of enemy dead, which, as usual, the enemy had not bothered to recover.

The 'enemy' mentioned here were of course the very Australian dead that Englezos and Selby sought. In the same correspondence, however, Dr Fuchs cautioned that 'only the history of RIR 21 mentions the burial of the Australian dead. A search of the archives of the Regiment and the Division found nothing'. In other words the graves were noted *only* in the post-war published unit history. The *Kriegstagebuchen* and *Gefechtsber-ichte*—war diaries and action reports—of RIR 21 had been scrutinised but nothing was found. The *Official Bavarian History of the War* revealed just five lines about the battle itself.

At first glance this was disappointing, for it appeared to dash all hope that the passage in the regimental history could be verified and expanded upon through records generated at the time of battle—the all-important primary sources. But Dr Fuchs did not say the war diaries and battle reports *did not exist*, simply that he could find nothing of relevance within them.

It should be understood, however, that the scale of Bavarian record-keeping was monumental, especially during the extended period on the Western Front when the German Army was standing largely on the defensive. A single divisional war diary and its appendices may contain many hundreds of thousands of pages of text, plus a myriad associated maps, plans, orders, letters, messages, drawings, photographs, panoramas, reports (typed, mimeographed and handwritten), receipts, captured documents, etc. In Munich these documents are kept in hundreds of *Bund,* heavy string-tied bundles, each of which comprise thousands—sometimes tens of thousands—of pages. Evidence relating to an *uneventful* day could run into hundreds of sheets. One may even follow the evolution of a document from the first handwritten draft through numerous rewrites, to the final typed version that was printed and circulated. Battles and raids—the very essence of the conflict—receive almost gratuitous attention to detail. *Kriegstage-buchen* chronicled daily occurrences down to the most mundane detail, while *Gefechtsberichte* described offensive and defensive incidents in the same surgically incisive and self-critical manner.

Alongside these abundant and varied records—which were of course compiled at the front itself by the soldiers concerned—sits the equally monumental resource of 6 BRD's parent unit, *Armee-Oberkommando 6* (AOK 6). AOK 6 observed the situation in both a tactical and strategic light, themselves reporting to their army *Gruppe* who in turn reported to OHL: German high command. A concerted exploration of a single action therefore requires much time and great patience on the part of the researcher. The astonishing Bavarian anthology of Fromelles-related documents would soon be found to number many hundreds of thousands of items. The two sheets of paper that would later help set in irreversible motion the wheels of the project that culminated in the location, recovery and reburial of 250 soldiers were indeed present in the vast military archive.

So why was the key information not found by Dr Fuchs at this time? There are several possible explanations. First and foremost is that the Munich military archive suffers from the same malady as many regional and regimental military archives: lack of funds, and thus lack of staff.

The papers could have been filed in several distinct categories of *Bund*:
battle reports, reports on the clearance of bodies from the field, intelligence
files, orders for burials, reports on burials, orders for grave relocations, or
padres' and chaplains' diaries, and the supply of names and other particulars to divisional HQ, including details of significant papers, maps, letters,
etc., found on bodies. Or indeed such papers could have found their way
into a range of AOK 6 files. (During conversations with the curators and by
scrutiny of introductory notes, I later established that the Bavarian records
had actually been 'weeded' during the 1970s. No precise details had been
kept as to which or how many documents had been destroyed. Although it
was impossible to ascertain whether Fromelles material was included in the
process, it appeared unlikely.)

Second, the heavily overloaded schedule of Dr Fuchs meant he had
meagre time to devote to this task, but did the best he could under the
circumstances. The third and most likely cause of failure, however, lay
in the explicit nature of Walter Dumps' request: to find information on
Australian dead. If Dr Fuchs applied himself to seeking only references to
Australians, he would have found little among 6 BRD's operational papers
of the July 1916 era. The reason is mundane but surprising. During this
period of the war, as long as the enemy were *Weiss Engländer*, the Bavarians
habitually recorded all 'Empire-related' troops as English. Apart from rare
exceptions, only in intelligence reports and prisoner interrogations were
white enemy soldiers routinely assigned their correct ethnic group. Both
classes of document were of course extraneous to Dr Fuchs' search parameters, for he was seeking information on *burials*. On the Western Front in
June and early July 1916, therefore, Australians were simply looked upon as
an alternative breed of Englishman.

There is, however, one further and compelling cause for the lack of
success: the chill mists generated by the events of the Second World War
that still linger over Germany. Although evaporating beneath the sunlight
of time, trade, knowledge and the great internet-driven surge in geneal-
ogy, in 2004 both academic and popular interest in early 20th century
German military history was but a shadow even of what it is today. There
were then in Munich no specialists in the subject. The military archive
reading room might be full of researchers, but none would be studying

the First World War. That conflict lay deep beneath the shadow of 1939–45. It still does, and for many years to come German academic and popular interest in 1914–18 is likely to remain but a fraction of that seen in the Commonwealth nations. One might say that historical research has been repressed by history itself.

Whereas in Britain or Australia one may readily find an enthusiast or expert whose knowledge of a particular unit or event is practically encyclo-paedic, and who is also willing to freely advise, assist and share information, in Munich there were no such specialists to turn to. No one, not even the staff, was sufficiently familiar with the resource. Indeed, with their help, I had on one occasion to scour the city's universities for anyone, student or teacher, who would lend a hand during a research visit. Only one historian, a professor of mediaeval history, was willing to immerse himself in what he called the *Morast* (morass) that formed the First World War papers of 6 BRD. He had never seen the like.

By comparison to other conflicts, the Great War is therefore practically unexplored. Being few, and fully occupied with readers researching other eras and topics (the Bavarian archives carry resources dating from the 16th century), the staff have little opportunity to become adequately acquainted with the vast scope of the collection.

At the end of the initial 'Fuchs' process, the Pheasant Wood theory had been enhanced, but Englezos and Selby still lacked sufficient evidence. I emphasised the necessity for further exploration in Munich: it was essential that the files were carefully and thoroughly sifted by someone familiar with the subject matter and with time enough to devote to the task. A visit was obligatory. Englezos asked if I myself could do the work; at that time it was not possible.

―――――

For some time the outlook did not improve. The theory that undiscov-ered bodies still lay at Pheasant Wood had been rejected by the Australian Senate in July 2003. In February 2004 the Director of the OAWG, Air Vice-Marshal (retired) Gary Beck, stated categorically, 'I stress finally that without concrete evidence of Australians' remains at Fromelles, there is no prospect of a search being conducted'.

By the beginning of 2005, Englezos, Selby and their colleagues never-theless remained undaunted. The story was still a recurring topic in the Australian press, not least as a result of advice offered by Jeroen Huygelier, a Belgian historian. Huygelier had drawn attention to the existence of a potentially valuable and easily accessible resource: the Red Cross Wounded and Missing Enquiry Bureau (RCWM) files. Apart from the short piece in *Generalmajor* von Braun's regimental history, this 'discovery' was the most important development to date. Ironically, the files were held not in Germany nor in the UK but at the Australian War Memorial in Canberra, just a short flight across the Snowy Mountains from Englezos' home town of Melbourne. More ironically yet, RIR 21's regimental history had for decades been in the Memorial's archive as part of a collection of German unit histories initiated by a Captain J.J.W. Herbertson. An English officer, Herbertson was a friend and colleague of Charles Bean, the celebrated war correspondent and author of the revered twelve-volume *Official History of Australia in the War of 1914–1918*. Both men have roles to play in the Fromelles story.

The nucleus of the RCWM collection comprises material accumulated during the war by the German Red Cross, converted into lists and passed to the Red Cross offices of the Entente nations via the International Commit-tee of the Red Cross (ICRC) from their headquarters in Geneva.

One of the key components in the AWM collection—*and an element not supplied to Geneva or indeed to any agency outside Germany during the war*—were many thousands of small index cards. Each card, written in German, related to the fate of an individual Australian soldier. They are today digit-ised and freely available via the Memorial's website. How the records came to be there is also an integral part of the Fromelles story, because there is a direct link between a Digger officer who fell into Bavarian hands on 19 July 1916 and the existence of the cards in Canberra. The War Memorial's complete RCWM collection comprises 305 boxes and occupies 55 metres of shelf space. It contains not only the cards but a mass of supplementary records relating to approximately 32 000 individuals.

Selby and Englezos were now joined by colleague John Fielding, who had earlier visited the Pheasant Wood site and set pulses racing by er-roneously reporting that the burial pits there were obvious for all to see on the ground. Another long-time affiliate was Robin Corfield, a close friend of Englezos who had first privately published his account of the battle, *Don't Forget Me, Cobber*, in 2000. Together, they set about researching the records of every man listed as missing as a consequence of 19/20 July 1916, scrutinising rolls of honour, cemetery listings, the German cards and any associated documentation they could find. Within the wider AWM collection lay several additional levels of information, the most important being files generated as a result of requests to the Red Cross for information about missing relatives. Here were conserved the original letters of enquiry, replies from the Australian Red Cross and their colleagues in London and Geneva, plus correspondence from German personnel who had been requested by International Red Cross headquarters *during the conflict* to search for information on specific individuals. In addition, the files relating to missing Diggers contained immensely valuable (although sometimes perplexing) eyewitness accounts: the personal testimonies of soldiers at the front, on leave, in hospital and in German prisoner-of-war camps relating to the capture, wounding or death of missing comrades.

One file in this category, that of the late Second Lieutenant John C. Bowden (Jack to his family) of the 59th Battalion AIF, created a stir. Not long before the action of 19 July 1916, Private Bowden had become an officer. At the time of his death he was a second lieutenant, but certain papers found on his body by the enemy related to pre-commission service. The documents revealed confusion over whether the Bavarians might have noted him as an officer or a private soldier. Among the file was a letter from *Herr* Grusingen of the Central Committee of the German Red Cross Societies in Berlin. It was dated 21 January 1918—some ten months before the Armistice—and stated as follows:

> It is no longer possible to establish with absolute certainty whether Lieutenant J.C. Bowden of the 59th Aust. Batt. and Private John Charles Bowden of the 59th Aust. Batt are identical. The possibility of it rests on the fact that the report of the death of the Lieutenant J.C. Bowden was only made on receipt of the paybook. His identity disc may well have read Private John Charles Bowden, as it is possible that, as an officer, he had not yet renewed his disc. After the battle on the 19.7.16 the identity

discs were removed from all the fallen men and sent in. The name of Bowden is not reported in the lists of graves. It may be assumed that possibly Lieutenant Bowden was buried in one of the five large British collective graves before the Fasanen-Wäldchen (Pheasants Wood) near Fromelles, or in the collective grave ... in the Military Cemetery at Fournes. There are no materials here for further investigations concerning those buried in the graves concerned.

Whether the body of the 36-year-old bank manager from South Yarra, Victoria, lay in the graves at Pheasant Wood would not be ascertained for nine decades, but in September 2004 his Red Cross file finally provided concrete evidence *produced contemporaneously* that none could dismiss or ignore: the site had been named by the Germans themselves as a place of mass burial of enemy troops. It also revealed the level of care employed in the recording and reporting of Allied casualties: in my opinion, it provided further encouragement to invest time and effort in searching for the primary source documents from which all Fromelles-related Red Cross files could only have been compiled: the records of 6 BRD in Munich.

By 1916 a German organisation called the *Zentralnachweisebüro* (Central Information Bureau) had long been established. No matter what an enemy soldier's fate, information was communicated from the bureau's Berlin headquarters to the International Red Cross in Geneva (and thence to waiting families across the world). During the Great War, data from Berlin arrived in Geneva in the form of five categories of lists, each consisting of names classified according to the circumstances of each individual.

Gefangenenlisten (Prisoner Lists) reported the capture of a soldier, his physical state, the nature of any wounds, the place where he was captured, his name, unit, number, rank, home address and next of kin, transfers between prisoner-of-war camps, illnesses while in captivity, etc. Through these lists it is possible to follow a soldier's narrative of imprisonment.

Lazarettlisten (Hospital Lists) covered injury, sickness and hospitalisation at any stage of a man's period of captivity, appearing in different formats according to where the records were compiled: a dressing station or field hospital, a military hospital, a camp infirmary, etc.

Nachlasslisten (Property Lists) itemised the effects of an individual. For a soldier to appear on such a list it was not necessary for him to be alive, dead or indeed in German custody, i.e. it listed items that may for tactical or intelligence reasons have been removed from a corpse in No Man's Land, or perhaps simply found on the battlefield—a common practice. Such lists had disappeared by 1918, but were prevalent throughout 1915 and 1916 when the two key battles at Fromelles were fought.

Totenlisten (Death Lists) spanned the entire war and in late 1918 and 1919 occupy many entire volumes, a substantial proportion recording deaths from influenza. Given the several ways in which it was possible to die in war, these lists appeared in several forms, some of which also indicate burial site, and indeed much more.

Gräberlisten (Grave Lists) related to burial places and appeared more sporadically. Unlike other forms of listing, their arrival in Geneva did not follow the chronological order of the conflict: it is not unusual, for example, to find 1914 graves being notified in 1918.

All five of these lists were relevant to the narrative of Fromelles. Jack Bowden's name never appeared on a Graves List, but the AWM files showed that information concerning his possible death had been sent from Berlin on a *Nachlassliste* dated 8 August 1916, just nineteen days after the battle. My research in Geneva revealed that on that date Bowden's name appeared *alone*, with no other Fromelles-associated soldiers present. The lists containing the other British and Australian victims of the battle emerge later. This means that Jack Bowden was the first Australian soldier reported by the Germans to Geneva. 'His' list was received by the ICRC on 26 August, whereupon the details were copied and immediately sent to London. The document signified, however, that only his *effects*—personal items—were recovered; from other papers we know these comprised an elephant ornament, a wristwatch and a tin box. They were despatched from Berlin to Geneva on 1 January 1917 and forwarded via the Australian Red Cross in London to the family in the Sydney suburb of Wahroonga. It was also made clear to the Bowdens at this time that the presence of their son's name on the list did not signify that he was in German hands, either dead or alive, but that the registration was part of an established procedure which required that *everything* recovered from the battlefield be sent to the AOK 6 intelligence officer, a *Hauptmann* (Captain) Fritz Lübcke, for scrutiny. There was, therefore, still a possibility that Jack Bowden had survived and was a prisoner, perhaps hospitalised.

It was probably because of the German confusion over his rank that for so long the family remained ignorant of the true circumstances of Jack's fate. The Red Cross files reveal that on a number of occasions their personnel made enquiries of other members of his battalion who had taken part in the 19 July attack. A Lieutenant 'Laidlaw' (actually Liddelow) said John Bowden was most likely a prisoner; Lieutenant N.B. Lovett, who knew him well, believed him to be dead and was 'quite sure Jack's body was not recovered by the British, and that the Germans could have picked him up'; Private J. Church saw him in No Man's Land with his 'left leg covered in blood, and his left arm strapped to his side by some of his equipment. He looked awfully bad'; Private John Wood explained that he and Bowden left their trench together and that the lieutenant held up the barbed wire for him to get under; they went on and when the officer fell he thought he had been shot dead, but couldn't stop to check; Private Ernest Blackmore stated that he saw Lieutenant Bowden hit and fall in No Man's Land. The final eyewitness said he was just behind and to the left of him during the advance across No Man's Land; he felt 'pretty certain he died about 100 yards from German trenches on 19th July'. Despite the testimony of the informants, the aggregated data remained inconclusive: it was still possible that Jack Bowden may have survived and been taken prisoner. Not unnaturally this is what most families preferred to believe when their loved ones were unaccounted for.

This single instance reveals how the fog of war drifted from the battlefield of Fromelles to Berlin, to Geneva and London, and thence across the world to Sydney and Melbourne. For many a family, resolution was not always easy to achieve. Eventually, after considerably longer than the statutory six-month period without fresh news, Jack Bowden's classification as 'Missing' was changed to 'Killed in Action'. The sad conclusion, finally communicated to the family on 2 January 1918, was that their son had indeed died of wounds on 19 July 1916. A letter of 8 July 1918 from Mary Stocks (Jack Bowden's sister) to the Australian Red Cross then revealed that although the family were unaware of the nature of the burials at Pheasant

Wood, referring to them as 'the five soldiers' graves in the Cemetery at Fromelles', they were of the belief that the likely location of his body was in the pits by the wood or in the cemetery at nearby Fournes, where it was known other Diggers had been interred. Throughout the last year of the war they continued to gently exhort the Red Cross to interview wounded men of the 59th Battalion who 'may have seen Jack 'ere he passed away. I wish we could get some information from someone who had seen him after he was picked up by the Germans'. The family were far from alone in that yearning.

Through their evaluation and cross-referencing of the AWM Red Cross files with every name on the roll of honour in *Don't Forget Me, Cobber*, Englezos and his colleagues managed to produce for the first time an estimate of the number of men they believed to have been buried at Pheasant Wood. That initial calculation was 169, and each was now associated with a name and an individual record. Although there were still no clues as to whether or not the graves had been cleared after the war, it was an important and potentially persuasive development. Media interest was strongly rekindled. The Families and Friends of the First AIF and other associations and individuals took up the gauntlet of research as the Englezos theory crept slowly towards reality.

Chapter 2

FIRST FROMELLES: THE FATEFUL DAYS

—⟫⬦⟪—

At first there will be increased slaughter—increased slaughter on such a scale as to make it impossible to get troops to push the battle to a decisive conclusion. They will try to, thinking that they are fighting under the old conditions. The war, instead of being a hand-to-hand contest in which the combatants measure their physical and moral dominance, will become a kind of stalemate, in which neither army being willing to get at the other, both will be maintained in opposition to each other, threatening the other, but never being able to deliver a final and decisive attack. Everybody will be entrenched in the next war. It will be a great war of entrenchments. The spade will be as indispensable to a soldier as his rifle . . . all wars will by necessity assume the character of siege operations . . . soldiers may fight as they please; the ultimate decision is in the hand of famine.

Jan Gottlieb Bloch, *The Future of War*, 1898

And so it proved. Having advanced with their French allies to meet the German invader, the two Army Corps of the British Expeditionary Force almost immediately found themselves faced by forces superior in every department. They were driven into chaotic retreat, and after two weeks of heavy loss the commander-in-chief, Field Marshal Sir John French, was mired in confusion. France's General Joseph Joffre's colossal counter-offensives in Alsace-Lorraine produced little gain but ghastly casualty figures, largely as a result of abundant German medium-range artillery that routed his field batteries at arm's length and broke up infantry assaults before they could properly form. On one day alone, 22 August, the French suffered 27 000 fatalities. Although Anglo–French resistance constrained their anticipated momentum, the Germans were nevertheless slowly but surely pushing forward in all sectors.

The crisis reached its peak when on 3 September 1914 the invader crossed the River Marne and began to bear down upon the capital; Parisians could clearly hear gunfire. Should their city fall, it would probably mean the end of the war for the French.

That the combined Entente forces might arrest the onslaught was looking ever more doubtful. So far the enemy had made few tactical errors. British military minds were torn between the hope that something advantageous might happen at the front, and a growing preoccupation with how to defend the poorly protected channel ports. The Empire itself was at risk, and the finest way to avoid invasion of British shores was to bind the enemy to a Continental battleground. In the absence of counter-attacking opportunities, French high command elected to try to dig in and buy time until drafts of fresh troops arrived.

Opportunity was finally presented through an uncharacteristic German strategic blunder. In early September two armies, General von Kluck's First and von Bülow's Second, were advancing towards Paris. As they approached to within 50 kilometres, both shifted south-eastwards to try to enclose the still-retreating French. In so doing a 48-kilometre gap appeared between the two. It was spotted and reported by Allied airmen, and a combined Anglo–French force (assisted by almost 6000 reinforcements who famously travelled to the front in a great fleet of Paris taxi-cabs) pushed as fast and as hard as they could into the breach—and beyond. The 9 September counter-offensive created a role reversal: the Germans, now split and soon themselves in retreat, were in danger of being enveloped and annihilated. The British and French then advanced almost 65 kilometres, pushing the Germans back across the River Aisne until on 13 September the fighting finally subsided on the high ground north of the river valley. Here both sides entrenched, and here the lines would remain for the next three years. Over two million troops had clashed in this, the First Battle of the Marne. Although the strategic laurels might have gone to the Entente, the invader was still within striking distance of France's heart. He must be driven out at the earliest opportunity.

It was in October 1914 that the British found themselves in the Fromelles and Aubers region. Having departed the now-stabilising Aisne and Marne battlefields, marching by night and resting by day they had headed north to try to arrest further German advances, on the Somme, in Artois, and then in French and Belgian Flanders. It was the period known as the 'Race to the Sea' when the Germans, baulked in their hopes of excising Paris from the east, sought to outflank their enemy and swing down upon the capital from the north. The fighting was to surge further and further northwards until it reached the coast. When Belgian engineers opened sluices at Nieuport to flood great reaches of the polder plain with sea water, the Germans were forced back inland to the nearest higher and dryer ground—at Ypres. Clashes in the neighbouring Lille region formed a part of this unpredictable and shifting era.

The great cities, such as Antwerp and Liège, were 'invested' by the Germans, that is, besieged before they were stormed, but elsewhere there was comparatively little destruction. There were as yet no trench lines: the enemy had to be sought out and engaged in open warfare. It was a case of patrolling, identifying, reporting and then skirmishing through fields and villages. French civilians remained in nervous occupation of their precious homes, businesses and farms, waiting, as they had done so many times down the centuries, for the fighting to pass them by. But the tempo was soon to change dramatically. Lille, little more than a dozen kilometres north-east of Fromelles, fell on 17 October; over two thousand properties there were destroyed.

In Fromelles at this time, a civilian might on the very same day distinguish British, French and even Indian troops. The front was fluid, with patrols moving to and from all points of the compass. Many were mounted, bands of horsemen brandishing lances and sabres (the British infantry officer went to war with a sword). Save for the presence of rifles, carbines and revolvers, the scene was frequently reminiscent of mediaeval warfare, producing sudden galloping arrivals that often terrified more than a salvo of bursting shells. Rumours of murder, rape, theft and wanton destruction multiplied, and fear of the unknown seethed from community to community. In this frightful period of waiting, the sole comfort was that the grain crop had been safely gathered in and starvation avoided.

On 20 October elements of the British 19th Brigade, alongside troops from General Louis Conneau's Mounted Division, some on bicycles, patrolled the ridge between the villages of Aubers and Radinghem, looking to push forward. One of the first to use a spade in anger at Fromelles was 2nd Royal Welch Fusilier Private Frank Richards (real name Francis Woodruff, 1883–1961), later the author of the popular memoir, *Old Soldiers Never Die*:

We moved off again at daybreak and relieved some French troops the further side of Fromelles: two days later we retired back through Fromelles and dug our trenches about four hundred yards this side of that village. Little did we think when we were digging those trenches that we were digging our future homes . . . each platoon dug in on its own, with gaps of about forty yards between each platoon . . . We dug those trenches simply for fighting; they were breast-high with the front parapet on ground level and in each bay we stood shoulder to shoulder . . . sandbags were unknown at this time. A part of our trench crossed a willow ditch and about forty yards in front of us we blocked this ditch with a little bank which was to be our listening post at night. The ditch was dry at present.

On 21 October German troops in field grey appeared en masse. Their approach was announced by gunfire, the heaviest that many had yet encountered. Both Briton and Frenchman were forced into withdrawal. On the morning of 23 October a defensive line was established between the settlement of La Boutillerie and a small area encompassing a tiny hamlet on the flat plain below Fromelles village known as Rouges Bancs (the derivation of this name has yet to be uncovered). Here, the troops dug primitive trenches and used roadside ditches for cover. To east and west, the Germans now owned all of the low, mean, but significant ridge in front of them as far as the eye could see.

For the next two weeks a sequence of hostile assaults was beaten off, enemy fortunes often being hampered by heavy mists typical of the area. One night towards the end of the month Frank Richards notes the British hearing mysterious noises: he and two others volunteered to crawl out and discover what the invisible but audible enemy was doing:

> . . . when all of a sudden the mist blew away, and there, a little over a hundred yards in front of us, were new enemy trenches. The enemy were taking advantage of the mist and working on their parapet: some were a good thirty yards from their trench—they had been levelling some corn-stacks so as to have a clear line of fire.

The enemy was *digging in.*

> *The 29 October, 1914, was a miserable rainy day . . . The night before a party of Engineers had come up to our trench and had driven some posts in the ground about fifteen yards in front with one strand of barbed wire stretching across them. It looked like a clothes line during the day . . . The Old Soldier of the platoon remarked that the British Government must be terribly hard up, what with the short rations, no rifle-oil* [they were employing Vaseline], *no shells, and now sending Engineers up to the front line to stretch one single bloody strand of barbed wire out, which he had no doubt was the only single bloody strand in the whole of France, and which a bloody giraffe could rise up and walk under. It was enough to make good soldiers weep tears of blood, he said, the way things were going on . . .*
>
> *Well, it was still raining on the night of 29th when heavy rifle-fire broke out on the extreme right of our front* [the trench sub-sector in front of La Cordonnerie Farm]. *At the same time our listening posts sent back to say that the enemy were getting out of their trenches, so the post was called in at once, and presently we could see dim forms in front*

of us. Then our right platoon opened out with rapid fire. We opened out with rapid fire too. We were firing as fast as we could pull the trigger: no man can take a sight in the dark so we were firing direct in front of us . . .

We kept up a continuous fire on our front, but one by one our rifles began to jam . . . In a short time mine and Smith's rifles were the only two that were firing in the whole of the platoon. Then ours were done up too: the fact was that the continual rain had made the parapet very muddy [no sandbags] and the mud had got into the rifle mechanism, which needed oiling in any case, and continual firing had heated the metal so that it was impossible to open and close the bolts. The same thing had happened all along the Battalion front. About a couple of hours before dawn, word was passed along the trench for every man to get out and lay down five paces in front of the parapet and be prepared to meet the enemy with the bayonet. When everyone was out Buffalo Bill walked up and down the platoon and told us all that we would have to fight to the last man.

Eventually the platoon returned to the trenches, which in the days to come they began improving and extending. During the next fortnight the Entente was to halt German advances at Messines and Armentières to the north, and Lens, Loos, Givenchy and Fauquissart to the south. Richards and his comrades of the 2nd Royal Welch Fusiliers were in fact witnessing the first embodiment of the fixed lines that would scar the landscape of French Flanders for years to come. Civilians were still living in Fromelles at this time.

There is nothing unusual about the Aubers–Fromelles battleground. French Flanders was part of a wider region that had been fought over so many times down the centuries it had long been known as 'Europe's cockpit'. The terrain may have lent itself to the mobile skirmishes and pitched battles of earlier times—generally brief encounters with a defined beginning and end—but it was peculiarly unsympathetic for the prosecution of long-term, trench-based siege warfare. The geology made a struggle not only of fighting but of everyday life.

The higher ground was almost universally German-held, and it was their forces that dictated the position and 'shape' of the line when positional warfare was being established. One factor in these decisions was climate. They realised in the late autumn of 1914 that the approaching winter required reflection: if and when fighting was interrupted, the troops required positions that were as safe, dry and commanding as possible. German divisions were content for regimental commanders to think tactically in association with neighbours on either flank. Whether that entailed a forward push or a retirement (in which they saw no loss of face), they were encouraged to take advantage of every contour and landscape feature.

The British approach to the onset of trench warfare almost beggars belief. The general staff were imbued with the doctrine that the offensive was the soul of the defence; even when immobile, the British Army must still act and be seen to act with belligerence. Regardless of tactical, topographical or sanitary suitability, the order went out: the troops were to hold the positions from which the last German attack had been repulsed. Facing a winter in primitive trenches and hastily prepared and primitive field fortifications, the troops occupying the Flanders plain were all too often denied permission to withdraw even a few metres to drier ground and finer cover. Pleadings by company commanders and engineers fell upon deaf ears: General Headquarters (GHQ) looked upon the trenches as merely temporary, and a spring advance merely a formality—it was only a matter of months away. Until this time the commander-in-chief required 'as much pressure as possible' to be brought upon the enemy, which included the symbolic pressure of not giving away an inch of territory. Those who believed that a withdrawal to healthier and more practical positions—an entirely different manoeuvre to a 'retreat'—was judicious were seldom courageous enough to express their concerns and brave the wrath of the 'old and the bold'. The posturing led to a dislocation between staff officer and field commander that created not only an underlying bitterness throughout the war, but widespread and prolonged discomfort, injury . . . and death.

On 15 November 1914 the 2nd Scots Guards took over the Cordonnerie Farm sub-sector and on the 27th a small party led by Lieutenant Sir Edward Hulse crept through unharvested turnips to make the first British raid in the neighbourhood. The enterprise reflects the primitive nature of early trench warfare, and stands in stark contrast to the forays of 1916, which by comparison look extraordinarily meticulous. In a letter to his mother Hulse described the venture:

29 November 1914

My Dearest Mother,
The enemies' trenches in front of us had been extraordinarily quiet for several days, especially at night, and we had ascertained that they were only occupied by snipers and digging parties by day, and they retired at night into their second line of trenches (main position), leaving just a few sentries and snipers. It was thought desirable that something should be done to find out, and they detailed a raiding party of one officer, one N.C.O. and eight men to carry this out. I got an N.C.O. and eight men to volunteer with great ease; we were to have started at 11 p.m., but there was a bright moon, and we stood over till 1.30 a.m., when it was pitch dark and raining. The CO. and Adjutant came down to see us off and give us instructions, namely, to get right up to the trenches, peep over if not spotted, select our marks, fire two rounds rapid, and kill all we could, and then each man for himself. On an ordinary night we could probably have done this, as their trenches were lightly held and sentries apt to be sleepy; but when we had got half way some firing opened away on the right, I think by the Border Regiment. This put the enemy on the alert, and by then I had satisfied myself that there were just as many of the enemy in their trenches as of us in our trenches, an unpleasant conclusion to arrive at when we were supposed to be raiding a lightly held trench! A little further on I made certain of this as I saw five fires, or rather the reflections of them (as they were in dug-outs and bomb-proofs and one could just see the reflection on bits of smoke which penetrated through) within a space of 50 or 60 yards! These were charcoal fires with a bit of wood burning probably. The fire I was making for was a proper wood fire shewing a lot of smoke, and it was there that I hoped to be able to peep over and find a little group of men to polish off. Progress was very slow indeed, as it was all crawling on hands and knees over turnips, and only four or five yards at a time, and then 'lie

doggo' and listen. Their sentries to our front were firing every now and then at our trenches, but all bullets passed over us, and we could locate them by the flash of the rifle. All went well up to about 15 yards, when I extended from single file to the right, towards this fire. We did another 5 yards and I had given instructions that directly I loosed off my rifle we should double forward, select marks, do all damage possible, and make off. I had seen where the sentry in front of me was, and told the scout to fire at the top of the parapet, in case he had his head over, and that I would fire at the place where the flash of the rifle appeared. We could only just make out the line of the top of the parapet at ten yards' distance. We were just advancing again when the swine called out in King's English, quite well pronounced, 'Halt, who goes there,' and fired straight between the scout and myself; he immediately fired where I had told him, and I fired at the point of the flash of the rifle, and there was a high-pitched groan; at the same time we all doubled up to the foot of the parapet, saw dim figures down in the trenches, bustling about, standing to arms, and my N.C.O. fired the trench bomb right into the little party by the fire. The other fellows all loosed off their two rounds rapid; there were various groans audible in the general hubbub, and we then ran like hares. The minute the alarm was given they threw something on the fire which made it flare up, and the machine gun, which we knew nothing about, opened just to my left . . . They had already stood-to-arms by the time we had turned tail, and they and the machine gun opened a very hot fire on us. I ran about 30 yards, and then took a 'heavy' into the mud and slush of the ploughed field and lay still for a minute to find out where the machine-gun bullets were going. They were just over me and to the right, so when I got up again and turned half left instead of half right, as I had been going originally, and did another 30 yards or so I found that the bullets were all round me, so fell flat and waited another half minute or so, until they seemed to alter the direction of their fire a bit. Then another run, and a heavy fall bang into our barbed wire, which was quite invisible, and which I thought was further off. These short sprints were no easy matter, as one carried about an acre of wet clay and mud on each foot. I had to lie flat and disentangle myself, and at that moment their machine gun swerved round and plastered away directly over my head not more than 2 or 3 feet. I waited again till it changed, and then ran like the devil for our trenches. I had lost direction a bit, and came on them sooner than I expected, and took a flying leap right over the parapet down about 9 or 10 feet into the trench. We had gone out on our extreme right, up the above-mentioned ditch, and I found that I came in about 50 yards to the right into the Borderers' trenches . . . Barring my rifle hitting me a good thump on the head as I fell into our trenches, and a bullet hole through the skirt of my coat, I was sound and whole, although extremely out of breath, and with a completely dry and salt taste in my mouth (the latter chiefly attributable to the intense anxiety to avoid the machine-gun fire) . . .

The great thing was that we found that the enemy had brought up machine guns, tripled their numbers in the trenches, and were very much awake and could stand to arms at a moment's notice; all of which was very different from reports about them from our scouts on previous nights. The C.O. and Adjutant frankly told me that they did not expect many to get back, and it was by lying flat that we avoided more casualties.

. . . I went out quietly alone to within 25 yards of the trenches at a different point last night, and heard talking, saw fires, and established that the other part of the line is more strongly held also than hitherto. They have an absolute network of trenches and communication—ditto to the rear.

Best love to all—send me all news possible.

Ever your loving

Ted

This escapade may smack of boy scouts and catapults, but it serves to illustrate one of the greatest difficulties in positional warfare: knowing what was happening within and behind the opposing trenches. As we shall later see, the description also contains many an unchanging feature. Hulse's letter confirms that the lines were now firmly fixed and the Germans already installing a designed defensive infrastructure. During the coming four years, every unit that occupied this and every other sector on every front in every theatre would face the same problem: how to force a permanent breach in the opposing bulwark. The great siege had begun. Although the enemy was 'camped' just a few hundred metres away (and in many places, much closer), it became no less difficult to know what he was doing, and how his defences were arranged. Thus it was that raids gradually became ever more regular, complex and carefully planned, to the point where by mid-1916 they resembled grand offensives in miniature.

Some 40 kilometres to the north in Belgian Flanders, on 22 November the First Battle of Ypres had also shuddered to a bloody halt, leaving both sides on their knees. The old British Expeditionary Force (BEF) was but a shadow of its polished pre-war self, and a confident young German Army lay torn and traumatised. General Sir Douglas Haig, then commanding I Corps and 'hero' of the battle, informed his colleagues at the War Office that in this hour of profound peril Britain was in need of 'patriots who knew the importance of the cause for which we are fighting'. The enemy was unlike any the British Army had had to face in a hundred years, the German people, noted Haig, having been 'impregnated from youth with an intense patriotic feeling, so that they die willingly for their country'. He was of the opinion that few Britons felt such a powerful allegiance to their nation, and advised sending out 'young Oxford and Cambridge men as officers: they understand the crisis in which the British Empire is involved'.

As the European winter took bitter hold, it might have been thought that both sides would take stock and lick their wounds. In places this was true. But the French generals, Ferdinand Foch and Joseph Joffre, were unwilling to allow the invader a chance to catch his breath; this was their land, and the jackboot must not be allowed to tread the precious earth of the Republic for a moment longer than necessary. Despite the conditions, aggression would be sustained. Unsurprisingly, the French requested British support-ing action; Sir John French was in no position to refuse. In the lead-up to Christmas, therefore, a sequence of limited attacks was launched in Belgian and French Flanders.

The December 1914 action at Fromelles was the very first set-piece attack in the sector. The battleground selected lay between the Sailly-sur-la-Lys–Fromelles road (the Rue Delvas, later christened the *Tommy-Strasse* by the Germans) and a track south-east of La Cordonnerie Farm. It was exactly the area that would be assaulted by the British 8th Division on 9 May the following year, and again by the 5th Australian Division in July 1916, over a year and a half hence.

The orders given to the 2nd Scots Guards and the 2nd Border Regiment (Borders) on 18 December 1914 were chillingly similar to those issued to the Australians in July 1916—and so was the way the action unfolded. Their attack was also timed for 6.00 p.m. but, being European mid-winter, this made it nocturnal. The troops, carrying spades and sandbags to consolidate the expected gains, were required to assemble in No Man's Land and upon the whistle rush and hold the German front trench. Should it be unoccupied they were to push on to the second line. The Scots Guards assumed responsibility for the right-hand sector facing Rouges Bancs, which includes the area today occupied by the Australian Memorial Park, while to their left the Borders attacked positions immediately west of Delangré Farm. The war diary of the 2nd Battalion Scots Guards written by Captain Giles Loder described the endeavours of his own company, LF:

At about 3 minutes to six the men were hoisted over the parapet and lay down. I blew my whistle as loud as I could, but owing to the noise of our gun-fire it appears that it was not generally heard. F Coy. being on the right and LF on the left, we began to move forward. After advancing about 60 yards I could see that in several places the line was not being maintained, some men moving forward faster than others. I could see this by the flash from the guns. I collected the men nearest me and I found myself practically on the parapet before the Germans opened fire. There was no wire entanglement at this point. We bayonetted and killed all the Germans we could see in the trench and then I jumped down into it . . . I ordered the men to make firing positions in the rear face of the trench. This was not easily done owing to the depth of the trench. I also told off some men to watch the flanks and if the enemy appeared to make traverses . . . I remained in the trench some time, about an hour, and then thought I had better try and see what had happened at other places in the line. I left [them] in charge of Lieut. Saumares and *told them to hang on. I found it impossible to get any information but could see a good many dead bodies lying close to the German parapet. I decided to come back to report to Captain Paynter and explain what the situation was, and suggest that if the trench was to be held reinforcements would have to be sent up. This he reported to the Brigadier. As it then became apparent that the attack of the Border Regiment had failed and also that F Coys. right had only succeeded in getting into the enemy's trench in a few places, he was ordered not to send forward the remaining two companies. I was then ordered to organize a digging party to sap to the German trench* [i.e. to dig towards the enemy's position with a narrow trench]. *This was attempted, but owing to a continuous German fire it soon became clear that the distance of 180 yards was too much . . . During this attack the Germans don't seem to have used any bombs or hand grenades. The cross fire from well-placed German machine guns played a big part, and this accounts for our very heavy casualties.*

The encounter concluded with Captain Loder being the only unwounded officer. Lieutenant Saumares' party escaped before dawn without loss. The battalion's casualties were approximately 180 killed and wounded—50 per cent of the force. On their left A and C Companies of the 2nd Borders attacked a quarter of an hour later. The war diary notes that 'The Companies were not in position until well after dark and consequently no one knew exactly their correct front or point of attack. At 6.15 the Companies advanced, strength about 300 men.'

They came immediately under fire, suffering numerous casualties from British shells falling short. Upon arrival at the enemy parapet they were forced—for the same reason—to withdraw 50 yards (46 metres), lie down, and wait for instructions. After an hour fresh orders arrived: attack again. The second attempt also failed and the party once more retired, this time lying down in front of their own breastworks (head-high defence works). Major G. Warren collected the remnants, added two platoons from B Company, and advanced a third time to a ditch in front of the German line. Here they found they had insufficient wire-cutters to breach the entanglements. Warren went back for more. On returning with three pairs ninety minutes later, he found the entire party had returned to their own trenches. The brigadier then drew proceedings to a close.

It left the Borders with 128 casualties, several of whom still lay in No Man's Land. For voluntarily bringing in wounded 'by daylight on 19 December 1914 under heavy rifle and machine-gun fire', Privates Abraham Acton and James Smith, both of the 2nd Border Regiment, were awarded the Victoria Cross—the origin of the place name 'VC Corner'. Early on the morning of 20 December observers noted an 'extraordinary' episode at Rouges Bancs. Edward Hulse was again an eyewitness:

The morning after the attack, there was an almost tacit understanding as to no firing, and about 6.15 a.m. I saw eight or nine German shoulders and heads appear, and then three of them crawled out a few feet in front of their parapet and began dragging in some of our fellows who were either dead or unconscious. I do not know what they intended to do with them, but I passed down the order that none of my men were to fire, and this seems to have been done all down the line. I helped one of our men in myself, and was not fired on at all. I sincerely hope that their intentions were all that could be desired with regard to our wounded whom they fetched in. I also saw some of them, two cases, where the two Germans evidently were not quite sure about showing themselves, and pushed their rifles out to two of our wounded and got them to catch hold, and pulled them onto their parapet, and so into their trenches.

Far the most ghastly part of this business is that the wounded have so little chance of being brought in, and if heavy fire is kept up, cannot even be sent for. There were many conspicuous acts of gallantry that night, in getting in the wounded under fire, but many had to be left out. One notices that sort of thing so much more when the two lines of trenches are very close, and the morning light reveals not only the bag, but also the pick-up! To put it plainly.

Five days later on exactly the same piece of ground one of the most celebrated events of the war took place. Captain Loder once more presents a colourful but tragically ironic glimpse:

25th Xmas. Fine and frosty. One man wounded. On the night of Christmas Eve the German trenches opposite those occupied by the Battalion at Fromelles were lit up with lanterns and there were sounds of singing.

We got into conversation with the Germans who were anxious to arrange an Armistice during Xmas. A scout named F. Murker went out and met a German patrol and was given a glass of whisky and some cigars, and a message was sent back saying that if we don't fire at them, they would not fire at us. There was no firing during the night. Early on Xmas morning a party of Germans of 158 Regiment came over to our wire fence, and a party from our trenches went out to meet them. They appeared to be most amicable and exchanged souvenirs, Cap Stars, Badges etc.

Our men gave them plum puddings which they much appreciated. Further down the line we were able to make arrangements to bury the dead who had been killed on Dec. 18–19 and were still lying between the trenches. The Germans brought the bodies to a half way line and we buried them. Detachments of British and Germans formed in line and a German and English Chaplain read some prayers alternately. The whole of this was done in great solemnity and remorse. It was heartrending to see some of the chaps one knew so well, and who had started out in such good spirits on Dec. 18th lying there dead, some with terrible wounds due to the explosive action of the high velocity bullet at close range.

Throughout the future conflict, truces specifically arranged to collect, separate and bury the fallen were far from uncommon. Properly agreed between the combatants, they formed one of the universally accepted unwritten rules of war.

On Christmas Day orders had also been issued for the BEF to be formed into two armies, the First under General Sir Douglas Haig, and the Second with General Sir Horace Smith-Dorrien as its commander. Every mind was now focussing upon how to fight this unfamiliar and unexpected war for which the British had been and indeed still were unprepared. How were trenches to be designed, built and defended? What kind of weapons were required for static warfare? Where might they swiftly be procured? How could troops be kept healthy under such conditions? And where and how should attacks—both small and great—be launched?

Chapter 3

OVERTURES

———⇒◦⇐———

The beginning of 1915 saw wet and stormy weather, cancellation of leave and a huge effort by the British to try to put the Fromelles trenches into habitable order. The troops were in a mess, struggling against water, mud, frost and bitter cold. They lacked almost every resource for trench warfare and in many places positions were so flooded that men could neither sit nor lie down. Several stretches of the earliest workings—which often consisted of converted ditches—were abandoned, and against orders the troops had had no choice but to pull back 10 or 20 metres to begin work afresh, this time with forethought.

At first the newly straightened line consisted of a string of 'forts', small defensive redoubts with poor cover and shoddy communication between. As supplies of wire, sandbags, hurdles and timber increased, they began to construct breastworks; frozen troops were happy enough to be occupied, especially if the activity helped avoid their demise. Waterproof shelters which also offered protection against shell fragments or 'splinters' appeared, and in many places trenches were brick-paved. Digging parties gradually connected the forts, and in true siege-warfare style the artillery began testing the capacity of shrapnel shells to cut enemy barbed wire; the steel thickets across No Man's Land grew denser by the week. Soon, practice attacks were taking place behind the lines. They included exercises with a variety of wire-cutters and instruction in the use of the newly introduced and hazardous home-made 'jam-tin' bomb; the troops were unimpressed.

By February fortification was everywhere in progress around the clock, and with so much activity there were many cases of soldiers accidentally exposing themselves to the enemy: on both sides, sniping became a serious menace. The exhibition of charity and compassion seen during the Christmas period had been firmly stamped upon by GHQ. There was to be no more fraternisation; the soldiers' duty was to grasp every opportunity to kill the enemy.

The first British offensive of 1915 began on 10 March. In reality it was an Anglo–Indian (British First Army) endeavour fought largely because a fractious Sir John French wished to silence French taunts of British offensive indolence. The Germans had been in possession of the small village of Neuve Chapelle since October of the previous year, the whole of the sector in which it was situated being garrisoned by parts of Crown Prince Rupprecht of Bavaria's Sixth Army. Neuve Chapelle lay some 3 kilometres south-west of Aubers, the lines protecting it forming a shallow salient (forward projection in the line). The prospective battleground was a narrow 3 kilometres, and the first enemy line of defence just a single lean breastwork protected by apparently derisory wire entanglements. Behind it lay further trenches, all unfinished and in the process of development.

Despite its comparatively diminutive scale, Sir Douglas Haig's ambitions for the enterprise were characteristically robust. After Neuve Chapelle had fallen, neighbouring Aubers would be attacked. Then, some 12 kilometres beyond, the defences of Lille would form the final British objective. Although only ten days were available for preparation, the tactical planning and supply of matériel was swift, and deployment of troops efficient.

The battle began with a hurricane bombardment by an unprecedented array of 372 artillery pieces, at that time the greatest display of firepower in British military history. It lasted thirty-five minutes. At 7.30 a.m. the guns spoke. Inspired by their sound and fury, and relieved to finally break out of crowded and sopping jumping-off positions, at 8.05 a.m. British and Indian troops began an assault that in the next four hours was to sweep over four enemy lines and into the fields beyond the village. In support lay massed cavalry, ready to exploit the breach and cause the havoc that would secure the ridge. Surprise—the greatest of all allies—was achieved, and in less than an hour Neuve Chapelle was occupied and consolidated. The tactics had worked and everything was progressing according to plan.

But almost as the first messages of success reached Haig's HQ the edifice began to crumble. Although the 'box barrage'—a newly introduced tactic that isolated a position by laying down curtains of artillery fire that cut off both enemy evacuation and reinforcement—was effective (it was at Neuve Chapelle that the term 'barrage' first appeared in reports), control within the now invisible fighting zone beyond the village began to dissipate. The attacking troops had advanced well, but their lines were fractured and dog-toothed. Commanders were not only losing track of the dispositions of their own troops, but the location and activities of the enemy. Signals became irregular and runners confused, and officers in the thick of the action received only intermittent orders from ill-informed headquarters; many that came through were already obsolete. Meanwhile at pre-arranged rendezvous beyond the village, scouts awaited the arrival of support battalions. They did not appear. To cap the confusion, the Indians and Scots on the two critical flanks both lost direction and advanced *too far*, leaving behind them vulnerable gaps and untouched pockets of enemy troops. It robbed the central assault of protection against lateral as well as frontal counter-attack, a fundamental requirement if momentum was to be maintained.

The few reports to reach HQ were faulty, leading to already fatigued troops being asked to press forward into areas thought to have been captured, but in truth still occupied by an increasingly organised and hostile enemy. By dusk the advance had long since ceased. Overnight the Germans hustled fresh troops into the sector, including elements of 6 BRD, a unit that British and Australian troops were to come to know only too well in the coming eighteen months.

On March 12 and 13 the British attempted further advances, but were fiercely rebuffed. According to the regimental history of RIR 21, this was 'primarily due to the exceptional effectiveness of the Bavarian and Saxon artillery, and in particular the battery commanded by *Hauptmann* von Parseval, which moved into position across open ground and inflicted very heavy casualties on the enemy . . . Although he [the enemy] employed fresh units and even had a cavalry division standing by to exploit the expected breakthrough, he achieved not the least success. The German supporting batteries smashed the enemy's waiting reserves.'

Ultimately, the British cavalry turned and headed back out of harm's way. It was not the last time that mounted troops, groomed and prepared to rout the 'Boche', would remain unemployed. Although after the battle the village of Neuve Chapelle remained British property, it was a meagre and disappointing reward.

In Berlin, the propagandists went to work, describing 250 British soldiers dressed as Germans luring the Bavarians into ambush and massacre, and mass desertions, especially by the Indians. What they did not need to embellish, however, was that the scale of British territorial success was grossly disproportionate to the casualties sustained: 2500 dead, and over 10 000 wounded and missing. The figures were made light of by British GHQ, which, not for the last time, would portray the engagement as useful for 'nurturing offensive spirit'. Without doubt, they pronounced, such actions disseminated within the enemy a feeling of 'disappointment' or 'disquiet'. How the conclusion was reached remained unspecified. It was, they said, still only a matter of time before the enemy were routed.

In August 1914 the British artillery had arrived in France expecting open warfare and therefore equipped with the means to fight in the open: shrapnel, fired by light and mobile horse-drawn field guns. But after Neuve Chapelle, Haig's attitude towards the gunners' contribution began to alter. He no longer saw it solely as the *provider* of a breach for infantry and cavalry to exploit, but something more complex, coming to believe that the '*extent* of a penetration might depend upon the amount of ammunition available'.

Neuve Chapelle's greatest legacy, therefore, was in convincing British and indeed French commanders that, given sophisticated preparation, enough guns and a sufficient supply of shells, the artillery was capable of delivering a platform for advance upon advance. The days of surprise attacks were over, and the war of the guns had commenced.

During the early months of 1915 Germany and Austria–Hungary, with some Turkish assistance, concentrated their efforts on waging war in the east against Russia. This, it was believed in London and Paris, presented the British and French with not just an opportunity but an obligation to attack in the west. Three offensive schemes, all French-led, were drawn up for the spring. The most important was General Joffre's plan to open up a vast battlefront in Artois, the region adjoining French Flanders some 12 kilometres west of Fromelles. With enhanced numbers of British Territorial and Canadian troops now occupying most sectors north of the La Bassée Canal as far as the boundary with the Belgian Army beyond Ypres, discussions involving diversionary actions to assist grand French attacks were opened. Joffre's scheme for May 1915 involved a vast battlefront some 19 kilometres in breadth extending from the Notre Dame de Lorette Spur overlooking the great coalfields of Artois to the Point du Jour, a low but strategically vital hill east of Arras. The intention was to precipitate an advance upon Lens, and—via the infamous Vimy Ridge—possibly Douai. Should it succeed, key German road and rail communications would be cut, and Lille would automatically become vulnerable. Anglo–French discussions commenced about possible British diversionary actions to assist French ambitions; the result was an agreement for a restricted enterprise involving a strictly limited number of First Army—Sir Douglas Haig's—troops.

On 1 May heartening news reached London: to relieve Russian pressure on their Austro–Hungarian allies, the Germans were about to launch an offensive of their own at Gorlice–Tarnow in the Carpathians. It was a development that weakened garrisons in France and Flanders, for during April the full ten infantry divisions of the Eleventh German Army had been transferred eastwards. Twenty-fours hours later the battle near Cracow began—and simultaneously General Ferdinand Foch, commanding the Artois Offensive, informed Haig that his own Northern Army Group preparations were almost complete. In turn, Haig notified Sir John French that he would be ready to attack in five days time.

As part of Prince Rupprecht's AOK 6, 6 BRD had now become fully embedded in French Flanders. Having served in the Ypres sector since October 1914, the troops were already experienced by the time they reached Fromelles the following year. Commanded since 26 December by *Generalleutnant* Gustav Leofried Ignaz Scanzoni von Lichtenfels (von Scanzoni), the division was composed of four regiments: the 20th and 21st Bavarian Reserve Infantry Regiments (RIR 20 and 21), which formed the 14th Bavarian Reserve Infantry Brigade (14 BRB), and RIR 16 and 17, their parent brigade being 12 BRB. After Neuve Chapelle the division was transferred a few kilometres north-east to the neighbouring Aubers and Fromelles sectors. For seven weeks there was little but hard labour, working on defensive fieldworks, but before two months had passed they were once more in action facing another British assault, again centred upon Rouges Bancs where the momentous events of late 1914 had taken place.

The Battle of Aubers Ridge would especially influence the fate of the 5th Australian Division, for on 9 May 1915 the Tommies of the British 8th Division would attack the same battlefront and indeed temporarily occupy the same German positions as would the Diggers of 1916—almost to the metre. In critical addition, although the strategic objectives were different, the tactics employed on both occasions were practically indistinguishable. As a result the two battles unfolded in alarmingly similar fashion.

———⊷⊶———

The British approached Aubers with optimism. There were to be two separate assaults, both pressed by First Army divisions under Sir Douglas Haig. The southern enterprise, once more in the Neuve Chapelle sector, involved a battlefront of 2.5 kilometres. Here four divisions were to break the line and surge eastwards. At Fromelles, some 7 kilometres to the north, two British divisions prepared to assault the enemy trenches on a front of 1.5 kilometres The battleground was boundaried by two features: the Sugar Loaf Salient, a small outward bulge in the enemy line, and Delangré Farm, a moated farmstead some 100 metres within German territory.

Following a south-westerly angle of penetration, the plan was for two brigades of the 8th Division to swiftly seize and consolidate the ground up to and including Fromelles. Through this breach the supporting

7th Division would drive beyond the village, swarm across the meagrely defended plateau beyond, and converge with the Indian Corps from the southern attack, thus enveloping Neuve Chapelle, Aubers and Fromelles. The British envisaged the conventional 'pincer' movement producing a foundation for assault not only upon the rest of the ridge but Lille itself. At a pre-battle conference on 6 May, all agreed that the scale and range of artillery was adequate. Sir Douglas Haig placed his supreme trust in the combination of guns and an overwhelming superiority in troop numbers: an estimated eleven to one.

In reserve, ready to exploit success at the very earliest opportunity, lay three infantry divisions and two corps of cavalry. To ameliorate the communication problems that had crippled the action of 10 March, the Royal Flying Corps (RFC) were tasked to have machines constantly in the air, updating infantry commanders with progress by signalling to and from the ground with specially designed equipment and codes.

Zero for both attacks was set for 5.00 a.m., and each was to be preceded by a forty-minute bombardment. A total of 190 artillery pieces had been allocated. They included two 15-inch and four 9.2-inch howitzers, and twenty-eight 4.7-inch guns for the bombardment of Fromelles and Aubers and selected targets behind the German lines such as fortified farms and key approach roads, and of course for the neutralisation of hostile gun batteries identified by aerial observation. The smaller-calibre weapons would concentrate upon wire-cutting and the destruction of the enemy breastworks, trench intersections, dugouts and suspected rallying points.

At 4.06 a.m. Sunday 9 May, the day dawned dry, bright and cool at Fromelles. The two leading 8th Division brigades had been in their allocated positions either side of Rouges Bancs by 2.30 a.m. The night had been quiet and confidence was high. Like their commanders, the troops were said to be in 'excellent spirits'.

———

Since their arrival in mid-March, the 6th Bavarians had made rapid progress in improving the line. They realised that with every passing week the forces opposing them in Flanders were growing stronger, with a steady influx of British and colonial troops; the increasing imbalance in numbers made work essential. Mirroring the activities of their enemy, the original 1914 positions were in several places abandoned, but instead of stepping back to build breastworks, von Scanzoni's men moved forward, thus leaving a convenient network of ditch-like channels—the original front lines—to the rear of the 'new' front line. They were now employed to enhance drainage. The defences were as yet uncomplicated and unrefined: fieldworks in progress. Nevertheless, like the humble shell- or fox-hole, they were eminently defensible by well-trained troops. The line predominantly consisted of a single breastwork parapet, although in places where the opposing trenches were close and thus more susceptible to attack, a basic parados (a mirror image of the breastwork parapet, but at the rear of the trench) had also been constructed. There were as yet no trench railways, no light-signalling stations, no power supply and no buried telephone cables. To the rear, there was also no established second line of defence; once a breakthrough had been achieved an attacker was therefore faced with lightly fortified cottages, farms and outbuildings.

Most importantly perhaps, the front-line breastwork had been raised and widened. For this to be possible, a huge body of earth had been 'won' from before and behind the structure. The resulting excavations were known as 'borrow pits'. Those at the foot of the steep glacis (the sloping face) facing the British were up to half a metre deep and 5 metres wide, and filled with thickets of old and new barbed wire, timber and steel pickets, *chevaux-de-frise* (spiked obstacles used to close gaps in the barbed wire) and general debris designed to impede. They often contained water. Before them stood a more formal belt of wire fixed to wooden stakes. Within the breastwork itself, now several metres broad, over 2 metres high and reinforced with timber and logs, were installed small shelters to protect the garrison. They were largely waterproof, bullet-proof, shrapnel-proof, and probably best described as 'almost' shell-proof—as long as the shell was of small calibre. There were as yet no concrete pillboxes or underground dugouts.

That a British attack was likely to be centred astride Rouges Bancs was no surprise to the Germans. The close proximity of the opposing trenches along a substantial stretch of line meant that No Man's Land could be swiftly negotiated: it was the most vulnerable and therefore the most logical place for hostile assault. In addition, for some weeks aerial photographs had revealed features behind the British line in the sector, which were correctly interpreted as assembly trenches. When the guns opened fire early on the morning of Sunday 9 May, the location of the impending assault was instantly confirmed.

Post-battle Bavarian reports recorded: 'at 5.50am an intense bombardment by artillery of all calibres was directed at our trenches in Sector III a-e, accompanied by heavy shrapnel fire on the ground between the front line and Fromelles. The shelling continued at this intensity for about an hour and, as later became clear, was heavy enough to destroy our wire in numerous places.'

Some British observers remarked that the shelling 'appeared to lack the intensity of the Neuve Chapelle bombardment'. More importantly however, they complained that many rounds were falling upon their own positions. The assault was disrupted before it had begun. The 2nd Rifle Brigade war diary noted that, 'When our bombardment opened a good many shells dropped short. Some of our men began to retire from the advanced sap [abandoned 1914 trenches, now in No Man's Land] and from the fire trench. The movement was stopped, but our first line suffered severe casualties from our own shell fire'. Before the assault, therefore, there were already British dead and wounded awaiting evacuation, obstructing the crowded trenches and making movement difficult.

In the sector east of Rouges Bancs the British launched the attack with mines. Beneath the enemy front line two 900-kilogram charges had been secretly planted by 173 (Tunnelling) Company, Royal Engineers. While working beneath No Man's Land the sappers had suffered severe difficulties with quicksand and poor air quality, but as the barrage lifted from the German front line the mines were blown with gratifying results, producing craters 10 metres deep and 40 metres wide. The earthquaking effect shook down breastworks and collapsed dugouts; according to their own reports, forty-eight Bavarians were buried. During the period of chaos and shock that followed, four companies of the 13th London Regiment (Kensingtons), shrouded by the smoke and fumes, dashed across the 70 metres of No Man's Land—the narrowest on the battlefront—entering the enemy lines astride the right-hand crater, exactly as the Diggers were to do in fourteen months' time. As 6 BRD reported to their command at AOK 6 on 29 May 1915:

Under cover of this smoke a tight formation of enemy troops left their trenches on a frontage of about 50m and broke into our positions through the breach blown by the mines. The break-in occurred in several waves. The first wave did not stop at our front-line trench but immediately ran on for a further 150–200m to the rearward strongpoint at the small farm known as 'mit dem toten Schwein' ['Dead Pig' Farm, later referred to as 'Tote Sau' by the Bavarians, but known to the British and Australians as Delangré Farm] *and the adjoining communication trench, where they went to ground and took up defensive positions. Subsequent waves occupied the captured section of trench and began to enlarge the lodgement by driving back our trench garrisons to left and right with hand grenades. The enemy storming column was exceptionally strong and forged ahead regardless of casualties.*

As a result of unchecked machine-gun fire on their left, the Kensingtons suffered losses while crossing No Man's Land; on arrival in the enemy line casualties became progressively heavier. Occupying the same positions which later would become temporarily familiar to the 8th Australian Brigade, they found Delangré Farm—the key objective—'hardly touched' by British shelling: it appeared to contain two machine guns and several riflemen. In addition, notes their war diary, 'The machine guns of the West Riding Division were firing into us. There was no sign of any British troops on our right or behind us. Our right flank was completely in the air and the whole line was suffering from fire from Delangré Farm.' The Kensingtons were isolated.

Two battalions of the West Riding Regiment holding the British line beyond the left flank of the attack had been tasked to suppress Bavarian fire east of Delangré Farm, i.e. beyond the unattacked left flank of the incursion. The Yorkshiremen's shooting was ill directed, streaming among the Kensingtons trying to push westwards along the Bavarian front line. Those who drove eastwards towards Rouges Bancs hoping to link with Rifle Brigade comrades were thwarted by a barricade built by parties under the command of *Leutnant* August Bachschneider. Despite eventually being hemmed in on both sides, Bachschneider's men would not only hold out, but assist in pushing the British out.

At Rouges Bancs itself, the British artillery, assisted by a gun firing at almost point-blank range through an aperture in the breastworks, managed to blow a breach in the Bavarian parapet for the 2nd Rifle Brigade and 1st Royal Irish Rifles. No Man's Land here was also narrow because of the presence and employment of the old 1914 trenches, features that would become sanctuaries for many an Australian on 19 and 20 July 1916. The primary objective was to swiftly install a strong force within the enemy lines astride the Rue Delvas and to link with the Kensingtons on the left and East Lancashire Regiment (East Lancs) on the right. Hostile machine guns in the sector should thus be quickly neutralised, allowing units of the supporting division to cross No Man's Land in relative safety, pick up the attacking gauntlet, and surge forward to the ridge.

A weaker 2nd Rifle Brigade force than had been anticipated now advanced over the broken wire, through the 20-metre-wide breach created by the howitzers, and into the section of the enemy line that today lies within the Memorial Park (between the Digger statue and the Rue Delvas). Aiming to link with the East Lancs, a party of riflemen drove west before being blocked after about 100 metres by another barricade erected by a platoon under *Feldwebelleutnant* (Sergeant Major Lieutenant) Isidor Neher. No further progress was to be made in this direction, and a key German machine gun (No. 3) was left critically untouched. A similar blocking action protected No. 5 gun, which was able to continue firing in enfilade across the ground that the 2nd East Lancs and 2nd Northamptonshire Regiment (Northants) were required to traverse to reach their objectives. Before they could make their assault, however, the East Lancs were punished by poor British artillery observation and gunnery; their war diary noted 'shells falling short into the Fromelles trench, in the parapet, in rear, and in the assembly trenches behind the parapet. As the Regiment was being rapidly annihilated by our own artillery it was withdrawn behind the parapet to the west side of the Fromelles Road.'

Although the Rifle Brigade and Royal Irish Rifles got quickly in among the enemy, the two companies of Lancastrians that eventually made the first assault across the rapidly diverging expanse of No Man's Land west of the road were cut down within moments of breaking cover. They had exited through narrow sally-ports (hidden doorways cut through the breastworks); congestion and casualties caused slow egress, making them easy targets. A second wave was 'mown down within 25 yards'. A courageous third attempt almost reached the Bavarian wire—which was uncut. In support, the 2nd Lincolnshire Regiment (Lincolns) were unable to advance more than a few metres beyond their own parapet.

The 2nd Royal Berkshire Regiment (Berks) now joined the tangled ranks of the Rifle Brigade and East Lancs in the jumping-off trenches alongside Rue Delvas, joining in the second leap towards the Bavarian line. Before they reached the enemy wire, however, retreating parties of first-wave riflemen came surging back shouting 'retire at the double'. Many heard the exhortation, and duly withdrew to the chaos of the starting line. There they were told to move eastwards and prepare to reinforce and re-supply the Kensingtons on the left flank.

Despite the chaos, by 8.30 a.m. the British had nevertheless achieved small yet still potentially significant gains, penetrating the Bavarian line at several points and capturing approximately 600 metres of trench. In two places they occupied deeper positions within the hinterland beyond. There was still reason for optimism. Whether the slender advantage that had now been fashioned could be converted into the significant tactical victory that Sir Douglas Haig had planned depended upon whether the breaches created by the 8th Division could be widened and consolidated so that the 7th could use the positions as a gateway and springboard for assault. Resistance had been more robust than anticipated; it now had to be crushed by pushing in as much support as possible.

The principal challenge for Bavarian commanders was to prevent British reinforcements from reaching their first-wave comrades. RIR 16 later provided this report to 6 BRD of what happened next:

> The former task fell to the artillery and was admirably accomplished in all respects. The barrage fire which began at this time and continued throughout the day, combined with the vigilance of the neighbouring infantry units, ensured that all attempts by the British reserves assembled in their rear to link up with the troops that had broken into our trenches were thwarted. No further British troops entered the German forward positions after 7.00 a.m.

Nevertheless, those elements of the 9th and 10th companies that were cut off between the two lodgements on the right flank found themselves in a very difficult situation. Deprived of half their strength and with British troops behind them, they were obliged to defend themselves on three sides. Realising that they needed to capture that section of trench in order to form a continuous front, the enemy began bombing from the flanks, while some of the troops that had advanced beyond our line turned around and attacked from the rear with bayonets and with rifle fire. That all such attempts failed, and the garrison of the isolated section of trench was able to hold out against overwhelming odds until evening, attests not only to the tenacity of the individual defenders but also to the intrepid leadership of the officers commanding them: Leutnant Bachschneider of 10/RIR16 and Feldwebel-Leutnant Neher of 9/RIR16. The former took command of the whole section and ordered barricades to be erected and flanking positions constructed, defended by grenade throwers. The British made repeated attempts to outflank these defences and take the position from the rear, but they were annihilated, some by rifle fire as they closed, and those who succeeded in getting into the trench in close-quarters fighting with bayonets and trench clubs.

The Bavarian tourniquet had been swiftly applied; now it was tightened, not only until the British were starved of support and supply across No Man's Land, but until there was no way in—and no way out. By late morning the Bavarians were in a position to draw breath, take stock and decide how best to re-occupy the lost trenches. The report went on:

Such was the situation at 12.00 noon. The crisis was past. The confusion engendered by the surprise attack and the shock of the mine explosions had dissipated; the officers commanding in the front line had acted decisively and reorganised the defensive structure; the flanks were secured, and the artillery was laying down a defensive barrage to protect against new incursions from the enemy rear. The British troops that had broken into our lines were cut off and had become defenders rather than attackers. The only route still open to them was towards Fromelles, but pressing their attack forward in that direction was impossible without

the reinforcements that were unable to reach them from their rear.
It was now only a matter of time before the lost positions would be
recovered, either by our troops on the ground taking the initiative
themselves or in an operation ordered by local commanders.

Hostile artillery, guided by observers in trees and tall buildings in and
around Fromelles, was now causing grave problems within the British
trenches. Both walking and stretchered wounded blocked routes that had
been earmarked for advancing support troops. Shrapnel continually burst
over No Man's Land. In expectation of just such an attack, the Bavarian
gunners had pre-registered their targets. It was just as well because British
shellfire had severed Bavarian telephone lines as early as 6.45 a.m., causing
serious problems at command posts. As 6 BRD later reported to AOK 6:

While the battle was unfolding, higher command at Regiment, Brigade
and Divisional level remained almost entirely uninformed until about
noon. Every conceivable interruption and obstruction that could
possibly have affected communication in such a situation came into
play. All the telephone lines went dead as soon as the enemy artillery
opened fire; in the excitement of battle, the officers commanding in the
front line either forget to send back reports or the runners could not
get around the British positions, or they were killed, or were unable
to find the command posts. Division and Brigade therefore had to rely
on reports reaching the 14th Brigade second-hand from non-engaged
units in neighbouring sub-sectors, which were inevitably vague or gave
a distorted view of events. It was known that the British had broken
through, but for some time neither where nor in what strength. A clear
grasp of the situation only emerged gradually from the reports of officers
sent forward into the front line and in particular from one superb report
sent back by Leutnant Bachschneider of 8 Battalion.

In the late afternoon the Kensingtons continued their forward surge,
occupying Delangré Farm but forming a somewhat porous flank. This was
the most advanced position that the British were to reach on 9 May. They
were prevented from encroaching further eastwards by *Leutnant* Schmitt

who, operating from a flanking position east of Delangré and supported by several platoons from RIR 21, broke up the assault, driving them back in the direction of the Bavarian front line. Ultimately, the Kensington remnants found themselves holding on by their fingertips in the same abandoned, waterlogged trenches that were to be vainly defended by the 8th and 14th Australian Brigades on 19 July 1916.

The Sugar Loaf was assaulted by the 2nd Northamptonshire Regiment, their task being to widen the breach to over 1500 metres and in so doing prevent hostile machine guns from baulking the passage of the 7th Division to Fromelles and beyond. Forming the right flank of the whole enterprise, the assault carried a heavy responsibility. The troops were separated from their East Lancs comrades by the Laies Brook, the stream which ran beneath the Bavarian breastworks in the Sugar Loaf and across No Man's Land, joining the British lines at the *Tommy-Brücke* bridge. Rather than run the risk of crossing the stream, it was simply avoided.

The Northants' advanced jumping-off trenches ran along the edge of an orchard of a farm bordering the Rue Delvas, and were the same as those employed the following year by the 59th and 60th Battalions of the 15th Australian Brigade. The position was already actually known as the 'Orchard' to the British (and the *Obstgarten* to the Bavarians). Before the assault, D Company under the command of Lieutenant O.K. Parker had moved into the Orchard to clear and extend the old trenches and cut lanes through the British wire. The two lead companies, A and D, assembled here, with B and C in support to the rear. A and D had been instructed to attack ten minutes *later* than the East Lancs, the objective being the north-east face of the salient. It lay some 260 metres away, across fields of dense weeds, grass and yellow flowering self-seeded oilseed rape. The ground was inter-sected by a network of ditches lined with pollarded willows. Having been subjected to a battering by 6-inch howitzers, the salient looked vulnerable.

The responsibility to follow up the East Lancs' assault—to consolidate the gains and thus forge a link with the Northants when they breached the Sugar Loaf—belonged to the 1st Sherwood Forester Regiment (Sherwood Foresters). Their war diary states that the enemy parapet 'appeared entirely untouched by our artillery fire, and between points 375 and 373 there were eight machine-guns, some in fixed positions; others were being fired from the top of the breastwork without tripods'. The first wave of East Lancs was held up only 20 metres into No Man's Land. Thus the first two attacking companies of Foresters were ordered to swing half-right and assault the enemy line to the left of where the Laies Brook flowed out beneath the Bavarian breastwork. The closest they got was about 35 metres from the wire: 'This part of the enemy's line appeared to be even more strongly held . . . The wire was only cut by our guns in one place, making a gap about 4 yards wide.' In several places it was noted that *chevaux-de-frise* were sunk into the borrow pits in front of the breastwork. No advance beyond this point was possible.

Meanwhile, the two companies of the 2nd Northants had left their forward trenches at 5.50 a.m. and advanced gingerly only to come under heavy enfilade fire. The culprits may well have been two machine guns possibly mounted upon wheels, situated in raised positions *behind* the Bavarian front line and firing over the top of the breastworks. The Northants' war diary states that the party:

> . . . *continued to push forward losing very heavily, only part of D Company under Lt. Parker reached the enemy trenches, which had been breached by our artillery. Lt. Parker had about 30 men all told and established himself in the enemy's parapet. A Company were nearly all wiped out. B Company advanced in support of A and D Companies at 6 a.m. but immediately on quitting the orchard came under heavy enfilade machine-gun fire and were unable to reach the enemy's parapet . . .*

The corresponding Bavarian narrative explains how Lieutenant Parker's successful incursion was able to take place:

> *The positions occupied by the right flank platoon were completely destroyed in the heavy bombardment of Sector f [i.e. the 'nose' of the Sugar Loaf] by artillery of all calibres that began at 5.00 a.m. At about 6.30 the enemy lifted his fire to the ground behind our positions, without*

reducing its intensity. Meanwhile the enemy infantry had worked its way up to our trenches under cover of the smoke cloaking the whole position, exploiting the landscape of drainage ditches and tall oilseed rape, and a force of about 70 men poured into the shattered trench. Because of the intense shelling, the company had evacuated this position and the garrison had withdrawn to right and left. The enemy was unable to drive eastwards because the spoil [from the blown-in breast-works] formed an impenetrable barrier, with the isolated parties of the company in position behind it, and progress to the west was rapidly halted by a vigorous counter-attack. At the same time the oncoming enemy infantry were bombed to a stand-still with hand grenades and did not dare to press on to support those who had broken in earlier. Instead, they went to ground in the field of oilseed rape and the ditches, and attempted throughout the day to work their way back to their own lines individually. But they were kept continuously under fire and suffered heavy casualties.

The crew of a British machine gun that was brought forward to within 50m of our trenches were shot down to prevent the gun from being brought into action. The troops who had initially broken in were first halted and then systematically driven back and annihilated. Those who took to their heels over the parapet were shot down by our men. As the enemy artillery was still firing on our front line trench and the strongpoint, a small number of British troops were trapped and left behind inside our lines. Contact was eventually established with our men at the eastern end of the trench and the last remnants of the enemy force were then overwhelmed by concerted pressure from east and west. By 7.00pm there were no enemy troops in the trench. The company took no prisoners.

The result of the assault on the Sugar Loaf was a splendid teaching aid for the Bavarians, whose positioning and deployment of machine guns, and performance of protective artillery proved practically flawless: their ranks having been withered in the killing ground of No Man's Land, the British had been unable to install an effective force. That evening, when darkness had enclosed the battleground, just four men led by Lieutenant

O.K. Parker cautiously made their way back through the oilseed rape. As the report above reveals, the rest of his party had been shown no mercy. Later, twenty men of D Company crept in from their hiding places in No Man's Land—they had not reached the enemy breastwork.

There is a critical aspect to the Northants' chronicle that is especially pertinent to the events of the following year. It concerns the evacuation of the Bavarian trenches under British shellfire. In May 1915 a temporary 'departure' from locations that were being severely mauled by Allied guns was officially sanctioned by von Scanzoni; this was not the case in July 1916, not least because, as we shall see in the next chapter, improvements in Bavarian fieldworks made it largely unnecessary. Had the Sugar Loaf been fully manned on 9 May it appears unlikely that Lieutenant Parker and his men would have been able to force an entry.

The Bavarian Divisional Reserve arrived in Fromelles at 2.15 p.m. By that time their deployment had already become unnecessary because the two incursions had already been brought fully under control. Only when later messages confirmed that part of the line was in fact still occupied by the British were I Battalion RIR 16 and one company from 14 BRB given orders (at 6.00 p.m.) to prepare a counter-attack. They later reported: 'By about 7.30 p.m. the whole trench was back in our hands with the exception of a 50-metre stretch astride the Rouges Bancs–Tommybrücke road, where the enemy held out doggedly until 2.00 a.m. when 4/RIR 16 (Divisional Reserve, *Oberleutnant* Gebhardt) stormed their position and forced them into submission.'

The 1915 battle concluded in exactly the same place and in exactly the same way as the 1916 encounter: in and around the site now occupied by the Australian Memorial Park. On May 29 von Scanzoni was able to report to his superiors at AOK 6:

The total casualties of the Division on 9 May were 13 officers and 630 NCOs and men (264 dead). In 9 and 10/RIR16, which bore the brunt of the enemy attack, 180 men fell at their posts. Our victorious troops took 141 prisoners and captured 7 machine guns. Burying the British dead took a week. Hauptmann Schmitz, Oberleutnant Gebhardt, Leutnant Bachschneider and Feldwebel-Leutnant Neher

were awarded the Iron Cross, First Class. The action at Fromelles is a
feather in the cap of this Division. All arms contributed to the victory,
but once again the laurels must go to the infantry.

The following year *Oberleutnant* Gebhardt was an RIR 16 battalion commander with the rank of *Hauptmann*; on 19 July he was again deeply involved.

Before news of the colossal British casualty count reached First Army HQ, Sir Douglas Haig and his staff were considering renewal of the offensive during the night or at dawn the following day. There were insufficient troops to guarantee success and no worthwhile artillery to support them, the guns having worn barrels and tired mechanisms. Low shell stocks completed the negative equation. Discussions continued until lunchtime, when all became fully aware of the shocking cost of the previous day's encounter. Finally, Sir John French abandoned the venture. Thus ended the 'second' battle of Fromelles.

No Man's Land in front of Rouges Bancs presented a ghastly sight, with hundreds of corpses entangled within thickets of German wire. If the battle's architect, Lieutenant General Sir Henry Rawlinson, had gazed upon the sight—or even the photographs taken by the Bavarian victors— he might have been less inclined to record on 10 May his 'fear' that the East Lancs and some battalions of the 25th Brigade got 'cold feet' and did not advance with 'the dash they ought to have done in the first instance'. It was, he wrote, 'doubtful if they tried very hard'.

The Bavarian narrative states that 'Burying the British dead took a week'. So it had after the action of December 1914, and so it would in July 1916. British 8th Division losses in the attack at Rouges Bancs on 9 May 1915 were 4682. In their assault upon the Sugar Loaf the 2nd Northants lost 426 men.

The combined casualty count for both 9 May attacks was over 11 500 killed, wounded or missing. In July 1916 the Australian casualty figure would reach 5333. An aggregation of losses in 1914, 1915 and 1916 makes the sector astride Rouges Bancs a candidate for the title of the bloodiest battleground of the Western Front. It is little wonder that human remains are still recovered from these fields.

What of French prospects in the main feature at Vimy and Arras? After a promising and storming start, the Second Battle of Artois eventually concluded in dreadful fashion for Joffre and Foch. Losses totalled 102 000, for a gain of a few hundred metres. Along the 12-mile (20 kilometre) front eighteen French divisions had been stifled by a mere four of the enemy. So crushing had been the defeat that the efficacy of Aubers as a cooperative exercise was simply impossible to gauge.

Afterwards, German headquarters in Berlin was even more confident that the French and British would be unable to force a decisive breach on the Western Front. For them, this was especially heartening because events were taking a turn for the worse in the east. They needed to cripple Russia's potentially huge offensive power, and that meant drawing upon more and more units in the west. Having proven the worth of organised trench-based defences, even when garrisons were grossly outnumbered, the priority for the foreseeable future was to formulate a way of retaining the territory they now held until the moment when a decisive thrust of their own could be launched—whenever that may be. In Flanders it meant devising new field-works and defensive tactics that would endure any and every thrust the Entente was able to exert.

Chapter 4

A POOR SEASON

The Battle of Aubers Ridge was an overture to the 1916 action, and an ideal rehearsal for the Germans. Apart from the piercing of the Sugar Loaf, the two actions unfolded almost identically. If one substituted the word 'Australian' for 'British', the Bavarian post-battle report of May 1915 could comfortably apply to July 1916; indeed, many of the same German names appear in both narratives.

Although British casualty figures were similar to those suffered by the Australians fourteen months later, there are several differences in the way the battle has been regarded, remembered and commemorated. Over 1300 men remain missing as a result of the May 1915 action; but no memorial marks their passing, or indeed the importance and legacy of the engagement. It has never been fully studied either as a template or even as a hypothetical adjunct to the action of 1916. Although not one among their ranks would have known it, the Australians who stepped out upon No Man's Land on the evening of 19 July 1916 and advanced over the sprawled mortal remains of hundreds of their British comrades were playing directly into the hands of Bavarian tacticians. The ravaged endeavours of the 8th Division on 9 May 1915 formed the very foundation of the almost pre-destined ill fortune that the nation of Australia was at that moment embarking upon.

In the Dardanelles at this time the Battle of Krithia had recently claimed 30 000 Allied casualties. It brought Anzac losses since the landing in April to 8543. By the end of the month the British casualty count had reached almost 50 000. In August a further amphibious landing at Suvla Bay was designed to assist the Australians and New Zealanders at Anzac Cove to break out of their coastal enclave, and at the same time create the environment for a general advance that would finally shatter the deadlock. Suvla's Turkish defence comprised 1500 troops of the Anafarta Detachment. Commanded by a Bavarian, *Major* Wilhelm Willmer, in the coming weeks they stifled attack after attack by forces numbering over 20 000.

The spring of 1915 was one of the bleakest periods of the war for the British on the Western Front. The Germans had employed poison gas for the first time during the Second Battle of Ypres, and a response was obligatory; the *Lusitania* had been sunk; the North Sea and other waterways were riddled with sea-mines; the crews of scores of small trawlers had been captured and their innocent vessels destroyed; to cap it all, on the English mainland coastal towns with no strategic or military importance were being targeted by the German navy and zeppelins. Newspapers stoked the furnaces of fury against such 'Hunnish' behaviour; but what made it all the more unbearable was that time after time the Germans appeared able, almost at will, to crush massive and seemingly overwhelming Anglo–French attempts to lance the boil of stalemate. And the same was true of the Turks—led by a German. Public frustration and disgust revealed itself in anti-German sentiment and rioting, powerfully fuelled soon after 9 May by the 'Shell Scandal'.

Instigated by Sir John French and promoted by the London *Times* and the highest-circulation newspaper in the country, the *Daily Mail*, the public were made aware of not only a shortage of artillery shells but their poor quality, and it was largely at this dubious door that responsibility for the recent catastrophe at Aubers was laid. Although many knew it, especially in the trenches, none dared articulate that the blame for the lack of success lay not with faulty shells, but with a highly professional and efficient enemy.

On 14 May 1915 Charles a'Court Repington, military correspondent for *The Times*, wrote, 'It is certain we can smash the German crust if we have the means.' The 'means' was an unlimited supply of shells. But the 'crust' was more robust than anyone could imagine.

The failure—and thus the loss—at Aubers was publicly laid by Sir John French at the feet of the government department responsible for shell production: the Ministry of Munitions. Some now believe that the commander-in-chief was guilty of crudely diverting attention from his own failures. It is true, however, that for weeks before the spring actions French had several times begged the British government to concentrate urgently on production. In his 1919 account of his actions at this time, Sir John wrote:

> . . . on May 9 1915, when we commenced the Battle of Festubert . . . my mind was filled with keen anxiety. After all our demands, less than 8 per cent of our shells were high explosive, and we only had sufficient supply for about 40 minutes of artillery preparation for this attack. On the tower of a ruined church I spent several hours in close observation of the operations. Nothing since the Battle of the Aisne had ever impressed me so deeply with the terrible shortage of artillery and ammunition as did the events of that day. As I watched the Aubers Ridge, I clearly saw the great inequality of the artillery duels, and, as attack after attack failed, I could see that the absence of sufficient artillery support was doubling and trebling our losses in men. I therefore determined on taking the most drastic measures to destroy the apathy of a Government which had brought the Empire to the brink of disaster . . . If any additional proof were required of the hopelessness of any relief coming from the War Office, I found it waiting for me when I reached Headquarters that afternoon, in the shape of a telegram from the Secretary of State for War, directing that 20 per cent of our scanty reserves of ammunition was to be shipped to the Dardanelles. I immediately gave instructions that evidence should be furnished to Colonel Repington . . . that the vital need of high-explosive shells had been a fatal bar to our Army success on that day.

Public outrage led to the fall of Asquith's Liberal government, the formation of a coalition, and the installation of David Lloyd George as head of a newly created and independent Ministry of Supply. Under his leadership the situation improved swiftly and markedly. But the war still had to be won.

A few weeks later, others of influence were assessing the situation in a different light. The following diary entry is by General Sir Henry Rawlinson, whose troops had been annihilated and humiliated at Rouges Bancs:

21.6.1915. The chief cause of failure was the dugouts and cellars into which the garrison withdrew during the bombardment so that when the moment came for the assault they were able to rush out and line their trenches without having suffered to any serious extent from the hellish bombardment we had given them. The moral effect of the heavy shells is neutralised by this form of semi-permanent fortification which the enemy has had ample time to prepare in the last six months in soil well suited to the purpose at all times of year.

While the British bickered and fumed over their failure, the Germans looked at the 'Shell Scandal' from an entirely different angle. Their narratives make no mention whatsoever of faulty British ordnance; to them, the hostile gunnery in May and June had been excellent, and the shelling not only seriously destructive but deeply disturbing from the point of view of fortification procedures.

They therefore elected to make the colossal investment in time, human effort and matériel by installing a second line of defence. In addition, all key timber structures were everywhere to be replaced—where time and geology allowed and tactical considerations demanded—by concrete emplacements and, for command posts, deep, tunnelled dugouts. Communication was of vital importance—telephone wires must be buried. The critical question was whether the British would grant them the time to carry out the work and make the investment pay.

During the two months before Aubers, 6 BRD had captured only a single British prisoner and one Lee-Enfield rifle. On 10 May they were able to record a bag of 141 men and two officers, five machine guns and

617 other weapons. The action was indeed a feather in their cap. Most important of all, however, was that the 8th Division's incursions, limited though they had been, were to date the sole instance of enemy penetration into the *Hintergelände*—the name given to the territory between the two main lines of Bavarian defences.

The study of the events of 9 May provided the basis for Bavarian tacticians to construct strategies to manage future assaults. If the British elected to attack again, they were likely to have similar objectives as on this occasion: the ridge and Lille. It was this strategic scenario upon which all future planning must be based. All of 6 BRD's efforts were now invested in producing a defensive system that would—without fear of failure—reproduce a similar outcome because: if the ridge could be made safe, Lille and its key supply and communication network was equally safe.

The fate of the 5th Australian Division and the 61st South Midlanders in 1916 may well have been sealed on 9 and 10 May 1915. Had Charles Bean been able to fully research that battle from both sides, his Fromelles narrative would almost certainly have assumed a different complexion.

Despite the catastrophes of March and May, the bloodshed around Fromelles was by no means over for 1915. As part of a much wider scheme, involving several limited actions in Belgian and French Flanders, on 25 September a second set of diversionary attacks was launched on either side of the Aubers–Fromelles sector to assist a huge Anglo–French offensive between La Bassée Canal and Arras, and another colossal French thrust in Champagne. The purpose of the British 'subsidiary attacks' in Flanders was to deter German commanders from sending support troops to Artois. As with the 9 May enterprises it was once more envisaged that, with the help of extra guns and more reliable shells, a twin breakthrough could be achieved and the two forces might link and consolidate along the crest of the Aubers Ridge.

On 25 September in the Action of Bois-Grenier (the sector adjoining Fromelles to the north-east), a place that Australian troops would also later come to know, on a frontage of a little over a kilometre, the 25th Brigade (8th Division) went over the top at 4.30 a.m. assisted by a mine and a smoke screen. They once more surprised and swiftly penetrated the German defence, capturing 123 men of RIR 16—the self-same enemy unit that had vanquished the British in May. But by noon the Bavarians had recovered composure and were pressing hard with sustained counter-attacks; by 2.00 p.m. the positions held by the Lincolns, Berkshires and Royal Irish Rifles had become untenable, and they were ordered to withdraw. This time losses totalled 1335, including fifty-two officers. It was a heart-rending case of *déjà vu*.

On the same day, some 5 kilometres away at the Piètre Salient next to Fauquissart, a similar fate befell the Meerut Division (Indian Corps). Jumping off at 6.00 a.m. an impressive initial thrust began with the quick capture of over 200 prisoners, before gradually turning into a nightmare similar to that of May. The Germans, well equipped and intimate with the terrain, bombed their way forward, biting and holding trench after trench until a general British retirement once more became unavoidable. The combined losses from these two actions were 3017.

When Joffre had first mooted another offensive in Artois, Sir Douglas Haig, whose First Army were tasked with the main supporting attacks at Loos, was entirely against the plan. He was dissatisfied with the terrain as a battleground and, on more than one occasion, professed a preference for a fresh and enhanced offensive in the Neuve Chapelle–Fromelles sectors (as indeed did Sir John French) where he also favoured the use of poison gas in assaulting the Aubers Ridge. Joffre's rejoinder was emphatic: without a British attack on his immediate left he could not guarantee the French Tenth Army would annexe the Vimy heights, and thus the prime strategic objective would be unattainable. In August Haig expressed further fears, advocating an impressive artillery demonstration with limited infantry assaults.

Joffre intervened, speaking with Field Marshal Lord Kitchener, who spoke with Haig, who as a result was guaranteed two full divisions in reserve and as much chlorine gas as he wanted. Spirits rose. So great became Haig's ever-simmering optimism that he privately began to express a growing confidence in total German collapse during the coming winter. But Joffre's second great offensive thrust in the Vimy and Arras sectors also failed, as did almost a month of British attacks at Loos: despite poison gas and a superiority of seven to one there were over 61 000 British casualties and nothing of note to show for it. The Champagne Offensive suffered a similar fate, with the French registering an extraordinary 190 000 losses.

On 29 September 1915 when the Loos battle was but a few days old, Sir Douglas Haig reported to Lord Kitchener: 'My attack, as has been reported, was a complete success. The enemy had no troops in his second line, which some of my plucky fellows reached and entered without opposition. Prisoners state the enemy was so hard put to it for troops to stem our advance that the officer's servants, fatigue-men, etc., in Lens were pushed forward to hold their second line east of Loos and Hill 70.' However, Sir John French had so positioned the reserves that they could not be swiftly called upon to take advantage of the initial success. It was this fundamental error, suggested Haig, that shifted the entire balance from one of great potential to a humiliating catastrophe, after an 8-kilometre breach had been forced to a depth of 4 kilometres.

Though there was some truth in the claim, numerous other errors of judgement that today appear elementary were made, especially when the lessons of previous months are taken into account. Not least was the fact that the enemy had installed a robust second line of defence—and it was from here that British hopes were dashed.

Kitchener's New Army divisions battled bravely but inadequate training and inexperience aggravated the situation: they would have benefited from a longer period at the front before going into offensive action. The failure meant that detailed information about the newly strengthened German defences was either unavailable or insufficiently studied. As at Aubers, mines had been planted to effect shock and surprise, but they had been blown before zero, thus alerting the enemy. Although smoke screens were effective, the poison gas was not. Releases had been sanctioned despite conditions clearly being far from ideal: in places the gas drifted back upon British troops. The artillery bombardment proved insufficient to cut wire and destroy defences; machine guns and hostile gun batteries were again not neutralised, and German reserves appeared to be able to enter the fighting zone with relative impunity. British trench designs were unsatisfactory, and traffic flow and logistical organisation behind the lines failed to facilitate reinforcement or casualty evacuation. As at Neuve Chapelle, repeated communication breakdown made it impossible to know where British troops were, which again meant that protective and supporting artillery fire was frequently not viable; support from the Royal Flying Corps was in any case handicapped by poor weather conditions. To cap the catastrophe, modifications to the catering arrangements before the battle meant that thousands went hungry into action.

In so many ways, 'The Big Push' as it was optimistically known beforehand, was a blend of Neuve Chapelle and Aubers writ large. It offered Prince Rupprecht's Bavarians, many of whom took part, a fresh array of invaluable tutorials. Having added the most important constituent—the unforgiving gimlet eye of self-criticism—they circulated their conclusions throughout every sector of the Western Front.

———

Save for the dubious prize of the single tiny village of Neuve Chapelle in March and a few acres of ground at Festubert in May, nothing undertaken by the Entente in French Flanders throughout 1915 yielded any substantial tactical fruit. Almost everything that could go wrong did go wrong, and in the trenches it left spirits low and the troops' belief in high command bruised. For the Germans, a period of further strenuous repairs and preparation lay ahead for, as sure as day followed night, another Allied spring offensive would undoubtedly follow the war's second winter. This was the time to act.

Meanwhile, in the Dardanelles the first moves were being made to ensure that Rupprecht's Bavarians would face a fresh enemy in 1916. On 3 October General Sir Charles Monro, recently appointed commander-in-chief of the Mediterranean Expeditionary Force, commenced a visit to all three sectors on the Gallipoli peninsula. The following day he advocated—for the first time—evacuation. On Thursday 4 November, just as the Turks launched yet another abortive attack against the Anzacs, Kitchener set sail for Gallipoli in order to form his own personal assessment. Upon arrival on the 10th he examined the strategic situation, gathered views widely, and came to the conclusion that not only was an evacuation necessary, but it might be achieved without crippling losses. On 22 November, as Kitchener prepared for home, the decision was made: the peninsula must be and would be abandoned.

First to leave were the French. Between 28 December, when the exodus began, and 8 January, a total of 35 268 troops, 3689 horses and mules and 127 guns were evacuated. Remarkably, no casualties were recorded during this period. Having finally escaped the place where as many men became casualties to sickness and disease as enemy action, most Gallipoli 'veterans' then travelled to Egypt for rest, refitting and training. Their future destination was as yet undecided.

Debate over the supreme Imperial military leadership had been fermenting since May and the Shell Scandal. In the late autumn of 1915 it rose strongly to the surface, and the name constantly on politicians' lips as a replacement for the ill, dejected and multiply defeated Sir John French was the commander of First Army, General Sir Douglas Haig, who had himself (alongside the King) surreptitiously nurtured a lack of confidence in the field marshal. After the Loos debacle changes were inevitable, for the Western Front was deadlocked and since the landings at Gallipoli in April no strategically worthwhile gain had been registered. The government could not on any account afford to lose public support for the war. A new and energetic hand was required on the tiller.

At noon on Sunday 19 December 1915, while the Gallipoli evacuations were in full flow, Sir Douglas Haig became commander-in-chief of the British Expeditionary Force. Command of First Army was assumed by General Sir Charles Monro, now returning from a short period of command in Salonica.

Haig had a coterie of close and trusted associates. Among them were Brigadier-General John Gough (his chief of staff at First Army) and Lieutenant-General Sir Richard Haking (commander, XI Corps, also part of First Army). Both assisted in the demise of Sir John French by telling the King 'startling truths of French's unfitness for the command' (Haig's diary) to promote the ascendance of their comrade. A third associate was Lieutenant-General Sir William Robertson, a man who exerted a powerful influence on the new commander-in-chief, and indeed the war itself. Having begun his working life as a household servant with minimal education, Robertson certainly had remarkable life experience (he is presently the only soldier in British Army history to rise from private soldier to field marshal). On 23 December 1915 he was promoted from chief of staff of the British Expeditionary Force to chief of the Imperial general staff. Deliberations with the French government and military, and especially General Joseph Joffre, began almost immediately.

If 1916 was to be the year of victory it was essential that the Entente put the internecine squabbling of the previous twelve months behind them and act as a united force. On 5 January 1916 in a letter to Haig, Robertson delivered a personal collective character portrait of the upper echelons of French command:

> *I am very pleased to hear you like Joffre. I always got on well with him. He is not brilliant but he is sound and honest. As a whole, the French Commanders and Staff are a peculiar lot. Now and again in some respects they are quite good, but on some occasions they are most elementary and impracticable. The great thing to remember in dealing with them is that they are Frenchmen and not Englishmen, and do not and never will look at things in the way we look at them. I suppose that they think we are queer people. It is a big business in having to deal with Allied Commanders, and one has to keep oneself in check and exercise great tolerance . . .*

As he was throughout 1915, General Joseph Joffre would remain the key French military figure for much of the following year. Indeed, discussions about policy for the coming season were convened at Chantilly in November 1915. In terms of manpower, Britain's establishment of almost sixty divisions (grown from six in 1914) was still significantly exceeded by France, but British influence was increasing. As Secretary of State for War, Kitchener provided a seven-point instruction to Haig as the new C-in-C. Point number five spoke volumes about the calamitous twelve months that was now passing into history: 'In minor operations you should be careful that your subordinates understand that risk of serious losses should only be taken where such risk is authoritatively considered to be commensurate with the object in view.' 'Minor operations' . . . 'subordinates' . . . 'risk' . . . 'authoritatively' . . . 'commensurate'. Kitchener's instructions left the commander-in-chief with ample flexibility to follow his instincts. As long as the wording for any approvals he sought for proposed actions was careful, responsibility for the outcomes could be laid at the doors of others.

The onset of winter 1915/16 would have been the second perfect moment in the war for all parties to have called a halt and produced a peace plan, but still no such course was envisaged. The situation was now infinitely more complex than twelve months before.

Despite the war's fathomless maw, somehow the governments of all the protagonists still managed to fund it. The British public had been persuaded that the increased sacrifices being made in France, Turkey, Flanders and at home were not only logical, worthwhile and judicious, but obligatory. There remained no effective pressure for a negotiated peace. On the German side of the Western Front a rigid siege mentality was now firmly in place, and it is probably safe to say that no unit was more deeply imbued than the troops of Prince Rupprecht's AOK 6. Defiant resistance was their primary role and his Bavarian commander at Fromelles and Aubers, Gustav von Scanzoni, was by nature, training and strategic necessity, a perfectionist.

Chapter 5

THE BULWARK

As the 1915 spring turned to summer Lord Kitchener advocated a purely defensive Entente stance in the west until manpower and matériel could be brought to a level whereby a truly fatal blow might be guaranteed. To a man, the French military hierarchy dissented. The suggestion was not just pitiable but heretical, they said; such a wretchedly feeble course could only have been proposed by someone whose native soil did not bear the imprint of a German boot. Their posture was explicable: Britain was not yet under threat of invasion and, despite the powerful influence the nations of her empire were now exerting upon the conflict, she yet remained the junior partner. Hostility would be maintained. Nevertheless, both sides required breathing space to recover from the deep rifts slashed in their ranks by the spring battles.

The strategy that Kitchener now proposed was precisely what Prince Rupprecht's forces in Flanders and Artois desired. It was also largely what they received, since the only remaining 1915 offensive on their territory was the Battle of Loos in late September. The longer the French and British disputed and debated, the greater the German opportunity to create an enduring bastion. The very moment the Aubers fighting ceased, therefore, the Bavarians began evolving a range of defensive fieldworks that in resilience, forethought, ingenuity and human effort would, for specific strategic reasons, far outstrip anything the Allies produced. The bastion that began to appear would have no equal in any other theatre. Unless the Allies could break it, and break it decisively and permanently, there was no hope of British or French offensive success on the Western Front. It is for this reason that a chapter must be dedicated to explaining exactly what the Tommies and Diggers faced in 1916. By the turn of the year tens of thousands of Allied prisoners from both fronts, east and west, were working to produce new roads, bridges, telegraphs, railways, camps, depots, dumps, factories, sawmills and electricity and water supplies, all to be operated and maintained by them and other sources of forced labour.

The vast and comprehensive scale of the Germans' record-keeping reflected their expectation of victory—so that in years to come subsequent generations would appreciate the care, effort and sacrifice necessary for the expansion of the empire and enhanced wellbeing of their people.

In the Munich archives one finds invoices and receipts for groceries, bread and hardware, agreements for rental of land, contracts and deals with local businesses, arrangements with *mairies* (council offices), records of the treatment of sick and injured civilians, punishment of wrongdoers (both French and German), and swathes of detail illustrating the ever-shifting nature of the forced intimacy between invader and invaded. The collection offers an extraordinary socio-military narrative of the greatest upheaval France and indeed the world had ever known. Despite a large part of French Flanders being under martial law and everything that entailed in civil control, curfews, shortages and anxiety, one can in several places distinguish a careful psychological subtlety and indeed skill in German dealings with the native population. A degree of nurture was obligatory, for troops and animals must be fed, machinery repaired, and a colossal quantity of raw material sourced—preferably locally—to fight a defensive conflict in a foreign land. The Germans could not do this alone. They were there to stay, in their opinion, so the development of a stable relationship from the earliest days was not only beneficial but simpler and less costly to administer than a regime based solely upon violence and fear. Make no mistake, however: fear was ever-present. Some of the more enlightened British Imperialists would have recognised the model.

Based in Lille, *Armee-Oberkommando 6*, the parent unit of the 6th Bavarian Reserve Infantry Division, sought to achieve harmony without too often wielding the stick. Most of the younger French male population were of course absent, fighting against the very forces who now largely controlled the lives of their families and friends. For people living on the Entente side of No Man's Land, information was able to travel fast and efficiently between the Allies, and thus to anxious families awaiting news; behind German lines however, reports of battles and the fates of the dead, wounded, captured or missing could derive solely from enemy sources. So, just as the Germans were reliant upon local people to assist with and enhance several aspects of production and supply for their military, especially foodstuffs, the annexed civilians were reliant upon the Germans for information about the most important facet of their lives: the fortunes of loved ones at war. Representations for news about missing men could be made to the relevant *Ortskommandant* (local commander) via the local *mairie*. How much effort the Germans might choose to invest was entirely up to the commanding officer and his staff, but it was clear that manipulation of the anguish of relatives could be employed as a tool to both oil the wheels of productivity and aid civil control: if there was unrest, theft or sabotage, the flow of information from battlefield, hospital and prisoner-of-war camp could soon dry up.

And yet with occupation, the Bavarians also brought unexpected benefits that before the war were often unavailable to civilians. Young children were inoculated against diseases, and they profited from regular check-ups for tuberculosis and other ailments prevalent at the time. Protecting the local populace protected the Germans. The Munich records produce many a surprise. It transpires, for example, that rather than simply commandeering land for military purposes, the German authorities dutifully applied to the local *mairie* for leases. Ground for military cemeteries was rented—per year, or for fifty years. Perhaps one of the strangest and most ironic examples reveals that the Germans fully acknowledged the importance to French rural culture of hunting game: *la chasse*. Printed sheets were circulated giving the closed seasons for the various quarry species; strict adherence was expected from the troops. No such seasons existed for human prey.

———➤●◄———

The Germans were masters of resistance and resilience because they chose to be. At Fromelles one is presented with a microcosm of their defensive doctrine as applied on the wider Western Front.

The true test of field defences is whether they afford troops not only protection from bomb, shell and ground attack, but the means to deliver fire, to move support and ancillary troops, to supply matériel, to communicate between all arms, and to provide multiple platforms for counter-attack. By mid-1916 the scheme at Aubers and Fromelles was based not just upon a single trench line, but on a broad belt of terrain. It included No Man's Land, because command of that all-important ribbon of contested terrain was paramount if they were to have maximum prior warning of enemy approach. It was scrutinised at all hours of the day and night—from within, from above and below, and from the trenches themselves.

When one studies contemporary aerial photographs and maps, the Bavarian positions *appear* more simple and primitive in design than those of the British and Australians. But while certain features, such as trenches and tramways, are clearly discernible and identifiable even to the layman, conclusions about what was taking place within buildings and woods—and especially underground—could only be reached by informed speculation or indeed plain guesswork. The ultimate purpose of camouflage is to conceal the fact that one is concealing something, and in this the Bavarians admirably succeeded.

The geology of the plain—a shallow layer of fertile loam sitting upon a deep bed of impervious clay—meant that soon after positional warfare had commenced both sides quickly accepted that the digging of trenches was largely impracticable. It was not that the water table was high, but simply that the clay did not allow percolation. Digging a trench was therefore like installing a bathtub without a plughole: when it rained, the trench filled with water, and if that water had nowhere to drain, pumping or baling was required to carry it to a place where it could be naturally evacuated, in this case the Laies Brook.

Because in 1915 the German strategic mindset on the Western Front was radically different to that of the Allies, at an early stage they invested far greater effort in making positions defensible, serviceable and indeed comfortable for their troops. This was, after all, not simply a line of trenches across Europe, but the new border of the *Reich*. Across No Man's Land, the Allied lines had a multiple purpose. They were a springboard (the *only* springboard) for attack and thus potential victory, and at the same time the first line of defence not only of France and Britain, but the Australian nation and indeed the entire British Empire. That springboard might be called into use at any moment, so garrisons were required to design, construct and keep it in a state of readiness for *offensive* action, while at the same time employing—but to a much lesser degree—the same defensive mindset as their enemy.

Both sides soon discovered that although it proved possible to dig hundreds, indeed thousands of kilometres of trenches during periods of good weather, come winter their upkeep required greater manpower and matériel than could ever be made available. Post-war Royal Engineer histories note that trenches were more often ruined by neglect of drainage and maintenance than by hostile shelling. Under almost perpetually damp conditions, sandbags had a limited lifespan and timber revetment was subject to rot, especially if fabricated with inferior materials. But one could not simply shift unwanted water by pumping it elsewhere. To achieve effective amelioration, huge areas were simultaneously and permanently 'bled'; on the Allied side, the Royal Engineer Land Drainage Companies eventually installed a system that involved the simultaneous treatment of 30 square kilometres (12 square miles) of forward zone, including Aubers and Fromelles. Because of the geology and hydrology, defences were erected upwards rather than dug downwards. Although referred to as trenches, the resulting structures were actually 'breastworks'—constructions that in their creation demanded many times the human effort necessary for a conventional trench.

To any front-line Digger or Tommy, the enemy's breastwork was the most evident and indeed mysterious feature within their field of view. It resembled an ancient rampart and stretched in both directions as far as the eye could see. Producing an effective protective barrier of this kind required a vast quantity of earth, which was 'won' from 'borrow pits' in front of and behind the position. In the Fromelles sector the 1916 German breastwork was over 2 metres high, screening the garrison from all Allied observation save from the air. Its 'thickness' of up to 10 metres offered soldiers in its lee ample protection from rifle and machine-gun fire, shell splinters, shrapnel, rifle grenades and light shellfire. The 'front face', i.e. what Allied eyes saw across No Man's Land, was a glacis, a steeply sloping earth rampart stabilised with sandbags and timber. During 1915 the Bavarians gradually and clandestinely enlarged their breastworks. Work was carried out under cover of darkness, but the frequent Flanders mists meant that it could often continue well into the morning. By 1916 the breastwork shield was linked with screened road and rail routes, allowing improvement and maintenance to take place at almost any time.

It is important to note that, contrary to popular perception, weather patterns were no different during the First World War than before or after. It did not rain every day, the troops were not permanently wet and cold, and mud was often entirely absent. Warm and dry periods—even droughts— were as commonplace as they are in France today. At such times the clay-rich ground baked, becoming so hard that digging was forcibly abandoned. Dust, rather than mud, then became problematic. Close human confinement carried with it a pest that soldiers from time immemorial would have recognised. The troops on both sides of No Man's Land were in a constant struggle to control body lice. The Bavarians enjoyed the benefit of a special shower and de-lousing train that every four weeks brought its welcome services to troops at rest behind the lines. The British converted farms and especially breweries into de-lousing stations, bathhouses and laundries. Other flying beasts were a yet more serious cause of concern. After summer rains, untended surface water quickly stagnated, and from mid-May until September flies and mosquitoes bred at an alarming rate, feeding upon the quick and the dead alike. Flies were inquisitive feeders; to them No Man's Land was a meaningless concept: they roamed wherever they wished— carrying sickness. They form an aspect of the aftermath of battle that occupies a surprisingly important place in the Fromelles chronicle.

In heat-wave conditions an increased supply of clean drinking (and washing) water was required. Meanwhile the soldiers, trapped in their maze of trenches, sat and sweltered, safe from bullets but robbed of a cooling breeze by the high sandbagged fire bays. Rats and mice abounded, and one finds German evidence of the paid acquisition of 'civilian' cats to counter the problem, healthy specimens commanding higher prices.

One of the strangest discoveries in the Munich archives is a document ordering the procurement of in-season bitches. Having noted an increased prevalence in the British use of message dogs, it was seen as worthwhile to select a night with a favourable wind, tie the bitch to a post near the parapet . . . and await developments. It has not been possible to establish the efficacy of the scheme, but it illustrates the ingenuity and effort expended for any and all tactical benefits.

By October 1916 the effects of the Somme Offensive were to lead to radical transformation of German defensive tactics across the entire Western Front. At the time of the Fromelles battle in mid-July, however, OHL still adhered to the established system of *Halten, was zu halten ist*—hold what there is to hold. The battlefront of 6 BRD at Aubers–Fromelles was divided into four sectors, one to each regiment. The dispositions and nomenclature for July 1916 can be found in the map section. A regimental sector was partitioned into four sub-sectors, a to d, each usually held by a single company, but occasionally by a mix of several. The battlefront's two key elements, the Sugar Loaf and Wick Salients, are respectively to be found in sectors IIIa/b, and IVa. The map shows that Bavarian sectors were given a corresponding alpha-numeric equivalent on the opposite side of No Man's Land. The boundaries of sector II, for example, had its direct British equivalent; company sub-sectors designated IIa, b, c and d, simply became IIA, B, C or D.

Should an assaulting force manage to negotiate No Man's Land and the Bavarian barbed wire, the *I Stellung*—the foremost enemy trench system—was the initial bastion that they would be required to overcome. Failure at this first hurdle, of course, meant that further progress was impossible. In true mediaeval style, grapnel hooks, storming ladders and scrambling mats were required in order to cross wire, scale the steep glacis and descend into the enemy trench. Speed at this critical point was essential, because ascending a glacis too slowly meant being subjected to showers of grenades. To ensure that any hostile approach was detected in sufficient time to allow adequate response, the Bavarians had installed scores of *Horchposten* (listening posts) at the end of saps (short sections of narrow trench that emerged from a screened sally-port in the breast-works and writhed forward beneath the wire and out into No Man's Land). They are frequently erroneously identified as machine-gun posi-tions. Spaced along the entire divisional front and intended for a crew of two or three, they probed up to 30 metres beyond the entanglements. Although employed primarily during the hours of darkness, the sap heads were frequently used as the starting place for daytime patrols. In order that their enemy was at all times visible, and thus a good target, the Bavarians cleared grass and undergrowth across substantial areas of ground in front of the posts, breastworks and wire using saws, scythes and even weed-killer. Searchlights (there were four on the 6 BRD front), Very lights and star shells were variously employed to illuminate the night-time scene.

Also in true mediaeval fashion, wherever the lines were close enough, underground warfare was underway. This was primarily a private conflict fought by specialist engineer troops; it was largely unseen and unknown by the infantry. Defence, rather than offence, was the main preoccupation of the tunneller—blowing in enemy galleries underground. From time to time, however, an offensive chance presented itself, and great craters, many of which still exist, were blown to assist with the customary 'surprise, shock and awe' that frequently aided the beginning of assaults great and small.

What the opposing breastworks contained, i.e. what they concealed, was largely a mystery to Tommy and Digger. If the enemy was prudent in his working practices, as both sides tried to be, aerial reconnaissance could be practically valueless, save for reporting the transportation and stock-piling of matériel, and the appearance of fresh trenches, tracks, railways, and other features that by their nature could not be camouflaged. Tactical elements were made invisible or subfusc, their potential existence remaining the subject of educated guesswork. The most comprehensive and valuable answers as to the strength and nature of an enemy position were supplied by a personal visit: 'trench raids' were necessary but hazardous pursuits that often failed to repay the investment in lives.

A tour of the Bavarian positions just before the battle in July 1916 would have revealed mined (i.e. tunnelled) headquarters dugouts installed *beneath* the breastworks at a depth of 5 metres on a scale of two or three per regimental sector. There were scores of individually designed timber, steel or concrete 'artillery shelters' built on or slightly below ground level *within* the breastworks for troop and weapon accommodation. They offered security from small shells, splinters and shrapnel, but nothing more. 'Cubby holes', even smaller refuges at the foot of the breastwork to hold one or two men, were ubiquitous. These were purely for temporary use, allowing the firestep (a narrow raised platform from which men could observe and fire over the parapet) to be instantly manned when the alarm sounded. There were also purpose-built light and medium mortar positions with adjacent ammunition stores, plus small arms ammunition and grenade caches. The parapet was everywhere fitted with veiled timber loopholes for riflemen, snipers and observers—the equivalent of arrow-slits in the walls of a mediaeval castle. In the immediate lee of the breastworks were many hundreds of timber and corrugated-iron weatherproof, but not bullet-proof, shelters; these were for daytime use.

The foremost line of breastworks formed the *I Linie*: the most advanced trench line. Behind it, still in the process of development in July 1916, was the support line, the *II Linie*, encompassing similar facilities, but with more accommodation. Latrines could be found here. The ultimate Bavarian aim was to provide adequate and comfortable cover, both from the elements and hostile action, for the entire garrison, and to keep ammunition and weapons within immediate reach. In 1916 the Bavarian positions still differed markedly from place to place. Some sections had both a parapet and a parados, others were unfinished, 'open-backed', and thus more dangerous. The enclosed sections were narrow (less than a metre wide at floor level) and fitted with a firestep from which riflemen had a clear view of No Man's Land.

Approximately 2 kilometres behind *I Stellung* lay a second and ultimately stronger position. Being on the forward slope of the ridge near its sandier and easily drained crest, the *II Stellung* was a conventionally built trench system possessing a wider range of amenities. The ridge-top villages, including Fromelles, were incorporated into its defences, and it was here that the main dressing stations—often a courtyard farm—were situated, with operating theatre and access for motorised ambulances. Between the two *Stellungen* was the critical band of terrain known to the Bavarians as the *Hintergelände*—the 'outpost zone' to the British. This was a feature of great and equal tactical importance to both sides because, should the Allies break through the first line, the defences established here—individual strongpoints based upon the many dispersed buildings and farms—were designed to restrain, rupture and weaken an assault so that there remained insufficient momentum and power to threaten the *II Stellung*. At the time of the battle of July 1916, this region too was under development.

In the spring of 1916 the Fromelles *Hintergelände* was verdant, leafy and rural—and deliberately kept that way. Footpaths were concealed by hedge-rows, and in those places where no natural cover was present, routes were artificially screened. As in No Man's Land, fields of fire were kept clear, and each strongpoint was located, designed and equipped to offer support to its neighbours. The result was an integrated system of observation and enfilade cross-fire as orderly and treacherous as those devised to protect No Man's Land, while at the same time being largely veiled within existing landscape features and thus infinitely more difficult to neutralise with artillery.

Through this area zig-zagged the main communication trenches that allowed movement of men and matériel between *I* and *II Stellung*. They too were constructed *on* rather than *in* the ground, using as construction material substantial timber boxes filled with earth or sandbags which were built up like brickwork to form two walls. As arteries of the forward zone, these vital routes allowed support troops to pass to and fro unseen and relatively unmolested.

There was a comprehensive trench tramway network, a narrow-gauge 'push-line' (i.e. 'powered' by soldiers) that carried matériel not only to the breastworks of the *I Stellung* but throughout the forward zone. On the ridge behind the *II Stellung* it connected to a medium-gauge horse-drawn or petrol-driven track and, beyond that, to the standard-gauge French railway (which linked with canal and road systems). Along the entire divisional sector the track ran parallel with, and just a few metres to the rear of, the breastworks, making it invisible to the British from the ground and to a certain degree protected from shellfire.

Further labour saving was achieved by investing in a buried electricity supply. In a remarkable engineering accomplishment, the current was carried to the front through a series of transformers that reduced it in stages from the 15 000 volts at its source in Lille. In the forward zone it powered lighting, including searchlights, while to the rear a more powerful supply was distributed to hospitals, workshops and the ubiquitous concrete mixing stations. Most importantly for the Bavarian front-line soldier, perhaps, it powered water pumps, so they need not engage, as did the British, in tedious and exhausting manual hand-pumping. Also buried up to 2 metres underground was a telephone network. Finally, and certainly no less important than any of these features, was an interconnecting network of signal lamp stations, some electrical, some manual. In the event of telephone failure messages could be flashed almost instantly to key locations. Beyond the tactical aspect, the overriding principle behind such a heavy investment in infrastructure was to minimise the expenditure of human effort, keeping the troops fresh for their primary commitment: defence of the bastion.

The Allies invested in only a fraction of this work, for it exemplified a defensive mindset that was not just senseless but dangerous. Belligerence was the British watchword.

––––––––

The only elevated vantage points available to the Allies were from trees and buildings along the Rue Tilleloy, a Roman road that ran parallel to and close behind the British lines. Although many a photograph and panorama was taken from sites along this route, each site was plainly identifiable as an observation position and therefore regularly molested by Bavarian artillery. Offering little in the way of height, by the beginning of 1916 they were of little practical tactical use. As for viewing the opposing line from the British trenches themselves, discernible activity was scant: beyond the enemy breastwork lay an invisible and alien landscape.

Contrary to popular belief, for the Bavarians to view the British positions from ground level on the Aubers–Fromelles ridge was far from easy. The terrain between the ridge and the front lines was more heavily overgrown than elsewhere, partly due to the numerous stands of hardwood (Pheasant Wood was one such), but not least because of the greater conglomeration of dwellings clustered near the villages, many with long-untended gardens, hedges and orchards. Because they screened or concealed other defensive features, it was important that these remained in place. Although the ridge crest was raised above the level of the plain, the angle of view from the top was still too shallow for effective direct observation. The Bavarians therefore installed platforms in trees, and observation posts in church towers (before the war, Fromelles boasted the tallest in Flanders) and in factory chimneys; they also erected concrete structures *within* more lofty farm buildings. They made a world of difference, because although activity immediately behind the British breastworks remained concealed, traffic could be seen on roads, footpaths and tracks to the rear, and frequently within the many communication trenches that fed the front line. Platforms atop mature poplars (called crow's nests), abundant along the ridge, offered the luxury of an extra 30 metres of elevation. While a few posts were spotted by the British, many remained unnoticed and thus unmolested, offering a colossal tactical advantage. It was from places such as these that Bavarian artillery was both ranged and guided onto targets, and where fall of enemy shot was recorded and muzzle flash noted: the location of many a British battery was identified in this way. All posts were connected to the telephone network, and some contained signal lamp facilities (for rearward use). It may be thought that British lives were at risk from sniping from these eyries, but it was considerably more profitable for the Bavarians to leave their visible but unsuspecting enemy alone, watching and learning from their activities.

The key to observation at ground level, i.e. from patrols, was the command and control of No Man's Land. Bavarian documentation of this activity is remarkable, revealing a level of intelligence gathering and record-ing that almost borders on the implausible. Every night (and frequently during the day), when conditions were suitable, patrols consisting of three or four men slipped out from a number of listening posts along the divi-sional battlefront. Employing the latticework of ditches as 'trunk roads', they crept along and observed, noted, sketched and photographed. Later a comprehensive report was produced, and upon an integrated map of the sub-sector the patrol leader marked the route his party had taken and where 'discoveries' had been made. These documents, of which there are many thousands, reveal that the Bavarians not only patrolled to the very foot of the British glacis, but frequently entered British saps and unmanned listening posts. From time to time they had the temerity to *backfill* certain new workings.

British patrolling was also ubiquitous, but if anyone could claim to *control* this piece of key contested ground, it was the Bavarians. Allied narratives reveal that patrols seldom reported encounters in No Man's Land; commanders thus reached the reasonable conclusion that the enemy did not 'often venture out beyond his own wire'. Records show this was not the case. Bavarian policy was plain: observe and note, but do not engage.

Put simply, in any attack the Allies' primary goal was to ensure by generous artillery preparation that the opening assault met with success. Should it fail, the vulnerability of subsequent attacking waves increased many-fold.

Each Bavarian regimental commander therefore evolved defences to suit the eccentricities of his battlefront. Being one of the foundation stones upon which the unit's security was based, machine-gun disposition was of prime importance. Belt-fed machine guns had an effective range of well over 2 kilometres and a lateral arc of fire of around 500 metres. A well-maintained gun competently crewed could without difficulty sustain a rate of fire of 250 rounds per minute.

On 1 April 1916 the German Army created 200 independent *Maschinengewehr* companies, each with sixteen weapons. The 6th Bavarian Reserve Infantry Division employed several makes of gun, including captured and modified British, French and even Russian and Serbian weapons. Each regiment usually had at its disposal a total armoury of between twenty and twenty-two weapons. Not all were deployed in the front line, however, some being dispersed in the *Hintergelände* or safely stored in support positions, ready to be brought forward in an emergency. Only a small number were located along the *II Stellung*.

In the foremost breastworks there were considerably more pre-constructed machine-gun posts than there were weapons to fill them. No regiment at Aubers and Fromelles routinely deployed more than a dozen front-line guns. Having too many made both the team and the weapon more vulnerable to bombardment, which by the summer of 1915 the Bavarians were already aware was guaranteed to precede any hostile assault. Siting was the key. The pre-installation of multiple posts not only offered instant platforms for auxiliary or replacement weapons, but the opportunity for existing teams to move from place to place *during an action*. Certain posts were more fundamental to the security of the wider sector than others, and in these cases crews were expected to defend their weapon to the last man. To the rear of the front line more guns were located in camouflaged and often elevated positions within buildings. Since they were firing above the breastworks, their targets lay in No Man's Land and the opposing trenches. In the case of break-in they also offered an extra form of insurance, covering newly occupied positions, open ground, communication routes, roads, and of course each other, often in enfilade. In short, at Fromelles German machine guns commanded most of No Man's Land and the *Hintergelände*, and indeed considerable swathes of ground behind the *Allied* line. They were augmented by riflemen selecting individual targets either through loopholes or over the parapet. The arsenal was completed by a host of mortars of various calibres, teams of rifle-grenadiers, and a dozen 33-millimetre trench cannons. Alongside the artillery, it was their combined task to make the killing zone of No Man's Land so lethal that their own trenches became inviolable.

———

Hardly a metre of Bavarian front was 'straight', for it had long been recognised that an irregular line with many small salients made it more difficult for the enemy's artillery to effectively register. There was of course a limit to how irregular one's positions might be because the more bulges, bumps and angles one added, the longer one's line became and the more troops were required to build, man, serve and maintain it.

There were two key salients in the 6 BRD sector: the Wick and the Sugar Loaf. Both were labelled as such by British map-makers; neither had a German title. The features joined in a re-entrant (the opposite to a salient), called Noose Trench by the British, and thus supported each other's 'inner' flanks. The Sugar Loaf, which lay a few hundred metres north of the Wick, incorporated a kilometre and a half of battlefront.

Many are under the impression that this feature, because it appears to bulge so belligerently into No Man's Land, was a kind of towering fortress or redoubt, heavily manned by crack troops and bristling with armaments. This was far from the truth. It was not elevated, the garrison was of normal strength, and it contained no greater or lesser number of weapons than any other part of the Bavarian sub-sector.

In one respect, the Sugar Loaf was much more vulnerable than other parts of the line to hostile artillery because the trenches could be shelled in enfilade rather than perpendicularly. What made the position (and indeed any mini-salient of the kind) almost inviolable to hostile infantry attack were machine guns located on its flanks—in the Sugar Loaf's case, these were in trenches named Necklace, Novel and Nut by the British. Their angles of fire were roughly parallel to the salient's 'faces', so whether approaching the feature obliquely or perpendicularly, in crossing No Man's Land an attacking force would encounter multiple enfilade fire. Bavarian gun crews need only have an adequate number of weapons firing at the right moment and at the correct elevation, and an enemy force would be obliged to *walk into and through* several streams of bullets to reach the opposing parapet. Furthermore, the Sugar Loaf's guns protected the Bavarian positions east and west. Only two machine guns were located in the nose of the salient itself. Each and every post was closely associated with a shelter within the breastwork, inside which the team nursed their weapon and awaited the alarm sounded by a dedicated observer on the firestep. In the days before tracer bullets became standard issue, shooting at grass-top height, i.e. using the grass itself as a control for the correct elevation of the weapon, was an orthodox and highly effective practice during the summer months; with the land having temporarily escaped husbandry, grasses grew to above knee height, hence the term so often encountered that describes troops being cut down 'as with a scythe'.

The core Bavarian aspiration was, however, the bringing to bear of all arms at the earliest possible moment, the prime objective being to defeat an assault before it had any hope of thriving: in No Man's Land. If hostile troops did manage to breach the line, the aim was to ensure that they were too weak in number to hold or consolidate the position. They could then be evicted, captured or eradicated by counter-attack.

The Allies knew that should they fail to overrun the entire enemy line at the first attempt, they might nevertheless create a set of isolated break-ins, the ensuing alarm and turmoil helping to draw attention and fire away from troops still fighting to force a breach or make their way across No Man's Land; thus several simultaneous incursions would materially assist in achieving general success. The most likely locations for such incursions to flourish were of course where the opposing trenches were at their closest. There were three obvious sites on the 1916 Fromelles battle-ground: on the southern flank where the Fauquissart–Aubers road bisected the opposing lines, astride the Wick Salient, and on the northern flank of the battlefield at Rouges Bancs. Elsewhere, there lay a daunting challenge, with success being entirely dependent upon Allied artillery having suppressed or preferably destroyed hostile defensive capabilities.

The sector where No Man's land was at its widest was in the quadrant north-west of the apex of the Sugar Loaf. Here, the field of German fire was both broad and deep, and thus any assault against Nut Trench or the salient itself would require significantly more traversal time. It was at this point, on the afternoon of 19 July 1916, that the 2/1st Buckinghamshire Regiment (Bucks) and 2/4th Berks set out towards the Bavarian breastworks; before them lay no less than 420 metres of open ground.

Success also depended upon how one's attacking force emerged from cover: in waves over the top of the breastwork, or via sally-ports. The latter could be effectively targeted by mortars, rifle grenades and trench cannon; meanwhile riflemen selected individual targets leaving the machine guns to concentrate on enfilading the assaulting troops. A key Australian sally-port opposite the Sugar Loaf had been installed adjacent to the little bridge on the Rue Delvas known to the Bavarians as the *Tommy-Brücke*. It gave access to No Man's Land along the right bank of the Laies Brook. Bavarian patrols had noted its presence before battle, and several weapons (including a machine gun) had been installed specifically to cover the threat.

The Sugar Loaf posed an added complication in that the muddy, sluggish stream emerged from its eastern flank and bisected No Man's land. The orientation of the feature was vitally important, for in an attack against the north-eastern face (Novel Trench), where the opposing lines were at their closest, the stream could produce both a funnelling and a separating effect, making those who attempted to negotiate it using the several small bridges placed there for the purpose simple targets. Although not deep it was awkwardly wide with steep, slippery sides and a muddy bed. Importantly, the Laies flowed on behind the Allied breastworks, so that in order for Allied troops to reach *their own* front line in the Horseshoe and Cordonnerie sub-sectors, they were required to cross a series of forty-five bridges. Although drainage here was well managed and at this point the stream was just 25 centimetres deep, bank to bank the span was 8 metres: for rapid incoming support or outgoing evacuation, bridges were obligatory. Well aware of their tactical importance, the Bavarians frequently harassed them with plunging fire from machine guns in the Sugar Loaf and indeed from the ridge.

If and when the Allies breached the Sugar Loaf, they would be presented with a landscape yet more alien than that of No Man's Land. Despite careful observation with powerful telescopes and meticulous examination of aerial photographs, the British had little idea of the nature and location of the pitfalls and traps that had been carefully put in place to surprise, confine, contain and kill them. Daily intelligence summaries presented front-line officers with reports of suspected snipers' posts, machine-gun positions and suspicious activity in ruined houses, but only action could reveal the true situation.

Like all salients, the 'base' of the Sugar Loaf 'triangle' was robustly protected against deeper incursion. Immediately behind the feature ran the Bavarian section of the Laies Brook, an obstacle that *had* to be crossed if forward progress was to be made. Four bridges were available, each covered by machine guns and riflemen in nearby fortified ruins, positions that also enfiladed any potential incursion to the flanks. Several of these were known to the Allies, and described in a document produced for the benefit of commanders by II Anzac Corps entitled 'Report on Enemy's Defences about Sugar Loaf'. It noted that in the salient's front line there were four posts from which machine guns had been deployed; however, there were actually ten, serving four permanent weapons. It is a fact that an assaulting force, especially one that has failed, habitually returns with reports of overwhelming enemy machine-gun superiority, often grossly exaggerating the number employed. What the Germans did so well and for so long was to protect their garrison by merging the effect of magazine and automatic fire with other weapons. Breastworks, battered though they may be by shellfire, still offered adequate cover for clear line-of-sight shooting over eminently favourable terrain from carefully selected positions.

※

For 19 July 1916 the Anglo–Australian objective was twofold: to put hostile machine guns and/or their crews out of action before the attacks were launched, and to create the opportunity for an adequate force to traverse No Man's Land before hostile artillery and mortars could deluge it with shrapnel and high explosives. By this time the Allied axiom had long been 'Artillery conquers, infantry occupies'.

To achieve victory their gunners had to obliterate Bavarian wire and breastworks, and the dugouts cosseted within, along the entire battlefront: the fewer pockets of resistance that remained, the swifter success could be attained and the shorter the casualty list. The fact that the opposing lines were based upon a breastwork defence was problematic because although the gunfire might strike the entanglements, the wire itself, like a wave on the seashore, was often driven up unbroken against the glacis by the forward 'throw' of the shellburst, thus remaining an obstacle, albeit damaged. Entanglements installed in borrow pits in front of the breast-works were difficult to destroy because the cutting effects of shrapnel and the lateral blast of high explosives were largely neutralised. If wire remained unbroken, those casting about to find a breach in the entanglement, or indeed trying to cut it, often 'herded', becoming simple targets for riflemen and grenadiers—which was, of course, one of the prime tactical functions of barbed wire. It was for this reason that the Germans repaired gaps at every possible opportunity, often during a bombardment.

By mid-1916, the adequate destruction of entanglements on a front of more than 5 kilometres demanded a colossal artillery presence manned by proficient gunners, and well-maintained weapons with a variety of calibres, fuse types and ranges: field and naval guns for wire-cutting and longer-range counter-battery work respectively, and howitzers for shorter-range destructive shoots, all supported by as many mortars as could be mustered. Allied problems with faulty shells and fuses had been largely eradicated;

a gun's effectiveness now depended primarily upon the proficiency of the man firing it. In June 1916 British artillery notes suggested that six 18-pounder shrapnel shells per yard (metre), bursting 'as close to the wire and as low as possible', was sufficient to destroy entanglements: the 374 lead shrapnel bullets (balls) contained within each shell should break the wire into small pieces. The amount of ammunition required to create widespread satisfactory results could thus be calculated; time after time it was supplied in full. The problem that remained was the demolition of targets beyond the easily visible enemy front line. For any and every one of these targets, Allied guns required guidance.

The year 1915, and to a great extent 1916, pre-dated the era when fire was routinely delivered 'by the map', i.e. ranging one's guns upon pre-determined coordinates using trigonometrical calculations adjusted for variations in wind, barometric pressure and temperature. This was partly because the ultra-accurate standardised universal trench mapping that allowed such 'indirect' or 'predicted' fire to take place was still in development. Registration was therefore still the domain of two agencies. First, there were the FOOs (forward observation officers), whose task it was to secrete themselves in an advanced position and guide batteries or individual guns onto targets by observing and noting fall of 'sighting shot' and indicating adjustment, usually by telephone, to correct what was known as the 'error of the day'. To achieve this, they needed an adequate view and uninterrupted communication, either telephonic or by coded 'buzzer'. On a battlefront where the enemy dominated observation and was able to deploy guns that were hidden, numerous and accurate, neither was easy to achieve. The second agency was airborne: shellfire guided onto hostile batteries by aircraft, the muzzle flash being the initial indicator. Once a battery had been located and targeted, fall of shot was reported in the same way.

One of the keys to resistance throughout a spectacularly successful German defensive year had been the development of artillery pre-registration before battle commenced, i.e. accurately lining up pre-selected targets. Likewise, they had enhanced their ability to conceal not only batteries themselves but the fact that there were batteries present. In this early evolutionary period of aerial reconnaissance, if guns were both well secreted *and* seldom fired, they were unlikely to be spotted from aircraft or observation balloon, and thus unlikely to be molested by counter-battery fire. At Fromelles and Aubers Bavarian gunners were in the happy position of occupying a ridge that included many screening terrain features, both man-made and natural. It made accurate Allied counter-battery work challenging, both in the delivery of fire and in observation, for the enemy positions themselves were practically invisible except from the air. There were also numerous dummy batteries—complete with dummy gunners. How did the Germans manage to pre-register so accurately without their batteries being spotted? Given that the guns were in good working order and gunners well trained and experienced, patience was the key: registration simply took place by means of test firings during periods when RFC aircraft were absent from the skies.

The supremacy of Bavarian observation meant that few British gun batteries escaped detection, and thus their location, calibre and targets were swiftly revealed. Without a considerably enhanced artillery presence and total domination of the air, there was little the Allies could do to improve the situation.

Bavarian ranging within the forward zone—upon No Man's Land and features within the Allied lines—was regularly 'adjusted' to make sure weapons remained correctly laid when called upon. The enhanced observational capabilities allowed swift modification, so that once battle was in progress and conditions favourable, guns *outside* an area of attack could be re-laid and re-registered through telephonic communication as the action was taking place. Because of the 'shape' of the battlefront, they were also frequently able to produce treacherous enfilade fire, a fact repeatedly noted by British observers. This was especially troublesome because angled fire could often mean muzzle flash became practically invisible, making counter-battery action exceedingly difficult to deliver.

Unknown to the British and Australian troops who would converge upon the Fromelles sector for the action of July 1916, they were already 'up a gum tree' by reason of the events that had taken place more than a year before. Beyond an ever-growing British and French infantry and artillery presence, by the spring of 1916 German high command had discerned no changes in Allied offensive procedures; should the Entente's strategists choose to employ similar tactics as in May 1915, Prince Rupprecht's Bavarians had every right to look upon their defences in French Flanders with confidence. The Allies, meanwhile, continued to consistently underestimate their foe.

Chapter 6

CARELESS TALK

———◦◦◦———

It is difficult to place too much emphasis on the importance of the events that took place in the three months leading up to 19 July 1916. It was during this period that the belligerents were able to become intimately acquainted—seeing and touching the fabric of their opponents' fieldworks, observing and noting the idiosyncrasies of each other's lives, rifling and destroying, and especially closing and killing, face to face and hand to hand.

It was an epoch of trench raids. Literally battles in miniature, they represented the very essence of war, and were yardsticks by which experience was measured, and a recurring topic of conversation in the *estaminets* (small cafés). They were also seen as the finest tool with which to instil that essential element, *esprit de corps*, and thus an obligatory part of a soldier's introduction to the Western Front. Thousands were undertaken during the war. The prime purpose was to identify the opposing enemy unit and to take prisoners, whose subsequent interrogation added the thickest layer of paint to the canvas of intelligence upon which plans for both defence and offence were superimposed.

No matter what the outcome—for they were perilous and often costly—on a number of levels raids were considered 'good' for a unit. Referred to as 'winter sports' by Sir Douglas Haig, they were frequent throughout January, February and March 1916 and would soon offer the Australians their first encounter with the new German foe.

In Egypt at this time, the troops that had been evacuated from Gallipoli were joined by draft after draft of reinforcements. While there, the AIF doubled in size, allowing the creation of a 5th Australian Division. The men were instructed in trench-digging and road-building; they staged mock battles and in the heat and dust endured gruelling, character-building route marches, at every step encircled by flies—six of which, it was said, were issued to every man upon arrival in the country. The soldiers attended grenade schools, learned the technicalities of Lewis and Vickers machine guns, and were introduced to a brand-new weapon, the 3-inch Stokes quick-firing mortar.

Whether the 5th Division would find itself in Salonica, Mesopotamia or France would not be known until a month after 25 April 1916, the first official commemoration of the Gallipoli landings. Only in mid-June did the fully equipped division gratefully embark for Marseilles and the cooler climes of the Western Front. Under the command of Major-General the Honourable James Whiteside McCay, upon arrival the force numbered around 18 000—almost maximum establishment.

To the exasperation of many, including military correspondent Captain Charles Bean, when the first Diggers had landed in Marseilles a local newspaper printed photographs of the 1st Australian Division striding towards the railway station. British journalists revealed their entrance by simply extracting and publishing material derived from imprudent French official *communiqués*. This kind of information, and more, continued to appear upon the desks of grateful German intelligence officers, who swiftly disseminated it along the Western Front. Although the key information—where the Anzacs were to be deployed—was fortunately not leaked, it was an inauspicious beginning to a new campaign.

It took a week (23–30 June) and more than thirty trains to transport the 5th Division and its supplies to Flanders. By the time McCay's men finally disembarked at Hazebrouck, von Scanzoni and the staff of the

6th Bavarian Reserve Infantry Division were in possession of comprehensive first-hand details about the Gallipoli campaign and its effect upon the morale of their new foe, partly through intelligence supplied by Turkish allies and partly from other more surprising sources. They knew about training and reinforcement in Egypt, and the establishment, weaponry, disposition and organisation of an Australian division bound for Europe. Such a level of intelligence was not unusual.

German sources in every theatre delivered their findings to Berlin, who sifted the data and, according to relevance, passed it to *Armee-Oberkommando 6*. *Hauptmann* Fritz Lübcke, AOK 6's intelligence officer, received information relating to a wide variety of units, not least because some were guaranteed to appear opposite certain of his own divisions: should troops from these units subsequently fall into his hands the material could be most useful, for prisoners tended to be considerably more forthcoming if they believed their interrogator was already aware of certain facts via other sources. Such knowledge helped to dispel the sense of guilt when 'spilling the beans'. Report B No. 6073, for example, held in the Munich archives, was headed 'Extracts from papers taken from prisoners and bodies'. Dated 12 July 1916, it contained extensive excerpts from letters and diaries written by soldiers when serving in Bombay, Egypt, East Africa, France, Ireland, Britain and Rhodesia. Lübcke underlined sections that were especially illuminating, and occasionally text with little apparent importance, such as this piece from the diary of a man of the 2/4th London Regiment who, like the Diggers, had served at Gallipoli and trained in Egypt:

The weather here is not as good as it was in Egypt, although it has been warmer in recent days. After the peninsula was evacuated, we had quite a good time in Egypt. We were quartered about 600km south of Alexandria. The heat there was 'hellish', but of course we did very little and generally had roll-call out of the way by 10.00 in the morning. We then slept for the rest of the day until tea-time. At night it was very cold, and in the evenings we used to have fun playing football matches between the platoons. My platoon was the favourite. Some Derby men have arrived in the camp. They did not exactly receive a warm welcome. This war is an insane business and I think it is time for 'them' to think about packing it in. I saw some [German] prisoners this morning; they looked very smug. Whenever I see one of those sausage merchants, I have an urge to run him through. I like the Turks much better. They are good fighters and proper sporting with it.

The writer displayed exactly the outlook and attitude required from the Australians by British GHQ. It existed already; after defeat at Gallipoli and the frustrations of Egypt, the Diggers were more than ready for a scrap.

On 2 June 1916 AOK 6 received a message from the German General Staff Intelligence News Service. Part of it read:

The 61st Division (second line Territorials) was reviewed by the King in camp at Salisbury on 6.5, which suggests that it was about to be shipped out. Newspaper reports now confirm that it apparently left England in the middle of May, and it is therefore assumed that the 61st Division is in France. It is possible that elements of the Division have already been deployed in 'nursery positions' at the front.

The message was copied and distributed to German infantry brigades, artillery, engineers and aerial reconnaissance units in northern France and Belgium. It was largely correct. By the time the ships carrying the 5th Australians docked at Marseilles, the South Midlanders, the British division with whom they were to link on 19 July, were already in training behind lines presently held by I Anzac Corps. Another report, No. 5011 of 17 June, records 'changes in enemy behaviour' in the Aubers sector. AOK 6 suspected that the 38th (Welsh) Division had been relieved; confirmation was required and patrols were detailed to prepare raids. The following day Report No. 5020 included a red-outlined description of papers found on the body of a soldier of the 7th Devonshire Regiment (Devons) by an RIR 17 patrol: the man's paybook was marked, 'attached 2/8 Worcester Reg.', a unit known by Lübcke to be part of the 183rd Brigade, 61st Division. The South Midlanders had arrived in the line.

For those Diggers who had served only in Gallipoli, the Western Front must have been an agreeable culture shock. On the peninsula they had effectively been captives of the coastal battlefront. There were no cafés or *estaminets*, and no interaction with local people; no egg and chips, beer or wine, and certainly no hope of association with the opposite sex. And there was no escape, save through injury or illness. Flanders was different in so many ways. It may have been flat and monotonous, with trenches frequently flooded and in a poor state of repair. Perhaps the hostile artillery and mortar fire was often heavier and more persistent, and maybe there was always the threat of gas, a form of warfare that no Anzac had yet had to face. But instead of the Aegean Sea and the desert wastes of Egypt, there now lay behind the Anzacs the vast green hinterland of northern France. Although intersected by line upon line of auxiliary defences all the way back to the channel ports (and indeed beyond), here was a fresh and 'civilised' country, people and culture. There were cities, towns and villages, shops and cafés—and women. Everything was once more different from home, but much more recognisable. Six shillings a day left the Diggers well equipped to enjoy all the facilities. For those lucky enough to be granted leave, the United Kingdom, where so many had family and friends, was but a few hours away by train and troop ship.

By now the original Australasian Corps had gone through a metamorphosis. First it had been the Australian and New Zealand Army Corps—the derivation of the acronym 'Anzac'—containing one Australian division and one New Zealand brigade. In June 1916, with the creation of several new divisions (including a full New Zealand division), the force was hefty enough to be divided into two corps: the I Anzacs under Lieutenant-General Sir William Birdwood, and the II under Lieutenant-General Sir Alexander Godley.

The arrival of II Anzac in Flanders in the summer of 1916 coincided with the period when the frustrating and un-winnable battle with the elements had at last drawn to a close, and every sector was being put in order for the campaigning season. With temperatures rising and rainfall declining, it was a passable time to arrive on the Western Front. Part of II Anzac, the 4th and 5th Australian Divisions reached their billeting areas in mid-June. They were joining three Canadian, two Australian, one New Zealand, and forty-one British infantry divisions; plus five mounted cavalry divisions. This force was occupying 130 kilometres of line in Belgium and France. By 8 July the transfer of the AIF from Egypt was complete.

Disguising changes in trench occupation was essential, for a hostile attack during a relief (always a nocturnal exercise) could be catastrophic, especially if the incomers were neophytes. Secrecy was paramount. As the breastworks of both sides were under permanent mutual scrutiny, they were also the prime place for deception. As the Tommies filed out and the Diggers filtered in, the simplest ruse—and an effective one—was to leave a British cap or two on the parapet. Soon after dawn it could be removed, but until then its presence signified that Imperial troops were still in occupation. Practised subtly from time to time, a humble hat might fool the enemy for weeks. In Flanders the ploy worked well until the day the first Diggers were captured, almost four months before the arrival of the 5th Division.

As part of the 5th Brigade, 2nd Australian Division, the 20th (New South Wales) Battalion—a unit that had spent the final five months at Gallipoli—arrived in France in March 1916 to be sent as part of I Anzac Corps (along with the 1st Australian Division) for acclimatisation to sectors south of Armentières. At 11.30 p.m. on 10 April the battalion completed its relief of the 103rd Brigade of the 34th (Imperial) Division and began adjusting to the cadence of Western Front life.

By the beginning of May they had made their home in and around the Le Bridoux Salient, part of the Bois-Grenier sector, immediately east of Fromelles. At the closest point the trenches were within 150 metres of the enemy—a Prussian unit. There had been plenty of sniping, and hostile artillery and mortar activity had occasionally been brisk, especially during recent days, but despite a few losses the most common early entries in the war diary were 'quiet day', 'nothing unusual', and 'night passed quietly'. Patrols crept out on most evenings, but all returned safely. Daily aerial duels were a fascinating distraction, and there had been a gas alarm or two, but little of especial note had occurred. It looked like the first month in the line would pass with an average of two casualties per day—a most acceptable figure for 'natural wastage'.

A couple of months earlier, on 21 February 1916, the Germans had initiated what was to become the Battle of Verdun, one of the greatest and most costly clashes of the war. Anzac commanders had quickly become aware that their enemy was by no means solely concentrating his hostile attention on north-eastern France; there had been minor attacks in Picardy and Artois, at La Boisselle, Saint Eloi, Vimy Ridge, Arras and Ypres, and many a raid in French Flanders. For their part, the Germans were aware that France's allies would be duty-bound to help relieve pressure at Verdun, and thus that a hostile summer offensive was assured. But would it be a French, a British, or an Anglo–French enterprise? Where would the blow or blows fall? And how heavy might they be? That Australian and New Zealand forces were now a part of the equation was common knowledge, but the Germans urgently required extra intelligence.

Outside of a battle, prisoners could best be taken either through the ambush of a patrol in No Man's Land or during a trench raid. The latter could deliver multiple benefits, such as the identification of enemy units, the examination of fieldworks, shelters, mine workings and weaponry, and, if possible, some material destruction. Documents, newspapers, maps and weapons could be procured, and unusual portable items brought back for evaluation. A successfully planned and executed raid could also have a debilitating psychological effect on the enemy; a series of raids was even more effective, provoking a wearing anxiety as to when and where the next might take place. The most susceptible troops were of course those who had not long been in the line.

The shape of the Bois-Grenier sub-sector and the proximity of the enemy there made it a prime candidate for surprise German action. When the first blow fell on 5 May an officer and ten men of B and C Companies of the 20th Battalion had the misfortune to become the first Australians on the Western Front to fall into enemy hands. It happened during a raid by the 230th Prussian Reserve Infantry Regiment (50th Reserve Infantry Division), an experienced unit who, before transferring to Flanders in December 1915, had served in the eastern theatre in 1914 and in France during the Second Battle of Champagne. With the intention of acquiring information about tunnelling activities (mines were one of the infantry-man's greatest fears), destroying shafts and capturing booty and prisoners, the venture was exceptionally profitable for the Germans.

Captain Charles Bean was nearly an eyewitness. His role as official war correspondent meant personally following the movements of all Australian divisions and producing reports and articles for home consumption that would illustrate their remarkable wartime odyssey. He had reported throughout the Gallipoli campaign—being wounded in the leg in the process—and followed the Anzacs to France. He was therefore at hand to chronicle many events during the period of acclimatisation. 'Embedding', as we today might call it, entailed touring the trenches both day and night, being 'illuminated' by the staff, and meeting and greeting the men in and out of the line. The task also necessitated being wherever action occurred, for everything of potential note had to be recorded.

On the day of the raid Bean rose at 4.00 a.m. and went with Captain J.J.W. Herbertson, a British intelligence officer attached to I Anzac, on a tour of observation posts. At the invitation of Major S.S. Butler, the chief intelligence officer, he afterwards occupied himself with an activity that was to become particularly important in the coming weeks: the scrutiny of aerial photographs. Surprisingly perhaps, given Bean's quasi-military status, Butler felt that Bean should learn how to interpret aerials in order to help confirm intelligence reports. It was Bean's first venture into the rapidly evolving discipline, and he found it fascinating.

That evening Bean and an Australian padre were taking a post-prandial stroll when they noticed an intense flickering accompanied by rumbling shellfire coming from the Australian-held sector. Rather than go to bed, Bean decided to stay at HQ, 'to see what came next'. Presently the fire subsided and soon afterwards he was handed a note, saying that the enemy had been seen to leave their trenches opposite the 5th Brigade but things had quickly quietened down.

It was after breakfast the following day that the full facts emerged. Butler informed Bean, 'I'm afraid the Germans had us last night. It appears that a party of them did reach our trenches and they seem to have some prisoners.'

Accompanied by Butler and Herbertson, he immediately set off for Bois-Grenier. Upon arrival enquiries were made with 2nd Division staff. 'I'm afraid it is not a very good affair from our point of view', reported Butler, 'the Boche seem to have done pretty well what they intended to do'. The Australian trenches had been bludgeoned by shell and mortar, and it was feared that close to one hundred casualties may have been sustained. It also transpired that several men were unaccounted for, and two Stokes trench mortars missing. There was no sign of any German dead or wounded.

Curiously, it was the loss of the mortars that was considered most serious, for explicit instructions had been issued that the newly introduced weapons were not to be taken into the front line. Bean noted at the time:

This order seems to have been utterly disregarded. There were two officers and each seems to have thought that the other had seen to it. It is this sort of hopeless casualness and slackness, which is probably worse in the Second Division than in the First, that counterbalances the good qualities of our Australian troops. Here is a class of officer who will not take his work seriously until he learns a fearful lesson, and sometimes the lesson is too expensive for the result. The incident was simply and solely due to bad soldiering—nothing wrong with the men (except that they would mostly be equally casual) but everything wrong with the officers. It is a most disappointing, mortifying beginning. However, we may make up for it. My word, they will poke this up against us in all other Corps.

The diary then lists indisciplines, such as men breaking out of billets to go to *estaminets*, being drunk on duty and other examples of 'dissipation'. In all cases, the culprit was seen to be weak command: officers, suggested Bean, seeking popularity rather than efficiency.

Anzac HQ took immediate action. Although none of the German troops fell within the Australian positions, during the raid they suffered nineteen casualties, of which four were fatal. Four Australian officers and ninety-one other ranks were killed or wounded. British and Anzac commanders looked upon the engagement as disgraceful, and although the troops were fresh to the trenches and subjected to a bombardment 'worse than anything endured at Gallipoli', the battalion commanding officer (CO) was sent home. Both General Birdwood and General Sir Herbert Plumer, commander of Second Army, considered the loss of the Stokes mortars especially 'inexcusable', and the event received a deal of emphasis within the military establishment. On Tuesday 9 May, Field Marshal Sir Douglas Haig mentioned the raid in a letter to King George V, reiterating Bean's sentiments about leadership.

> *I inspected the Australian and New Zealand Divisions. They are undoubtedly a fine body of men, but their officers and leaders as a whole have a good deal to learn . . . A portion of their front was shelled last Thursday night and a small party of Germans entered their trenches. I understand that the severity and accuracy of enemy's artillery fire was a revelation to them!*

Possibly because they were the first Diggers to be captured on the Western Front, Charles Bean's *Official History of Australia* devotes considerable space not only to the raid, but to the prisoners' subsequent interrogation by the Germans:

> *The story is completed by the statements of captured Australians, made upon their return from Germany after the war. They say that the wounded prisoners were treated at a German dressing station, and then all were sent to Lille . . . At Douai the prisoners were examined by officers of the German intelligence staff, and the enemy on that day ascertained that the 2nd Australian Division was in the line southeast of Armentières, with the 1st Division on its right. The German reports further show that the captured Australians, when questioned by the enemy's intelligence officers as to the artillery and billets behind their lines, gave no information, but spoke of general matters such as the severity or otherwise of the German artillery fire, and the food they received.*

Bean then adds a supporting footnote:

> *There is no question that the prisoners were sturdily determined to give away no intelligence of value. The only really safe course, however, and one permitted by the rules of war, was for a prisoner to refuse to give*

any information, except as to his name and number. Men captured in
battle were usually under an intense strain and suffering from shock,
and it was comparatively seldom that they absolutely refused to answer
questions. The majority endeavoured to fence with the examining
officers, giving replies which they considered safe. The enemy—like the
British—seems generally to have respected a man who would not speak.

In producing these highly unusual, indeed almost unique, passages in
defence of the prisoners' integrity, Charles Bean states that he was influenced by their later statements. Here, he is referring to the contents of
Australian War Memorial file 30 B6.14. 'Statements made by Prisoners
of War, 2nd Australian Division, 28.4.16–15.5.16. 5th Australian Brigade,
20th Battalion', where one may read the testimonies of nine of the eleven
men captured that night. Their words do not tally with Bean's account in
the *OHA*.

Upon his return to England, on 2 December 1918 Norman G.
Blanchard, the sole officer in the party, was interviewed; he made no reference to being questioned by the Germans. Seven weeks later Corporal
H. Jewiss, one of Blanchard's battalion's bombers, offered his version
of events:

I was with a bombing party of eight which was in charge of Lieuten-
ant Blanchard at the head of the Bois Grenier salient, when we were
surprised by an enemy raiding party, surrounded, and some of us taken
prisoners. I was not wounded. Lieutenant Blanchard was wounded.
Four of us, including Lieutenant Blanchard, were taken to enemy lines,
searched and questioned. We gave no information.

Out of nine available files, Corporal Jewiss' is the only account that
mentions interrogation. Given that the men were the very first Australians to be captured on the Western Front, it is perhaps unsurprising that
Bean felt it necessary to invest time and space on the incident, for soldiers
naturally place implicit trust in their comrades not to give away potentially harmful secret information. That Bean's defence of their integrity was
based upon the statements above is, however, a little difficult to accept.

Perhaps other statements exist, although there is at present no evidence to support this. Given Bean's tremendous propensity to harvest, check and correlate fine detail, it seems peculiar that he did not take the story further. He offered, in the *OHA*, a detailed report of the action itself taken from the regimental records of the German unit involved. Through his contacts in the Potsdam archives he already knew that the officer captured during the raid, Lieutenant Blanchard, commissioned in the field at Gallipoli, had indeed vouchsafed certain details to the enemy. That lead was apparently not followed up.

The most curious aspect of Bean's 'defence', however, is the assertion that *German* reports admired the tight-lipped response of the Australians. In fact the prisoners were exceedingly communicative, offering a mass of invaluable information that not only guaranteed and assisted subsequent raids on Australian positions, but almost certainly influenced the outcome of events at Fromelles some ten weeks hence. In 2007 the interrogation report—B No. 4730—was found in the Munich archives by the author. An important document, it is here reproduced in full:

Information obtained from 1 officer and 10 men of 'B' and 'C' companies. 20th (New South Wales) Battalion, 5th Brigade, 2nd Australian Division (Australian Imperial Expeditionary Force)

To the north: 17th (New South Wales) Battalion, 5th Brigade, 2nd Australian Division

To the south: Battalion of the 1st Australian Division

Taken prisoner at 8.30pm on 5 May, south-east of Touquet on the Bois Grenier–Bridoux road

Joined the army: August–September 1914

I. Personnel information

After completing its training, the battalion was transported to the Dardanelles with the rest of the 2nd Australian Division at the end of June 1915. The 1st Australian Division was sent at the same time. The battalion served in the trenches in the area of Sed-ul-Bahr until approx mid-December. The 2nd Australian Division was then relieved and, after a 10-day rest period on the island of Lemnos, was shipped to

Egypt, where the 20th Battalion was employed on railway construction and digging trenches. Around the middle of March the 20th Battalion was shipped via Alexandria to Marseille, and from there transported directly by rail to Abbeville (Somme). After a stay of 4–5 days in that town, the battalion was route-marched in stages to the area of Armentières. After 5 days' rest, the battalion went into the trenches for the first time in the Bois Grenier sector around the middle of April. The 17th and 19th battalions, 5th Brigade, which were the first to go into the front line, relieved the 103rd (Tyneside Irish) Brigade. The 17th Battalion relieved the 28th/Northumberland Fusiliers. The 18th and 20th battalions went into the line a few days later. They again relieved Northumberland Fusiliers.

During the night of 1–2 May the 20th Battalion was rotated into the front line for the third time, relieving the 18th Battalion. On 5 May, at about 7.00pm, their positions came under heavy German artillery and Minenwerfer fire, followed, after about an hour and a half, by a raid by a German patrol numbering about 40 men. The well-directed fire completely destroyed the front trench and, in the estimation of the prisoners, killed most of 'B' and 'C' companies.

Reserves: the 5th and 7th brigades were in the front line positions. The 6th Brigade was in support positions in farm buildings immediately behind the front.

Senior officers: OC 2nd Australian Division, General Lake. OC 5th Brigade, General Holmes.

Staff HQs: Divisional HQ is reportedly near Erquinghem. Brigade HQ was in a village on the Bois Grenier–Erquinghem road, but was moved further to the rear after it was shelled by German artillery.

II. *Factual details*

1. *Reliefs: 2 battalions of the Brigade are always in the front line positions, with 2 battalions in the reserve trenches or immediately to the rear of them, in farm buildings. The front trench is always garrisoned by two complete companies, with one in the support trench and another in the first reserve trench. Units are normally rotated every 14 days.*

2. *Artillery:* According to the officer, the division brought its own artillery with it from Australia. It comprises guns of all calibres, some Australian, some British. The prisoners are unable to give any information about the gun positions, as they are forbidden to approach them. They know only that there is a lot of artillery behind their positions.

3. *Uniform, badges:* The Australian battalions wear slouch hats, the left side of which is folded upwards and held in place by the badge.

   On both upper arms, below the shoulder, the battalions wear a patch in the form of a square standing on its point. For the 5th Brigade, the lower half is green. The upper half is black for the 17th battalion, violet for the 18th battalion, brown for the 19th battalion and white for the 20th battalion. The prisoners do not know the colours of the patches worn by other battalions and brigades of the 2nd Division.

   The badge consists of a rising sun over a crown and the inscription 'Australian Commonwealth Military Forces'. The same badge is also worn as a shoulder title, with the battalion number in Arabic numerals.

4. *Weapons:* The men are all armed with the British 'short rifle'.

5. *German operations:* The men are more afraid of the German heavy artillery than of the fire of our Minenwerfer.

6. *Replacements:* The Battalion has received no replacements since it has been in France.

7. *Gas attacks, gas protection:* As usual the men are equipped with two 'tube helmets'. There are many Vermoral sprayers. Gas protection equipment is inspected daily under the supervision of an officer and a medical officer. There have been a number of practice gas alarms, during which it was found that the men need 10–20 seconds to put on their gas masks. The prisoners have never seen any preparations for a gas or smoke attack by their side. Before the battalion went into the trenches, a training exercise was carried out, in which gas was released upwind of their practice trench. It blew towards the trench in a greeny-white cloud. Some men who had not put their masks on properly were overcome by the gas, but very quickly recovered.

8. *Sector frontage: Each company holds a frontage of 220–230m.*

9. *Health: Very good.*

10. *Order of battle: The officer confirms the order of battle of the 2nd Australian Division in all particulars. He further states that the 13th Australian Light Horse, which is also attached to the division, is en route to France, or may even have arrived already.*

11. *Hand grenades: In each battalion there are 80 specially trained 'bombers' under the command of the 'Battalion Bombing Officer'. The 'Mills bomb' is the only hand grenade issued, and all the men have received instruction in its use.*

12. *Ages: 18–35. In Australia men are allowed to enlist up to the age of 46.*

13. *Machine guns: Each battalion has a machine-gun company comprising 16 Lewis guns and 64 men under the command of a 'Battalion MG officer'. There is also a Brigade machine-gun company comprising 10 Maxim-type machine guns and 60 men under the command of a 'Brigade MG officer'. The heavy machine guns are left in position, but units take their Lewis guns with them when they are relieved. There were apparently 9 machine guns in the front line trench, but the prisoners think that most of them were destroyed by our artillery fire. The machine-gun teams are trained to use all types of MG, including German ones.*

14. *Ammunition supply: Good. SAA and artillery ammunition is made partly in Australia and partly in Britain.*

15. *Communications: Mainly by telephone, which is installed in the front line trench. Sometimes by runner. The prisoners have never seen carrier pigeons used. According to the officer, a 'Detectiphone'* was installed in the front trench, with which good results had been achieved in intercepting our telephone traffic. The officer is unable or unwilling to give more detailed information. Cover names are apparently not used (it is known that we have a listening system and the men are therefore instructed to conduct conversations in whispers).*

   *Possibly a version of the French overhearing apparatus designed in August 1915 that intercepted telephone messages wirelessly. It

was found that unless telephone systems were properly earthed and insulated, the signals passed not only through the wires but through the ground itself: conversations could be overheard. Being underground, hidden and close to the enemy positions, mine galleries were ideal locations for listening equipment.

16. *Future plans: The officer claims to know that a major British attack will take place in the near future. A German attack is not expected, as our forces are not considered to be strong enough. The men do not believe that there will be a British attack.*

17. *Officers: The Battalion CO is Colonel Lamerik, 'B' company is commanded by Captain Ferguson, with Lieutenants Barley, Connor, Francis and the prisoner, Lieutenant Blanchard. 'C' company is commanded by Major Paul, second-in-command is Captain Hoskins. The men do not know the names of other officers who have only recently joined the company.*

18. *Trench guns, trench mortars: There were 4–5 trench mortars in the sector held by the battalion. They were distributed between the front trench and the support trench and changed their positions regularly. Two of these mortars fell into our hands. The battalion does not possess any flamethrowers. A captured German flamethrower was demonstrated to the men while they were in training behind the lines. They wore protective goggles during the demonstration. They were not very impressed by the flamethrower, as its effect is less damaging than it appears.*

19. *Unit strengths: The ration strength of both companies is approx. 225. Their combat strength is about 180–190 men.*

20. *Positions: The British positions are said to be essentially much the same as the German ones, although the latter are somewhat better constructed. According to the OR prisoners the front line trench, which is about 100m from the German front line, has 3–4 small splinter-proof shelters, 5–6m deep, each for 3–4 men. The support trench, about 20m to the rear, has about the same number of dugouts, but they are bigger—for 10–12 men—and deeper—8–10m, and they have two entrances/exits. The first reserve trench is about 40m to the rear of the support trench and*

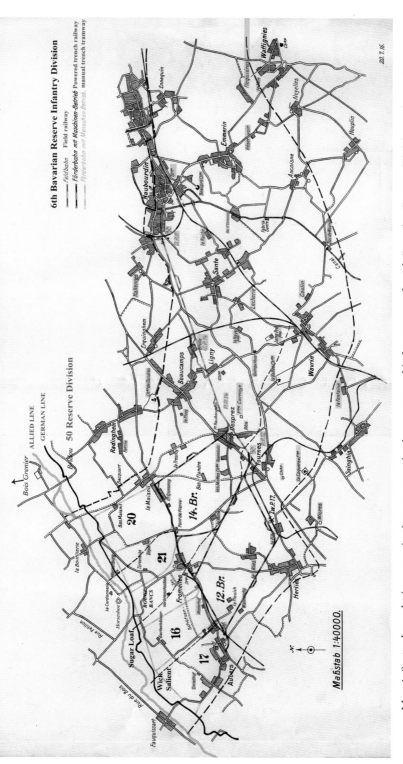

Map 4: Sector boundaries, organisation, communication routes and infrastructure for 6th Bavarian Reserve Division as it was at the time of the action of 19 July 1916. (Kriegsarchiv, Munich, 6 BRD Abt 1a, Bund 20 Akt 1)

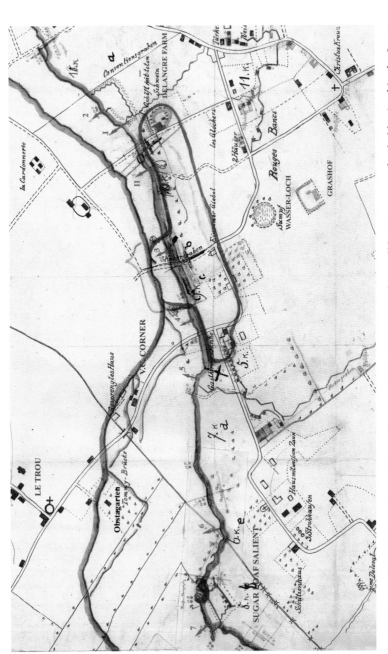

Map 5: Extent of British incursion at Rouges Bancs on 9 May 1915. Note the small but temporary foothold gained in the Sugar Loaf. The locations of Bavarian machine-guns are marked with (enhanced) green arrows. The boundaries of this incursion should be compared with those of map 7, showing the Australian positions on 19 July 1916. Note that Bavarian unit boundaries are different for the two actions; in 1915 the Rouges Bancs sector was occupied by RIR 16. (Kriegsarchiv, Munich, 6 BRD, Bund 8)

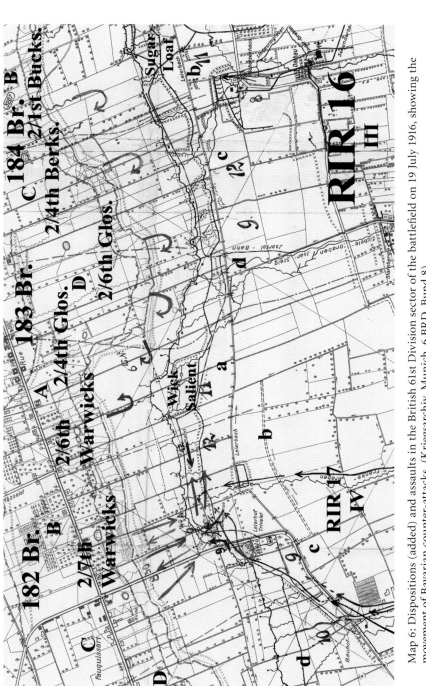

Map 6: Dispositions (added) and assaults in the British 61st Division sector of the battlefield on 19 July 1916, showing the movement of Bavarian counter-attacks. (Kriegsarchiv, Munich, 6 BRD, Bund 8)

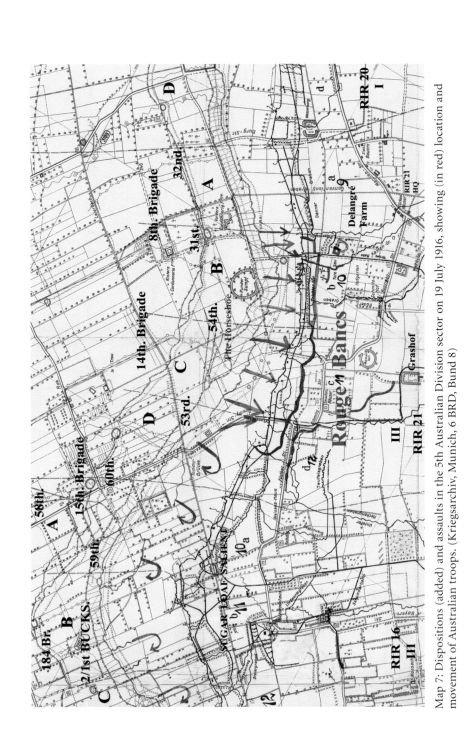

Map 7: Dispositions (added) and assaults in the 5th Australian Division sector on 19 July 1916, showing (in red) location and movement of Australian troops. (Kriegsarchiv, Munich, 6 BRD, Bund 8)

Map 8: Bavarian map showing the assault pattern and results of the British attacks at Fauquissart and the Wick Salient. The red crosses denote places where there are 'many dead'. (Kriegsarchiv, Munich, RIR 17, Bund 17)

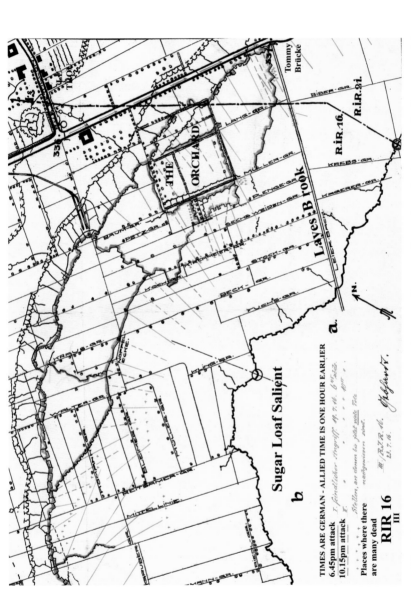

Map 9: Gebhardt's map showing the results of the Anglo–Australian assaults against the Sugar Loaf Salient on 19 July 1916. The red crosses denote places where there were 'many dead'. (Kriegsarchiv, Munich, RIR 16, Bund 18)

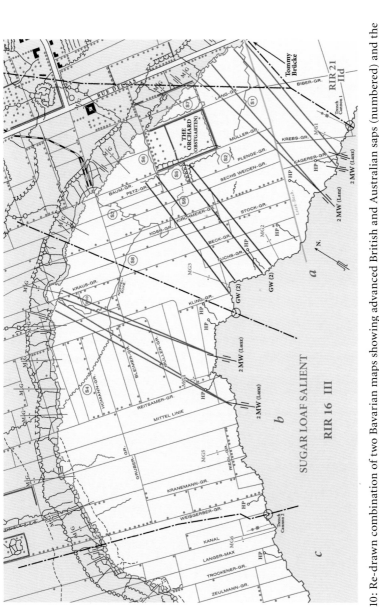

Map 10: Re-drawn combination of two Bavarian maps showing advanced British and Australian saps (numbered) and the suspected positions of allied machine guns on 19 July 1916. The locations of front-line RIR 16 machine-guns defending the Sugar Loaf are clear. Also included are HP = *Horchposten*/Listening Posts, MW = *Minenwerfer*/Mortars. The light, rapid-firing *Lanz Minenwerfers* were employed in pairs, as were the *Granatenwerfers* (GW). The pre-selected targets for the *Minenwerfers* and *Granatenwerfers* have been marked. (From the originals in Kriegsarchiv, Munich, RIR 16, Bund 14)

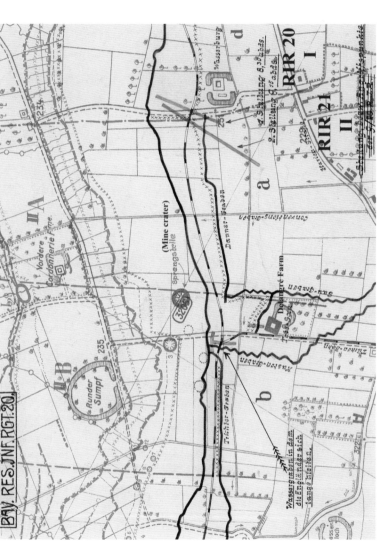

Map 11: RIR 20 detail of the Australian left flank showing the 19 July mine crater, the complex of trenches on the junction of RIR 21's sub-sectors IIa and IIb; also the *Kasten-Graben* and Delangré Farm (*Tote Sau*). Note that the Bavarians have specifically marked the flooded ditch occupied by the Diggers. (Kriegsarchiv, Munich, RIR 20, Bund 3)

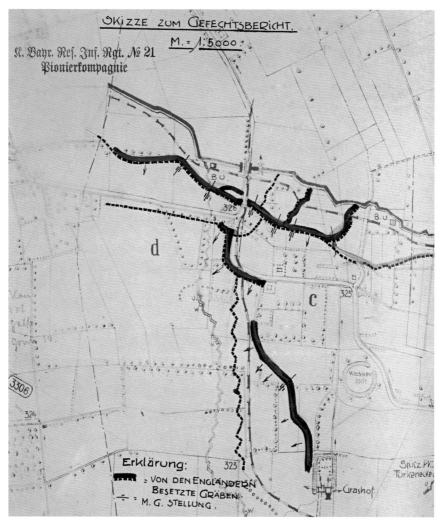

Map 12: RIR 21 map showing enemy-occupied trenches about Rouges Bancs, and the location of the Diggers' unauthorised 'excursion' to Grashof; note the symbol denoting an Australian machine-gun. BU = *Beton Unterstand*/concrete pillbox. (Kriegsarchiv, Munich, 6 BRD, Bund 8)

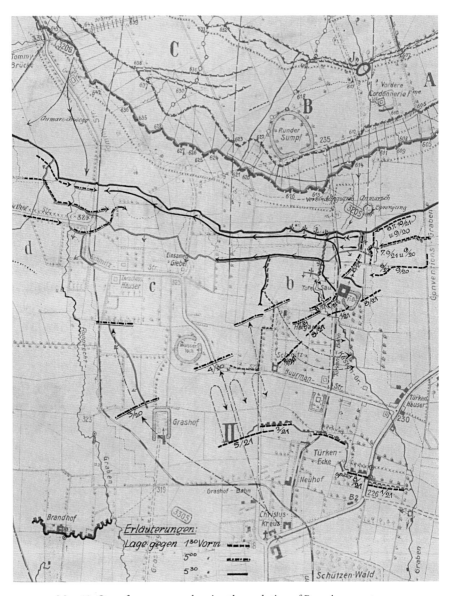

Map 13: One of many maps showing the evolution of Bavarian counter-attacks. This one generally describes manoeuvres between 1.30 a.m. and 5.30 a.m. on 20 July 1916. RIR 20 and 21 troops can be seen have moved to seal the Australian incursion in the centre and on the right flank, whilst elements of RIR 16 can be seen driving in from the left. In IIb the mine crater (*Sprengung*) and eastern communication sap (*Verbindungsgräb*) across No Man's Land are also marked. (Kriegsarchiv, Munich, 6 BRD, Bund 8)

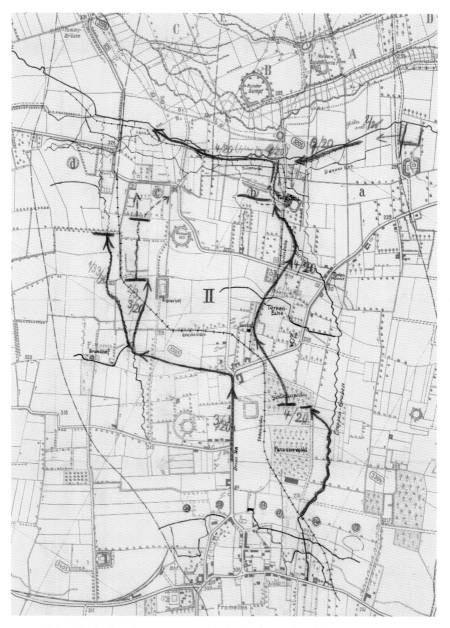

Map 14: The Bavarian counter-attacks in relation to the village of Fromelles and Pheasant Wood as the action was drawing to a close. The site of the Pheasant Wood grave pits has been added (red rectangle). Note the *Forderbahn* routes. (Kriegsarchiv, Munich, 6 BRD, Bund 8)

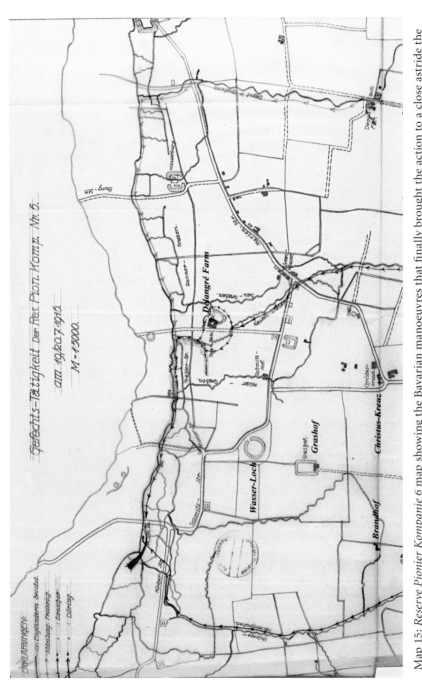

Map 15: *Reserve Pionier Kompanie 6* map showing the Bavarian manoeuvres that finally brought the action to a close astride the Tommy-Strasse/Rue Delvas. (Kriegsarchiv, Munich, 6 BRD, Bund 8)

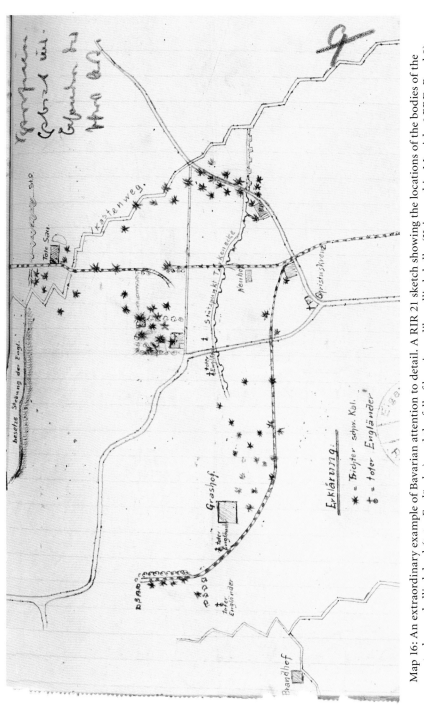

Map 16: An extraordinary example of Bavarian attention to detail. A RIR 21 sketch showing the locations of the bodies of the most advanced allied dead (*toter Engländer*), and the fall of heavier-calibre allied shells. (Kriegsarchiv, Munich, 6 BRD, Bund 8)

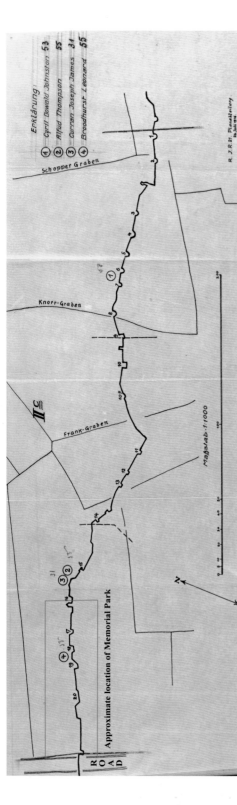

Erklärung:

1 — Cyril Dewald Johnston 53
2 — Alfred Thompson 55
3 — Curran Joseph James 31
4 — Broadhurst Leonard 55

Schopper Graben

R. J. R. 21. Plänabteilung.
26 Juli 1916.

Knorr-Graben

Frank-Graben

II c

Maßstab. 1:1000

N

Approximate location of Memorial Park

R
O
A
D

(*Above*) Map 17: One of two RIR 21 1:1000 scale maps showing numbered firebays in sub-sector IIc, and the locations of fallen Australians. This example names four Diggers found close to the Bavarian parapet. The men are all likely to have been buried at Pheasant Wood. The remains of Leonard Broadhurst and Cyril Johnston were certainly interred there, for they have been identified through DNA testing and now have a named CWGC grave. (Kriegsarchiv, Munich, 6 BRD, Bund 21)

(*Below left*) Map 18: RIR 21 (and the other three 6 BRD Regiments) produced many thousands of patrol maps. This example, composed after a nocturnal venture on 26 July, shows Bavarian progress in the backfilling of the Australian eastern communication sap across No Man's Land; it was reported as 'filled' with enemy dead. Craters 1 and 2 were the result of the two 9 May 1915 mine explosions. The 19 July crater is not marked. (Kriegsarchiv, Munich, RIR 21, Bund 12)

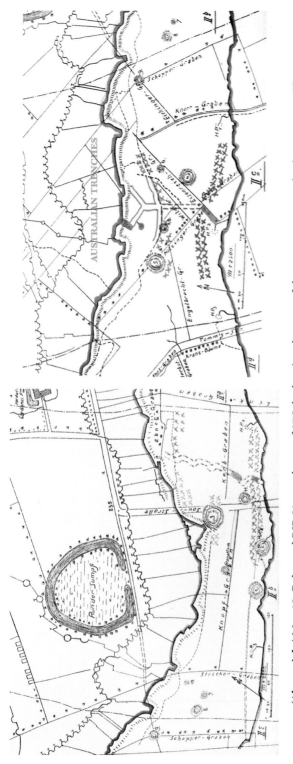

(*Above right*) Map 19: Enhanced RIR 21 patrol map of 27 July showing the trace of the western communication sap across No Man's Land in sub-sector IIc. The sap formed the only 'protected' Australian evacuation route on the morning of 20 July; like its eastern counterpart, it is also being backfilled. Note that it had been connected to Bavarian listening post number 2, and in their 'half' of No Man's Land, the Digger engineers had incorporated some abandoned early British trench positions (dotted lines) into the scheme. Note also the *Tommy-Strasse* (Rue Delvas) at left. (Kriegsarchiv, Munich, RIR 21, Bund 12)

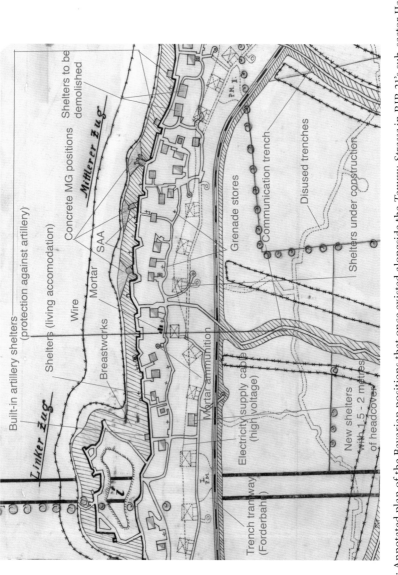

Map 20: Annotated plan of the Bavarian positions that once existed alongside the *Tommy-Strasse* in RIR 21's sub-sector IIc. It is now the site of Memorial Park on the Rue Delvas. *Linker Zug* and *Mittlerer Zug* translate as left and middle sections. See also images 2 and 5. (Kriegsarchiv, Munich, 6 BRD, Bund 13)

about 60m in front of the second reserve trench. The number and design of the dugouts in these trenches is much the same as in the support line.

Contrary to what the other ranks say, the officer asserts that the front trench and those behind it all have 3–4 concrete dugouts capable of accommodating 40 men. All the trenches are protected by a densely laid-out wire entanglement about 1.2 metres high. According to the prisoners, there are no saps or mines. There are Australian sappers in the trenches, but they are only employed on maintaining and improving the positions.

During the day, the front trench is garrisoned by about the same number of men as the trenches further to the rear, but at night about 300 men are brought up from the rear trenches to reinforce the front line. 4–6 man patrols under the command of an officer or an NCO are sent out approximately every other night. Double sentries are posted between each of the fire-bays.

21. *Morale: In general, morale is good and the mood of the men is confident, but their enthusiasm has waned somewhat since they went into the trenches. The confidence in victory that the men had when they left their homeland was shaken by the failure of the Dardanelles campaign, but was then revived by the belief that the Australian divisions were to be given the task of spearheading the breakthrough in France. They were told that we were chronically short of ammunition and that an Allied victory was assured. As far as the latter point is concerned, the men are now convinced of the opposite. The officer, however, thinks that the Allies will win the war by the end of this year.*

22. *Activities behind the front: Exercises and demonstrations of all kinds take place in the rest areas.*

23. *Leave: The block on leave was lifted three weeks ago. Now, one man at a time from each company is given 6 days leave to be spent in England.*

24. *Casualties: Up until our trench raid, the battalion had incurred few if any casualties.*

25. *Rations: Very good and plentiful.*

26. *Miscellaneous: The officer prisoner, Lieutenant N. Blanchard, was a grain merchant in civilian life and enlisted in the army in Sydney on 11 August 1914. After only 6 days, he was sent to German New Guinea, returning to Sydney in February 1915, when he was assigned to the 20th Battalion as a Sergeant. In the October he was commissioned as a 2nd Lieutenant and was promoted Lieutenant in December. He was in line for promotion to Captain in the near future.*

  The pay of the Australian troops is as follows: a private receives 6/- a day, a corporal 10/-, a sergeant 10/6d, and a sergeant-major 12/6d. 1/- a day is withheld, either to be paid to the man at the end of the war, or to be paid in regular instalments to his dependants. Lieutenants and 2nd Lieutenants receive the same pay, 21/- a day, of which 3/- is withheld for mess expenses.

  According to the officer the 1st Australian Division arrived in France about a month ago and its three brigades are now in position to the south, alongside the 2nd Australian Division. The boundary between the two divisions is the Bois Grenier–Bridoux road. The 3rd and 4th Australian divisions are reputedly en route from Egypt, or may have already landed in France, and the 5th Division is currently being assembled in Egypt. The officer thinks that the Australian/New Zealand Division is also in France, but he has not yet seen any New Zealanders. None of the prisoners know the whereabouts of the 34th Division.

27. *Conditions in Australia: In addition to patriotic reasons, many of the men enlisted for the high rates of pay. There is still quite a lot of enthusiasm for the 'Mother Country' in Australia, but it may now be declining as the war drags on. That would affect recruitment, and the prisoners doubt whether much more than another division could now be formed by voluntary enlistment. The officer thinks that the imposition of conscription in Britain will result in the introduction of compulsory military service in the colonies too. The war has not yet had any dramatic effect on economic conditions in Australia. As Australia produces more than it consumes, there is unlikely to be any significant increase in the price of food.*

All factories are working feverishly on the production of ammunition
and war materials under the direction of specialist British managers.

As usual, within thirty-six hours the document had been mimeo-graphed and distributed to selected personnel in AOK 6, and thence to specific individuals throughout the German Army, but under conditions of strict confidentiality.

Ironically, the capture of prisoners had been listed as a 'subsidiary' objective of the raid, but it will be immediately evident just how much crucial secret data had been obtained—and perhaps why the capture of two Stokes mortars elicited so little German excitement. Here was a mass of fine detail about a newly arrived, maximum-establishment, Anzac unit. A photograph of two Diggers, at least one of whom may have been captured during the raid, was taken from a prisoner and copied. An annotated sketch was then produced, and distributed to show German troops what an Australian soldier looked like. The Germans could take it as read that other Australian divisions (and possibly New Zealand units) occupying adjoining sectors were likely to employ similar administrative arrangements; the same could be assumed for those yet to arrive. The data offered superlative material for comparison with British units. It also allowed planning of front-line garrisons, support and reserve strengths and dispositions, and the adjustment of fieldwork defences and tactics to counter hostile assault of the kind that might be launched with the forces and weaponry affirmed by the prisoners. Whereas German raiders were able to personally note the effect that their own artillery and mortars had had upon the enemy's breastworks, shelters and associated fieldworks, it was only interrogations that furnished the necessary data to calculate calibres and concentrations for the destruction or harassment of other key localities, some well behind the opposing front line. It had been handed to them on a plate.

After a successful raid such as this, the Germans were able to site or re-site small arms ammunition and grenades, select features for the attention of aerial reconnaissance, adjust troop concentrations and deployment, and of course plan future raids upon the Diggers with a hugely enhanced platform of knowledge. When the time was judged to be ripest, selected material from the interrogation report could also be supplied to the

German propaganda department. OHL in Berlin did not, however, allow all information garnered on 5 May to reach the German press; in this instance secrecy was essential, and only the blandest details were published. The careful 'amendment' of operational data before its delivery to the press is one of the most fascinating and illuminating aspects of the Fromelles story; it will be illustrated later.

There were further serious implications for the Diggers. The fact that the prisoners revealed that the 1st Australian Division had moved into the line in front of Fromelles required corroboration, i.e. a 'confirming' German raid was guaranteed. The Germans' planning for 'Bamberg', an action that will be described in the next chapter, began almost immediately.

The Bavarians were especially encouraged by item 21 on the interrogation notes, which indicated waning confidence: that confidence must be kept on the wane by an increase in artillery and mortar activity—they had just been supplied with fresh targets.

Item 26, telling of fresh Australian divisions being en route for Europe or assembled in Egypt was exceptionally magnetic. In the original document this section was heavily underlined in red, and appended with a large exclamation mark. For reasons that will become clear later in this chapter, item 16 also attracted the attention of the intelligence officer for it chimed with intelligence data recently collected in the Somme sector. It had just been confirmed that a potential 40 000 Australians were now in theatre; it was essential that the German intelligence network kept the closest eye on the whereabouts and movements of the further 55 000 Diggers potentially destined for the trenches of Flanders: the 3rd, 4th and 5th Australian Divisions.

At the same time, the senses of German artillery observers were sharpened to note any changes in behaviour, including fresh battery positions and new types or unusual calibres of weapons or shells. Every shift in enemy habits, no matter how minute, was recorded. While the full report reproduced above was only disseminated among a few senior officers, a carefully edited summary was quickly issued by the 50th Reserve Infantry Division.

The post-war prisoner statements (which were actually compiled to assist Bean in the production of the *OHA*) make it clear that not all the 5 May men were interrogated in the same way. Corporal D.W. Austin of

B Company, for example, was not initially interviewed at Douai. During later questioning at Charleville, back in Australia, he mentions the Germans being 'well informed of all our movements and especially about the salient in which they had captured us. They knew how many Stokes Guns there were, and knew exactly where they were. Their objective during the raid were the Stokes Guns.'

The passage reveals shrewd German psychology. As we know, the raid had not at all been planned around the capture of mortars, but it was typically judicious to persuade prisoners to believe and indeed spread the belief that it had.

Why did the prisoners sing? It is a fact disclosed within the several bound volumes of intelligence reports in Munich, and many documents elsewhere, that most prisoners were to a lesser or greater degree forthcoming, and apparently without duress. In this particular case, however, the men need actually have said very little.

Questions could have simply been answered by, 'I don't know', a response which in countless other interrogations the Germans are seen to accept. This was especially applicable to non-commissioned ranks. But of course, no one was to know that.

Was a form of persuasion employed? Scrutiny of post-war statements reveals evidence of poor treatment of the wounded, abominable food, rough handling in camps, overwork on 'commando' (the German term for forced labour), and many other instances of abuse, but no evidence that the 'third degree' was ever meted out during interrogation. No returning prisoners mentioned any coercion other than psychological, and this was often something they only came to recognise later.

Interrogators were genial, and the process far from disagreeable. Deliberately. The Germans relied upon the prisoner's sense of self-preservation. From the earliest days of the war German interrogation policy was to treat prisoners with a degree of care and respect that was sufficient to put them at their ease and quickly alleviate the fear of violence that newly captured men, apprehensive of the alien circumstances, are bound to feel. It was found that in this way information would be *freely offered*, perhaps in gratitude for the tendered humanity. (Whether what the prisoners were saying was true or not, of course, was for the intelligence officer to decide, and his comments are to be found appended to most statements.) This was not initially the British procedure: physical and mental abuse remained a feature of their interrogation regime until it was realised that more data could be extracted if they employed the more benevolent German strategy.

The post-war prisoner statements may be taken as an accurate indication of German conduct, for upon their safe return there was nothing to be gained by a soldier understating anything that took place after his capture and during incarceration. Indeed, all the men interviewed understandably appear keen to record instances of maltreatment and want, often providing harrowing detail. None spoke of violence during interrogation.

It is interesting to note that no offensive tactics were divulged by the 5 May prisoners. This was because the Australians were still to engage in their first action on the Western Front and had not yet been required to draw up operation orders or put them into practice: as yet, the Diggers were entirely unaware of any offensive schemes they might take part in.

Every three or four days, *Armee-Oberkommando 6* updated and circulated a document entitled *'Feststellungen über der Gegner vor der Armeefront'*—'Information about the Enemy on the Army Front'. In the bulletin of 10 May 1916 they immediately incorporated some of the data derived from the questioning of the 20th Battalion men. Among other things, it noted that:

> The deployment of the 2nd Australian Division in the Bois Grenier sector, south of Armentières, has been confirmed by the captured Australian officer belonging to that division. He says that the sector immediately to the south of his division is held by the 1st Australian Division, which was already suspected to be in France. If that is correct, the 1st Australian Division has presumably relieved the 35th Infantry Division. Confirmation of this is required.

Also:

> The Australian officer also says that the 3rd and 4th Australian Divisions are being shipped from Egypt to France, and may even be in France already. That may well be correct in the case of the 3rd Australian

(or perhaps Australian/NZ) Division, which is believed to be ready for deployment, but is less likely in the case of the 4th Australian Division, which is newly formed and not yet fully trained or equipped. It is at most conceivable that this division is intended for eventual deployment on the French front and that it might be brought to France sooner rather than later to acclimatise and undergo further training.

This document is more significant than might immediately meet the eye, for it was elements of this very bulletin that were brought to the attention of Charles Bean on 6 May 1926 by his English colleague Captain J.J.W. Herbertson. As a witness of the event in question, Bean would therefore have been well aware that the 'Australian officer' named above could only be Norman Blanchard of the 20th Battalion. One might have thought that such a strategically sensitive entry would have provoked in Bean a request to see the original interrogation papers, not least because in recording the testimony of the first Australian prisoners to be captured on the Western Front they were also *historic* documents. Had he viewed and elected to use them, the May 1916 section of the *OHA*—and indeed many subsequent sections—may today read rather differently.

But Bean's extended and repeated vehemence in the men's defence is a little disconcerting. Here was information that the Australian nation would not be pleased to see—and of a nature far more reprehensible and perfidious than the loss of a couple of mortars: some would happily have called it treachery. Did Bean see the reports and choose to suppress them? We shall perhaps never know, but their existence changes not only long-accepted history, but our perceptions of this critical period of the war, and indeed the way we need to look at Fromelles.

Although sensitive information about the 19 July attacks clearly could not have been divulged at this time because the action had not yet been settled upon and approved, the Germans were now, crucially, aware of fine comparative detail of two Australian divisions. Should relieving units also be Australian, such as the freshly arrived 5th Division or the soon-to-arrive 4th, they were likely to employ similar operational configurations; it was equally probable they would pitch up somewhere in French Flanders.

It is for these reasons the 5 May raid heralded a sequence of German 'investigative' trench raids that would only conclude three days before the Battle of Fromelles itself.

———————

The Australians themselves were now about to move into offensive mode. According to Charles Bean, their own raiding scheme was planned 'in order to give confidence to the troops, encourage a fighting spirit, and, if possible, inflict losses on the enemy and damage the morale of his garrison'.

A second reason was the ever-growing necessity to assist their allies. France was fast sliding towards breaking point, and grand Anglo–French plans for a Somme offensive were almost daily being undermined by news of fresh emergencies at Verdun, some 280 kilometres south of Picardy. The offensive was still haemorrhaging French lives. One by one, the divisions Joffre had earmarked for the Somme were absorbed and vaporised in the maelstrom, tumbling from thirty-nine at the turn of the year to thirty at the end of April 1916, and twenty-five a month later. In early June they were to fall further still to just sixteen. Each downward reassessment of the French contribution loaded responsibility for the upcoming offensive more heavily upon the shoulders of Sir Douglas Haig. His private papers reveal an anxious man. On 29 March he wrote, 'I am strengthening the long line which I have recently taken over. I have not got an Army in France at all really, but a collection of divisions untrained for the Field. The actual fighting Army will be devolved from them.' Incoming Australian divisions presently fell into the 'untrained for the field' category. For his grand opportunity on the Somme to succeed, Haig required every possible assistance from every possible quarter. Five days later an urgent directive from GHQ warned that 'Army Commanders must be prepared to mount an attack of considerable scale on their fronts and they must have their schemes prepared for this purpose'.

It is at this point that one of the leading characters in the Fromelles story comes to fully inhabit the frame: General Sir Richard Haking, commander of XI Corps, whose responsibility it would be to plan and execute Sir Douglas Haig's requirements on his 'patch' in Artois and French Flanders.

Haig and Haking were kindred spirits—aggressive believers in the inculcation and constant enhancement of an offensive attitude, and profoundly discontented when 'treading water'. Wherever defence was—temporarily— necessary, it must at least be an active one.

The enemy, they decreed, must never perceive the slightest material or psychological weakness in their British foe; he must be harried and massacred on every possible occasion. If in seeking this end no major enterprise was possible, then every effort must be made to carry out minor ones: trench raids, patrols, tricks, traps—anything that would keep infantry on their toes and shed German blood. In the spring of 1916 Haig was especially appreciative of Haking's tireless pursuance of 'cumulative aggression'; in positional warfare, he was perhaps a model leader.

On 19 March at a Corps conference, Haking decreed that, regardless of the present shortage of ammunition for the guns, as a result of it being transported 'elsewhere', brigade and battalion commanders were to pursue raids and ruses with the utmost vigour. Assault parties could be made smaller if necessary, he said, but it was essential that the offensive spirit 'that had been created and nourished during the last few months in the Corps' was maintained. It was only by 'getting into the enemy's trenches and driving him out' that his men would be rendered 'fit for greater operations later on, when we shall end the war with one or two great battles'. The provision of fitness by aggression and bloodshed was General Haking's principal maxim. Nothing diverted him from that belief. Here was a man with absolute confidence in his convictions. After Loos, for example, he had condemned the idea that short shooting by British artillery had contributed to the lack of success.

Troops that have failed in an attack are very apt to believe that they have suffered from their own shell fire when really it was the enemy's, and many cases of this nature have been investigated and it has been found that there was no real foundation for the allegation.

The striking certitude illustrates Haking's 'style'.

The nature of the XI Corps battlefront meant that the efforts Haking expended in this task had to be prodigious, not least because it incorporated a 'nursery sector': divisions were often attached to his command for limited periods, sometimes a month only. However, the greatest problem for those in the highest echelons of command was that although their senior subordinate officers may have understood the benefits of relentless trench raiding, the Tommy in the trenches, who always bore the bloody brunt of such activities, was seldom made aware of the wider strategic purpose; what the 'ordinary' soldier often perceived was no valid gain for a great deal of pain.

On the night of 26/27 June a raid by a party of 2/8th Royal Warwickshire Regiment (Warwicks) north of Neuve Chapelle, for example, left the enemy with fifteen English prisoners, one of whom was 29-year-old Captain G.C. Field, second-in-command of D Company. In a tight-lipped interview Field deflected, diverted and stone-walled. Fritz Lübcke, feeling thwarted, reported: 'Insofar as he answers questions at all, the prisoner otherwise confirms what his fellow prisoners have said.' But of the raid itself, Lübcke noted that Captain Field spoke 'with bitterness' about the attack, saying, 'The idea for it had come from the Brigade commander, who evidently wanted it to get him noticed'; the whole enterprise, he said, had been, 'pointless from the outset'.

In this and numerous other examples, a certain sullen resentment of Haking's tactics can be seen to exist long before July 1916. Given that the interrogation of Captain Field took place on 29 June 1916, the prisoner's most valuable deflection appears as point 5 in Lübcke's report: 'A general major offensive in the west has been talked of for so long and at such length that no one now seriously believes that it will ever happen.'

Chapter 7

RAIDING SEASON

It was before the arrival of the Anzacs that the Germans first became aware that something suspicious was afoot in the Somme region of Picardy. Aerial reconnaissance suggested preparations were underway—hutting, bridging, road and rail works—but the most critical data once again came from trench raids. This time it was British prisoners who confirmed the build-up of divisions in the region—a region which OHL in Berlin had already identified as the likely stage for a strategic Allied response to France's difficulties at Verdun. Although for some time they were to erroneously believe that a counter-offensive would be a solely British affair, the Germans were nevertheless alert to the way their enemies usually functioned.

Joffre requested substantial British assaults to ease his nation's troubles at Verdun. French reserves were being significantly drawn down, but although a great body of 'Kitchener's Army' of citizen volunteers now swarmed in France, sustaining sufficient combat strength for the approaching Somme campaign was uppermost in Haig's planning. He advocated that, if carefully planned and executed, smaller enterprises would both preserve British potency for the grand offensive ahead and at the same time be effective in stopping the Germans thinning garrisons elsewhere and despatching support to Picardy. On 27 May he issued the following decree: 'Preparations for deceiving the enemy should be made . . . Raids at night of a strength of a Company and upwards on an extensive scale into the enemy's front system of defences. These to be prepared by intense artillery and trench mortar bombardment.'

In French Flanders the order was acted upon by First and Second Army on 1 June 1916, with both Sir Charles Monro and Sir Herbert Plumer instructing corps commanders to devise plans that would 'wear out' the Germans, mislead them as to where 'real' attacks might take place, and by repeated molestation generally reduce enemy morale and fighting efficiency. Soon after this sequence of 'muggings' began, however, another event would influence the fortunes of all belligerents.

The Brusilov Offensive was a Russian surprise attack launched on 4 June against the Austro–Hungarians in the Ukraine. General Alexei Brusilov crushed the Austro–Hungarian army to the point where it was never again capable of launching a major attack without German support. The enterprise also achieved a second fundamental objective, by forcing Germany to transfer so many reinforcements to the east that its attacks on Verdun had to be halted. During the offensive an astonishing 25 000 square kilometres of ground was recaptured—but at a cost of nearly half a million Russian troops. The Austrians were crushed, their losses reaching an extraordinary 1.5 million, a figure that included almost 400 000 prisoners.

Meanwhile, in Flanders, the fighting was still over metres, and prisoners counted by the handful. The first German soldier to be captured by Australian troops on the Western Front was a *Pionier* (engineer) of 20th Bavarian Reserve Infantry Regiment. Although the Diggers had been trying to 'snaffle a Hun' for some time, his capture in No Man's Land on 28 May 1916 was unprofitable. He had little to say for himself. On the same night and in the same sector two Digger sappers fell into Bavarian hands. This time Fritz Lübcke found they were 1st Australian Division men:

The captured NCO, Hedley L. Stevens, is badly wounded and has so far only been able to give a small amount of information. He is 22 years old, by trade a precision engineering worker, and joined the army in 1915. He left the camp where he received his training shortly before Christmas with 250–300 men of the 8th Reinforcement transport of the 19th Infantry Battalion, 5th Australian Infantry Brigade, sailed from Fremantle (south-west corner of Australia) on 1 January and landed in Egypt on 23 January.

In mid-February the prisoner was reduced in rank and assigned to the 2nd Battalion, 1st Australian Brigade, and was then posted to the 1st Pioneer Battalion at the beginning of March. At the end of March this Battalion, which is attached to the 2nd Australian Brigade, 1st Australian Division, was transported by sea to Marseille and from there by rail direct to the Hazebrouck area. After spending some time working in the rear, it was sent into the trenches for the first time about a fortnight ago. On the night of 27/28 May, A Company was detailed to repair the parapet in the front line trenches. When the work was finished, he and the officer in charge, Lt. M.B. Dobie, went out to see how it looked from the enemy side. They strayed too close to the German positions and were surprised by a patrol, which threw hand grenades at them and brought them both in badly wounded. The officer succumbed to his wounds without regaining consciousness. The prisoner can give no information about the composition of the 1st Australian Division, or about his own unit or neighbouring units. He knows only that the 1st Pioneer Battalion is attached to the 2nd Australian Infantry Brigade and that the 2nd Pioneer Battalion is attached to the 1st Australian Infantry Brigade. The Battalions of the 2nd Brigade manning the front line at the moment are apparently the 6th and 8th.

Each Pioneer Battalion has 4 Companies. Their work is confined to the construction of defensive positions. Wiring, mining, etc, are the responsibility of the infantry or special Tunnelling Companies.

The CO of the 1st Pioneer Battalion is Colonel Nichol (or Nicolsen). The prisoner professes not to know the names of the Divisional commander or any other officers. A Coy is based in a place near Estaires, the name of which he does not know.

*The prisoner admits the possibility that the 2nd Australian Division
and New Zealanders might be in that area. However he claims to have
no certain knowledge.*

Lieutenant Dobie's letters to his mother, which were taken from his
body, were translated, copied and circulated, adding a few more fragments
to the intelligence jigsaw. It was now clear that the region south of Armentières had been selected to introduce Anzac divisions into the line—at least
another three—and that the whole sector was in a state of flux. The shifting
circumstances again pointed towards major action elsewhere: the Somme.
What was extracted from Corporal Hedley Stevens was added to earlier
data, but more information was required on who was where, how long they
might be there and where they were ultimately bound. To acquire it, the
Bavarians produced their own raid plan.

The most significant German raid of May 1916 was the previously mentioned
Bamberg. It took place on the 30th. This time it was a 6th Bavarian Reserve
Infantry Division enterprise, the purpose being to 'identify beyond all doubt'
(in case the unit had been relieved and transferred) the troops facing the
21st Reserve Infantry Regiment. Planned by its commanding officer, *Oberst*
(Colonel) Julius Ritter von Braun, the raid was so intricately designed that
one would be forgiven for thinking it was a far greater endeavour.

Sanctioned by von Scanzoni on 15 May, preliminary registration by
twelve-and-a-half batteries of assorted artillery supported by ten mortars
of four different calibres (including the famously malicious *Ladungswerfer*,
or 'Flying Pig') commenced on the 22nd. Von Braun's operation orders
directed that a model of the sector be prepared and that selected men
be separated from their comrades in order to keep the place and time of
attack as secret as possible. There was to be no mention of the venture
over the telephone, even by code-name, for fear of enemy interception.
The 120 raiders practised day and night for two weeks for an operation
that was planned to last a mere quarter-hour. In the event, Bamberg, led by
Leutnant Brassler, 'overran' by two minutes. Part of Brassler's post-action
report reads:

At 10.00 p.m. the two patrols were ready at the exits, and provided with hand-grenades. During the bombardment of the enemy's front line from 10.15 until 11.15, the men were kept in recesses as much as was possible. Those who were not so accommodated remained at the parapet and took cover from our own mortar and HE splinters coming over from the enemy trenches. The enemy did not reply against our trenches . . . At 11.03 p.m. all left their recesses and assembled at the exits. At the same moment, whilst our fire was still on the enemy's front line trenches, two pioneers from each patrol left the trench and cut lanes through our wire. Exactly at 11.05 the patrol advanced. Watches had been checked several times during the day.

Because of thick smoke the point of entry in the enemy trench fixed by day could not be seen as we went forward, but owing to the short distance to be traversed the correct place was reached. In crossing No Man's Land the patrol was molested neither by artillery nor infantry or machine-gun fire. On arrival at the enemy trenches the groups at once took up the place that had been indicated for them, and no one stood idle. In a moment touch was established throughout the entire patrol; also all the reports on the blocks arrived quickly.

The left blocking group moved leftwards about 12 metres from the point of entry and suddenly found themselves faced with 6 of the enemy, one of whom fired his rifle. The group were not able to block the trench. They attacked the enemy with hand-grenades, but because of lack of ammunition (the reserve supply was not yet to hand) they had to retire to the point of entry. There, four men from the left rear blocking group came to their help with grenades. I also sent from the reserve group four men with sacks of grenades as reinforcements. As a consequence the left flank group were able to check the enemy, who had also turned a machine-gun on them which consistently shot too high. They silenced the machine-gun and heard the cries of the wounded.

The party left the Australian trenches at 11.22 p.m. (German time— as today, one hour later than the British). The following day von Braun reported to his 14th Bavarian Brigade superiors:

The placing of our artillery and trench mortar fire was excellent. The enemy wire at the points of entry was completely swept away, although in the last days it had been considerably strengthened. The front part of the enemy parapet was not so much destroyed as I had imagined. The main effect was in the enemy trench, which was for a great part levelled, so that the exact nature of its bottom (whether drained or duck-boarded) could not be established. The approaches to the communication trenches were blocked with earth which made their discovery and recognition as they were shown during instruction very difficult, all the more so as thick clouds of smoke from explosive shells still lay in the trenches and made it impossible to see.

The effect of the fire must have been fearful. Bodies, buried and torn in shreds, were found in great number, and also very many dead, apparently unwounded, were seen in dugouts. On this account, in spite of the strong garrison, only ten prisoners were made. These were taken from several dugouts which had been collapsed in an opportune manner, and first had to be freed. Only a few enemy were in a position to offer resistance. They were overcome. The enemy belonged to the 1st Australian Division.

The [artillery] lift having been made to secure the security of our own troops, the enemy quickly recovered from his surprise and began to defend himself, and indeed to work his machine-guns, whose radius of fire, however, was fortunately too high. Thanks to the smartness of the blocking group, and to a barricade of spikes and wire which had been brought for the purpose, the enemy was shocked and was fought down gradually with hand-grenades. In other parts of the trenches only a few of the enemy showed resistance. Shots came, however, from one half-buried dugout, but a few hand-grenades quickly settled the garrison. The rest of the enemy preferred not to betray their presence by any sign, so that individual members of the patrol had to enter the dugouts, light them with their pocket lamps. Unteroffizier Frank, in this manner, fetched out five or six men . . .

This account is typically Bavarian: objective and straightforward, rather than heroic and embroidered—seeking solely to record reality in order that future enterprises might better prosper. By way of contrast, in his report to the 3rd Australian Brigade, the 11th Battalion CO Lieutenant-Colonel S.R. Roberts minimised the event, downgrading it to an 'attempted' raid. In the unit war diary he stated:

> ... I accept as an established fact that a small party of the enemy did actually reach our trenches under an intense bombardment and under cover of the dense smoke, but the party withdrew at once and were not seen by the men manning the debris immediately the bombardment ceased. At the point of attack mining had been very active and no doubt the object of the raid was to destroy our mining chambers. I am inclined to the view that only the enemy's scouts were able to reach our lines. The prompt manner in which the breach was manned after such a heavy bombardment, and the valuable aid given by our machine guns made any raid an impossibility. The party which reached the parapet did no damage whatever to our lines and I venture to assert it was unable to return by the way by which it came. I regret to say I lost one Lewis Gun ... The casualties were heavy being Killed 36 other ranks, Wounded 2 officers and 59 other ranks, and Missing 6 other ranks. With regard to the missing personnel, whole portions of the line were blown up and no doubt the men were either blown to atoms or smothered in the several craters which were formed in the lines.

Colonel Roberts was probably correct about the fate of his own missing, for the nine Australians brought in by the Bavarians did not belong to his unit but the neighbouring 9th Battalion: four infantry and five pioneers. It is curious that at no time does Roberts consider that the enemy were primarily seeking prisoners. Expecting to have captured more Australians, both RIR 21 and 6 BRD were somewhat disappointed. As usual, they make no attempt to estimate the number of enemy casualties, but may well have been surprised by the split: 108 Australian to just two Bavarian. The lack of yet greater success was attributed by Brassler to 'stupidity'. The captive Diggers were marched off to the detention centre at the citadel in Lille. Here they vouchsafed significant information on orders of battle, troop movements, locations of headquarters, and training. Lübcke's report also incorporated the following:

3. _Divisional headquarters_ thought to be in Sailly-sur-la-Lys.

4. _Relief:_ The infantrymen claim not to have been relieved, even within the trench system, since they went into the line. The pioneers remain in the trenches for 2 days at half-company strength, then get two days rest at Sailly or Laventie.

5. _Artillery:_ The Division brought its own artillery with it.

6. _Insignia:_ The (whole of the) 3rd Brigade wears a blue rectangle on the upper arm at shoulder height. The Pioneer Battalion wears a crossed rifle and pick on the shoulder.

7. _Weapons:_ Lee-Enfield rifle.

8. _Replacements:_ Two of the captured infantrymen belong to the 14th draft of reinforcements that the Battalion has received since the war began. The Pioneer Battalion received 200 replacements from Egypt a week ago.

9. _Gas protection:_ The usual Vermoral sprayers and gas helmets. They know nothing about their own gas warfare apparatus.

10. _Hand grenades:_ All the men have been trained in bombing.

11. _Age range:_ 18–45 years old.

12. _Company frontage:_ 175m.

13. _Machine guns:_ One of the prisoners attended a Maxim MG training course in Egypt and belongs to the MG reserve, although he carries out infantry duties. The number of MGs in the company sector is not known, but there are both Lewis guns and Maxims, the latter belonging to the Brigade.

14. _Communications:_ There are telephones in the front line trench.

15. _Trench mortars:_ There was a trench mortar in the sector, the crew of which withdrew when German artillery fire began.

16. _Unit strength:_
    Infantry: 4–5 officers, 200 men (per Company)
    Pioneers: 4 companies each of 250 men

17. _Defensive positions:_ There are only two lines of trenches, approx 75m apart. In the front line, in addition to small funk-holes,

there are some 15–20 foot deep dugouts. Patrols are sent out frequently, usually made up of men from different companies. The men know nothing about mining. The Pioneer Battalion was only involved in improving and maintaining the trenches and making dugouts.

18. *Casualties: In France, minor: mainly caused by German minenwerfer fire.*

19. *Interception of communications: It is known that the Germans have listening devices (tapping = abzapfen). The men do not know what precautions are taken against this.*

20. *Miscellaneous: The infantrymen were brought by train from Etaples to a place behind the front. The journey took from evening until 1.00pm. They then marched for 5 hours to Sailly, where they were assigned to the different companies. The infantry and pioneers are paid 6/- a day, of which 1/- is withheld.*

21. *Morale: Morale is very good. The men constantly emphasise that they are 'volunteers'. The prisoners do not think that universal conscription will be introduced in Australia; popular sentiment is not in favour of it.*

The following day, after further questioning, a supplement was added, which included:

The prisoners had the following to say about the New Zealanders:

About three weeks ago approximately 100 New Zealanders spent two days in the trenches of the 3rd Australian Brigade for training purposes. According to some of the prisoners, they are now deployed in the area of Armentières. The New Zealanders' uniform is similar to that of the Australians, but their slouch hat is somewhat smaller and has a red band instead of a khaki band.

The Maori, of whom the prisoners saw 100–200 in Laventie, wear the same uniform as the New Zealanders and the same smaller slouch hat with a red band. They are attached to the New Zealand Division, and the Australian troops regard them as equals, as they are civilised in every respect.

In the estimation of the prisoners, there are around 2000 Maori in France, among them numerous officers. The prisoners themselves had seen several officers in Laventie. They are all powerfully built and their skin colour is similar to that of half-castes. They have fuzzy hair, which they wear cut short.

<u>*Australian cavalry*</u>*:*

A contingent of the Australian Light Horse came to France from Egypt at the same time as the 1st Australian Division, and is presently operating behind the front: guarding railway lines, etc. In Egypt these troops were assigned to transporting ammunition, for which they used only mules, but the contingent sent to France has come with its horses. According to some of the prisoners, these troops are waiting impatiently for the opportunity to take part in a cavalry offensive in order to place their riding skills, honed since childhood, at the service of the Motherland. They are almost all 'bushmen' and ride only the best horses. Some of the prisoners take the fact that they have been brought to France to mean that an offensive is imminent, in which the cavalry will play a significant role. The prisoners do not know the strength of the Australian cavalry stationed in France . . .

<u>Discipline</u> is said to be very strict. Thus, for example, one of the men had received 28 days 'Field Punishment No.1' for being drunk in quarters. On another occasion, when he was 10 minutes late on parade, he got 6 days punishment duties in the trenches while his comrades went to the rest camp.

If a man leaves the confines of his quarters without special permission, he is liable to a minimum sentence of 3 years imprisonment, to be served after the war, and if he re-offends, he is shot without right of appeal (This sounds to me to be an exaggeration: Intelligence Officer).

There is a <u>trench railway</u> that goes as far as the second-line trenches.

The men wear their slouch hats in the trenches, usually with the brim turned down, when they are not wearing their helmets.

Bamberg was looked upon by 6 BRD as a fine accomplishment. A great swathe of added intelligence had been harvested, all of which harmonised with the results of Lübcke's earlier interrogations. The picture was building and the Australian model becoming considerably clearer. In typical Bavarian style, the raided section of the opposing breastworks was panoramically photographed *Vor und Nach der Beschiessung*—before and after the attack. In the 'after' image wire defences are seen to have been utterly swept away; the ground is pulverised, all vegetation gone, and the earth appears to be seething. Von Scanzoni and his staff were especially pleased with the performance of mortars and artillery.

The efficacy of the German bombardment was confirmed by the CO of the 3rd Australian Brigade, Brigadier-General E.G. Sinclair MacLagan. MacLagan was obliged to apologise for the delayed delivery of his report to 1st Australian Division HQ; its lateness, he explained, was due to evidence having to be 'collected from men who were to a great extent stupefied by the *minenwerfer* bomb explosions, for about 24 hours'.

Regular infliction of loss upon the enemy was a permanent objective. This included the morning and evening 'hate', short but intense periods of shelling designed to annoy and destroy; the Bavarians preferred the term 'prayers'.

Patrols occasionally achieved success, but raids were the best vehicle for killing, capturing and learning. Since early 1915 the British had looked upon them as good for morale, and General Sir Richard Haking was one of their most fervent advocates, for they were especially useful for 'blooding' inexperienced troops, offering an invaluable introduction to the wholesale butchery that larger enterprises would sooner or later demand. Men had to be mentally and physically prepared for what they were required to do and to see. Losses, as long as they were not excessive (a calculation normally computed by those whose names did not form a part of the casualty lists), were balanced against the results. To this calculation the perceived wider benefits of 'personal development' were added. Fighting one's way into and along an enemy trench demanded teamwork and trust. It also contained many of the desensitising ingredients required to attain effective performance in the prime object of warfare on the Western Front: ultimate victory through homicide. Training in close combat was essential, for trench fighting was the ubiquitous essence of the war, and no matter how great or small the venture, trenches had to be captured and cleared before consolidation and/or further advance could take place. If the infantry were not in secure occupation, an objective could never be classed as captured.

Trench raids demanded very specific tactics. Having broken into the enemy line, it was a case of working in both directions and systematically clearing each fire bay in a method known as 'rolling up'. The party was often accompanied by engineers armed with mobile charges to throw into dugouts, shafts, stairways or inclines. For the infantry, however, the focal procedure involved 'the three B's'—bomb, bayonet and butt—in an orchestrated surge from fire bay to fire bay. It required careful planning, prudent selection of men, energy, determination, split-second timing and absolute ruthlessness. Two lead bombers threw grenades over or around the corner of a traverse into the adjacent fire bay; the moment the bursts were heard they moved on to the next traverse leaving a brace of bayonet-men to follow up and further incapacitate or despatch wounded and stunned alike. The final *coup de grâce* was delivered by shattering blows to the skull with the rifle butt. If carried out by a well-drilled team, the method could be highly effective, and especially terrifying for those who could discern the gradually approaching sound of combat.

To counter the procedure, 'trench blocks' were installed—bundles of timber and barbed wire that could be swiftly rolled or pulled into a trench to slow enemy movement while at the same time baulking the assault, turning the attackers into static targets for defensive bombing. The taking of prisoners depended solely upon local conditions. Experience showed that the more ruthless the approach, the more likely it was that defenders would lay down their arms and surrender.

Given the restricted nature of the attack that would be planned for 19 July, the procedures devised for raids were to play a major role in the outcome of the battle, for in counter-attack the enemy employed identical practices. In the Fromelles excavations of 2007, clear visual evidence of the 'three B's' was widespread in the Pheasant Wood graves.

Unless the enemy had been neutralised by artillery or forced to withdraw, a bombing battle during a full-scale offensive might last not just minutes or hours, but days. Trench raids, however, were short and furious, and casualties more than just likely. This too had its advantages. The death of comrades engendered the primal and militarily useful desire for revenge, a slumbering human instinct. It could be especially 'inspiring' if one was attacking an enemy at whose hands one's unit had earlier suffered. The emotion of earlier events could be deliberately rekindled before every subsequent action—make the enemy pay. Fromelles was to be a working example. The location of the sector within the wider battlefront, and its topography, made it the perfect place for both small-scale tactical experimentation and larger-scale strategic diversion.

—————

Every army, corps, division, brigade, regiment and battalion on the Western Front was aware of the most vulnerable localities on their 'patch': where No Man's Land was at it narrowest and could thus be swiftly traversed, and where the profile of the lines made defensive enfilade least effective. For both the Australians and the Bavarians at Fromelles the prime candidate was the Horseshoe sub-sector, where No Man's Land was less than 100 metres wide. It mattered little whether the enterprise was a raid or a grander assault, such places were guaranteed to receive special attention.

In the case of a limited but substantial attack, such as that of 19 July, the need to capture and consolidate one's flanks was fundamental to the success of the initial assault, and to the permanent linking of the newly captured positions to one's own. Brassler's left and right blocking parties during Bamberg offer an excellent small-scale illustration of what was required. Their task had been to hold the two flanks while specialist searching groups met the prime purposes of the raid. In larger enterprises, flanking units provided critical protective bulwarks for the main body of assault and for support, communication and supply. Thus the boundaries of a battleground were usually established where solid flanks could be most effectively and easily created and held—the narrows. Again, Fromelles provides a textbook illustration.

—————

Given that one was unlikely to be able to subdue a nocturnal hostile barrage (in any case, fieldworks could always be repaired) the prime defensive objective was to keep an enemy raiding party out of one's trenches by destroying or weakening it in No Man's Land and especially at one's wire. Hence the need for *Horchposten*—listening posts. If hostile artillery and mortars had done their job by destroying wire and resistance at the point where an enemy party had elected to enter, and were able to block avenues of escape and support throughout the action, this left flanking fire as the only way in which the infantry might halt hostile progress. To defend a carefully coordinated assault supported by effective, precise and devastating shell and mortar fire was a colossal challenge even for the most experienced of troops. It required supreme watchfulness, training, leadership and, most important of all, early warning and the capability for immediate *organised* response. To achieve such a response required time and practice.

Britons, Bavarians and Australians were about to experience a period where both method and mettle would be tested. From the beginning of June activity around Aubers and Fromelles became more lively by the day. Shelling and mortaring of all calibres increased, likewise the frequency of nocturnal (and in the case of the Germans, diurnal) patrols. Things were clearly happening, and intelligence-gathering was the order of the day. On both sides of the line, rumours abounded.

On 24 June the Somme preliminary bombardment commenced. The Germans, knowing an offensive was imminent, arrested the supply of ammunition to Verdun: the efforts of France's allies were gradually releasing the nation from her shackles; now it was Britain's turn to help smash the final locks on the gates that should lead to open warfare. Throughout this tumultuous period, raids—both Allied and German—continued to produce prisoners and intelligence.

On the night of 28/29 a small but highly successful enterprise by sixty-two men of the 1st Battalion, 1st Australian Brigade, against the 20th Bavarian Reserve Infantry Regiment sector near La Boutillerie created serious consternation. The Diggers evaded hostile listening posts, crept unseen through the long grass (this was blamed by the Bavarians upon a shortage of scythes and herbicide) up to the enemy wire, waited just 50 metres behind an accurate barrage, and then bombed their way into the enemy trench. Their orders were to capture prisoners, wounded or unwounded, to kill the enemy to collect material for unit identification, and to seize or destroy machine guns and trench mortars. Although the raiders were unable to keep to the precise plan of attack, the effect was far-reaching.

RIR 20 recorded nineteen dead, thirty-six wounded and two missing (both prisoners): a heavy loss for a foray that, including the barrage, lasted only twelve minutes. Another raid on the same night in an adjacent sector resulted in a German captain and fourteen men being taken prisoner. These events had the effect of forcing the Bavarians to augment front-line garrisons, not only in the RIR 20 sector, but elsewhere.

Observing, *Oberst* von Braun noted with concern that after a short artillery preparation, the enemy had attacked in six to seven waves each numbering about twenty. In one sector the first wave were wiped out; jubilant at their success, the Bavarians had then congregated at the break-in point to inspect the enemy dead, leaving the breastwork to either side unmanned—which had allowed the next wave to enter the positions and drive in from both sides, killing and wounding numerous men. It was a serious failure in established practices. The raid had a profound effect. This was complacency of the highest and most serious order. An immediate enquiry was carried out, blame allocated, and penalties imposed. Hostility was increasing; British and Australian artillery especially were exacting an ever-heavier toll. The Germans took the increasing frequency of raids to signal mounting British confidence in their Dominion comrades. By closing with the enemy face to face, Diggers were learning how to fight and survive in a realm which every soldier must at some time face—that of the great offensive.

Chapter 8

THE DAY OF
SUPPLICATION

Religious faith was the cornerstone of Sir Douglas Haig's military and personal life. On the eve of the Somme attack he wrote the following note to his wife:

> You must know that I feel that every step in my plan has been taken with the Divine help—and I ask daily for aid, not merely in making the plan, but in carrying it out, and this I hope I shall continue to do until the end of all things which concern me on earth.

Charles Bean became familiar with the commander-in-chief's convictions through Padre Dexter who on 17 June had mentioned that the army's senior chaplain was to have visited him, but that 'he was unable to come because things might be taking place in another direction. He said that Field Marshal Haig had told him a great event might be coming off in a few days, and had asked him to get three-quarters of the other chaplains together to pray, for all the prayer that they could offer would be needed.

He believed that success could not be too earnestly prayed for. Dexter said that it depended, he understood, on whether the French needed this help in connection with Verdun. It seems just a little bit like the Roman Consul seeing to his Pontifex before a campaign or an Indian Chief bringing out his medicine men.'

When the morning of the 'great event' finally arrived the prayers and supplications of collected clergy and hundreds of millions of less pious souls cut little ice with the Almighty. As darkness finally fell on 1 July 1916 British Third and Fourth Armies had suffered over 57 000 casualties, their French ally around 2500. There were over 20 000 dead. Long before noon Joffre and Haig's strategy and expectations lay in ruins. The offensive failure—or perhaps more correctly the German defensive success—was to create the environment for another five months of tumult in Picardy that would generate a million more casualties. There was no question that the Somme show had to go on, and a key immediate requirement was to enhance diversionary action in sectors geographically divorced from the Somme.

The next attack upon 6 BRD was already in the Diggers' tactical pipeline. It took place on the night of 1/2 July 1916 against Necklace and Nephew Trenches, in RIR 21 sector II, sub-sectors c and d bracketing the Rue Delvas—the *Tommy-Strasse*. British XI Corps intelligence summary (these daily reports were known throughout the British Army as 'comic cuts') for this day observed that recent examination of enemy prisoners exposed great 'variations in morale, individuals in the same regiment expressing quite different sentiments on the subject'. The most striking section, however, was the last line where Anzac Corps intelligence staff noted that 'in several cases lately prisoners have expressed the opinion that the majority of their company would be only too glad to be captured if they got the opportunity': a most heartening passage.

The assault party of 153 men of the 9th (Queensland) Battalion, 3rd Brigade, commanded by Captain M. Wilder-Neligan, was split into three groups, each led by an officer. All were volunteers, and all had undergone a 'heavy course of training'. Theirs was to be a 'silent' attack. Although no shelling of the target area would take place, a diversionary bombardment would be dropped on the north-eastern face of the adjacent Sugar Loaf Salient directly opposite a newly dug sap protruding diagonally into

No Man's Land from the Australian front line adjacent to the *Tommy-Brücke*. The sap itself was part of the ruse, for it had been specifically dug to encourage the enemy to expect activity in the area. On receiving the code-word 'gallop', two Vickers machine guns were to keep hostile heads down by peppering the enemy parapet, with a further four (located 2 kilometres to the rear) firing indirect protective barrage patterns onto selected positions behind each flank.

With blackened faces, carrying scrambling mats to assist in scaling the glacis, and ladders to enter and exit the enemy trench, the party formed up in No Man's Land. To inhibit coughing, everyone had been issued with chewing gum. As soon as the artillery opened distracting fire upon the Sugar Loaf, the two parties cut the wire and forced entry. Having independently pierced the enemy line, they then successfully linked.

The subsequent Bavarian report estimated that the hostile party consisted of 'about 100 men': 'The raid began at 2.00 am with a lightning barrage by light and medium guns and heavy trench mortars. All was quiet again by 2.40 am. The enemy was in our trenches for about 10 minutes and his incursion cost us total casualties of 9 dead, 21 wounded, 25 missing and the loss of one German machine gun. The enemy raiding force left behind two men dead and one wounded.'

The report is remarkable and so illuminating that the attack section is reproduced here in its entirety:

Account of the attack:
The enemy fire-strike came very suddenly and was monstrously heavy. Those men who were not designated as look-outs or trench sentries took cover in the artillery shelters and the new concrete dug-out to the west of the Tommy-Strasse (in this latter, about 15 men of the right flank platoon of IId, which was under heavy fire).

In the sector to the east of the Tommy-Strasse, the men moved sideways, away from the artillery fire, and crowded into the middle platoon sector in IIc, coming to a halt some 30 metres to the east of the Tommy-Strasse. They were joined in this lateral movement by the crew of MG no 8, which had previously been firing over the parapet in enfilade on the ground in front of IId.

The following events then followed one another directly in rapid succession:

A man from listening post 3 in front of IIc (Infantryman Schürfer of 7/RIR 21) rushed into the trench to report that 7 or 8 men were climbing over the breastwork at the boundary between IIc and IId. Whether these were enemy troops or displaced members of the patrol from the left of the Tommy-Strasse (whose presence he was aware of), he could not tell. When he jumped down into the trench, Schürfer landed beside Reservist Schwab of 7/RIR 21, and it was to him that he shouted his message. Schwab looked out over the breastwork and saw about 6 of the enemy entering the trench at the Tommy-Strasse. Schwab then ran to the right, past a trench sentry who had just been killed by artillery fire, to the men who had moved away to the right, and shouted to them that the enemy was breaking in at the Tommy-Strasse and that they must quickly go back to the left, otherwise the enemy would spread out further to the right. This movement was then promptly carried out, under the command of Unteroffizier Wittmann of 7/RIR 21.

The time elapsed between the move to the right and the return to the left was only about 5 minutes, but this was long enough for the enemy troops to kill the second man in listening post 3 in front of IIc and make off with the abandoned machine gun.

Having broken in at the two points already described, the enemy went west along the trench from break-in point 1 and east from break-in point 2, killing the trench garrison with hand grenades and taking prisoner the 15 or so men sheltering in the concrete dug-out. Of the defensive patrol out in front of the wire, only one man returned, and it seems that the rest were likewise taken prisoner.

The machine gun in IIc appears to have been taken not by the main raiding force but by a few men who went off to the east of the Tommy-Strasse, perhaps as a blocking party.

By the time the garrison from IIc that had moved away to the right returned and spread themselves out beside the Tommy-Strasse, the enemy had already withdrawn from our trench. The men say that the enemy was in the trench for not more than 10 minutes.

To the west of break-in point 2, which was at the junction between
the 1st and 2nd platoons in IId, Leutnant Reuter and Vizefeldwebel
Thiel, both of 8/RIR 21, rushed to the right flank of their company
sector as soon as they heard that the enemy had broken in. Leutnant
Reuter immediately had machine gun no 9 set up in a firing position
on top of the breastwork to provide flanking fire to the half-right, while
Vizefeldwebel Thiel took a squad of about 10 men further to the right
along the trench, where he was initially held up by gas shells and then
took up position on the upper edge of the trench and began firing to
the half-right towards the Tommy-Strasse, where the enemy could be
seen moving to and fro in the light of the flare fired by Leutnant Reuter.
Thiel believes that he inflicted casualties on the enemy.

In the area between the Tommy-Strasse and point 667 there was
evidently ferocious fighting at close quarters. Vizefeldwebel Wagner and
Vizefeldwebel Hegelein (both officer-candidates) of 8/RIR 21 were both
found, severely wounded by hand grenades, with their emptied pistols
still in their hands. (See also page 1, 'Casualties'.)

Observations:

1. At 2.30 am the enemy fired a number of single red flares high into the
   air from the direction of the Tommy-Brücke, which then burst, releasing 7 greenish stars. This was evidently the signal to withdraw. At the
   same time, the enemy's artillery fire greatly increased in intensity.
2. From his viewpoint in IIb, the company commander believes that by
   the light of the numerous flares fired all along the line, after 1.00am,
   he saw 6–7 waves of gas within a period of one and a half hours, in
   the area held by the Saxons, or even further to the north.
3. In my opinion, the object of the raid was to take prisoners. Perhaps
   the concrete dug-out had been identified on aerial photographs.

The destruction of the drainage tunnel on the Fürther-Strasse, which
has often been cited in the past as the reason for the heavy bombardment of that sector, was evidently not the objective, as no attempt was
made to attack it with hand grenades, demolition charges or other
similar means.

That the principal purpose of the raid—apart from unsettling the front—was to take prisoners seems to be borne out by the fact that when the prisoners were taken away, their weapons, equipment, etc, were left behind.
Signed: Weiss

The entire escapade took place within 50 metres either side of the Rue Delvas. 'Break-in point 1' lies within the boundaries of today's Australian Memorial Park—where similar ventures had taken place in 1914 and 1915.

The report has worth on multiple levels, illustrating clear-eyed and frank Bavarian scrutiny and the habitually keen self-criticism. However, nothing is ever quite what it seems. The event is a textbook illustration of the value of primary source research, for the customary enquiries by RIR 21's commander, *Oberst* von Braun, revealed certain aspects that dramatically change not only the complexion of the raid, but our perceptions of it, for the Bavarian records disclose that the reasons behind the Diggers' success were not, as their own narrative understandably evokes, entirely down to skillful Australian planning and execution

Von Braun found that—without being commanded—his troops at the *Tommy-Strasse* had moved sideways to avoid the shelling; in order to engage the enemy, they had to be *led back* to the position by *Unteroffizier* (NCO) Wittmann. The machine gun was abandoned by its crew—a crime that became the subject of a military enquiry, as did the conduct of the NCO (non-commissioned officer) who surrendered with his men in a concrete dugout after the two officer-candidates present had been severely wounded. The action of the searchlight crew was also subjected to official scrutiny. Although the remainder of the garrison appeared to have conducted themselves well, said von Braun, it was noted that Bavarian artillery was very slow to react. A defensive patrol that was out in front of the attacked sub-sector reported simultaneously with the alarm bells that about fifteen raiders were approaching IId. One of the two men in another post in No Man's Land also saw and reported the enemy incursion. He escaped, but his comrade was later found stabbed to death in the listening post, with his hands tied. The success of the raid was therefore based upon a mix of Australian competence and serious Bavarian transgression.

The brigade commander, *Generalmajor* Danner added a handwritten adjunct to von Braun's report:

> *Part of the trench garrison of IId on the left flank undoubtedly failed completely under the impact of the intense artillery and trench mortar fire. However, I see from the report of the Battalion commander that the majority rapidly regained their composure, but unfortunately too late to engage the enemy effectively.*
>
> *I have no doubt, given the often proven good conduct and courage of the men of RIR 21, that such an incident will not occur again. The Regiment has taken the necessary action, and the commanding officer assures me that the men themselves are eager to make amends.*

The Australians sustained six dead, twenty-three wounded and three missing. They 'definitely ascertained' fifty-three enemy killed and a very large number of wounded. The revised Bavarian casualty figures for the raid were in fact nine dead, twenty wounded, twenty-four missing: a coincidental total of fifty-three. According to Captain Wilder-Neligan's report, three of the dead were enemy prisoners. When being taken back across No Man's Land, he wrote, they 'began to get troublesome' and had to be 'quickly despatched'; a fourth—an officer—died in the Australian trenches, ironically as a result of German retaliatory fire. These four men would be among those noted by the Bavarians as 'missing'. Twenty-one prisoners were taken, plus the abandoned machine gun. It was a most acceptable outcome for the Diggers.

The raid was said to have fully satisfied the requirements of Brigade, Division, Corps and Army, and plaudits were liberally distributed. The Australians had effected the all-important element of surprise, its colossal value being manifest in the Bavarian narrative. From the point of view of future enterprises, the most vital point in the brigade commander MacLagan's subsequent report was probably his first: 'Owing to all the officers and several of the Sergeants having been killed or wounded and the strenuous opposition met with by all the parties when in the trenches, no information of the hostile works is available, except that the breastworks are higher than most of ours, the parados appear to be better, and some of the dugouts under the front breastwork have their entrances under the fire step and are difficult to get at in a hurry.'

So brief and frenzied had the raid been, that an adequate inspection of enemy fieldworks had not actually been possible—an important point, for they were the same positions the 14th Australian Brigade were to assault some eighteen days hence.

Two dead Diggers and one man with serious leg wounds had to be left behind. The injured soldier was Private Louis Braganza, a 29-year-old former farm labourer from New South Wales. He was questioned while receiving treatment in a field hospital. His interrogator notes: 'The prisoner was visibly in great pain and was very weak, and it was therefore necessary to discontinue the interrogation several times and to confine it to the most important points.'

Braganza provided a description of the composition of the 1st Australian Infantry Division and its leadership. He was from the 9th Infantry Battalion (Queensland); he described the battalions' responsibilities and the purpose of the raid in this way:

> A Battalion normally stays in the front line for 18 days, usually followed by a similar period of rest at Sailly sur la Lys. The trench garrison lives in dug-outs directly behind the front line.
>
> While one battalion manned the forward positions, another was in readiness in reserve positions behind it. When the 9th Battalion was in the line, three platoons of each Company occupied the front line trenches, whilst the fourth carried out working party duties behind the lines. On 2.7.16 the 9th Battalion had been in the front line for 8–10 days.
>
> Each company held approx 400m of front, and the Battalion frontage was 1 mile = 1600m. The fighting strength of the company was approx 200 men.
>
> 3. The purpose of the raid was to bring in prisoners and identify the positions of our machine-guns, which they perceive as a constant threat. Preparations for the raid were made over several nights. Exits from their own trenches were created, and 100 men were drilled specifically for this operation. The prisoner was not originally selected to participate in the operation, but had to take the place of

*a man who went sick. Shortly before the raid 5–6 of the 100 men
reported sick, as they 'didn't want to go'.*

Having then itemised his battalion's arsenal for Fritz Lübcke, Braganza
concluded:

6. *The prisoner has not seen any <u>cavalry</u>. He has heard, however, that
   there is British cavalry behind the 1st Australian Infantry Div. front.*
7. *The prisoner has no knowledge of the installation of any <u>gas cylin-
   ders</u> or other preparations for a gas attack. The smoke seen rising
   from the Australian trenches comes from cooking fires.*

> *Everyone expects the British to launch a <u>major offensive</u>, but no-one
> knows any details. The Australians do not care how the war ends; they
> just want it to end soon; they do not want to attack.*
>
> *The recruiters in Australia told them that men were needed to defend
> the Dardanelles. They did not know that they would be sent to France.
> If people in Australia knew what it was like here, there would not be so
> many men willing to volunteer. The men of the 9th Battalion are all
> very war-weary.*

Louis Braganza died on 4 July, unaware of the colossal Anglo–French
offensive launched on the day of his capture, and of the result of his
own venture. The 'purpose of the raid', as he had described it, was not
achieved: Bavarian machine-gun positions were not identified. But it was
through this interrogation and information gleaned elsewhere that the
Bavarians confirmed that the British 31st Division had been relocated
and the 61st Division and the 1st Australians were now adjoined—opposite
the Sugar Loaf.

On the night of 2/3 July the Diggers raided yet again, with a party of
11th Battalion troops under Captain F.G. Medcalf. The 3rd Brigade war
diary shows that the operation was considered 'a complete success' by
Brigadier-General MacLagan, revealing 'excellent' and 'thorough' organisation. The cooperation of the artillery and trench mortars was 'more than
excellent', with 'the shooting so good that considerable damage was done

to hostile personnel and works, and its accuracy was such that our party were able to lie within 60 yards of hostile parapet while bombardment was in progress, with complete confidence': a point to be noted. Again, a prominent aspect of this raid was its careful preparation. Planning began two weeks beforehand, the target was selected and patrols reconnoitred the ground every night.

In the 'lessons learned' section there are several points that, in the light of the action that was to take place in a little over a fortnight, sound a rather hollow ring. Point number one notes that 'by the good use of Artillery, Trench Mortars and Machine-Guns a comparatively long frontage of the enemy's forward line can be completely subdued, rendering it possible to cross No Man's Land in safety'. One might glean from this statement and the results of the previous raid why on 19 July both staff and troops may have invested so much confidence in the bombardment and the words of their brigadiers. Point seven noted that 'by studying aerial photographs, particularly when they are enlarged, you can familiarise yourself beforehand of the trenches to be raided'. It had certainly worked for Wilder-Neligan's men. Commanders thus became confident that they could accurately 'read' the physical nature of their objectives from aerials. Lieutenant-Colonel Roberts concluded with the declaration that the raid 'has certainly had the effect of considerably increasing the morale of the Battalion and particularly that of the party engaged'. Several machine-gun posts were also located in the raid, but only one gun observed. The raid ticked pretty well all the necessary boxes.

Captain Medcalf's comprehensive account records that unlike the venture of 1/2 July, his party had plenty of time to inspect enemy positions. Although the artillery had reduced the opposing front line to a 'shambles', destroying much of the parapet and 'wrecking many dugouts', there was plenty to explore and take note of. Among many small shelters, 'What appeared to be an officer's dugout was visible. There were three bunks built in ship fashion to the wall, two tables in the dugout, and a candle burning. The dugout was estimated at 30′ by 6′ by 6′ and was in the parados of the communication trench . . . two searchers spent three minutes in this dugout but could find no official papers.' The raiders' failure to find documents on almost every occasion they entered the enemy line was cited as an example

of Bavarian good practice, and as a result Australian troops were fiercely
exhorted to do as their foe and not leave any papers, private or otherwise,
in front-line shelters and dugouts.

Ostensibly, the raid had been a mirror image of its predecessor, but
there was one important difference. So effective was the bombardment that
it left no living Bavarians. This was a heartening result from the point of
view of the gunners' growing prowess, and thus future prospects, but at
the same time disappointing for infantry and intelligence personnel—for
there were no prisoners. 'Although we traversed 150 yards of the trench',
reported Medcalf, 'only one live German was seen, and he was bayoneted
by the first bayonet man who entered the trench.' In addition, no opposition meant no test, and no test meant insufficient practical benefit for
the troops. 'Valuable' papers and photographs were however taken from
Bavarian dead. Brigadier-General MacLagan concurred, saying it was
'regrettable that no active opposition was met with by the raiding party to
more thoroughly test their organisation, which appears to have been excellent'. Although Captain Medcalf's party were only able to slay one German
soldier, they estimated fifty enemy dead. Total Bavarian divisional losses
were in fact thirty-eight dead and sixty-six wounded; of those, neighbouring RIR 21 noted thirteen and sixteen respectively, primarily from accurate,
heavy and sustained artillery and mortar bombardment. Most casualties
had been buried. Fortunately for 6 BRD it was the last offensive action that
the 1st, 2nd or 4th Australian Divisions were to undertake in the Fromelles
sector: by 9 July they had all departed Flanders for Picardy.

Von Scanzoni was shocked at how the enemy had managed to reach his
line undetected. The next day his divisional orders informed every unit that
British attacks in Picardy were still in full swing, and that further night
raids were therefore to be expected. Such attacks, he said, must find every
trench garrison ready and waiting on the firing line to staunchly defend
their positions. Avoidance of heavy enemy gunfire by moving out of sectors
under fire into neighbouring sectors must never occur at night and, given
the present circumstances, could not be contemplated during daylight
either. As a result of the two raids, Bavarian tactics were altered, for the
lessons learned from every perceived weakness could be equally applied to
any greater hostile enterprise.

It had been reported from various parts of von Scanzoni's sector that the enemy was 'bringing unusually large amounts of ironwork into his positions. In view of other reports that he is also raising the height of his breastworks, it is not beyond the bounds of possibility that the enemy may be installing gas cylinders.'

Bavarian suspicions were absolutely correct: the Special Brigade were indeed planning an attack on the 6 BRD front. Von Scanzoni ordered grass in front of listening posts to be cut over a wider area and other appropriate measures taken to permit earliest observation of hostile movements. It was, he noted, 'essential that secure recognition signals are in place for use during night fighting in the forward trenches'. The reasoning behind this was simple: 'The enemy troops wearing steel helmets who broke in to sector IId could evidently not be distinguished in the dark from men of RIR 21 wearing helmets without spikes' (the German *Pickelhaube* was a leather helmet with or without a spike on the crest).

Dugouts were to be provided with loopholes and caches of hand grenades to enable the occupants to keep the enemy away from entrances, and materials were to be kept close to hand to allow all fighting trenches to be swiftly separated into defensible segments by the construction and installation of movable barricades, provision of wire 'hedgehogs' and stocks of ready-filled sandbags.

The action continued. Private Alfred Jones fell into German hands. It happened during a British raid mounted opposite the village of Fauquissart. Jones, a 26-year-old former tin worker serving in the 2/4th Gloucestershire Regiment (Gloucesters), gave this description of the raid to Fritz Lübcke, whose comments are in brackets here:

On the evening of 4 July, after the 2/4th Gloucesters had relieved the 2/6th Gloucesters, C Coy received orders to mount a raid on the German trenches opposite with 50–60 men, led by several officers, (although the prisoner <u>himself saw only one</u>), and 'bring back what ever you can lay your hands on'. (So the purpose of the raid was to gather information). For identification in the dark, the men wore a white armband on their left arm. The raid was preceded by an hour-long artillery bombardment, after which the infantry attack went in.

The artillery fire had damaged the German wire defences, but not badly enough for it to be easy to get over them. Corridors had been cut through their own wire in advance. As soon as the prisoner reached the German front line trench he received a blow on the head and therefore knows nothing about the subsequent course of the attack.

Although Jones divulged little to Lübcke, the officer was nevertheless able to correctly identify his brigade and division, and thus their movements.

    1. *Divisional and Brigade Staff HQ locations not known. Battalion HQ in a village near Laventie.*

    2. *No <u>gas</u> installations. No gas attack planned.*

    3. *Prisoner does not know of any impending conventional large-scale attack.*

    4. *Has not seen any cavalry, Australians, Indians, or Maoris . . .*

    11. *<u>Morale</u>: he and his comrades are war-weary and would like to go home sooner rather than later.*

    12. *<u>Rations</u> were passable and just about sufficient.*

The 2/4th Gloucesters had only entered the line on 3 July, beginning their first tour in the Fauquissart trenches. The previous few days had been taken up with training, a rather inauspicious period that resulted in two men accidentally killed and three wounded.

The action that began at 1.10 a.m. on 5 July is particularly useful when studied from both sides, and issues a powerful caveat against accepting the narrative of only one belligerent. Although composed of four officers and 138 men plus six engineers, the raid on Noose Trench on the east flank of the Wick Salient was a disaster, with only three British soldiers (dressed in boiler suits and with blackened faces) actually entering the German trenches. The Gloucesters' report notes, 'several dugouts were cleared and it is thought that heavy casualties were inflicted on the enemy'. An estimated '15 to 20 Germans were killed'. Bavarian records of III Battalion of RIR 16 note two privates and two officers wounded (*Leutnant* Wildegger suffered eye injuries, and *Leutnant* Peters severe leg wounds). There was only one fatality, *Vizefeldwebel* (senior NCO) Josef Bauer. All five casualties were caused by a single British hand grenade. No dugouts were 'cleared' because rapid barricading restricted the raiders to a single fire bay. Von Scanzoni's note on grass length had not yet been acted upon. At this time neighbouring 2/6th Warwicks noted the enemy wire was almost impossible to distinguish among the long summer grass—a great advantage to raiders because their approach, although a little noisy, might be invisible. On the approach, the ditch network offered splendid cover.

As was so often the case, the game was given away by preparatory artillery fire. From 1.00 a.m. onwards, British guns poured heavy shrapnel onto the sector, causing defensive patrols to withdraw to the cover of listening posts. Meanwhile, in anticipation of imminent action the entire Bavarian garrison stood-to in the fire trench, with NCOs and half the men standing on the firestep observing over the parapet and the other half in shelters below. In addition to the officers and senior NCOs detailed for trench duties, commanders and reserve commanders were all with their platoons. *Leutnant* Wildegger had left his command dugout to be in the fire trench and had established contact with the command post by telephone in a forward artillery dugout; *Leutnant* Peters was in the same shelter. Soon after 1.45 a.m. the left-hand platoon was alerted by the look-out (a soldier named Wiedmann) that there were *Engländer* outside the wire, and at almost the same moment a man came in from a listening post reporting the same. The entire garrison immediately mounted the firestep and opened fire. The captain of machine gun No. 7 brought his weapon into action without waiting for orders and *Vizefeldwebel* Sauerer, who was with the centre platoon, fired three red star-flares calling for defensive barrage fire, which commenced almost immediately. The report takes up the story:

As soon as the alarm was raised the duty corporal, Gefreiter (Alois) Meier, ran from his position to the nearby dugout shelter of Leutnant Wildegger and reported to him that Engländer had been sighted in no-man's land. He asked for more light-pistol cartridges, of which Leutnant Wildegger had a large supply. The duty officer of the left-hand company, Vizefeldwebel Bauer, had also rushed to Leutnant Wildegger's position and was standing outside the shelter. As Gefreiter Meier set off back to his platoon with the cartridges, three Engländer suddenly leapt over the breastwork above the shelter. At that moment Leutnant Wildegger had the telephone in his hand, evidently reporting the situation to the Command Post, when one of the Engländer threw a hand grenade into the shelter, wounding him, Leutnant Peters and two orderlies, and killing Vizefeldwebel Bauer.

Feldwebel-Leutnant Schnellrieder then rushed up and, as the first Engländer thrust at him with his bayonet, shot the man dead with his revolver. The second Engländer attempted to get away but was felled by a blow from the rifle-butt of Feldwebel-Leutnant Schnell-rieder's orderly, Infantryman Goldbrunner. The impact shattered the butt of Goldbrunner's rifle and this man was only wounded. The third Engländer was killed by several hand grenades thrown at the same time by various members of the trench garrison. Feldwebel-Leutnant Schnellrieder then barricaded the trench to the right, while Vizefeld-webel Sauerer did the same to the left. Support came a few minutes later when bombing parties from sub-sectors b and d arrived.

As soon as the alarm was raised, the trench garrison had driven the enemy raiders back from the wire with small arms fire and, in conjunction with the machine gun, was now firing on the three groups of Engländer retiring across no-man's land, each of which was estimated by common consent to be 30–50 men strong. The Engländer were also caught in perfectly placed artillery barrage fire and in flanking fire from sub-sector b, on the right, which had been ordered to open fire with MGs and rifles by the Company Commander, Leutnant Plenge. The retreat-ing enemy carried a large number of wounded or dead back with them.

A strong reconnaissance patrol sent out immediately in the wake of the enemy's retreat brought in one dead Engländer, seven rifles with fixed bayonets and several bags of hand grenades from the strip of ground directly in front of our wire. There are three dead Engländer still lying just outside our wire and the tall grass in no-man's land probably conceals several more enemy casualties.

An inspection of the entanglement in front of the left-hand platoon in sub-sector c found no evidence of attempts to cut the wire. It had however been very badly damaged by shellfire, which allowed the three

Engländer to slip through the entanglement under cover of the very dense powder smoke. After the raid, the sector was completely quiet.

The subsequent British report observed that 'severe casualties occurred on the way back'. It is interesting to note the strength of the British party being estimated so accurately by the Bavarians. Remarkably, through their records it is possible to say that Alfred Jones, whose part in the enterprise ceased when he 'received a blow on the head' as soon as he reached the enemy line, was probably felled by *Infanterist* (infantryman) Goldbrunner. Jones' two comrades were clearly both killed. The leader of the raid, Captain Frederick Hanham, died of wounds soon after returning to his own trenches. He was recommended for a Victoria Cross by battalion commander Lieutenant-Colonel J.A. Tupman, who said it was 'undoubtedly due to his splendid dash and courage and noble example that our party reached the enemy parapet'. The award did not materialise.

The exploit had allowed recently introduced Bavarian contingencies to be tested, as their report indicates:

1. *The distribution of a large number of light-flare pistols was thoroughly vindicated during this action. They allowed no-man's land to be illuminated without delay.*
2. *The newly issued red star-flares were clearly recognised by the Command Post as our signal for barrage fire.*
3. *The searchlight crew reported that it was not possible to illuminate no-man's land with the searchlight because their position was so heavily engaged by hostile flanking fire that the searchlight could not be brought into operation.*
4. *The alarm was recognised without delay, not least because several of the look-outs threw hand grenades into the wire. The fact that all officers and NCOs were in the fire-trench at the time proved most advantageous, as good discipline was maintained throughout the action.*
5. *Telephone communications with all four sectors were maintained throughout the bombardment, thus proving the worth of burying the cables. Line c was out of action for 2 hours from 3.15am.*

6. *Our artillery performed splendidly. When called for, it opened fire very quickly.*
7. *The following especially distinguished themselves: Feldwebel-Leutnant Schnellrieder, Vizefeldwebel (Hans) Sauerer, Infantrymen Ascher and Goldbrunner, and the gun-captain and crew of MG No. 7.*

Through Alfred Jones' interrogation the Bavarians also learned of a potential numerical imbalance in combat strength between Australian and British infantry companies: numerous Digger prisoners had already confirmed a figure of 200; Jones spoke of 120.

At 11.20 p.m. on the same foggy night a company of 2/7th Worcestershire Regiment (Worcesters) raided RIR 17. They did 'considerable damage with bombs to Germans in trenches and dugouts', notes the war diary. British casualties were two dead and thirty-five wounded. Although only four men entered the enemy trench they managed to kill five Bavarians and seriously wound eleven others. Messages of praise and encouragement arrived from 61st Division commander Major-General Sir Colin Mackenzie, who said, 'though we have had casualties they are out of all proportion to the effect which this attack must have had on the enemy's morale, apart from the losses he has actually suffered'.

The raid did not affect enemy morale. The Bavarians' two-page report with sketch map confirms they were puzzled by the event, not least because when the alarm sounded, no one reported seeing any enemy troops except those posted near the points where the British had entered and exited—a matter of 6 metres. Knowing they were probably streaming back, neighbouring German rifles and machine guns blazed across No Man's Land, but remained unaware of the results of their efforts. RIR 17 had certainly been caught napping, but it merely appeared to be a somewhat bizarre local failure. Their own report noted: 'Of the four British rifles found, two were lying on top of the breastwork and two were propped up against it, exactly as their owners had left them as they hurriedly climbed out of our trench. The *Engländer* were fortunate in that the breastwork at the break-in point was not as high as elsewhere.'

At the combined cost of seven dead and forty-six wounded, neither side had learned anything of real value. In contrast to the Diggers on the nights of the 2nd and 3rd, the raid was a model illustration of why such enterprises were so detested by the troops.

Despite the recent attacks, the Bavarians remained comfortable in the capabilities of their defensive garrisons and armaments. It was simply impossible to erase the risk of enemy incursion at night; but with careful and constant planning and training, damage could be minimised. Adjustments were made. The primary concern remained hostile artillery, which appeared to be growing more competent by the day.

A few days later in a congratulatory signal XI Corps commander General Sir Richard Haking said that the raids were 'far more successful than was at first believed'. The general's intelligence sources are not revealed, and we therefore cannot be sure whether this was bluster for the sake of troop morale, or a sincere conviction. Whatever the motives, only those raiders who had actually taken part were aware of the full truth of the matter.

Two weeks later the 2/4th Gloucesters would attempt to force entry into exactly the same piece of trench garrisoned by exactly the same troops armed with exactly the same weapons. So too would the Tommies and Diggers of more than a dozen other battalions. But this time in broad daylight.

Chapter 9

THE SOWING OF
THE SEEDS

The enemy offensive straddling the Somme stalled on 3.7.16 after some localised successes and efforts to re-launch it in some places on 4.7.16 were unsuccessful. On our Army front, raids by small infantry formations and bombardments by artillery and trench mortars have continued.

Further hostile night raids are to be expected. A major enemy attack is unlikely.

Divisional Order B. Nr. Ia 3634, 6th Bavarian Reserve Infantry Division
Divisional HQ, 5.7.1916, 4.00 p.m.

Since September 1915 the 6th Bavarian Reserve Infantry Division had been daily enhancing, adjusting and correcting their defences, preparing for the very day that was approaching. Every hostile shell was now plotted: its origin, estimated calibre, perceived target, and the result. Outcomes were compiled in tables, charts and graphs, and carefully studied for patterns. June 1916 in French Flanders saw no indication of a build-up of artillery, and information from other sources failed to reveal that unusual quantities of ordnance had been delivered anywhere except Picardy. Patrols continually reported conditions as 'normal'. Likewise, there were no reports of troop concentrations behind the British lines in Flanders, just the regular comings and goings. No supplementary trains had been recorded, and traffic on the roads remained typical. Allied prisoners mentioned various calibres of weaponry, but as they were commonly infantry, airmen or engineers, and not gunners, their statements were largely inadequate. Those same prisoners had now provided the Bavarians with a tidy model of how the *Engländer* organised their positions, number of men per metre of trench, types and dispositions of weaponry and the location of supports. Some had offered a great deal more. Conclusions about the quality of the opposition had also been reached, and there was no cause for undue alarm. However, with the Somme campaign in progress, and in anticipation of continuing harassment, it was considered wise to introduce reliefs every four days (instead of seven) until further notice.

For von Scanzoni and his men it was a case of business as usual until something unusual happened. What was undeniable, however, was that day by day Allied gunnery was improving: although molestations were slight, since the beginning of June fewer and fewer shells were falling upon stony ground, and every day some kind of repair was necessary. The Bavarian rule was to live in permanent expectation of hostile action. Von Braun ordered enhanced patrol reconnaissance. Notable observations such as the concentration of artillery and trench-mortar fire on particular sectors, bombardment by large-calibre guns, or the shelling of places that did not normally receive artillery fire, were to be reported immediately by telephone. Battalions manning the front line were to continually check telephone links, optical signalling apparatus, signal flares, stocks of ammunition and hand grenades. 'There *must not* be any failures or deficiencies when these are needed', he directed.

When required, the entire accessible garrison was to be available, and every NCO or private seconded outside their own company was to notify the battalion where they were deployed and whether their presence there was essential. Every man was clearly and specifically told where he was to report, and officers overseeing construction works instructed to immediately rejoin their companies if and when the siren sounded. Regimental Order No. 3666 of 16.5.16, 'Instructions in the event of an alarm', was to be read and re-read until commanders were satisfied that their companies were thoroughly familiar. Frequently amended, the document always concluded with the irrevocable exhortation: 'The front line is to be held at all costs!'

During the first days of July, the French attacked astride the Somme River and made substantial gains. On their immediate left flank the British produced spectacular results in the southern sectors, but their triumphs were entirely un-mirrored in the central and northern battleground where not a single metre of ground was gained. The commander-in-chief was evidently only mildly discouraged, however. His private tactical barometer remained high. Given the weight of British high explosive, the enemy, who was numerically considerably weaker, must surely be suffering at least as greatly as his own troops. Haig and Joffre were both of the opinion that with the Germans being now engaged in the two vast enterprises at Verdun and on the Somme, plus a host of raids both planned and in progress, they would be hard pressed to conjure sufficient reserves to baulk sustained Anglo–French firepower. If the enemy were as weak as his intelligence advice suggested, there still remained a splendid chance of bursting through, widening the breach, 'rolling up' the enemy lines and pushing the cavalry into the vast expanse of thinly defended open ground beyond. The Allies *must* press on.

As the 5th Australian Division marched through Flanders towards Fromelles, the following order was received by II Anzac Corps:

> It is imperative that raids and all possible offensives should be undertaken at once by both divisions of the corps in order to make a certainty of holding on our front such German troops as may now be there. Raids must therefore take place immediately and must be on a larger scale than has hitherto been attempted—about 200 men or a company.

GOC (general officer commanding) II Anzac, Lieutenant-General Sir Alexander Godley, acted at once, charging his commanders to 'fight now, at once, in order to give help to our comrades fighting desperately in the south, and that however little we may be ready, or however difficult it may be, we should never forgive ourselves if we did not make the necessary effort, and, if necessary, sacrifice, to help them'.

During the first week of July the 50th Prussian Reserve Infantry Division at neighbouring Bois-Grenier began to express doubts that they still faced Australians. No proof could be produced, but there were several indications of change, mainly involving things that were *not* happening, such as outbursts of song and laughter. On their left flank 2/RIR 20 were also vigilant. The commander reported 'seeing Australian hats on the parapet and on posts in enemy sector IA5'. He suspected a deception, possibly to disguise a relief by a British unit; when the Diggers had taken over the sector, the Tommies had attempted a similar ruse. All units were ordered to maintain the closest observation. The question that still primarily concerned AOK 6 was who supported whom, especially with regard to the Australians and New Zealanders: were they working as an Anzac team? If one of them attacked, would the other act as a reserve to follow up the initial success?

The general feeling was that this was not the case, but final confirmation was provided by three exceptionally loquacious New Zealanders of 1st Canterbury Battalion captured south-east of Armentières during a German raid at 11.00 p.m. on the night of 8/9 July. They confirmed that the two arms of the Anzac Corps were indeed separate entities. Among a mass of operational details, they added that, apart from a general war-weariness, morale was good and the troops optimistic. The war would soon end because Germany would be forced by the effects of the Allied blockade to sue for peace—probably before winter. No leave was being granted at present, they said, because such a large proportion of Australians in England behaved so badly. As a result of this interrogation, by noon the next day *Hauptmann* Fritz Lübcke was able to note in Intelligence Report B No. 6070 that his knowledge of the Australian and New Zealand divisional structure and organisation might now be regarded as 'definitive'. That same day von Scanzoni further warned that exhausted English units from the Somme were likely to be exchanged with fresher British and Australian divisions now known to lie opposite 6 BRD.

Unlike 6 BRD, the Australian units facing them were clearly at full establishment. Before the rash of raids in May and June, when all members of the
Bavarian garrison including NCOs were present on the firing line, front-
line combat strength had been calculated on the basis of one rifle for every
three metres of breastwork. Hostile artillery and raids were nibbling at that
figure. Allowing for listening-post teams, patrols, company runners, and
the fact that NCOs were unable to remain permanently on the firing line
because of other duties, by 2 July it had declined to an unsatisfactory one
rifle per 3.5 metres: a cause for concern. Brigade headquarters were warned
that if casualties were incurred as a result of artillery fire, 'gaps of 20 metres
and more can easily open up that can only be filled by men brought up
from the support lines, which takes a certain amount of time. If the destruction and levelling of stretches of the trench by artillery fire is then also taken
into account, it is clear that at night a bold enemy raiding party that comes
across a section of trench that is very lightly garrisoned, or even completely
unmanned, is very likely to be able to get into our trenches.'

Von Scanzoni and his staff pondered the implications: the division
was likely to be placed under growing pressure. Their comrades struggling at Verdun and defending and counter-attacking on the Somme were,
not unnaturally, receiving the bulk of reinforcements and transfers; until
OHL obtained intelligence that indicated serious Allied intent in Flanders,
so that situation would persist. For the foreseeable future, 6 BRD should
expect no assistance. With two belts of entanglements now in place—one
about 50 metres into No Man's Land, the other close to the breastworks—
it was already proving difficult to find troops to repair wire, which in
many places was damaged. It was decided that front-line strength should
henceforth remain the same during the day as it was at night. The increasing frequency of nocturnal raids, however, meant that garrisons would be
further augmented each evening. Rest periods were reduced, and support
units moved to positions closer to the front.

In his preparations for significant action in Flanders, the thrusting
General Haking was well ahead of the game. On 9 May 1916 at one of the
regular corps conferences, divisional commanders had been informed

that he was considering 'a more powerful and extended offensive to be carried out by XI Corps in conjunction with the Australian Corps on our left, the ultimate object being to gain the Aubers and Fromelles Ridge'. With the consent of First and Second Army commanders Monro and Plumer, Haking had already spoken with General Godley about possibilities and permutations. Keen to see his troops take part in their first major Western Front action, Godley was open to suggestion and discussion. Six weeks later Haking's proposal had been written up and delivered. It was now a question of awaiting developments.

On 5 July General Sir Herbert Plumer received instructions from Brigadier-General Sir Launcelot Kiggell, Chief of the General Staff, for commanders of the British First and Second Armies to 'select a front on which to attempt to make a break'. Plumer wrote to Monro to say that the only logical and functional place for action was where their two armies conjoined; if his colleague agreed, then perhaps they might make a 'joint arrangement'. At that time the boundary between First and Second Army bisected the Sugar Loaf Salient. Cooperation was agreed, and at a First Army Conference on 8 July, Monro confirmed to Haking that he was at liberty to propose XI Corps' plans. Having earlier produced an outline strategy, on the very next day Haking was able to report that he had prepared a scheme to capture the section of ridge between Aubers and Fromelles, and connect the flanks with the existing British lines. One First Army division might be selected to attack alongside another from Second Army, who had also agreed to provide additional artillery.

The Aubers Ridge was not Sir Charles Monro's first choice. As alternatives were debated GHQ received notification that nine enemy battalions siphoned from AOK 6 had been despatched to Picardy. With the arrival of this fresh intelligence, the choice of sector became considerably more simple. On 11 July Monro wrote to Haking and other corps commanders approving an attack at Aubers–Fromelles, still the ideal location from which to implant fear of assault against one of the most important German centres of command and communication, Lille.

The transfer of German troops, however, coincided with Sir Douglas Haig's plans to correct the disasters of the first week of July with a massive resumption of the offensive on the Somme. This scheme caused Haking's plans to be diluted: the attack against the ridge was postponed. The next day Haig wrote to his army chiefs saying that the recent raiding policy had 'undoubtedly been very effective in preventing the transfer of German reserves', a statement that called for further discussion and potential readjustment. Haig's fresh operations were due to begin on 14 July, from which date GHQ staff were certain that German forces in French Flanders would surely be further 'milked'.

After long consultation, the general staff and Sir Charles Monro considered that Haking's ambitious original concept might be replaced with a less costly but potentially equally effective 'artillery demonstration', perhaps with 'a few raids' for good measure. If a combined array of First and Second Army artillery could deliver three consecutive days of bombardment upon a 15 000-yard (14-kilometre) front, the *perceived* threat of a major assault might well be sufficient to cause German sphincters to tighten, and for OHL to retain their troops in French Flanders.

On the eve of the 14 July attack, Sir Douglas Haig's deputy chief of staff, Major-General Sir Richard Butler, met Sir Charles Monro to discuss 'distractions' in Flanders. During the course of deliberations the question was posed as to what might follow the artillery demonstration. Brows furrowed when it was contemplated that three days may not be sufficient for Lieutenant-General Sir Henry Rawlinson's Fourth Army to achieve their objectives on the Somme. There could be no guarantees. To the demonstration, therefore, was now attached an infantry assault, with First Army providing two divisions and Second Army, one. Haking's plan was back on the table and in a yet more muscular form. In a secret memorandum Butler confirmed that: 'The role of the First Army is to fully occupy the enemy on its front and prevent the detachment of hostile forces towards the south. This role has hitherto been fulfilled by constant raids, bombardments, wire-cutting, and gas attacks, along the whole front. Some more incisive operation, however, is required, in order to obtain the best results, and for this purpose the attack on the left of XI Corps assisted by troops from the Second Army, under General Haking, has been projected.'

As Haking returned to his drawing board a confirming order arrived from GHQ. It demanded offensive operations 'as early as possible on the front Fauquissart–Trivelet road to La Cordonnerie farm'. The battlefront had shrunk from 14 to 5.5 kilometres, but Haking now had at his disposal three infantry divisions—the 31st, 61st South Midland (both First Army units), and 5th Australian, loaned from Second Army by Plumer. Most importantly, he had the use of their artillery plus whatever extra hardware First and Second armies could procure. There would still be a three-day preliminary bombardment—which dispensed with any hope of surprise in the accepted sense. But surprise was neither required nor sought, for the longer the enemy was induced to remain on a state of nervous alert, the less likely they would be to sanction troop transfers.

The Bavarians had already experienced and learned from all the tactics presently available to the Allies, and had acted according to their knowledge and instincts. The only significant unknowns were whether the British would employ gas and/or mines, and the exact moment of attack.

There was now some concern expressed over the participation in the operation of Major-General McCay's 5th Australian Division, the last Anzac unit to arrive in France from Egypt. On 8 July Plumer had been made aware of its lack of experience, being advised by the chief of the general staff that it would be beneficial to invest in several more months of active service before employment in operations other than minor instructive trench raids. This was disputed by Lieutenant-General Sir William Birdwood, the influential GOC of I Anzac. He held that the troops were as well trained as any of their predecessors and would perform competently. Four Australian divisions were now in theatre. The 3rd was yet to arrive in France. Although the 1st and 2nd had been present for some months, neither had been blooded in major combat. They, plus the 4th, were presently en route for Picardy. An important outcome of the discussions, however, was that 4th Division gunners were not yet considered qualified for a major enterprise and should remain in Flanders for further instruction and experience. They were therefore available to Monro and Haking.

McCay was keen for his men to be the first Diggers in serious action, and on the evening of 13 July he is said to have rejoiced at confirmation of the order that the 5th Australian Division were to move a few hundred metres south, link with the British, and prepare for action under the temporary command of XI Corps.

On 14 July the 31st Division, recently involved on the Somme, were detached from the equation, and moved out of the projected battle zone to take up positions south-east of Fauquissart on the right flank of the 61st Division, who themselves shuffled northwards to link arms with the Diggers on the army boundary: opposite the Sugar Loaf Salient. This revision had become necessary as a result of Sir Herbert Plumer's late decision to retain some of his promised Second Army artillery. Losing a division and the extra guns was a disappointment, but Haking decided that the attack could still take place on a reduced frontage of 3600 metres with two infantry divisions supported by the artillery of the 61st South Midlanders and 4th and 5th Australians, plus whatever additional non-divisional weapons could be made available.

It is at this point that guns and gunners assume a yet more critical role in the build-up to battle. XI Corps staff working on barrage plans became aware that the 5th Australians had only minimally trained trench-mortar teams—an essential adjunct to the modern battle—and that their gunners were even less experienced than their 4th Division comrades. Both had critical roles to perform: wire-cutting, certain destruction of selected key targets, defensive covering fire, and counter-battery work. Heavy and medium mortars could meanwhile help blow breaches in parapets, while quick-firing light Stokes guns were able to hound the enemy, 'peppering' the parapet and causing hostile heads to stay low while the infantry made their moves. The preparatory bombardment therefore not only formed the essence of infantry expectations, but in the initial moments of attack provided the mechanism for their salvation and thus success: if the first line could not be seized, finding and holding the second was simply impossible. Although there remained insufficient time to fully acquaint gunners and mortar crews with either their weapons or the terrain they were expected to terrorise; an artillery programme was nevertheless drawn up, and as Monro and his First Army staff awaited news from the Somme, initial registration and wire-cutting began.

Saturday 15 July was an exceptionally eventful day at Fromelles. Sir Douglas Haig read and endorsed XI Corps' plan of attack, noting in his own hand at the foot of the document: 'Approved, except that the infantry should not be sent in to attack unless an adequate supply of guns & ammunition for counter battery work is provided—This depends partly on what guns enemy shows.'

That evening the Bavarians were further alerted to potentially imminent Allied aggression. A gas attack was suspected, and wind direction had already been signalled as dangerous. At 8.30 p.m. a green mist was seen to emerge with a hissing sound from several points halfway up the British 61st Division parapet opposite RIR 17 in the Fauquissart sector. The dense clouds 'rapidly fanned out into a greenish-yellow wall of gas about 3 metres high that drifted across the ground towards our positions', their subsequent report noted. Some of the chlorine-phosgene mixture settled treacherously into the trenches, dugouts and shelters, while the majority passed slowly over, heading towards *II Stellung*. It did not reach Aubers or Fromelles but upon meeting slightly higher ground veered north-east along the face of the ridge, drifting parallel with it before completing a 180-degree curve by turning north over the Bavarian front line beyond the Sugar Loaf. It then engulfed the trenches on the *opposite* side of No Man's Land, primarily those in the process of being taken over by the British 60th Brigade, just arrived from Ypres to occupy the Australian left flank during the forthcoming operations. They suffered numerous casualties.

Despite the density of the clouds, the Bavarians coped with the attack without serious problem. Twenty-eight men were affected, seven of whom died, all as a result of 'errors on their own part'. In typical self-critical fashion, the subsequent report stated that 'Every case of gassing that occurred, without exception, is attributable to mistakes that could have been avoided.' One man, for example, had so much stubble that his mask did not seal against the skin; another tried to change filters during the attack; a third kept his spectacles on, the gas creeping in around the arms; two men failed to properly tighten their filters, while others removed their masks too soon. And three miners died because they failed to take their masks underground. It was established that during the attack not a single mask leaked and no filters failed; indeed, wiring parties and observers were able to continue their work unimpeded.

The report notes that rats, mice and cats died in large numbers, that the grass on the enemy side of No Man's Land was seen to have turned 'brown and shrivelled', and that 'rifles and metal equipment developed a thin patina that was initially blackish and later became rust-coloured'. The deposit was easily removed and all weapons remained serviceable. Telephone apparatus was not affected.

The first 'half' of the gas attack was profitable for the Allies, with the chlorine affecting to a greater or lesser degree the entire 6 BRD front. In the area of Pheasant Wood it was so dense that visibility was reduced to just 10–12 metres. Retaliation was obligatory, and having established the situation Bavarian observers called for a hostile response. The trenches where the gas originated were subjected to trench mortaring and shelling with high explosive and shrapnel. But the nature of the retaliation was noted by the Allies to be somewhat peculiar, for it appeared to be primarily focussing upon the Australian sector in front of the 'Horseshoe'—some 2 kilometres away from the point of gas release.

It soon became evident, especially to the Australians, that in fact the Bavarian shelling was unconnected with the gas: it presaged yet another trench raid. Known as Operation Kulmbach the strike had been planned for some time by 14th Bavarian Reserve Infantry Brigade commander *Generalmajor* Danner and RIR 21's *Oberst* Julius Ritter von Braun; by pure luck it had coincided with the British gas attack. It is of especial interest in the wider story of the battle for it was launched against the very heart of the sector from which the Australians were to attack four days later. In an illuminating pre-raid report, on 10 July Danner outlined his reasons for selecting the location:

The 'Kulmbach' raid will be executed against sector IIB. I came to this decision after discussions in person with the commanding officer of RIR 21 [von Braun] during the afternoon of the 9th for the following reasons:

The section of the enemy line selected for the raid is the closest to our own positions. As the operation is to be carried out on the 14th or 15th of this month and it will therefore be a moonlit night (full moon on the 15th), I consider this to be of decisive importance. Hostile machine guns have less opportunity for enfilading fire in this section than in any other part of the enemy position facing sector II. There is no reason to suspect that the enemy is expecting a raid at this point, and, with skilful registration of our artillery, it may therefore be easier to deceive the enemy here than elsewhere. As the operation is to be carried out comparatively soon, I believe the choice of this section of trench in IIB to be especially advantageous as our artillery, Minenwerfer and MGs still retain a measure of experience with this section of the enemy position from 'Bamberg'.

In view of the close proximity of the opposing positions, the section of IIB selected is likely to be more heavily garrisoned than elsewhere, thus increasing our chances of taking a large number of prisoners.

If taking prisoners proved difficult, the raiders' instructions were to inflict as many casualties as possible. On this occasion, *everything* proved more difficult than expected. The lingering gas caused the two assault parties to wear masks for a lengthy period before the raid, which meant that nothing could be done 'at pace' for it was impossible to breathe properly. Unusually, the Bavarians also experienced problems with their own artillery. The left-hand raiding party suffered casualties during its advance as a result of *Minenwerfers* firing short, and at least one heavy mortar exploded in mid-air killing the commander of a party and four men.

Von Braun's report notes that the right-hand party 'was less successful'. It too attacked head-on, but suddenly ran into heavy infantry fire and a shower of hand grenades, losing many of its most experienced men. The Bavarians wavered under this onslaught, fell back several times due to mounting losses, and had to be repeatedly driven on again by *Leutnant* Härder who later noted that 'much time was lost in consequence and the cohesion and discipline of the raiding party broke down as the attack turned into a grenade-throwing contest, in which some of our men doubtless fell victim to some of our own grenades. As a result, very few men actually made it to the enemy trenches. Nevertheless, they brought back one unwounded prisoner.'

———※———

After the triumph of Bamberg, Kulmbach fell short of expectations. But there were nevertheless some important findings and conclusions. It was confirmed that the 1st Australian Division had departed the Fromelles sector—for an unknown destination—and been relieved by the 5th Australian Division, a unit which had arrived in France from Egypt only a fortnight earlier and was thus facing the Germans for the first time. This was good to know, not least because it meant that the 1st Division artillery, who were becoming ever more proficient, had probably left with the rest of the unit. The Australian front line was found to be very heavily manned which, despite the inauspicious circumstances, at least facilitated the procurement of three prisoners—Privates Albert Dunn (34th Battalion), Joseph Skewes (40th), and James Semple (25th). They were the very first 5th Division Diggers to fall into enemy hands. In addition the Bavarians returned with a Lewis gun, five rifles and four revolvers, a self-rescue apparatus (for tunnellers), a blanket, several packs and greatcoats, and a 'large quantity of documents and newspapers'. Plenty of other booty had been piled onto the Australian parapet but could not be carried back.

Much of Danner's pre-raid reasoning was applicable to Haking's assault plan for the impending attack, now in the final phase of preparation. The Bavarians noted that there had been no Australian mortar retaliation and the artillery response was weak, for the weapons and crews of the 1st and 4th Australian Divisions had indeed departed and the new incumbents were in the process of installing their own guns. The key aspect in the equation, however, was enfilade. That part of the Australian-held sector between VC Corner and the Cordonnerie formed a wide, shallow convex salient: in the event of a Bavarian assault it was practically impossible for the defending Diggers to produce effective enfilade. In the event of an Australian attack, however, the reverse was the case: the shape of the salient favoured the Bavarians, and unless neutralised, their machine guns and artillery could make the crossing of No Man's Land—narrow as it was—a supremely hazardous exercise for enemy troops. Elsewhere, where No Man's Land was wider and open, the threat was diminished, for the greater the distance the enemy were required to negotiate, the more time was proffered to all arms of the defence. Opposite the Sugar Loaf it was almost luxuriously wide.

But this was all in the future. Given the imminence of the forthcoming action, at both XI Corps and 5th Division HQ there were deep concerns about what the three captured Diggers might have disclosed to the enemy. In the event, they were too new to the sector and too lowly of rank to be aware of key tactical information. Nevertheless, from their interrogation

Lübcke was able to confirm that organisational arrangements and garrison strengths mirrored those employed by their recently departed predecessors.

RIR 21 suffered nine dead, thirty-two wounded and seven missing: far too many for such an enterprise. As usual, von Braun delivered a detailed action report to his brigadier. Danner's view was that because the Bamberg raid had gone so smoothly on 30 May, those who took part in Kulmbach were expecting similarly excellent results and were surprised at the stiff opposition; he believed that more could have been achieved and more prisoners taken if the raiding party had had more English-speakers to employ phrases such as 'Give yourselves up!', 'Come out or we will bomb you out!', and 'Drop your weapons'. Von Braun's report, however, contains a very important observation:

> The opposing front line was very densely manned, and it is not beyond the bounds of possibility that the enemy was intending to launch a surprise attack against sector II without artillery preparation, following the planned gas attack in sector IV. The concentration of troops can have no other explanation in a sector that was explicitly described to the 5th Australian Division as a 'quiet sector'.

Von Braun's acuity is evident here. His enemy was indeed preparing for an attack—a much more substantial one, presently intended to begin at 4.00 a.m. two days hence. Although it would have been surprising for an inexperienced unit such as the 5th Australians to be put into battle so soon, the combination of events in Picardy and findings from recent raids had put the Bavarians firmly on the *qui vive*.

More importantly still, on this same day von Scanzoni modified his 2 July standing orders on defensive tactics, making changes that were critical to British and Australian prospects. Future defensive measures would take into account the need to ensure that *enhanced* front-line garrisons were ready for action on the firesteps in sufficient numbers and in good time to offer the best prospects of repulsing an assault. The evacuation of certain sections of trench subjected to particularly intense gunfire might still take place, but only on the orders of the officers commanding the front line, who would issue explicit instructions detailing the extent of the evacuation and the precautions to be taken. If a hostile infantry assault was *expected* there would now be *no evacuation*, for should a trench be vacated and the enemy break in as a result, the cost of regaining the position would assuredly be greater than the number of casualties sustained if the garrison had stood its ground. It was decided therefore that trench garrisons, including officers and NCOs, that came under heavy fire at night were to remain in situ. It was a decision that would profoundly affect outcomes on 19 July. Von Scanzoni's directive outlined the essential requirements that had to be met:

Enemy infantry advancing up to and through the wire must be detected in all circumstances. If a look-out falls, another man must immediately take his place. Replacements must therefore be stationed, under cover, in the immediate vicinity of the observation posts, and rigorous and energetic NCOs must ensure that trench positions are correctly manned.

If the enemy is approaching, the remainder of the trench garrison must get into position, ready to defend the firing line, in the shortest possible time. The look-outs, who are already on the fire-step, and those men who are sheltering behind the breastwork in the open trench, will be at their firing positions in seconds. Those who are in the reinforced dugouts will need longer to get into position. If the enemy jumping-off positions are very close to our trenches, or if it is believed that the enemy has advanced to the wire under cover of the bombardment, and also at night, a larger proportion of the company must be retained in the trench than would be the case during the day or where the enemy front line is far away, or the enemy infantry is relatively inactive. The distribution of troops will also depend on the strength of the company, the number of shell-proof dugouts available, and other local factors that cannot easily be enumerated.

To prevent the part of the company that is sheltering in the shell-proof dugouts from being taken by surprise by insurgent enemy troops, an observer must be posted at the entrance to every dugout to alert the occupants.

Communication between observers in their splinter- but not shell-proof positions on the surface and comrades in nearby subterranean cover was effected by speaking tube. To alert those in the more easily accessible cubby holes within the breastwork, a loud bell or gong was sounded. It had been noted on a number of occasions that certain companies had not allowed men to occupy shelters and dugouts but insisted they stood fast in the trenches, with some on the firestep and the rest crouching behind the breastwork. Von Scanzoni did not disagree with this course of action, for these troops were obviously available for instant defensive action. As preparation time for such raids was generally short, and the enemy frequently tried to cut lanes through wire while the preliminary bombardment was still in progress, he decided that, being on the spot, company commanders should have the final say in how best to man and defend their position in good time. His battalion commanders confirmed receipt of the new orders and assured their brigades that the new principles would be drummed in until they became second nature.

In trench warfare, the harvesting of the kind of intimate knowledge that assists raids or larger assaults is a slow process; for the Diggers there was time to glean only the most cursory insights. Personal acquisition of information about enemy defences was a hopeless aspiration, for the Allied bombardment was already underway and enemy listeners (now in posts with the surrounding grass cut) largely prevented Allied patrolling close to the Bavarian wire and breastworks.

The disappointed von Braun may have been more comforted had he been aware of the scale of Australian loss on 15 July, and indeed how his enemy felt about the Kulmbach raid and their new predicament. With forty-two dead, 105 wounded and five missing, the raid had been a baptism of fire for the 58th Australians. Stunned, the battalion had to be moved to a neighbouring sector, their trenches being temporarily occupied by a British unit, the 6th Oxfordshire and Buckinghamshire Light Infantry (Ox. and Bucks). Although the war diaries of both the 15th Australian Brigade and 58th Battalion record only ten enemy soldiers entering their lines, the clear-up was a lengthy and solemn affair. The diary of Private E.C. Penny DCM, one of the stretcher-bearers, vividly captures this demoralising period:

14 July—Our own artillery (4 Div) opened up and killed 4 and wounded 10 (B & C Coys)

15 July—Day quiet until evening when our troops on the right delivered a cloud gas attack which blew back on to our trenches. About two hours later the Germans opened up a terrific bombardment on our lines, with everything he possessed. Our artillery 4 Div. were being relieved by 5 Div. and so did not reply. This bombardment killed a great many and wounded more. We had over 400 casualties. B Coy had 93 left. Germans entered our trenches and took a machine gun. We killed 2 Huns. Was carrying out wounded under MG fire all night until 3pm the next day. Our men were badly shaken. D Coy had 2 killed and 17 wounded.

16 July—Was carrying wounded until 3pm when I had breakfast. Men who tried to shelter in dugouts suffered worse as they were all blown down. The Germans sent over all kinds of shells and minnies which killed a lot by concussion. Lost my rifle and also left some of my equipment behind being useless to me as a stretcher-bearer. The men spent most of day digging out the dead and repairing the parapets.

It was under these gloomy circumstances that the countdown to the 'third' battle at Fromelles began.

Chapter 10

STAND TO, MAKE READY

His Majesty's Government consider that the mission of the British Expeditionary Force in France, to the chief command of which you have recently been appointed, is to support and cooperate with the French and Belgian Armies against our common enemies. The special task laid upon you is to assist the French and Belgian Governments in driving the German Armies from French and Belgian territory, and eventually to restore the neutrality of Belgium . . .

In minor operations you should be careful that your subordinates understand that risk of serious losses should only be taken where such risk is authoritatively considered to be commensurate with the object in view.

Instruction issued in December 1915 by Field Marshal Lord Kitchener, Secretary of State for War, to Sir Douglas Haig upon his elevation to Commander-in-Chief

As a result of the army boundary falling astride the Sugar Loaf, the battle-front was somewhat unevenly divided between the two attacking divisions. The Tommies occupied some 2750 metres of line, and the Diggers, 1800 metres. More importantly perhaps, although both the 5th Australian Division and the British 61st were recently arrived after training, disposable troop numbers differed markedly. Whereas the Diggers were able to deploy a division at full combat strength, as a result of recent transfers to other more needy units the Tommies lacked over 30 per cent of the normal establishment. Indeed, the South Midlanders hardly lived up to their divisional title, for men from at least a score of other regional regiments had recently been attached to the Warwicks, Gloucesters, Berkshires, and Ox. and Bucks. Some had not yet had the opportunity to exchange old regimental numbers and insignia for that of their new unit, a situation that ninety-five years later was to create extra labour for researchers on the Pheasant Wood project. The numerical imbalance meant that the British would be unable to attack in the same 'density' as the Australians, a situation that was not looked upon as especially problematic as long as the artillery was properly registered and performed to Haking's expectations.

Wire-cutting and general bombardment began on 14 July and continued until the early morning of 17 July, when the attack was originally timed to commence.

On 16 July corps and divisional commanders assembled to iron out final details. There was great news from the Somme: the somewhat atypical battle plans devised by Fourth Army GOC Sir Henry Rawlinson and XIII Corps commander Lieutenant-General Sir Walter Congreve for the action of 14 July had been spectacularly successful. Artillery supremo Major-General Noel Birch had accumulated a devastating array of guns. Almost two-thirds of those deployed along 21 kilometres for 1 July attacks had for this semi-nocturnal enterprise been ranged upon a frontage of less than 6 kilometres. When they spoke it was an awesome spectacle: after three days of shelling to 'soften-up' the enemy, plus several confusing diversions, a five-minute hurricane bombardment presaged the 3.25 a.m. night attack. The Battle of Bazentin Ridge was a sensation, at last presenting Sir Douglas Haig with a genuine victory to celebrate, and Fourth Army, still shocked after earlier disasters, with renewed hope.

It was a glorious affair, our artillery was marvellous and when the artillery lifted their fire from the front line to the second line and our boys charged it was too much for Fritz and he bolted. Poor old Square-head—when I saw what our artillery had done I almost felt sorry for him. His wire had been smashed to bits and his trenches blown in. I never saw ground so ploughed up by shellfire and I know no fellow who's been out here since the beginning has ever seen anything like it. At the very moment the intense artillery fire lifted on to their second line we advanced. It was a most astonishing affair because of rifle and machine-guns all spitting fire at us, nothing happened. We crossed their front line and very few of us knew it. We were over their two lines in a very short time. In fact we pushed on about three or four hundred yards past their second line before we realised that we had actually taken their two lines.

Colour Sergeant Charles Wilson, 1st Gloucestershire Regiment,
Letter to his mother, 17 July 1916

The customary German counter-attacks duly arrived and were decisively driven off. Such was the story in every sector: wire cut, defences devastated, and defenders overwhelmed. The French were dumbfounded but delighted, and awaited news of further British thrusts in which they might assist. Critically, the result had been made possible by well-planned, carefully targeted, super-concentrated shellfire delivered by experienced gunners. 'The moment offered a splendid opportunity for a blow on the XI Corps front, where the enemy was known to be weak both in men and in guns', declared Sir Richard Haking to his assembled staff and divisional commanders.

The methods employed on the Somme could of course not be exactly reproduced in Flanders, but with the armoury at Haking's disposal a suitable outcome could certainly be anticipated, not least because it had been decided that the objective was to be limited solely to the capture of the Bavarian front and support trenches, a territorial excision with an average depth of under 200 metres. To help achieve it, said Haking, every round of artillery and trench-mortar ammunition was to be used. It should be possible, he added, with the ammunition available, to reduce the defenders to a state of collapse before the infantry attack took place.

Haking's 'lifts' were seen as one of the keys to success. The standard procedure thus far had been to bludgeon the enemy front line for a prolonged period, with the infantry advancing at the moment the fire lifted onto communication and support positions beyond. Recent actions in Picardy had shown that even with a colossal bombardment, success could by no means be guaranteed by this method, so Haking ordered that, having moved on to shell the enemy support trenches for a few minutes, the bombardment would suddenly *return* to the front line. The hope was that, having seen waving hats and flashing bayonets above the British parapet, German observers would believe the assault was about to begin and summon the garrison from their shelters, at which point the returning barrage—including a hail of shrapnel—would fall among them. Repeated several times, this strategy should visit death and destruction, shatter morale, and confuse the Germans as to when the real attack was going to take place. Ultimately, they would be too weak and traumatised to offer significant resistance, allowing the British and Australians to emerge from advanced positions in No Man's Land to occupy and consolidate the Bavarian trenches without suffering significant and debilitating loss. With 380 artillery pieces earmarked for the enterprise, there was some kind of gun or howitzer for every 10 metres of battlefront. Plus mortars and a fine array of machine guns.

On 16 July Haking attended a meeting with Sir Charles Monro and Sir Herbert Plumer. He found them in the company of Deputy Chief of the General Staff Major-General Sir Richard Butler, who had come in worsening weather to First Army headquarters at Chocques to discuss the commander-in-chief's latest reflections on the proposed attack. In part Butler was there as a result of a recent visit to the 5th Australians by GHQ staff officer, Major H.C.L. Howard. Howard had been shown the battlefront. The chief sticking point for McCay, and especially Brigadier-General Harold 'Pompey' Elliott's 15th Brigade, which was to assault it, was the Sugar Loaf. Although their section of front was limited to some 350 linear metres of the salient's north-eastern flank, the expanse of No Man's Land the troops were required to navigate in order to reach the enemy line was nevertheless seen as excessive, especially by Elliott. Despite having almost halved the distance by preparing advanced jumping-off positions in front of the Orchard and in the sap protruding from the *Tommy-Brücke*, it still left more than 200 metres to negotiate, an expanse that—as Elliott pointed out—recent French studies regarded as too extreme. The situation facing the Buckinghamshire and Berkshire troops on the immediate Australian right was considerably worse, with the opposing breastworks being almost 400 metres distant. According to a post-war article written by Elliott for *The Duckboard* (journal of the Melbourne branch of the Returned Services League), on being presented with the spectacle Howard went considerably further than simply acknowledging Australian concerns: the attack was likely, he was reported as saying, to be a 'bloody holocaust'.

Howard's concerns may well have been transmitted to Sir Douglas Haig, for Butler on his errand to XI Corps HQ arrived with a message that came as something of a surprise. The C-in-C, he declared, 'did not wish the infantry attack to take place unless it was considered that the artillery preparation had been adequate and that Commanders were satisfied that they had sufficient artillery and sufficient ammunition not only to assure the success of the attack but to enable the troops to retain and consolidate the trenches gained, so far as was humanly possible to foresee'.

The influence of recent actions on the Somme (and possibly memories of his own failures in Flanders in May and September 1915 against the same Bavarian foe) appear evident in Haig's words. Given improved British expectations in Picardy, and the fact that there was no intelligence suggesting that large numbers of enemy troops were presently being siphoned from French Flanders, it may not only be unnecessary to attack the following day, but to attack at all. 'It was not', said Butler, 'the C-in-C's intention to direct the attack to take place unless they were satisfied that the resources at their disposal of all kinds, including troops, were adequate for the operation'.

Butler went on. As prevention of withdrawal from the Flanders front was the purpose of the enterprise, why attack before any fresh movements had been reported? Sir Douglas was content to await developments and gauge German reaction to recent Allied achievements in Picardy with a view to attacking at a later date, if and when intelligence produced the strategic motivation.

Butler's memorandum on this meeting reveals that the notion of delay cut no ice with anyone present. Monro and Haking emphasised their complete satisfaction with the present plans, and their complete confidence in success; the artillery were capable and there was enough ammunition both to install a force within German territory and to guarantee it might remain there. To a man, they were against postponement, Haking adding that, 'the troops were worked up to it, were ready and anxious to do it, and they considered that any cancellation or change of plan would have a bad effect on the troops now, and a loss of confidence in the future when operations were ordered'.

This appears to be a remarkable statement, for the troops of both divisions had only recently arrived in their respective sectors and were in the process of not only preparing for action but becoming acquainted with their surroundings. At present they were still primarily engaged in the myriad tasks required by divisional relief. Some Australian battalions had not yet seen their new abode at all; none were yet aware of any detail of the battle plans; others would not set foot in the front line until the day of the stunt.

Regardless of Haig's reservations, both Monro and Haking were not just keen but determined to maintain the proposed schedule. The enterprise could not possibly disadvantage anything that was happening on the Somme, they said, so why should the present orders not hold good? The query was a shrewd one. Its posing by both an army and a corps commander seems to have put Butler on the back foot, as he later noted, 'On the question being put to me in this form I stated that there was nothing in the general situation to prevent the operation taking place.'

More assurances followed: there were enough guns, ammunition and troops, and the men were ready and anxious to go. At this point Butler appears to have crumbled, acceding to the combined influence and sanctioning the attack. It was something that could not have occurred without his having received Sir Douglas Haig's prior authorisation to do so.

Before departing for GHQ, however, Butler was placed under further pressure by Haking, who in his typical thrusting fashion asked whether in the event of little opposition being encountered, he might push on and assault the ridge. This time the answer was categorically negative: Butler almost certainly possessed no licence to go further.

The weather meantime had now completely closed in, with pouring rain combined with a dense Flanders mist. Heading back to GHQ along the muddy roads, it occurred to Butler that the potential meteorological conditions were an important matter that had not been discussed at the meeting, yet they had every bearing upon what had just been agreed. Ordering his driver to turn around, he arrived back at First Army HQ to find Monro and Haking had departed. A guarantee was therefore extracted from two high-ranking staff officers; they promised that Sir Charles Monro would be informed that, 'if the weather or any other cause rendered a postponement desirable', it was within his power to 'postpone or cancel the operation at his discretion'. Butler could have done no more.

It was at 3.00 p.m. on 16 July that XI Corps Order No. 58 was issued. The artillery were to begin their bombardment at 4.00 a.m. the following morning. It would gradually develop into drumfire and then, as zero approached, the sequence of lifts were to commence. Haking insisted on three key points: that the artillery maintain sustained and accurate fire upon the enemy wire and line, that the troops were ready and waiting in No Man's Land when the whistles blew, and that the assaults take place immediately on command and in a coordinated fashion. The infantry attack would take place at 11.00 a.m. The order survived a matter of hours before being rescinded. In anticipation of imminent action, however, Haking also dictated the following note to be read out to the troops:

Secret 16.7.16
When everything is ready, our guns, consisting of some 350 pieces of all descriptions, and our trench mortars, will commence an intense bombardment of the enemy's front system of trenches. After about half-an-hour's bombardment, the guns will suddenly lengthen range, our infantry will show their bayonets over the parapet, and the enemy, thinking that we are about to assault, will come out of his shelters and man his parapets. The guns will then shorten their range and drive the enemy back into his shelters again. This will be repeated several times. Finally, when we have cut all the wire, destroyed all the enemy's machine gun emplacements, knocked down most of his parapet, killed a large proportion of the enemy, and thoroughly

frightened the remainder, our infantry will assault, capture and hold the enemy's support line along the whole front. The objective will be strictly limited to the enemy's support trenches and <u>no more</u>.

This order to be read to all troops taking part in the attack.

Forwarded for information and necessary action.

Signed: H. Wake, Lieut.-Col., G.S., 61st Div. XI Corps

The fact that Haking directed that his note be read to everyone would leave no man in any doubt as to what was being asked of him, or under any illusion as to the purpose of the attack: it was designed to help achieve success not in Flanders but Picardy. Although the word 'sacrifice' was not present, nevertheless it was almost legible. And yet the document also contained encouragement and hope in abundance.

'Finally, when we have cut all the wire, destroyed all the enemy's machine gun emplacements, knocked down most of his parapet, killed a large proportion of the enemy, and thoroughly frightened the remainder, our infantry will assault, capture and hold the enemy's support line', is a sentence suffused with optimism, promises and confidence. It also suggests (and was surely designed to suggest) that those charged with drawing up the plan of attack had the best interests of their troops at heart: on their behalf resistance would be crushed before the assault. It was nothing less than a guarantee. If one accepts that they themselves were indeed true believers, Monro, Haking, Godley and their divisional commanders could hardly have been more honest with their men.

But continuing bad weather soon threatened to throw the entire scheme into disarray. The artillery of both attacking divisions plus attached 4th Australian Division batteries and heavy guns of XI Corps, I Corps, II Anzac and Second Army could not register. Meanwhile, the troops, in trenches eroded and slumping as a result of the incessant rain, were battling to complete what was a severely telescoped period of preparation. Many were already worn out.

The night passed slowly. The original start time of 4 a.m. came and went, as did Haking's revised start times of 8 and then 11 a.m. The mist still hung in the valley. Without observation the guns could not fire, and without artillery there could be no attack. Haking took the only logical route and postponed operations for twenty-four hours when, according to meteorological advice, the weather should have improved.

Monro immediately approved the decision, but took a long and unanticipated step further by telegramming Sir Douglas Haig to say that *he himself no longer wished the attacks to take place*. Haig's reply was both surprising and categorical: now the C-in-C wanted the operations 'to be carried out as soon as possible'. Knowing Monro had no choice but to obey, Haig added the slightly impersonal but mollifying rider that the general should be 'satisfied that the conditions are favourable, and that the resources at his disposal, including ammunition, are adequate both for the preparation and execution of the enterprise'. It was effectively an insurance policy against future personal blame.

By 17 July Haig's surge on the Somme was stalling. Even small hostile counter-attacks were already biting back chunks of territory that had cost thousands of British lives to annexe; Fourth Army found itself baulked by a series of woods within which the enemy seemed able to resist even the most colossal artillery firestorm. Operations were now suffering from the perennial problem of superlative German defence, and experience suggested that a heavy counter-stroke was certain to materialise soon. Haig was convinced, and indeed correct, that in the recent renewed action enemy losses had far exceeded his own, which meant that the milking of German forces elsewhere was probably already underway. A diversionary exploit at Fromelles had simply become necessary.

Had Haig concurred with Monro's request to cancel, it is hard to see how the action of 19 July 1916 could have gone ahead, certainly on the date desired by Haking. Perhaps it never would have taken place in the form that it did.

It was at 7.15 p.m. on the warm and dry evening of 18 July that General Sir Richard Haking issued Operation Order No. 60. Z Day was tomorrow, 19 July. At 11.00 a.m. a seven-hour bombardment would commence; it would be followed at 6.00 p.m. by the assault. He had also penned another note to be read out to the troops:

As you know, we were going to have a fight on Monday, but the weather was so thick that our artillery could not see well enough to produce the

very accurate shooting we require for the success of our plan. So I had
to put it off, and GHQ said do it as soon as you can. I then fixed 'zero'
for Wednesday and I know you will do your best for the sake of our lads
who are fighting hard down south.

In the week preceding battle *Armee-Oberkommando* 6 artillery flights recorded several changes in the dispositions of hostile artillery facing the 6th Bavarian Reserve Infantry Division. Five previously silent batteries were observed to be active, and new gun positions identified. Aerial operations of both sides were hampered by unfavourable weather, especially mist and low cloud, and it made both general observation and counter-battery fire difficult, yet day by day the Germans noted increasing enemy activity. In support of Operation Kulmbach, and in spite of the adverse weather conditions, the Bavarians had put up an aircraft to reconnoitre enemy activity and direct the fire of two 21-centimetre howitzers against the heavily dug-in four-gun Battery 63 which had survived repeated destructive shoots in the past. Sixty-one rounds were fired, and it was silenced. Battery 38, which had been mute during the period from 3–13 July, was now observed to be manned and in action—registering. More and more British guns were becoming more and more vocal. Something was in the offing. Whether it was a 'demonstration' or something more sinister was immaterial. No longer was an attack hypothetical; it was anticipated.

Report B No. 6106, 'Findings Relating to the Enemy' for the period 11.7.16–16.7.16, noted that:

It remains to be seen whether the 5th Australian Division has taken over
the entire sector from the 1st Australian Division. The 5th Australian
Division was only formed a few months ago in Egypt, where it under-
went training. It would be a departure from previous British practice
if the Division were to take over the whole sector without at least some
measure of prior 'acclimatisation'.

It was a dangerous moment for 6 BRD: they were unable to discern whether the entire 1st Division had departed, nor if the 2nd Division was still in the sector; the whereabouts of the mysterious 4th Division was still unclear, but it was known that the 61st Division had extended its boundary further east. If hostile action was indeed imminent, which of these units might be ranged in reserve? And what were their potentially combined artillery resources?

There has been criticism of the Allies' dispensation with the element of surprise at Fromelles. Given the precautions specifically put in place by the Bavarians to obviate that very aspect, it seems plain that the only form of surprise that could have been engineered was a nocturnal assault. Here, the chances of success would have been slim indeed, for before reaching the enemy wire (which would have been uncut) and negotiating the glacis in the dark, the troops would have had to neutralise hostile patrols in No Man's Land, plus listening posts, wiring parties, searchlights, and observers on a fully manned parapet. On this front surprise on a major scale could probably not have been achieved. In addition, none of the troops were trained for such an enterprise.

This was known to General Haking—and from very recent experience. Less than three weeks earlier, to coincide with other concurrent 'distractions' in the region, he had ordered a small diversionary attack against a position known as the Boar's Head Salient some 4 kilometres south of Fromelles. The units involved, the 12th and 13th Battalions of the Royal Sussex Regiment, had served in the sector since 18 March. They were acclimatised, knew the ground, and in preparation for the raid had received behind-the-line training on models. The attack was nevertheless a disaster, with 30 June 1916 later being labelled, 'The Day Sussex Died'.

According to the war diaries of the 12th and 13th Royal Sussex Regiment, the critical moment came when 'a smoke cloud, which was originally designed to mask our advance, drifted right across the front and made it impossible to see more than a few yards ahead. This resulted in all direction being lost and the attack devolving into small bodies of men not knowing which way to go.' Tactically and functionally the attack was effectively a Fromelles in miniature. There was no requirement for deep penetration or infiltration, and in the event of success, no arrangements for supplementary actions. The enterprise was primarily dependent upon artillery preparation and sustained support and supply to the newly captured ground. But 1128 Sussex soldiers were dead, wounded and missing: almost 60 per cent of the force. Haking's comment upon this failure was that the 39th Division, to which the Sussex regiments were affiliated, had not until recently 'shown much offensive spirit. I consider that this operation has greatly improved the fighting value of the Division.' The general was effectively saying that he had tried to do his job and, if the men were not capable, it was not his fault.

The clearest lesson to be learned from the botched enterprise, however, was that the enemy was alert, prepared, and fully aware of the procedures likely to be employed by the British. The Allies were not yet employing 'advanced tactics', which were in any case designed to sustain assaults that had already ruptured German lines. In mid-1916, therefore, despite the fact that commanders might have persuaded themselves of the sophistication of the means at their disposal, both in terms of manpower and gunpower, the war remained semi-mediaeval. There was still but one route: create a breach with artillery, mortars, mines, gas or a combination of the four, and go 'once more unto it' with the infantry.

At Fromelles, no one could rely upon the wind being favourable for gas. Haking had the use of several mines, but McCay elected to employ only one. In truth, both divisions were dependent upon whatever enhanced firepower could be assembled, the skill of the gunners and mortar crews to adequately destroy wire . . . and of course, the 'lifts'. The final line of Sir Douglas Haig's note in his approval of the offensive scheme did not appear in XI Corps' offensive equation: 'This depends partly on what guns enemy shows.' Deliberately and wisely, most enemy guns did not show.

Before battle commenced General Haking had one further message to convey. Typically optimistic and ebullient, it outlined the measures required for the retention of captured ground.

18 July 1916
Don't let the position go when you have once got it. Above all, look after, block and wire the enemy's communication trenches leading into the position and prevent the enemy from bombing you out of there. A counter-stroke across the open you can easily repel with rifle and machine-gun

*fire and with your artillery. Get your communications across to the new
line as rapidly as possible in the early part of the night, and have a good
fire position along the whole front ready by daylight on 20th. Have this
order conveyed to all ranks.*

On the same day Hans Gebhardt, commanding III Battalion RIR 16,
reported upon the effect of Allied shelling across his III sector, which
included the Sugar Loaf (sub-sectors a and b):

Morning: b [sector]: *80 shrapnel, 10 TM* [trench mortar]; *c* [sector]:
18 shrapnel, 10 medium HE [high explosive]

   *Afternoon: a: 30 shrapnel, 25 medium HE; b: 800 shrapnel,
500 medium HE; c: 250 shrapnel, 20 medium HE, 10 heavy HE;
d: 150 shrapnel, 30 medium HE, 15 heavy HE; Schützenhauswerk,
Dachau: 30 shrapnel, 30 medium HE; Starnberg: 25 shrapnel.*

   *The heavy gun fired from the left flank. Calibre not yet estab-
lished. Gruppe Wurm received shell fragments. Location of gun not
yet ascertained.*

   Machine gun fire on repair/reinstatement works.

   *Hostile artillery fire effectively countered by Gruppe Wurm
and Treuchtlingen.*

   *Water situation unchanged; electricity supply cable to front line cut
by shellfire; hostile aircraft directed the enemy's artillery throughout the
day and were not engaged.*

   *The position is in a completely defensible state, but sector b has been
quite badly knocked about today. With the exception of the right flank
of sector IIIb, the wire defences still offer protection.*

   *The whole of the battalion's wiring troop is working tonight on the
repair of this part of the wire. As authorised by the Regiment, the other
repair works in sector b are being undertaken by the Petzstadt platoon
of the 8th Company.*

   *The right flank of IIIb is potentially exposed to an enemy trench
raid. All necessary defensive precautions have been put in place. The
artillery has today re-registered its guns on the ground in front of the
right flank of IIIb.*

Despite the bombardment, the position remained in a 'completely defensible state'. The Sugar Loaf was sound. Von Scanzoni's infantry and artillery prepared for the onslaught. British and Australian fortunes now largely depended upon tomorrow's drumfire and Haking's lifts.

PART II

DER TAG

Chapter 11

OVER THE TOP AND
HOPPING THE BAGS

—————

It has been ascertained that the enemy is moving his troops from our front to resist the attacks of our comrades to the South. The Commander-in-Chief has directed the XIth Corps to attack the enemy in front of us, capture his front system of trenches and thus prevent him from reinforcing his troops to the South. Two Divisions are about to attack the enemy's line of trenches along a front of 4,200 yards. I wish all ranks to understand the plan of attack, and I trust them not to disclose it to anyone. There will first be a heavy bombardment the day before along a front some seven miles to the South of the attack. By this bombardment I hope to induce the enemy, who is very weak in artillery, to move some of his batteries in that direction. This bombardment will be continued on the morning of the attack, whilst our guns along the front of the real attack will be getting the exact range of the enemy's trenches without attracting undue notice. This order to be read to all troops taking part on the attack.

Operation Order, XI Corps. 16.7.16

Since the discharge of the first gunpowder weapon the psychological effect of explosives has been one of ever-increasing influence. Destruction, whether natural or by shell and bomb, remained (and indeed still remains) mesmerising to the onlooker. The curious gratification derived from violent but detached destruction is by no means reserved for headstrong youth: in war, the delight of a direct hit is exhilarating, partly by reason of the fascination, but also because it indicated fruitful instruction and duty done: no soldier—in any theatre—was there to provide humanitarian aid . . . he was there to kill.

At Fromelles on the evening of 15 July the Kulmbach bombardment had ravaged the Australian trenches; dugouts were blown in and men buried alive. Many heard or saw that firestorm; some were involved. Whether participant or onlooker, it was an arresting event, and a devastating introduction for the 5th Division. But . . . if twenty-six minutes of German drumfire could wreak such havoc, the Diggers and Tommies had every right to envisage General Haking's artillery fire-plan visiting equal if not greater devastation, loss and chaos upon the Bavarians. Indeed, they had been assured of it. When informed of the hardware drawn up on their behalf there was no cause to doubt the confidence and poise of their superiors.

It was for good reason, however, that Sir Douglas Haig demanded corps and divisional commanders be fully satisfied with artillery planning before confirming the assault. During the bombardment that recently heralded his great offensive in Picardy he had received assurance after assurance from artillery advisers that German wire would be severed and resistance neutralised. His gunners were not just *the* specialists, they were the *only* specialists. They and their trusted subordinates had been on the testing grounds, assessed the effects, commissioned production of the weapons and missiles, trained the crews, and invested trust in capabilities. Others were inspired and convinced by the confidence these men exuded. Haig was one such—he had no one else to consult.

It was self-confident officers from the same dignified military tribe to whom Monro, Haking, McCay and Mackenzie turned. There was no reason to suspect flawed or incomplete information, especially after 1 July.

In repeatedly demanding and receiving unconditional assurances, therefore, Haig did everything within his power both to protect the infantry,
and to help them prosper at Fromelles. And after the trauma of Kulmbach,
McCay instructed his brigadiers to let all their men know the battle was
'their chance of getting more than even'.

The artillery reports of the 6th Bavarian Reserve Infantry Division
subsequently noted that the earliest observed indication of hostile artillery preparation was on 16 July. The enemy had at that time brought up
a number of light-calibre, short-range batteries and the Bavarian front
line had come under intense artillery and trench-mortar fire, mainly from
light guns and medium and heavy trench mortars. On the 17th another
group of light batteries had come into action, while the batteries they had
detected the previous day virtually all remained silent. On the 18th both
were in action.

> There was no discernible build-up of medium-calibre artillery in the
> days preceding the attack. During the action itself, a slight increase
> was noted.
>
> The enemy did not bring his heavy artillery into action until the day
> of the attack.
>
> Remarkably, on the days preceding the attack, only some of our
> battery positions were engaged, weakly and without W/T-directed
> [wireless-telegraphy] observation, by hostile light and medium-calibre
> artillery. Our battery observation positions were not brought under fire.
> Only a small number of shells fell on the approach routes. A few bombs
> were dropped on positions on the Hochbahnstrasse [the road along the
> crest of the ridge] and on individual defensive positions.

The Bavarians responded by themselves targeting known and suspected
observation posts in buildings on the Rue Tilleloy, along and indeed
beyond the predicted battle zone, and repairing damage to wire and
breastworks either as it occurred or in the lulls between molestations. For
the British, the combination of poor weather and hostile shelling of their
observation positions made fall of shot almost impossible to efficiently

monitor. On the eve of battle RIR 21 were not unduly concerned; they recorded the following damage from the 'liberal' Allied bombardment:

IIa: *Wire badly damaged at the Conventionsgraben. No significant damage to breastwork.*

IIb: *Wire damaged in several places; in the centre and in particular on the left flank; major damage to the breastwork.*

IIc: *Wire damage bad on right flank, otherwise minor. Breastwork heavily damaged in places.*

IId: *Wire damaged throughout. Damage to breastwork not as bad as in IIc.*

Casualties were four dead and twelve wounded.

On the morning of Wednesday 19 July visibility finally improved, with the mist lifting and a mean cloud base forming at 3000 feet (900 metres). The gunners had at last been given their chance.

When hostile shelling increased, the Bavarian garrison quit the parapets for dugouts and shelters, leaving observers to warn of the slightest indication of enemy attack. In the early afternoon fire intensified, and at 12.30 p.m. a state of general alert and combat readiness was affirmed. As regimental staff made their way back to command posts, the flow of enquiries and reports increased dramatically. For 6 BRD only three questions remained. First, might all the commotion yet be a feint? Enemy aerial activity and traffic behind and within the enemy lines made this unlikely; but if it was the case, they should have no worries save for the Allied guns, whose threat was partially offset by improvements in fieldworks completed during the previous fourteen months. In any case, damage was reparable. Second, if not a feint, when would the blow fall? *Where* it was likely to fall was at present being strongly indicated by fall of enemy shot, which still suggested that the boundaries of the battle zone would extend from about *Leierhof Trivelet* (opposite Fauquissart) to *Wasserburg* (Cordonnerie sector): an area entirely within von Scanzoni's divisional sector. Experience warned that this too might be a ruse, but every preparation that it had been humanly possible to make was now made, and neighbouring divisions were at the same level of vigilance.

The third issue was both the most imperative and the most unanswer-able: what might the enemy objectives be? Fromelles? Aubers? The ridge? Lille? It was known that Allied troops facing 6 BRD were raw. Would they attack together or singly? Who was in reserve? From 16 July onwards a brisk flow of traffic had been noted between the rear and the front line during daylight, while at night heavy vehicle and trench-railway traffic could be heard behind the lines on both divisional fronts. There were, however, no indications of reserves being in place, so whatever its purpose, the enter-prise was unlikely to be hugely ambitious. Capture of a section of the ridge—including the two villages—surely had to be the minimum Allied goal. Dispositions were made accordingly. For the Bavarians, it was simply a question of watch, wait and, when the time came, act as swiftly as possible.

All indications were that fourteen months of thought, work and training was about to be tested, as were their final deductions. An RIR 16 report of 17 July provided the following observations relating to the enemy in sector III (the Sugar Loaf to Wick Salients) from 8 July to 15 July:

White Engländer were observed. Large numbers of trench periscopes in evidence opposite IIIc and d. Changes in the behaviour of the enemy trench garrison—sometimes very cautious and at other times observing from quite unreasonably exposed positions—suggest that a relief has taken place or new troops have arrived. On 12.7 at about 11.30 a green flare went up in IIIB, whereupon the enemy infantry ceased firing. A relief is assumed, as the enemy artillery also held its fire that night. Movements behind the front remained within usual levels.

These observations were acute. It was indeed during this report-ing period that the Australian relief took place opposite RIR 16 and 21, the change soon being confirmed by the three Diggers captured during Kulmbach. Their words, plus the behaviour of the troops opposite, verified the 'greenness' of the new arrivals.

Having moved to advanced headquarters in Sailly, Haking and his XI Corps staff were now close to the action. The seven-hour artillery overture began at 11.00 a.m. The Bavarians carefully observed and plotted all this, shell by shell, both from the ground and the air. Expectation on both sides of No Man's Land was reaching a peak. British and Australian bayonets were being fixed—the ultimate signal that the moment of no return was close.

When the final and heaviest phase of the bombardment began at midday, the Bavarians put up two aircraft. Initially, none of their guns were free to counter Allied artillery, as all suitable batteries were registered on other targets. However, one battery did become available for short periods, and with the aircraft guiding its fire, hits were made on key targets. In noting all this, Artillery Flight 201's report commented:

> The work of the Artillery Flight was greatly hampered throughout the mission by adverse meteorological conditions as the average cloud base was only about 1000m, with individual clouds at lower altitudes, and there was a dense mist illuminated by the sun lying between the clouds and the ground. The aircraft were therefore obliged to fly over the lines at altitudes between 400–1000m in order to observe, and were thus constantly exposed to the enemy's defensive screen of fighter aircraft and the heavy, well-aimed fire of motorised flak batteries. In the course of their mission the two aircraft engaged in aerial combat with two Vickers machines and one Nieuport (all biplanes). These encounters were inconclusive because the proximity of other enemy machines restricted the freedom of manoeuvre of their own aircraft.

With Bavarian artillery occupied with by far the most profitable activity—the disruption and destruction of British and Australian troops within and behind their own lines—Allied gunners were not at this time unduly hampered by counter-battery fire. The men of the 61st Division again noted many 'blinds', as did the 15th Australian Brigade. It was at 12.30 that Australian medical services reported their first casualties—one officer and eleven other ranks.

Although the Bavarians reported serious damage to breastworks and the area immediately to the rear, Haking's four 'lifts' can be only vaguely discerned among the many messages despatched at this time. They were planned to take place at 3.25 to 3.39, 4.04 to 4.09, 4.29 to 4.36 and 5.21

to 5.31. Between each lift the troops were directed to raise dummies and dummy helmets above the parapet, wave bayonets and holler as if about to attack. In a message of 3.56 p.m., the British FOO (forward observation officer) for the Right Group of artillery (Fauquissart sector) noted with concern that 'the enemy did not appear to man his parapets during the lift'. This seems to have simply been because most Bavarians had not actually noticed them: they were relying, as ordered, upon alarm signals being sounded when the attack actually commenced.

Because the lifts were indistinct, the Bavarians failed to act according to Allied predictions—and thus XI Corps' requirements. In fact, only one RIR 16 record (III Battalion) makes direct reference to such a tactic: 'At 4.00pm the enemy fire lifted to the rear and large numbers of English troops in battle order could be seen in the enemy trenches. Our companies prepared their defences, but then the enemy artillery shortened and began to shell our trenches again.'

The effect of Allied fire during the afternoon was mixed: heavy in places, but consisting primarily of light-calibre shells and mortars. Heavy and medium trench mortars appeared from time to time, 'always in salvoes of four', but there was no pattern to it. Inexperience was everywhere evident. On the left flank RIR 20 reported almost all of the 140 heavy-calibre rounds (over 20 centimetre) falling behind their line, thus causing negligible damage. The effect of such miscalculation would be far reaching. At Rouges Bancs, however, Allied shooting, especially by mortars, was considerably more accurate. Light weapons concentrated upon blowing 75-metre gaps in the German wire, while the medium and heavy weapons focussed upon parapets.

Convinced an attack was imminent, the Bavarians declared a state of alert and heightened combat readiness at 12.30 p.m. Their own guns responded, and at the same moment Lieutenant-Colonel D. Coghill (OC 32nd Battalion) reported, 'Hostile trench mortars and 18-pounders smashing our parapets and trenches to pieces. Many casualties.' By 1.00 p.m. every Bavarian soldier had received the order, 'Stand To', and soon a message arrived at 14th Brigade HQ in Fromelles telling of 'enemy infantry on the left in front of their own wire in IIIb': these were the British 184th Brigade troops of the 2/1st Bucks and 2/4th Berks gathering in the advanced saps opposite the Sugar Loaf. As the afternoon wore on von Braun made his preparations:

> Hostile fire then increased to the level of drumfire and in the case of some batteries, at least, was directed by aircraft. In preparation for a rapid response to the enemy attack anticipated later in the evening, and in order to have support on hand, I gave orders at about 5.00pm to the support battalion to place one section of the regimental reserve at the alarm bell posts and in the signal flare dugouts and to assign six runners to the regimental command post. I also gave instructions for communications with the front line to be maintained in all circumstances, if necessary by the use of runners. At this time a report was received from the artillery that the enemy was transferring men from the second line into his front line. I therefore ordered the regimental reserve to be brought forward to reinforce the garrison at the Türkenecke. The message did not reach our front line in time as all direct communication between the front line and BII had already been interrupted.
>
> There was now a danger that the front line—weakened by losses due to enemy artillery and trench mortar fire—might be unable to withstand an attack in heavily superior numbers long enough for support to be brought up from the rear.

The transfer of Allied troops from support to jumping-off positions was not an easy task. Whether in the trenches or crossing open ground, at every step the Tommies and Diggers were molested by Bavarian artillery, mortars and in numerous places rifle grenades. The thrill of the Allied bombardment had vanished; no longer was anyone counting hostile 'blinds'. Almost seven hours after zero, the point of no return was now approaching for the Diggers. Although somewhat tortuously composed, in his 'Instructions for Infantry Brigadiers' Major-General Sir James McCay's orders were ultimately simple:

> The mode of taking the trenches should be as follows—first wave stays at and clears enemy out of first row of enemy trenches in which any enemy are, whether they resist or not. Then advance further.

Meanwhile second wave passes first wave to next enemy row where resistance or enemy are; and so on until all works of enemy first line system, which in most places extends about 100 yards behind their front parapet, are taken.

Every work in enemy first line system is to be taken, but no troops are on any account to go beyond that line. See that communication trenches leading back from first line are not mistaken for parts of first line. These communication trenches must be blocked (with the double block where possible) and watched.

It is the rearmost row of enemy's first line that is to be at once fortified and held when it is taken.

Every battalion had also been issued with XI Corps' directive: 'the objective will be strictly limited to the enemy's support trenches and no more.'

Attacking formations followed an orthodox pattern: the 8th and 14th Brigades each deployed two battalions assaulting in four waves approximately 55 yards (50 metres) apart. In the case of the 15th Brigade, because of the greater breadth of No Man's Land in their sector the gap was 150 yards (140 metres). The third battalion was to form carrying parties for supplies and at the same time hold the original front line, remaining available as reserves if circumstances required. The fourth was held in close reserve, ready to act where necessary. Thus the entire establishment of every brigade was to some degree implicated in the enterprise. Once the first waves had made the assault, subsequent traversals of No Man's Land (until the several communication trenches had been cut across it) would take place in artillery formation, i.e. in file rather than wave.

To enhance crossing times, under the cover of the bombardment the foremost wave was to covertly deploy beyond their own wire in No Man's Land before the assault, the location and timing being dependent upon the nature of each battalion's battlefront. On 18 July, Battle Memorandum No. 56 had been circulated to all divisions. Its first points stated:

1. *It has been established in recent operations that troops should not assault a hostile prepared position from a distance of more than 200 yards. If the opposing lines are far apart, it is necessary to:*

>   a) *Establish a jumping off place within 200 yards*
>   *or*
>   b) *Form up for the assault under cover of darkness within this distance.*
> 2. *The detailed plan should be fully explained to all concerned and they should be made particularly to understand the exact place they must gain in each advance and their action on arrival, i.e. whether to consolidate, to organise and prepare for a second advance etc.*

'Recent operations' of course, referred uniquely to Allied offensives in which no Australian units had taken part. Troops traversing No Man's Land in the areas where it was wide would be assisted by the fact that others would hopefully have swiftly occupied neighbouring narrow sectors, putting pressure on the entire enemy line and thus diminishing the hostile response. This was an important aspect of every offensive scheme for, although desirable, the attainment of ultimate success was not necessarily dependent upon events unfolding exactly according to plan. Fromelles was as much a percentage game as any other action. Despite the limited territorial aspiration, the most important aspect of the post-initial assault phase was the establishment and maintenance of communication so that commanders might react to changing circumstances and instruct auxiliary arms—mortars, machine guns and artillery—accordingly.

Early on the morning of 19 July General McCay sent a message to all brigades: 'The G.O.C. relies upon you to get constant information back from front immediately events happen and to send it on at once.' The same request had been issued by scores of McCay's British colleagues on countless occasions during the previous eighteen months. But try as they might, at no time since the war began had it been possible for attacking troops to satisfactorily comply. Breakdown of communication with the assault was the ubiquitous and enduring affliction of every commander at all levels of combat. Fromelles was not about to break that mould.

In preparation for rapid response and in order to have assistance to hand, at around 4 p.m. Bavarian regimental commanders issued instructions for support battalions to place sections of reserves at alarm posts, in signal-flare dugouts, and at light-signalling stations, and to assign at least half a dozen trained runners to the numerous command posts across the sector. They too stressed that communication with the front line must be maintained in all circumstances, if not by telephone then by runners.

In several ways the nature of No Man's Land favoured the attack. It was green and lush, in parts marshy, and with many an overgrown pond—old shell and mine craters. In short the ground had returned to its innate biological state. Nature had taken advantage of the previous year's fighting, masking the damage with weeds, brambles, wild flowers, nettles, thistles and self-seeded crops. For a long time it had been practically untroubled by gunfire, for there was no profit in targeting an empty space until it was filled with targets worth shelling—men.

On the plain below Aubers and Fromelles, No Man's Land was therefore a ribbon of relatively undisturbed ground. Probably for the first time in centuries mother nature was left to her own devices. Because of war, it had become a sanctuary for wildlife. To the troops lining its boundaries on 19 July 1916, however, the perspective could hardly have been more different: No Man's Land was the prime focus of everyone's attentions, hopes and fears: it was *the* place to kill and to be killed.

Covered by British (60th Brigade) rifles in the trenches to their left, at zero the 32nd Battalion began to swarm across the narrow reaches of No Man's Land towards Negative Trench. Before them lay 10 Company of von Braun's RIR 21. This is the Bavarian report on what happened next:

From 1.00pm onwards the bombardment increased to drumfire with HE shells (mainly 8.3cm calibre [18-pounder]) and trench mortar rounds. Throughout the company sector, the men took cover in the trench shelters and the concrete dugout. Each platoon posted three lookouts. At about 4.00pm fixed bayonets were seen projecting above the parapet of the enemy front trench, whereupon the order was given to the men in our own trench to also 'Fix bayonets!'.

Vizefeldwebel Reindl, who happened to be in the Company commander's dugout at this time, reports that at 4.00pm the Company commander, Leutnant Keim, gave instructions for the papers, war diaries, etc, kept in the command dugout to be destroyed. At about this time a number of men belonging to the centre platoon were wounded and evacuated to the rear, among them Vizefeldwebel Tempelmeier, the deputy platoon commander. Those who were not wounded were dispersed in the trench shelters and the concrete dugout on the right flank of the left-hand platoon. The part of our position that Reindl passed through was already very heavily shot-up, as our trenches had been badly damaged by the bombardment of previous days, and only temporary repairs had been possible during the night.

After a short pause at 4.00pm, the barrage resumed. By then, Reindl was in a trench shelter roughly in the middle of the platoon sector with one other man. A look-out was posted nearby, and at 5.45pm he called out 'The enemy is coming'. At this, Reindl immediately mounted the firestep and saw enemy troops advancing towards Crater no 2. He could also see that the alarm had been heard, as the parts of the trench that were still defensible were largely manned. As Reindl immediately realised that there was nothing he could do in that place with only two men, he led them hurriedly about 30m to the right, where Leutnant Keim had garrisoned the breastwork directly to the right of his command dugout with perhaps 10 men from the centre platoon. These men engaged the oncoming enemy with rifles and hand grenades. The enemy assault column (strength approx. 2 platoons) divided at Crater no 2 [the northernmost of the two May 1915 mine craters]. *One section veered off to the left and the other jumped into the crater. The Company commander and the men around him were soon killed by hand grenades and rifle fire from the attackers. Reindl then became aware that he was the only unwounded survivor, and saw that the attackers had penetrated beyond our front line trench in the left-hand half of the platoon position and had already reached our support trench. No enemy troops had entered our trench at the point where Reindl was standing. Reindl moved to the rear and entered the Kastengraben beside the trench tramway track. He then made his way swiftly to the left-hand barricade at Tote Sau and there fired a number of shots at the enemy. In so doing, he observed that the enemy had changed direction and was now heading towards the Kastengraben.*

At this point Reindl decided to make his way as quickly as possible to BII and make his report, and this he then did.

Facing a No Man's Land averaging 80 metres in width, the 32nd Battalion required little time to form up, and on the whistle sliced through enemy resistance in quick time despite losses to enfilade fire from the left flank and initially stiff opposition at the Bavarian parapet, where the enemy garrison had immediately spotted the advancing Diggers and manned the breastwork. Initially, they fired on those closing on the centre platoon near the 1915 mine craters. According to Charles Bean it left a number of dead fallen on their knees or faces as they advanced.

Shortly after 6.00 p.m. the sappers of 2 Australian Tunnelling Company drove down the handle of their exploder, springing the 1200-pound charge designed to create both a 'moral effect' and 'protect the left front'. Its eruption had an instant effect, compelling the Bavarians opposite to move to the right where they then took part in the defence of the left of sector IIa. Resistance opposite the 32nd Battalion was thus successfully weakened, although not in the way that had been anticipated. A small number of enemy troops shifted left into the path of the main Australian assault; according to Bavarian reports, these men 'fell where they stood'. It was a promising start for the Diggers.

The seething mine crater appeared some two-thirds of the way across No Man's Land—in the perfect spot for its designed purpose—and on the boundary of sectors IIa, garrisoned by 9/RIR 21, and IIb. The commander of 9 Company, *Oberleutnant* Georg Luther, later reported:

A look-out standing in the centre of the left-hand platoon was the first to see the enemy and raised the alarm with a shout of 'The Engländer are coming', which very quickly spread along the line. By that time, the oncoming enemy had also been seen by the middle and right-hand platoons and the trench garrison rushed to man the breastwork. The right-hand hostile formation (as seen from our positions) left the enemy trenches some 40–50m to the left of the boundary between sectors IIa and IIb and advanced in columns of 8–10 men in company strength towards the Saustrasse [road crossing No Man's Land between Delangré Farm and the Horsehoe]. *This body of men did not leave the enemy trenches until the assaulting column advancing to their left had already reached Craters 1 and 2. As the first groups of men in the right-hand column left their trenches, there was a loud detonation as a mine exploded between the opposing positions and the high rim thrown up around the crater largely blocked the field of fire. At the same time several men from the 10th company arrived to report that the enemy had broken into the positions of the middle platoon in sector IIb. The garrison and MGs of sector IIa opened enfilade fire on the advancing enemy. Hostile machine guns then began to sweep our breastwork, inflicting substantial casualties and putting MGs 1 and 2 out of action. There must have been 4 or 5 enemy machine guns trained on sector IIa.*

The covering fire came from the British 60th Brigade, protectors of the Australian left flank. By neutralising two hostile machine guns they presumably saved several lives. The mine blow partly confused the Bavarians, and it was later reported as having 'no obvious purpose', for it had failed to destroy their trenches, as mines were habitually expected to do. With the crater on their left, the 31st Battalion 'hopped the bags' in front of the Horseshoe. Their target was Nib Trench, occupied by the central garrison of RIR 21; their wire, breastworks and indeed ranks had been bludgeoned by shell and mortar fire. *Oberleutnant* Luther's report continued:

The commander of the right-hand platoon, Offizier-Stellvertreter Keller, had gone over to Company F and was killed in their positions. The machine gun sited on the right flank of IIb had already been buried earlier during the bombardment. In the left-hand platoon sector, Vizefeldwebel Meier rallied the remaining men (about half a platoon in strength) on the right flank of the position. The machine gun located there was set up on the breastwork to fire in enfilade to the left, but was soon annihilated, together with the gun team, by a shrapnel shell. The enemy attacked the centre of the left-hand platoon sector and was vigorously resisted with rifles and hand grenades by the garrison, led, after Vizefeldwebel Meier was killed, by Leutnant Hain of the 11th Company, who was already injured and was then severely wounded again. Of these

men only Gefreiter Salmansberger survived to crawl to Rouges Bancs
and the Türkenecke. Four men succeeded in taking refuge in the [mine]
shaft and were able to emerge later to take part in the recapture of the
position by our troops.

This appears to have been the point at which the enemy first broke
in to Sector IIb, as the men were already locked in combat with the
attackers when they saw the enemy troops advancing against the centre
platoon. Time, approx. 6.00pm.

Ironically, the two May 1915 craters were of equal practical use to the
Diggers as their own mine. Easily entered, the great holes presented instant
cover for troops whose ranks had already, as a result of hostile artillery and
mortars and numerous 'friendly shorts', been depleted while forming up
within crowded trenches. Later they became staging posts for runners.

Prospects at this time may have looked promising, but the Diggers' pre-
attack losses were so heavy that, some time before the assault, the provision
of a sufficiently concentrated force to capture, hold and consolidate the
Bavarian positions was seen as under threat. A restructuring was therefore
ordered, with the planned third and fourth waves becoming one; reserve
battalions were placed on stand-by. Having exited through concealed sally-
ports, many secretly constructed at the last moment, the troops came under
flanking fire from sector IIa, sustaining further losses despite the narrowness of No Man's Land ahead of them. Although IIa was outside the initial
assault zone the plan was to consolidate the area where the *Kastengraben*
(known to the British as Negative Drive) communication trench joined the
twin lines of the Bavarian front trench system, infiltrate a little to the east,
and install solid and permanent trench blocks. The Germans in IIa, especially those near this critical boundary, therefore had to be subdued, and in
this effort the Australian gun and mortar crews performed excellently, as
Luther's action report testified:

The enemy's trench mortars came into action at about 1.00pm and
bombarded the middle and left-hand platoons and the old support
line (Dannergraben) with a very large number of heavy spherical and
cylindrical mortar bombs—some 700 rounds being counted between

*1.00 and 3.00pm. The right-hand platoon suffered less from the artil-
lery fire; only its right flank was bombarded with mortars and a number
of heavy HE rounds. The shelling continued throughout the afternoon
and became even heavier at about 5.15pm. In sector IIa the barrage did
not lift to the rear. As many of the men as possible were under cover in
shell-proof shelters and dug-outs, and the rest stood tight against the
breastwork. Look-outs were posted in every platoon sector.*

*The right-hand platoon was largely spared, but the middle platoon
was very hard hit. There were only 4 or 5 short stretches of trench
where look-outs could stand—everything else was shot up and one
12–15 metre section of trench was completely flattened. The right-hand
half of the left-hand platoon sector suffered only minor damage, whilst
the left-hand half was heavily shot up, but remained defensible with the
exception of two traverses. Casualties during the artillery preparation
amounted to approx 25 men.*

Beyond that flank RIR 20 received meagre attention from Allied artillery, registering just '40 light trench mortar bombs and 80 light shrapnel
rounds' after the enemy infantry had left their trenches. But with many
of RIR 21 dead or routed, the regiment's contribution now became critical
to Bavarian prospects. Soon after the first Australian waves had made the
initial incursion, the commanding officer of the defending II Battalion
issued the following orders:

1) *The enemy is attacking Sectors II, III and IV and appears to have
   already broken in to IIb and IIc.*
2) *All sections to combat readiness. Prepare barricading materials in
   case of need to block trenches. Sub-sector d to put a resourceful NCO
   and 18 men into the enfilading position covering the old communication trench to the Wasserburg in order to prevent the enemy from
   breaking in there. MG 8 to support.*
3) *MG 7 to enfilade no-man's land in front of Sector II.*

For the Diggers, it was point 3 that caused the greatest problems. In order
to take and firmly hold the critical left flank a stream of support troops,

runners, pioneers and engineers would be required not only to traverse No Man's Land, but work within it on the all-important connecting trench. The Bavarians were as yet still unaware of the eastern boundary of the Australian attack, but they naturally took measures to contain it. Nothing could be done about the mine crater, but it was found that from a little 'nose' in the line some 550 metres to the east, MG 7 commanded the assault by firing westwards down No Man's Land and thus across the line of enemy advance. Because of its angled alignment, the gun was to some extent protected from Allied bullets. To be certain of silencing it—and others that would soon arrive in the sector—Allied artillery and mortars would be required.

Oberst Julius von Braun's worries during the afternoon had been fully justified. At 6.00 p.m. most of his regimental sector was a shambles of blasted sandbags, splintered timber, tangled wire, and dead and wounded comrades. Arriving at his command post, BII, at 7.45 p.m. he found telephones and tramways useless and casualties debilitating. Half of his sector already belonged to the Australians. When the Digger attack burst in to IIb, c and d, the stunned survivors of his regiment were quickly killed or captured. They were surprisingly few—the Allied guns had done their work well. However, because it had been known for several days that this area was the most vulnerable, and therefore most likely to be successfully assaulted, precautions had also been taken. Some troops had earlier moved back to the cover of strongpoints, buildings and woodland in the *Hintergelände*. Unknown to von Braun, the entire left-hand platoon of 11 Company had evacuated their positions some five hours before the Diggers' assault:

Hostile fire increased in intensity from 11.00 a.m. and then escalated to drumfire from noon with the addition of hundreds of heavy trench mortar rounds. The left-hand platoon was exposed to the heaviest fire and at about 1.00 p.m. the Company commander ordered it to evacuate its position, as no enemy attack was expected during daylight. One man remained as an observer in the left half of the left-hand platoon sector and another look-out was posted at the boundary between the left-hand and centre platoons. Vizefeldwebel Aal remained in position directly to the right of the latter observer until about 3.30pm. The men of the three platoons took cover in the shell-proof dugouts and shelters in the centre and right-hand platoon positions. Look-outs were also posted in those sectors. The two machine guns belonging to the left-hand platoon were taken to safety on the right . . . Due to the recent drumfire and the constant bombardment over the three previous days, the left-hand platoon positions were very soon almost levelled, offering protection in only a few places and retaining very little defensive capability. The centre and right-hand platoon positions were also rendered almost indefensible in many places by the bombardment. Movement was often only possible behind the parados. Telephone connections were lost at about 2.45pm.

Our casualties during the bombardment were very heavy.

Action Report, 11 Company, RIR 21, 22 July 1916

With resistance weak and in places non-existent, the opening events of 9 May 1915 were soon replicated. The Australians swiftly secured the Bavarian front line between Rouges Bancs and Delangré Farm. Within minutes the first 11 Company prisoners were being sent back, and the process of regrouping and orientation within the alien enemy world had begun. Numbers of the enemy could be seen fleeing the onslaught; the Diggers—to their certain frustration—were under strict orders to resist the allure of the chase. Some did, some did not; several Bavarians fell to Australian snap-shooting.

Having been cut out of the battle plan that very morning, the capture of Delangré Farm was no longer a 32nd Battalion aim. This decision may now be seen as an error, for the moated ruin was a strongpoint, an observation point, a depot, a signalling station, a rallying point, a shelter and a communication hub. It was also slightly elevated. For these very reasons, it had formed one of the 8th Division's key objectives the previous year. With Allied guns having lifted to features beyond the Bavarian first line, the farm lay unmolested for hours after the assault, a fact that was quickly noted and taken advantage of: RIR 21 troops slipped quietly back into its ruins.

From within and about the farm hostile fire was soon enfilading the Diggers as they scanned the ground for the stated and final objective.

The Bavarian front line, trench tramway and parts of a support position were evident, but all other features looked defunct and neglected. Where exactly was the third line they were meant to occupy and make their own? Major J. Hughes, second in command of the battalion, arrived with the third wave to find his men destroying dugouts, cutting telegraph wires, dealing with pockets of resistance and sending back prisoners. About 120 metres inside enemy territory and practically adjacent to the farm, which now partly blocked the view to the east, he found troops of the second wave occupying a waterlogged ditch just over a metre deep. A more unsatisfactory place to defend could hardly have been selected for there was almost no protection to the front, side or rear. When quizzed by Captain Arthur White (D Company), Hughes replied that, according to the orders, this was indeed the assigned objective and for the time being the men must dig in as best they could. The two officers then saw Diggers advancing to their right. They themselves went ahead into the dust and smoke to see if better shelter existed deeper within the Bavarian position. The search was in vain, but the expedition cost Hughes a thigh wound and ultimately a long captivity.

Those troops who had pushed on were now called back and ordered to fortify the western extension of the ditch. In fact there was only one more trench between them and the Bavarian *II Stellung,* almost 1.5 kilometres away on the ridge. This was the *Türkenecke,* a strongpoint to which many of RIR 21's absconders from sector IIb had withdrawn to join three other sections of the regiment who had moved in during the afternoon. Two machine guns defended their position. It was clearly too far advanced to be McCay's objective.

This period of initial chaos presented certain leading elements of the 8th Brigade with some little time to find, assess and begin the consolidation of their positions before the enemy was sufficiently recovered to mount substantial organised counter-attacks. Until reports and observation had established exactly what had taken place and where, and the disposition of both hostile and friendly troops, Bavarian guns and mortars were likely to leave the area relatively unmolested.

Having established that the enemy trenches were firmly in Australian hands, 8 Field Company, assisted by reserves from the 30th Battalion, commenced the northern communication sap across No Man's Land.

This vital work demanded—under fire—the digging and subsequent linking of 'potholes' over a distance of almost 130 metres with a view to creating a continuous trench. In the first instance it was to act as an artery for supply and communication, but the ultimate plan was to develop it into the new Australian front line. The raised lips of the mine crater screened only a limited part of this area, making it a ghastly exercise. Men in parties of two or three per hole were forced to generate cover by sheer determination and muscle power. There was no opportunity to return fire—every pair of hands was required to wield picks and shovels. For their salvation they relied upon covering fire from comrades in the trenches.

Commander of the 8th Brigade, Brigadier-General Edwin Tivey, had suggested the sap scheme on 17 July. Division's response was that it was impracticable in daylight, but could go ahead as long as precautions were taken to avoid casualties from hostile machine guns, especially on the left flank. Bavarian artillery seems not to have been taken into consideration. Although toil continued after sunset, the costly creation was never to be manned as a fire trench.

Nowhere did the Bavarian positions resemble what the Australians had been led to expect. The slumped remains of the old 1914 trench they now held was indeed presently employed as a drain by the Bavarians, marked on their maps as a *Wassergraben*—a ditch receiving water pumped from dugouts and shelters. Rimmed with nettles and thistles, it contained old barbed wire, the mixed detritus of trench warfare . . . and the kind of mud uniquely generated by Flanders clay. It was with this 'running muck' that for hour upon hour the Diggers were destined to fill sandbags to create a primitive protective parapet, while at the same time trying to keep rifle mechanisms clean and anxiously awaiting support and vital supplies.

On the far left flank the 32nd Battalion's most critical task was to find a way to permanently withstand lateral assault from IIa, for it was here that their enemy was certain to strive to infiltrate. Suitable places for blocks needed to be located. Digger patrols probed along the *Dannergraben* (the Bavarian support line) east of the *Kastenweg* (also, a little confusingly, referred to as the *Kastengraben or Kistengraben*), a 2-metre-high double breastwork built of boxes filled with earth, the 'trench' being formed between them.

Facing them, Luther's 9/RIR 21 were equally concerned that their line might also be 'rolled up' eastwards:

The enemy tried repeatedly to push into the Conventionsgraben [communication route running centrally through IIa] *with weak forces, but was prevented from leaving the position by our lively fire. When the enemy had reached sector IIb, it was observed that he was moving forward into the Kistengraben and digging in there. There was brisk traffic between the two positions, with ammunition boxes, sandbags, etc, being carried over. This was disrupted as much as possible with infantry and MG fire.*

On the left flank of sector IIa, a shot-up section of trench was used as a natural barrier, but this was not attacked by the enemy, who evidently did not wish to spread out to the right. From his lodgement in the Kistengraben, the enemy began firing at the new position N in the Conventionsgraben, which has no cover against the left flank. The commander of the left-hand platoon (Leutnant Eckinger) thereupon detailed a section to return fire on the Kistengraben.

At about 7.00 p.m. it was noticed that the enemy was working his way along the Dannergraben and had already reached position a, presumably intending to attack the left-hand platoon from the rear. A patrol was sent into the Dannergraben and drove the enemy back with hand grenades, leaving an officer and 15 men dead in the trench. 8–10 men who were trying to reach trench IIb were shot down. The patrol pressed forward up the Dannergraben to a point level with the left flank of IIa and held off further attempts by the enemy to break through at that point.

As there was a danger that the very weak trench garrison of the left-hand platoon sector might not be able to withstand a determined assault from the flank, repeated requests were made for support for this sector, but none came.

Luther, OC 9/RIR 21

The Diggers' remodelling of Bavarian communication trenches now began. This primarily entailed the creation of McCay's 'double-blocks':

twin barriers of wire, timber, sandbags and earth. The theory was that while the enemy were occupied in trying to break through the first block, they could be bombed back from the cover of the second. It was a delicate exercise, because although the Mills grenade carried greater destructive power, a German stick bomb could be thrown considerably further.

The Australian bombers defending the block on the *Kastenweg* were commanded by a young bank clerk from Peterborough by the name of Lieutenant Eric Chinner, a name that will reappear later in this story. Some 30 metres in front of his 'new line' and adjacent to the *Kastenweg*, an advanced post equipped with a Lewis gun was established to cover the trench and its new blocks, and suppress hostile fire from the farm to the east and copses and buildings to the north. A heavier weapon, a Vickers, was positioned where the ditch and *Kastenweg* abutted. In command there was another bank clerk, Lieutenant M.A. Lillecrapp.

The complex sub-sector that the *Kastenweg* served is today largely covered by woodland, but at that time it was open ground. The area required resolute defence because within a lateral distance of 150 metres, two further communication routes—the *Rodergraben* and the *Saugra-ben* (which forked)—joined the front line, one on either side of *Tote Sau* (Delangré Farm). Including the Bavarian front and support lines, there were therefore six means of sheltered hostile access to the Australian left flank. Each demanded clearing, sealing, observing and defending, which meant heavy labour, an unbroken supply of grenades, the finding or fabri-cating of secure and dominating locations for machine guns and Stokes mortars, and lucid, decisive command. If this could be accomplished and the sap across No Man's Land completed, the 32nd's defensive prospects were considerably less daunting, because except for Delangré Farm, the surrounding terrain was virtually free of orchards, woods, hedgerows and copses: it presented an expansive and supremely functional field of fire.

The Diggers quickly found themselves short of vital matériel. Because they had not expected to have to construct a new defensive line, each man had been ordered to bring across just two sandbags; every third man carried a pick or shovel. These simple tools now replaced rifles and grenades as the most critical elements of salvation and success. Messages were urgently despatched by both runner and pigeon: more tools, more sandbags, more men—as soon as possible. After half an hour the Bavarians of RIR 21 were beginning to glean the scale of the Diggers' territorial ambitions: although a strong force had installed itself, the troops displayed no signs of a thrust towards the ridge. It was a little puzzling. Ironically, both sides were now creating trench blocks for the purpose of containing each other, and yet the only troops anxious to press forward were in fact the Bavarians.

The assault of the 31st Battalion followed a similar course to that of the 32nd. Orders were to leave the trench, negotiate their own wire, form an attacking line and lie down in No Man's Land. While the bombardment played upon the enemy parapet the troops would advance as one to the enemy wire, wait until the guns lengthened range, and then invade on the whistle. Watching fall of shot for almost an hour before the assault, battalion commander Lieutenant-Colonel Fred Toll gauged that many Allied shells were falling some 40 metres *beyond* the enemy breastwork. Adjustments were ordered and at 4.45 p.m. they started dropping on and behind *his own* positions. Toll's notes (later supplied to Charles Bean for his *OHA*) tell a torturous tale, tragically concluding: 'It will be seen that our casualties prior to attack were heavy and unfortunately very many must be accounted to our own artillery dropping short. Just prior to launching the attack the enemy bombardment was hellish, and it seemed as if they knew accurately the time set.' When the guns finally lifted the required 100 yards (90 metres) (indicating the narrowness of No Man's Land in the sector), a somewhat weaker assault force than anticipated rose to cross the Bavarian wire. The entanglements were adequately cut, which made for swift entry, but this battalion too had been deprived of many an officer and NCO in the period before attack.

Once the Diggers entered enemy territory, little quarter was given: there was no time or place for chivalry. Dugouts were systematically bombed. Bavarians were again seen taking flight, but Toll's Diggers were forbidden to follow. A few small RIR 21 parties escaped the carnage, creeping back to hole up at the *Türkenecke* and *Brandhof* strongpoints, there delivering the very first reports to comrades eager to hear the news and devise responses.

The second wave of Diggers had crossed by 6.00 p.m. Toll himself appeared with the last, following the Lewis guns which on arrival were set up in commanding positions alongside those of the 32nd Battalion: on top of the old enemy parapet where an optimum view of potential hostile activity might be had. At 7.14 p.m. the battalion was well established and able to report: 'Four waves well over 200 yards beyond enemy's parapets no enemy works found yet so am digging in.'

Why the target trenches—so clear to intelligence staff during their scrutiny of aerial photographs and upon which the objective of the entire enterprise had been based—did not appear to exist on the ground is one of the most peculiar aspects of the Fromelles story. As Charles Bean already knew from his own 'interpretation training' just a few weeks before, in aerial photographs breastworks and ditches bear little resemblance to each other: the first cast a deep shadow, the second do not. Light-reflecting water-filled channels would have been difficult to mistake for a constructed trench. The reason for the misinterpretation still remains a mystery. With the purpose of garnering precisely this kind of essential information, Allied balloon observers had minutely scrutinised the prospective battleground, and RFC airmen had flown scores of low-level missions.

Nevertheless, the same unsatisfactory saturated drain as occupied by the 32nd Battalion was presented to the 31st. It too offered meagre cover against fire from Les Clochers village and other isolated buildings and copses to the front, and was equally open to enfilade from Delangré Farm. The scarcity of officers and NCOs loaded a heavy responsibility upon the shoulders of those left in command, the majority of whom had never experienced action before. The Diggers were occupying unfamiliar terrain; they were short of time, matériel, protection and personnel, and under fire from their own guns as well as those of the enemy. The ground ahead was broken only by hedges and rows of trees; it was definitely devoid of trenches. There were a few buildings in sight, and of course the village on the hill—Fromelles— which now had evidence of burning fires. Unknown to the Bavarians, it was under no threat whatsoever.

As the men of the 31st dug for their lives, Colonel Toll, Lieutenant G. Still and a runner made a probing reconnaissance in search of more functional positions, creeping forward along a partially constructed communication trench (the *Rodergraben*) to reach a ditch bordering a road. Later Fred Toll was unable to tell Charles Bean exactly where this point was, but Bavarian records show it to be a few metres west of the

junction of D222 from Fromelles and the Rue Delvas. In open ground on
the far side of the road—known to the Bavarians as the *Graben-Strasse*—
lay a wired and fire-bayed trench. It was the *Schmitzgraben*, the western
extremity of the *Stutzpunkt Türkenecke,* one of RIR 21's key intermediate
defensive strongpoints. From here, the trench stretched some 350 metres
eastward, linking with the *Kastenweg,* at the far end of which the
32nd Battalion were at that moment battling with hostile bombers—and
mud. At such a distance from the front line, the *Schmitzgraben* could not
possibly be the objective.

Retracing his steps, Toll found his men trying to coordinate their defence
with elements of the 54th Battalion on the right flank. Soon afterwards
Toll's troops made contact with the 32nd on the left. Albeit fractured and
gappy, the Diggers were now forming a definite line between the *Kastenweg*
and Rouges Bancs. At 8.50 p.m. the 8th Brigade was informed by Toll that
the ground up to 350 yards (320 metres) beyond the enemy front line had
been explored without finding 'trenches or works of any kind to consolidate, merely open ditches full of water'.

On Toll's right the 14th Australian Brigade's prospects of capturing
at least the enemy front line had also been favourable, for their front
incorporated a substantial narrow stretch of No Man's Land. Being the
middle of the three Australian assaulting brigades, the key task for the
four companies of the 53rd and 54th Battalions was to secure the enemy
breastworks while at the same time remaining in contact with colleagues
from the 8th Brigade to the left and the 15th to the right. Their sector
commenced at the *Tommy-Brücke* and included the *Tommy-Strasse,* thus
incorporating the area occupied by today's Memorial Park. Unlike his
May 1915 predecessors, General McCay had elected not to employ the old
1914 trenches as advanced jumping-off points, so distances to the enemy
line ranged from 120 metres on the left (54th Battalion) by the road, to
280 metres on the right (53rd) next to the bridge.

Both the preparations for assault and the initial results were similar
to their 8th Brigade neighbours: the leading companies, C and D, were to
attack at 5.50 p.m. and 5.53 p.m. respectively. At 4.45 p.m. messages stated
that everything was 'going well', with observers reporting the enemy parapet
'in ruins'. Again, while moving forward and assembling in the congested

and battered trenches the Diggers suffered significant loss to artillery, both hostile and friendly. The OC, Lieutenant-Colonel W. Cass, later reported that the accuracy of enemy gunfire was so fine that he was certain that 'not only did the enemy know we were coming but that they could see the advance'. Cass himself was blown over while crossing No Man's Land, but was able to carry on. Upon the charge at 6.00 p.m. only a few Bavarians were in evidence: it was assumed that they had evacuated to escape the shelling. The battle report of 11 Company, previously quoted, reveals that this was indeed partly true.

At around 5.00 p.m. the 53rd Battalion had deployed behind the Australian lines in front of Le Trou behind the Orchard. Their arrival coincided with the fiercest hostile artillery concentrations of the day. Bavarian gunners were well aware that this was the principal opportunity to wither enemy ranks before the attack. With every communication trench choked with men hugging the walls, plus dead and wounded on all sides, confusion and turmoil reigned. Following orders, the troops rose from the crowded support line to move forward some 200 metres across open ground into the forward trench, from where they were to hop the bags into No Man's Land. Some found their own wire entanglements had not been properly cleared to assist the passage. Reflecting the events of 1 July on parts of the Somme battlefield, many Diggers were cut down before they could reach their own front line.

Under cover of the bombardment the first waves crept forward to form up on the far side of No Man's Land before the enemy wire; it was adequately cut. At 6.00 p.m., followed by three further waves at 100-yard (90-metre) spacing, they rose and charged the Bavarian line, quickly capturing both the front and support positions and throwing out patrols some 200 metres beyond to counter any initial hostile response. While the captured positions were prepared for defence, other parties struck out to the right to link with comrades of the 60th Battalion of the 15th Brigade. The 53rd's casualties at this early stage were slight, although one key casualty was their OC, Lieutenant-Colonel I.B. Norris, who was fatally hit soon after entering the enemy position. By contrast, Cass's 54th suffered a crippling catalogue of losses before and during the assault: there were no less than twelve officer casualties, three of whom were dead.

Despite this, prospects at Rouges Bancs looked fair, for once more the enemy had clearly been decimated. The 14th Brigade had produced a surprise attack upon trenches that were practically undefended; RIR 21's machine-gun capabilities lay in tatters; the Australian guns and mortars had excelled, paving the way for the infantry. That morning von Braun had had nine weapons deployed in his front line: six German, one English, one French and one Russian. At 9.00 a.m. a German gun was damaged and despatched by trench tramway for repair (it was returned at 6.00 a.m. the following morning). All the rest were crippled or buried before the attack— exactly what had been planned.

RIR 20 despatched two weapons to assist on the right flank in sector IIa. The first, a Russian gun commanded by *Infanterist* Bärnreuther, was probably the cause of many casualties among the 32nd Battalion, for it was this weapon that enfiladed men trying to create cover in the ditches, and drove back groups of Diggers pushing north along the *Danner-graben* and through the *Kastengraben*. The second, under *Leutnant* Püls, was positioned to command movements on the Australian left flank: it was responsible for many a casualty to support troops and runners, and to the vulnerable parties digging the eastern sap across No Man's Land.

At 8.15 p.m. *Oberst* Weiss, commander of RIR 20, and von Braun, commander of RIR 21, conferred. The situation remained unchanged and apparently unchanging, so the potential of a flanking attack through IIa was examined. Weiss had already organised all his reserves, including cable-layers, water-supply personnel and company artisans; he also had two ammunition wagons and one *Pionier* cart loaded with hand grenades held in readiness to move forward. He would be able to act as soon as orders were issued. But it was not yet time—6 BRD still had no accurate grasp of the magnitude of the assault, the ground lost, or the aspirations of their foe.

Having broken into the enemy positions astride the *Tommy-Strasse* most Diggers turned left, only a few men swinging right to try to link with the 60th Battalion along the northern flank of the Sugar Loaf. According to Bavarian reports, theirs was the very first hostile entry. It took place in the area of today's Memorial Park:

Between 5.30 and 6.00pm the enemy broke into the left-hand platoon positions with extraordinarily strong forces, completely undetected, as both look-outs in the left-hand platoon sector had been killed. By the time the alarm was raised in the centre platoon sector, the enemy had already occupied the left-hand platoon sector as far back as the trench tramway line and was fanning out towards the rear. In the right-hand platoon sector, the assault was vigorously resisted with all available hand grenades and a number of rifles until the enemy force eventually succeeded in overwhelming the weak trench garrison by enveloping it from both sides, while also attacking it head-on in ever increasing strength. The right-hand platoon sector remained under hostile artillery and trench mortar fire throughout the enemy assault. During this part of the action Leutnant Wolf, 11/RIR21, and Leutnant Wagner of the MG company were both killed. The company commander, Leutnant Hain, was wounded. By the time that Vizefeldwebel Aal and the men who had remained with him in the Company commander's dugout, some of whom were already wounded, were alerted to the situation by a medical corporal and an infantryman, the enemy had already broken in to both the left-hand and right-hand platoon positions. He [Aal] succeeded in fighting his way through to the Brandhof with part of the company. Seventeen men who had been in the right-hand platoon sector retired to the Türkenecke and joined up with the 2nd Company. Vizefeldwebel Aal placed himself and the remainder of the company at the disposal of the officer commanding the company holding the Brandhof, Leutnant Frank (3rd Company, RIR 21), and was directed to barricade the Schützenstrasse, the new communication trench leading to IId, and was then employed to reinforce the garrison at the Brandhof and to reconnoitre towards the Grashof.

The unwounded survivors were questioned, but no further information could be obtained.

Action Report, II Battalion,
21st Bavarian Reserve Infantry Regiment, 21.7.16

The most effective Australian tactical manoeuvre of the assault phase took place here; ironically, it is also where the battle would later be terminated. Whereas upon their arrival in enemy territory the neighbouring 8th Brigade almost instantly faced vigorous hostile pressure, at Rouges Bancs the situation for the 14th Brigade appeared considerably healthier. Minimal resistance gave them time and space. They found three clearly defined trenches. The first had a good 8-foot- (2.4-metre-) high parapet; the second—ten metres behind—contained basic sleeping dugouts. In the third the Diggers encountered comfortable billets, including headquarters dugouts. All could be made eminently defensible. Except on the left, the second line was in good condition, while an early message noted the third to be 'damaged in places but not much'. This was excellent news as, using matériel to hand, they could be quickly re-engineered to form a functional new front line.

The first essential tasks were to set up advanced posts to warn of enemy approach, and to establish union with the 15th Brigade, whose assault upon the Sugar Loaf was well underway. For an hour there was no contact, but at 7.18 p.m. they received their first message. It held a certain degree of promise: the 14th Brigade was informed by the 15th that '60th Battalion had taken front line and were bombing support line', and that the 8th Brigade was in the enemy's second line but 'now being shelled by own artillery'.

The latter was true—again the Allied guns had failed to lengthen their range. The former, however, was only partly accurate. A handful of 60th Battalion men had managed to enter enemy territory, but only by drifting left of their objective and sliding in alongside the 53rd Battalion: they were not in the Sugar Loaf. What the message omitted—because no one knew—was that the rest of their comrades in both the 60th and 59th Battalions were either dead, pinned down in No Man's Land, or back in their original line. No Digger was in any part of the Sugar Loaf. The 60th Battalion war diary is painfully brief:

Battalion established in [Australian] *front line trench by 4.20, Lewis guns excepted, a few casualties having occurred, some serious. Battalion scaled parapet and advanced in four waves, the first wave leaving at 6.45, the last at 7. Each wave advanced under very heavy artillery, machine gun and rifle fire, suffering very heavy casualties. Advance continued to within 90 yards of enemy trenches. The attack was held up, although it is believed some few of the battalion entered enemy trenches.*

From the moment the 7.18 p.m. message arrived, the only additional Bavarian territory that would be subsequently occupied by any Digger unit would be ground that was penetrated strictly against corps and divisional orders. Just seventy-eight minutes into the action, Australian and British progress at Fromelles had already reached an end. The awful unfolding of the battle's nucleus was about to begin.

Chapter 12

THE CARBUNCLES

><><

On the morning of 19.7 the whole of the Regimental sector came under heavy artillery and trench mortar fire, which at times also lifted to the strongpoints and communication trenches. At 1.00 p.m. the Battalion commander in the front line reported intense artillery fire, characteristic of an imminent raid, on the whole of Sector III. At about 4.00 p.m. it was reported that 'Some of the sentries in IIIb have seen English troops in no-man's land'. As the shelling continued and did not diminish in intensity, the Regimental staff set out for the command post at Meierhof at 4.30 p.m. and arrived there at 5.10 p.m.

Report on the action at Fromelles, 22.7.16, by *Oberstleutnant* Spatny, commander of 16th Bavarian Reserve Infantry Regiment, defending the Sugar Loaf Salient

The attacks on the Sugar Loaf on 19 July 1916 are, partly as a result of the Fromelles Project, almost as deeply engraved in the collective Australian psyche as any event in the nation's history. Most commentators portray the salient itself as being relatively small, comprising solely a blunt 'head' bristling with machine guns and rifles. Yet it is not the physical scale of the feature that we should be examining, but its influence within the wider Bavarian defensive scheme. The salient stretched across 1400 metres of battlefront and incorporated three Bavarian company sub-sectors. Unlike in the Cordonnerie, Red Lamp (which included the Wick Salient) and Fauquissart sectors, much of the enemy line here was too distant a target for Allied offensive mining (tunnelling) to be worthwhile. It could be captured only by the traditional fusion of artillery and infantry.

The plan was to have the 184th Brigade (61st Division) seize the enemy front line at the tip of the salient. Following on from that, the Diggers would assault the long northern flank, and surge through to link with the Tommies and consolidate the support system in the salient's interior beyond the *Leierbach* (Laies Brook). The objective was to create a robust defensive chord some 375 metres beyond the snout that might be linked with the captured trenches on either flank. It was less a traditional pincer movement than a coordinated convergence of forces.

The responsibility for taking the salient's head and therefore producing the initial advantage, upon which final success could be built, lay squarely upon the shoulders of the 184th Brigade—in particular, the troops of the 2/1st Bucks and 2/4th Berks. Their 18 July operation orders insisted it was 'vital for the success of the attack that the whole of our assaulting line is deployed in No Man's Land as close to the enemy's parapet as possible during our bombardment'. It was a complex request to fulfil because in the Sugar Loaf sub-sector the enemy was so distant, even from the extremities of the Rhondda Sap (known to the Bavarians as *Australierstellung*). By reason of the long grass and numerous ditches, it may have been possible to clandestinely reach an effective assault position in No Man's Land, but not in daylight. Deployment during the hours of darkness the night before battle, and then waiting all day for the assault with all the hazards that occasioned, was unthinkable. The troops were stepping into the unknown.

When the time came on 19 July, while moving forward and forming up, both battalions were pounded by enemy artillery; once in the saps and No Man's Land, they continued to sustain losses. The cause was quite plain:

they had been seen—hours before the assault. Long grass and ditches were no longer the saviours they had once seemed.

At 2.35 p.m. Bavarian observers reported '*Engländer* lying in No Man's Land in front of their own wire opposite IIIa, and the *Australierstellung* occupied'. The men were by no means 'close up' to the enemy line. For almost three hours before the assault, artillery and mortar fire was concentrated upon the area. Two extra batteries on the Aubers Ridge turned their muzzles towards the sector. At 4.00 p.m. sentries in the Bavarian breastworks reported, 'English troops in No Man's Land'; at 5.45 p.m., on the very threshold of assault, more were spotted, 'forming up in No Man's Land in front of IIIB'; Battery 4 opened independent fire on the sector. This time the '*Engländer*' were Australians. The narrative of 3 Company RIR 16 described the measures put in place to deal with an assembling enemy:

> *Flanking battery Giesing was ordered to put out observers in the direction of command post BIII and to open fire on sight of a red signal flare.*
>
> *At 4.20pm all the telephone lines to the front line were knocked out. Visual communication with the front line was established via Starnberg. At 4.30pm two runners were sent to each of the sub-sectors, a, b, c, and d, to ascertain the situation in the front line. At around 5.00pm runners arrived from the companies themselves and reported that the front line was under intense drumfire, casualties were heavy, and the trenches were badly damaged.*
>
> *At 5.45pm flare signals calling for barrage fire went up all along our Regimental front, and our light and heavy artillery, which had been continuously engaged in counter-battery work against the enemy artillery since midday, went over immediately to barrage fire on sight of the signals. Wurm's group and the heavy artillery had already been requested by the commander of III/RIR 16 on 18.7 to concentrate especially heavy fire on the Australierstellung if barrage fire was called for.*
>
> *Flanking battery Giesing opened fire on command when the barrage fire signal was launched from BIII* [RIR 16 central command post].

A torrent of shellfire fell upon the advanced saps. Before battle was joined, it had depleted the ranks of 2/4th Berks and 2/1st Bucks by at least

140 rifles. To further compound difficulties, the previous day A Company of the Bucks had lost seventy-eight men to a burst toxic-gas cylinder (the culprit was said to have been an Allied shell), one of many still remaining in the trenches after the aborted 17 July attack. Despite the best efforts of the Special Brigade and attached infantry, there had been insufficient time to clear all the gas installations. Now, with the troops waiting, inert and under concentrated hostile fire, they were an added hazard. Reserves were pushed in to replenish gaps in the ranks, but with the 61st Division now mustering an average battalion combat strength of just 600, as 6.00 p.m. approached the 184th Brigade was already in a serious predicament.

The distance the troops were required to traverse demanded that each piece of the battle plan fell neatly into place—starting with neutralisation of resistance by Allied artillery. If this was ineffective, the British were in serious danger of being too weak to seize the objective. Six hours before the assault the ineffectiveness of Allied counter-battery fire was already apparent.

Across No Man's Land the Bavarians were aware that defensive artillery had to react instantly. To make the shooting pay dividends, gunners had only the time it took for hostile troops to cross No Man's Land. Once they had made an incursion, pre-laid fire patterns were not exactly redundant, because the guns were useful against supporting waves, but they had failed in the primary aspiration. The less time it took an assault force to cross the killing zone, the more likely it was to flourish, hence the requirement for troops to steal their way as close as possible to the enemy before an attack began, while still leaving sufficient safe space for 'friendly' artillery to do their work on enemy wire and trenches.

In this sector the attacks of Tommy and Digger, although coordinated, were not conjoined at source. At the deepest part of the shared re-entrant facing the Sugar Loaf there was left a 300-metre gap between the two attacking brigades. It was filled with nine machine guns, their crews tasked to spray the opposing parapet and keep Bavarian heads low as the dual assault was made. The guns' utility depended upon a) being able to focus upon the enemy positions through the dust and smoke of both their own bombardment and hostile retaliatory fire; and b) the convergence of the twin infantry forces not taking place too soon, i.e. men straying into their

field of fire. When zero arrived for the British and Australian infantry, the
Sugar Loaf was indeed visible, but as was so often the case, as soon as
the assaulting troops came under fire, control and direction were quickly
lost. A recurrent feature of trench warfare was that this critical flaw was
never immediately apparent. Messages from Brigadier-General Elliott at
15th Brigade HQ to Division were initially encouraging but, as the true
situation began to emerge, their tone changed dramatically:

> *6.45 p.m. 59th Battalion held up half way across No Man's Land. Heavy
> casualties. 60th Battalion and others appear to have got across.*
>
> *7.18 p.m. Report from 59th that they cannot get on . . . the trenches are
> full of the enemy and every man who rises is shot down . . . report from
> wounded indicate the attack is failing for want of support.*
>
> *7.33 p.m. F.O.O. reports (message delayed) enemy observed retreat-
> ing across the open from N.8.d.4.0* [head of Sugar Loaf] *to their
> support trench.*
>
> *7.50 p.m. Reinforcements appear to be badly needed along all our
> fronts . . . at present we are just hanging on with men in some places
> of front trench . . . Greenway reports 59 and 60* [Battalion] *casualties
> very severe.*

The FOOs were all mistaken. There were no Diggers or Tommies in the
Bavarian 'front trench'. At 7.00 p.m. the 61st Division also believed that
British infantry had entered the Sugar Loaf, leading XI Corps to report at
7.25 p.m.:

> *Right and left Brigades 61st Division reported in enemy's trenches and
> enemy is shelling his own front trenches opposite centre Brigade from
> which inference is that brigade is in enemy's line although no definite
> report to that effect yet received. 5th Aust. Div. report attack of right
> brigade appears successful and musketry fire by enemy has practically
> ceased. Centre Brigade occupy enemy's trenches in front of Rouge Bancs.*

Quite how the conclusion that the Bavarians were shelling their own
trenches was reached is not revealed. It took two hours for the situation

to become clearer. Only at 8.00 p.m. was the 61st Division able to clarify the true situation: '184th Brigade report that they have not taken German trenches on their front . . . Germans still hold Sugarloaf.'

Once underway the attack must have been a shocking sight. The account of 11 Company RIR 16 is as unadorned as any in the Munich archives, and all the more pungent for being so:

Re: the English attack

Having lifted their artillery barrage the English leapt over the parapet or left their trenches via masked exits [sally-ports]. After leaving the trench they initially formed dense groups, then attempted to deploy in an attacking line. These lines [the attacking waves] then proceeded to assault but failed to keep formation. The enemy tried four or five times to form such lines but were mostly shot down whilst still in groups and before they could organise.

Some of the Australians only left the trench hesitantly, and this is when their officers moved up with drawn revolvers and tried to move them forward. It then became obvious which were the officers and they were immediately shot down.

Some groups that began to withdraw were apparently encouraged to renew the attack by those still in the trenches; they quickly fell to our machine-gun and infantry fire like the others, if they had not already been cut down by our artillery. The enemy were clearly of the belief that our defences had been so weakened that we would be easily overcome, so when we opened fire they were completely taken by surprise and lost their heads. In a diary that we found, the entry for 19th [July] reads: 'We are now about to take the German trenches; we think this will be very easy'. The failure of the attack in sector III is probably due mainly to the fact that our observers continued to pass on information in the most selfless fashion. Most of the losses in our battalion were amongst the observers. When one was killed, the next stepped up to the parapet and continued the work without any order having to be given. They spotted an attack was underway when they saw the first enemy troops leave their trenches, and just a few seconds later the entire garrison was at the parapet ready to fire, so the advantage of a surprise was foiled.

The writer, *Hauptmann* Hans Gebhardt (the battalion commander), employs not a single triumphalist adjective; one can almost detect a sense of regret. There was actually no more that needed to be said: the enemy was clearly as green as any that had ever been asked to perform such a daunting task, and well-laid plans executed by experienced and well-drilled Bavarian units had snuffed out their endeavour.

Part of the reason for Allied failure lay in the time it took to open sally-ports, the small 'doorways' through the breastworks selected by Haking as his preferred method of egress into No Man's Land. Although the ports had been largely completed the evening before, a thin 'skin' of sandbags was left in order to camouflage British intentions and avoid Bavarian attentions until the whistles blew. Given the chaos in the trenches as a result of hostile shellfire, sappers were unable to open all ports at the same time. They also found that the exit points became congested by their own men trying to leave. It led to catastrophic delays in deployment, the troops appearing and trying to form waves in No Man's Land over a period of several minutes instead of 'as one' as Haking desired. That delay conferred upon the enemy a tremendous advantage in both observation and response. They could distinguish not only the exits, but gauge the strength of the assault by the numbers appearing. Men who clambered over parapets were plain to see.

The war diary of the 2/1st Bucks describes the hostile fire as 'annihilating'. Those who reached positions close to the enemy line went to ground and waited for dark; they were few. Of a combat strength of around 600, the battalion sustained 322 casualties. Survivors later reported the wire at the Sugar Loaf being uncut, but Bavarian reports show this to be false; the truth was that hardly a single Allied soldier had been permitted to reach it.

In his later appreciation of lessons learned, Gebhardt noted 'the fact that the enemy attack was so completely repulsed is mainly attributable to the deployment of large numbers of machine-guns in the front line'. We now know that, of the ten deployed (eight German, two British) across the RIR 16 sector, four were in the Sugar Loaf itself, with only two in its apex, each covering a separate quadrant. A deal of damage was done by flanking weapons to the south-west. The same record reveals that not one gun was used from within cover, i.e. through pillbox loopholes: all were deployed from the parapets. Although numerous casualties were sustained by Bavarian gun crews, the enemy was brought to his knees long before the situation became remotely critical. In every case, Gebhardt deemed the standard issue of between six and seven thousand rounds of ammunition per gun 'sufficient'.

The machine guns did not work alone, of course. The same document records RIR 16 *Minenwerfers* firing 'continuously on the attacking enemy as long as their ammunition held out. In particular where they gathered in groups, the enemy suffered heavy casualties from our MW fire.' Once targets in No Man's Land had been neutralised, the weapons were free to re-focus on the British and Australian trenches; by the end of the battle supplies of ammunition were exhausted.

As regards small arms, by 11.00 p.m. on 19 July in sector IIIa—the nose of the Sugar Loaf—each Bavarian rifleman had an average of just thirty rounds left. This was despite ammunition being taken up to the front line as soon as the assaults began by specially trained carriers assisted by troops from support units. Every runner, stretcher-bearer and reinforcement going forward also delivered vital provisions. 'In total', said Gebhardt, 'some 2,500 hand grenades (packed in sandbags), 35,000 rounds of small arms ammunition, 60 boxes of machine-gun ammunition, 200 mortar rounds and quantities of light and signal flares were carried up to the front line'. The huge expenditure can be put down to the fact that across the battleground, but especially east of the Sugar Loaf, targets were constantly present.

It will be noted that Hans Gebhardt's 26 July action report is unique in being the only one that mentions both English and Australian troops in the same document, the reason probably being that 11 Company garrisoned sub-sector b of sector III: the apex of the Sugar Loaf. It was thus the only unit to simultaneously defend assaults by the Australian 59th Battalion, 2/1st Bucks and 2/4th Berks. It was Gebhardt's men who should have been cowed by Allied artillery and the machine guns located in the re-entrant. Despite No Man's Land being narrower on the Sugar Loaf's eastern flank, for the Diggers of the 59th and 60th Battalions initial results were almost identical:

At 5.45pm the enemy artillery fire lifted once more to the rear and the enemy infantry left their trenches, some over the parapet and others through previously prepared and carefully concealed sally ports. The enemy advanced towards our trenches in dense waves, carrying scrambling ramps and mats with them. In front of IIIa [60th Battalion] the enemy ignited several smoke-pots.

Our trench garrison was immediately alerted by the sentries and hurried to the breastworks. A barrage of machine-gun, small-arms and artillery fire mowed down the attacking enemy like a scythe. Only a small number reached our wire and were shot down there, while the remainder tried in vain to retire to their trenches.

Again, Haking's lifts were hardly noticeable. The only option now open to divisional commanders Mackenzie and McCay was to renew the bombardment where assault had met with failure, and hope that the present incursions were strong enough to resist until more successful attempts could be mounted. After the battle Gebhardt described the effects of Allied artillery in relation to RIR 16 protective measures in sector III:

4. *Protection against artillery and trench mortar fire: the mined dug-outs provided shell-proof refuges for some of the trench garrison during hostile disruptive fire of short duration. The entrances of these need to be made more secure with reinforced concrete frames.*

To avoid the risk of being taken by surprise during an attack, the mined dug-outs were evacuated, in accordance with standing orders, as soon as the drumfire barrage began. They were then used to good effect as telephone posts and emergency dressing stations. The mined dug-out at Starnberg [a command post in the Hintergelände] was used during the action to shelter reserves.

The artillery shelters afforded the men protection against shell splinters, but in a number of instances the concrete roof was penetrated by a medium-calibre shell or the shelter was completely destroyed by a direct hit because too little concrete had been used in its construction. As each shelter was occupied by 3–5 men, this resulted in substantial casualties.

The most effective cover the trench garrison was able to find was
by lying on the floor of the trench, under the firestep, or in the niches
of the traverses. Direct hits then only took out individual men, and
when the alarm came, every man was able to quickly assume his
appointed position.

The report flies in the face of received knowledge: the Allied bombardment was indeed effective at the Sugar Loaf. What was required was more
accurate and more prolonged shooting with heavier-calibre weapons.
Aside from the quality of XI Corps' planning and the talents of the
gunners, time and the weather had disallowed it. The Bavarians' own
defensive barrage was described as 'excellent', with the guns laying down
an 'impenetrable curtain of fire in front of our trenches' and respond-
ing 'impeccably to the demands of the infantry'. Signal flares—perfected
in recent months—calling for barrage fire were 'clearly seen and recognised, even in daylight'. Every British and Australian account adds force
to these fateful words, for at no point within and around the Sugar Loaf
were troops able to pierce the enemy line. In his battle report RIR 16
commander *Oberstleutnant* Spatny later noted, '*Not one of the English troops*
entered the RIR 16 sector' (italics reproduced as in the original document).
Spatny is, of course, referring to both British and Australian troops.
It was later noted in 61st Division reports that 'a number got into the
Sugar Loaf', and that the action was 'substantiated later by an eyewitness
of 15th Australian Brigade'. There is no evidence to support this statement. One message, however, contradicts Spatny. At 7.43 p.m. the
12th Bavarian Brigade received the following: 'Several groups of English
who broke into the middle section of IIId have been annihilated . . . One
MG buried in d. Sectors b, c, d absolutely firmly in our hands. There
are great masses of English dead 150 metres in front of b [the apex of
the Sugar Loaf].' Neither the war diary of the 2/6th Gloucesters, the British
unit opposite sub-sector IIId, nor the narrative of the only other battalion
who might have forced a breach, the 2/4th Gloucesters, makes any mention
of their troops reaching the enemy line.

Although Hans Gebhardt's post-battle map shows no enemy troops
reaching his line, it marks two concentrations of English casualties in a

mine-cratered No Man's Land close to the Bavarian breastwork. Another German divisional map, however, does show one incursion, so it remains possible and even probable that, unbeknown to their respective colonels and brigadiers, groups of Gloucesters—perhaps from both the 2/4th and 2/6th Battalions—entered the enemy trenches only to be 'annihilated'.

Curiously, it took a full two hours for the situation at the Sugar Loaf to become clear even to the Bavarians. Sector III (RIR 16) command post reported at 7.10 p.m. that 'Our positions appear to be still firmly in our hands.' At 7.15 p.m. was added: 'As far as we can tell, sector a is also firmly in our possession.' By 7.35 p.m. it was concluded that: 'The attack came from the Australian lines; there are large numbers of English dead lying 150m in front of the trenches. The English attacked in groups. Our losses appear to be tolerable.'

News from across the sector remained somewhat too nebulous, and perhaps even too surprising, to be accepted at face value. Commanders, remembering 'the events of 9.5.15, when our trenches were prematurely reported to have been cleared of the enemy', sought confirmation, which was received at 9.50 p.m. when two volunteer runners arrived with a single situation report—it was signed by all four regimental commanders.

Spatny's revised casualty list for the battle would later read: five officers killed and five wounded, eighty-six other ranks killed, 284 wounded and one man missing. Most of the losses, it was noted, were sustained in clashes during the coming night and the following morning. The casualties inflicted upon the enemy were to outstrip Spatny's own figure by a factor of four. But the real fight was only just beginning. Universal Allied failure left RIR 16 and 17 with ample combat strength to both defend the front line and counter lateral pressure resulting from the 14th Australian Brigade's incursion at Rouges Bancs until support and counter-attack troops arrived, a manoeuvre that had begun just ten minutes into battle.

The 15th Australian Brigade headquarters received notice of the failure of the neighbouring 184th Brigade as early as 7.35 p.m. Twenty minutes later Brigadier-General Pompey Elliott, who from his command post at Le Trou was able to hear but not see the enterprise, was requested to assist with a renewed attack. Employing part of the fresh support battalion alongside residual troops from the first assault, this was to be a yet more tragic endeavour. Elliott's report makes grim reading.

At 7.52 pm this Brigade [184th] asked us to cooperate with a fresh attack they were making at 9.00 pm. The Divisional Commander gave authority for half of the 58th Battalion to be used to support the attack . . . arrangements were completed by 8.45 pm. At 9.00 pm two companies of the 58th Battalion moved forward with great dash, carrying with them remnants of 59th Battalion, to a point about 100 yards from the enemy's trench where they were enfiladed by machine-guns in the Sugar Loaf and melted away. Major Hutchinson, who led this charge, fell riddled with bullets, close to the German parapet. At 9.37 pm the Divisional Commander informed us that the 61st Division (includes the 184th Brigade) would not renew the attack until next day. The failure of that Division to attack at 9.00 pm permitted the enemy to concentrate his whole strength at this point on our right flank.

The second assault need not have taken place. Slothful transfer of messages meant that XI Corps' order cancelling all offensive operations until the following morning did not reach the 15th Brigade until after the venture had been summarily extinguished by the Bavarians of RIR 16. According to Elliott, the reason the message did not arrive in time was because it had been sent via Division rather than direct from the 184th Brigade: there were no universal direct telephonic links between the HQs of the various brigades. An elementary mistake.

The Diggers were not entirely alone: at Red Lamp Corner the same misfortune afflicted Tupman's 2/4th Gloucesters. To their left and right the 2/6th Gloucesters and 2/6th Warwicks had both received cancellation orders at 8.20 p.m.

At 8.00pm I received an order to attack again at 9.00pm with the two companies not previously engaged—this was done, but only one Lewis Gun could be found available, three being out in No Man's Land; of the other three, one was in the reserve trench (under orders to come up), one was ready, and the third was hung up to the Right Sally Port.

The behaviour of the officers and men, under very trying circumstances was excellent and I very much regret A and D coy. did not get an opportunity of proving their mettle, as they went forward in a very gallant manner . . . after we had been driven back, there were many instances of men going out to assist to bring in wounded.

J.A. Tupman, Lt.Col. Commanding 2/4th Gloucestershire Regt.

The enemy did not recognise either assault as worth especial note, Spatny merely being moved to record:

At 9.15pm the enemy in front of IIIa launched a second attack, again with very strong forces, which was snuffed out by our artillery barrage and our MG and small-arms fire before it could develop. After the failure of this second attack, relative calm settled over Sector III. The enemy barrage fire was directed almost exclusively on Sector II. During the night of 19/20.7.16 Sector III experienced only light searching and sweeping fire; the infantry remained completely quiet.

It had been hoped that the Rhondda Sap and the other advanced trenches dug in the several months before battle would play a key role in successfully carrying the salient. Around the Sugar Loaf the width of No Man's Land varied from about 230 metres before the advanced works of the 15th Brigade to over 400 metres in front of the British 184th. Both exceeded recommendations for a successful 'trench-to-trench' attack, the latter being more than twice the suggested maximum. In August 1925 Pompey Elliott wrote to Charles Bean on the matter of the 15th Brigade, stating that he had been 'depressed by the prospect' of the attack, but that in loyalty and deference to his superiors concealed both his thoughts and feelings.

The deeply concave curvature of the line in Elliott's brigade sector lent itself to the installation of advanced jumping-off trenches. Some were largely already in place, having been dug by the 8th Division the previous year; they simply required preparation and expansion. Others were added by the Australians themselves in the weeks before the battle. Examples of the latter include a trench (the feature mentioned in Chapter 8, originally driven to attract enemy attention before a raid) that ran from the *Tommy-Brücke* to the southern corner of the Orchard, and another from the end of the Rhondda Sap towards the western corner of the Orchard. All were interconnected, and linked by communication trenches to the front line. They thus formed a multipart chord that dramatically narrowed approaches to the Sugar Loaf from the northern and north-eastern quadrants, reducing the width of No Man's Land by at least 30 per cent. All but the Rhondda Sap (ultimately shared by both Tommy and Digger) fell within Australian assaulting territory.

The Bavarians had watched the creation of this network with more than just curiosity. Their records reveal a period of what one might call counter-fieldworks, a remarkable episode where night after night in May and June 1916 freshly dug Australian trenches were backfilled by Bavarian sappers guarded by parties of infantry. The Rhondda Sap itself was more than once both reconnoitred and backfilled. A most careful weather eye was maintained on progress, and in Bavarian patrol files an extensive set of 'time-lapse' plans and reports can be found revealing in detail the development of the trenches, and a record of how many metres were backfilled each night and by whom.

This perilous Bavarian exercise was clearly impossible when their enemy was working, but it was in fact rain that created most danger, for the sploshing of earth as it was pushed back into the waterlogged trenches might be heard. Much the same happened when the British dug a chord across the re-entrant opposite the Wick Salient—their scheme received similar treatment by RIR 17.

According to Bavarian maps, the 59th Battalion's four assaulting waves universally employed the advanced jumping-off positions. In the 60th Battalion sector only the first wave used them: later assaults clambered over the original parapet. Few if any in the latter attack managed even to *reach* these trenches; indeed, because of the immediate ferocity of hostile fire, some failed to arrive at their own wire some 30 metres away. In not employing the advanced trenches to their full capacity, the Diggers offered the Bavarians a deal of extra time to react. Gebhardt's maps also show the flawed angles of initial attack followed by the 2/1st Bucks and 59th Australians.

Facing the Allies was a well-prepared, well-drilled, well-equipped regiment, fully expectant for several hours, and defending positions that had been designed to withstand molestation. In the weeks before battle, Bavarian patrols had distinguished alterations in enemy fieldworks, noted the location of potential sally-ports and ordered specific machine guns to cover the most dangerous of those exits—such as that installed near the left flank of the 60th Battalion immediately adjacent to the *Tommy-Brücke*. Two rapid-firing Lanz (light) mortars and a 37-millimetre *Grabenkanone* were ranged upon this very spot.

On Gebhardt's post-battle map there is a mass of small red crosses in front of this sally-port with the words '*Starke Feindl Verluste*': 'Many enemy dead'. The culprit was probably a machine gun at point S11 located in the front line some 140 metres north west of the Rue Delvas. From here, with minimal shift in its arc of fire, the gun had multiple utility: to target emerging troops, and to cut down men trying to cross the seven nearby bridges straddling the Laies Brook, or indeed any of the 60th Battalion who attempted to negotiate No Man's Land in the 375 metres between bridge and gun. Ironically, it appears that the weapon may have been a converted British Vickers. It was not alone; two others assisted in the task.

Bavarian machine guns produced both aimed fire upon pre-selected targets and devastating interlocking fields of enfilade. Their deployment on the evening of 19 July met every tenet in the German instruction manual. At the same time, only the most modest Allied counter-battery fire hindered the work of the gunners as they rained shrapnel and high explosive upon the battleground. The combination resulted in a slaughter that quickly replicated the ghastly scenes of 9 May 1915.

—————

Along the 61st Division front the 183rd and 184th Brigades everywhere failed to penetrate the enemy line, but the Tommies did force entry in two places at the western end of the battleground. At Devil's Jump on the extreme British right flank, the 2/7th Warwicks swiftly broke into sectors IVb and IVc. Despite the trenches being pulverised almost beyond recognition (including the destruction of two key machine guns) they almost immediately found themselves in a worse predicament than their Australian 32nd Battalion cousins on the far eastern flank. At just 150 metres wide their incursion was so narrow as to become instantly insignificant within Haking's greater scheme. By 7.30 p.m. 9 Company, RIR 17, had regained complete control of sector IVc and the left flank of IVb.

The Bavarian machine guns worked so successfully alongside the infantry, mortars and artillery that only a small force of Tommies managed a break-in. The area was immediately isolated by guns enfilading from both right and left, which explains the many dead in front of this position— not only the bodies of attacking troops, but those cut down as they later tried to make their escape; the casualties included German prisoners being sent back to the English line. Within forty minutes the 2/7th Warwicks' OC, Lieutenant-Colonel H. Nutt, was made aware that his men were under siege. He demanded a communication sap be driven across No Man's Land to connect with Devil's Jump, but before the order could be carried out it became clear that the game was already up: No Man's Land was a maelstrom of fire. Observers then confirmed that enemy troops were closing upon his men from three sides. By 10.00 p.m. when the attack had been fully contained (some fought on until the morning, but with little hope of success or escape), the Bavarian machine guns were able to be moved towards the Wick Salient to defend any fresh assault that might take place there.

Assaulting in unison, the 2/7th Warwicks' sister battalion in the 182nd Brigade, the 2/6th, also forced a breach, but one of insufficient strength to have any effect. The party that managed this feat is noted in Bavarian reports. At 8.43 p.m. 'several groups' of English are noted as having broken in elsewhere in IVb. The Warwicks' own war diary says the first waves reached the enemy parapet (of Navy Trench) and:

> . . . the leaders were seen to be inside the wire when machine guns handled with the greatest bravery by the Germans were raised on the parapet and mowed down the attackers. This was seen by our machine-gunners who at once opened on the Germans and caused them to jump down off the parapet and doubtless suffer some loss. Simultaneously with this B Company (Captain T. S. Wathes) now deployed, rushed forward carrying on the survivors of the leading Companies, and it was at one time reported that they had succeeded in entering the trenches.

Only ninety-five years later were details of their short-lived triumph confirmed. Bavarian maps show an area of Navy Trench again marked with a mass of red crosses. It appears that Captain Wathes and his party did indeed break in, but not a single man may have been left alive to tell the tale.

The neighbouring 2/4th Gloucesters assaulted out of Red Lamp Corner towards the apex of the Wick Salient—across the narrowest section of No Man's Land. Although the area was an active mining sector and Wick an ideal target, Bavarian listening and counter-mining had made it impossible for British tunnellers to plant a charge. Without this added assistance they were cut down by a gun commanded by Lance Corporal Christoff Liebl and a four-man crew.

These actions had been concentrated upon the capture of the second key carbuncle, the Wick Salient, which on 17 and 18 July the British had bombarded for several hours each day. Here it had been machine guns that had strangled British hopes. One weapon, knocked out before it was able to cause much damage, was a Vickers. The single French gun present 'proved a good weapon'. One spare gun was brought from the workshop in the *Hintergelände*. At 10.15 p.m., as fighting in the sector was drawing to a close, the regiment's two reserve guns were moved forward from the depot in Aubers. Ammunition was sent non-stop to the front line throughout the night from this same depot, with the result that a few hours after the initial assault all guns were fully provided for. It was also in this way, via carriers and runners, that communication with the front line was maintained. During the night four damaged guns were sent to Aubers for repair. Two of these were already back in position on the morning of the 20th, another on the evening of the 21st, while the fourth was despatched for further work.

The fact that not a single gun was lost to the enemy during the battle illustrates two things: the efficacy of Bavarian shelters, and the overall ineffectiveness of British artillery and mortars. RIR 17 captured three British Maxims and two Lewis guns. On 20 July they too were sent to the armourers, adapted for German use, and pronounced ready for deployment the following day, by which time the situation was considered sufficiently stable for gun numbers to return to the normal ten dispersed across the sector. The regiment was also later able to report the capture of forty-three unwounded and fourteen wounded prisoners.

The 6 BRD artillery had had no cause to occupy themselves with the RIR 17 sector. Indication of the likely area of assault during the days prior to the battle meant that the guns of the neighbouring 54th Reserve Infantry Division had plenty of time to re-lay their weapons. Without suffering any Allied counter-battery fire they were free to ravage British trenches not only opposite sector IV but also in parts of RIR 16's sector III—beyond the Wick Salient. In addition five 54th Reserve Infantry Division machine guns enfiladed No Man's Land from the west, peppered British parapets and delivered long-range barrage fire on support and communication trenches, and even molested advanced field artillery positions. The situation was mirrored at the other end of the battleground where on the Australian left flank fourteen guns of the 50th Reserve Infantry Division concentrated their fire between the Cordonnerie and Le Trou. The arrangement allowed von Scanzoni's gunners to select targets and focus their fire wherever and whenever it was required.

Haking was correct in his appreciation of 6 BRD's artillery capacity: it was hardly muscular, the total complement being sixty pieces. Capacity is one thing, however, and capability another. Against Haking's promised 348, the total number of guns in all three participating German divisions was 102.

———

By 8.15 p.m. the situation in RIR 21's sector II remained unclear. Where and how far the Australians had penetrated was still nebulous to 6 BRD. Most appeared to have gone to ground in and near the support trenches, yet two elements had clearly struck out beyond, the first towards *Grashof* and the other towards *Schmitzhof*. (It was a party of Toll's men that had been spotted 'advancing in file towards the *Schmitzhof*'.) A third had dribbled forward along the western flank of the *Kastenweg* but soon retired to dig in with machine guns; they were unlikely to move again.

There was still no counter-battery fire, and the second line on the ridge was unassailed. At 9.35 p.m. XI Corps was in 'a good deal of doubt about some of the information as communication is very difficult and interrupted'. To the Bavarians the attack was still not making any tactical sense, and no definitive indications of ultimate intent could be garnered. It made retaliatory action difficult to plan.

On the Australian right flank at Rouges Bancs Lieutenant-Colonel D. McConaghy, commanding the 55th Battalion, had on arrival in enemy territory at 10.10 p.m. expected the connection with the 15th Brigade to have been made. His two supporting companies, A and B, had earlier completed their traversal of No Man's Land with few casualties, and a telephone message from Captain N. Gibbins, OC of B Company, had informed him that although there were certain pressing material requirements and counter-attacks were expected, the troops 'can hold them easily'. McConaghy was surprised to come upon disorder and a serious shortage of officers. He despatched a reconnaissance patrol westwards along the enemy front line towards the Sugar Loaf. They did not return. A second party was halted by enemy bombers, working forward down the trench. The Diggers erected barricades, but this did not stem the advance, and the Bavarians commenced to reclaim lost ground metre by metre.

The problem here was that the Australians were split into two parallel forces. The only enemy communication trench in the area, the *Rupprecht-graben*, joined the front-line system at a point where there were not just two trenches to defend, but five; the Diggers had no choice but to block and garrison them all so that the enemy could nowhere steal unseen into their ranks. Defending this complex tangle of workings demanded significant manpower and a constant and adequate supply of ammunition and bombs, plus machine-gun cover.

The aspect of communication and supply remained the greatest difficulty, for there was no 'line' to patrol and report back from: individual parties were dispersed throughout a gridiron of unfamiliar trenches and breastworks, many being invisible to each other. Command and control could only be exercised by men on the spot. It meant that requests for manpower and matériel were slow to arrive at HQ dugouts in the newly captured lines, making it almost impossible to achieve the rapid reaction that was so critical to success.

For the Bavarians the correct timing of their counter-attacks was crucial. If the Australians intended to stay—and the indications were persuasive—they were certain to try to reinforce their positions. And if the present situation continued, von Scanzoni's planning must therefore include provision for substantial hostile movement across No Man's Land, and renewed nocturnal or dawn attacks. That the occupation of two small enclaves on both extreme flanks was not what the *Engländer* had hoped to realise was clear. But what would they do next? When night enclosed the battleground, von Scanzoni's advantage of dominant observation would vanish. For the moment, his regimental staff concentrated upon restraint and probing assaults to test enemy resistance and gauge garrison strengths.

At advanced HQs on the Australian side of No Man's Land—still under shellfire and surrounded by congested trenches and bewildered support troops, the majority as unfamiliar with their own positions as those of the enemy—there was a comparable but different form of confusion. Which parts of the attack had been successful? Where were the various units? Who was in touch with whom? How strong were the garrisons? Where was artillery support required? Messages arrived slowly and piecemeal; they had to be gradually harmonised to create even the simplest overview. Some reports never made it at all. Demands were still coming through for matériel, now including duckboards—an ominous sign. The most frequent plea was for ammunition, assistance and stretcher-bearers. Message sequences make harrowing reading:

> *7.32 Digging in here with our entrenching tools as we have nothing else and no help coming.*
> *8.25 Send all available sandbags shovels and working parties. URGENT.*
> *8.45pm. We are linked on right with 53rd and left with 32nd. Have sent fatigue party back and* <u>*must*</u> *get sandbags and shovels. Engineers have sent for pump—we are in water up to our waists in some places.*

> W.D. Harris, Captain (54th Battalion)

> *9.15pm. Flare just dropped from aeroplane. Have no pistols or flares here with which to reply, neither have I any flares for use tonight. Only illuminants as far as I can find out are one red and one white rocket*

which I have with me. Is it possible for a supply of flares and pistols to be sent here please?

H.R. Lovejoy, Lieutenant (54th Battalion)

Four hours into the action, Bavarian support was now fully mobilised and brigade and regimental reserves were either sheltering in ditches and hollows along the ridge awaiting instructions or en route from Herlies, Fournes, Wavrin, Santes and La Vallée. Every man was issued with extra pouches of ammunition and told to keep his gas mask at the ready.

As wagons loaded with ammunition and grenades converged on the sector, Allied artillery remained unfocussed. There was desultory shelling of Aubers, Fromelles and communication routes, but no concentration on obvious strongpoints in the *Hintergelände*, and minimal counter-battery fire. Within the next hour Bavarian supports had been committed, the troops resting in strongpoints and secure cover behind the Sugar Loaf. Splinter-proof shelters were prepared for sections and half-sections. There they awaited orders. Similar 14 BRB operations were taking place in the RIR 21 sector and on the eastern flank beyond Delangré Farm.

Within three hours of the assault, the results of hasty British planning were showing themselves in unnecessary suffering and needless casualties. The order remained in place: keep digging and make contact with neighbours. By 9.30 p.m. XI Corps had informed McCay that the 61st Division was 'withdrawing from the elements they have taken tonight with a view to fresh bombardment and attack tomorrow'. The men of the 14th and 8th Brigades were notified that the 5th Division would nevertheless be required to continue to hold their present positions. McCay made more troops available: two support companies of the 55th Battalion made their way across No Man's Land. This injection not only bolstered morale but finally made it numerically possible to form an almost continuous defended front.

A frightful harvest had already been reaped, but morning was still to come. Bavarian weather forecasters said the day would start still or with a weak northerly breeze. Clear after early morning mist. Rainfall: nil.

Chapter 13

THE SHORT REACHES
OF THE NIGHT

At 10.15 p.m. on 19 July when the evening light had all but faded, General James McCay received a wire from the neighbouring 3rd Canadian Division: 'Heartiest congratulations on your success', it said. A few moments later, through a message passed on by the 8th Brigade, he was made fully aware of the plight of his troops:

10.20 p.m. C.A. (31st Battalion) reports at 8.50 p.m. they have been to front as far as 300 yards in rear of front trenches, but there are no trenches to consolidate, merely open ditches full of water. Part of the battalion is attempting to consolidate but owing to heavy casualties from shell fire on front of left flank and our own rear, position is untenable. Small isolated parties are digging on our right front, apparently straightening front line. Material will be required and communication trenches opened up with our original trenches. We have suffered severely and may require assistance to hold position. Urgently require stretcher bearers and medical assistance as all bearers are casualties.

At 8.55 a thick curtain of smoke in front and cannot observe. Strength-
ening parados on first captured enemy line. Battalion broken up.
Reorganisation at present impossible. Send as many stretcher bearers
as possible. Ammunition required, also picks, shovels, sandbags, duck-
boards. 20 prisoners being sent in. 30th Battalion reports at 9 p.m.
heavy enemy artillery are firing on the trench. Can you silence them;
they are doing a lot of damage. Reports 9.10 p.m. ammunition carriers
wanted urgently to carry bombs and ammunition to front line of
trench. A Company are asking for duckboards for their new trenches.
No men are available here. I must have more men to carry forward.
32nd Battalion at 9.45 p.m. report front line cannot be held unless
strong reinforcements are sent. Enemy machine-guns are creeping
up. No star shells. The artillery is not giving support. Men bringing
sandbags are being wounded in back. Water urgently required.

This desperate missive encapsulates almost every problem faced by the
Diggers since zero. The objective was still unclear and the line fractured;
they did not know the terrain and were still enduring friendly fire; both
flanks were insecure and under pressure, and the location of the enemy and
his strength was nebulous. It was proving impossible to silence Bavarian
artillery because hostile batteries had not been located and Allied gunnery
was in any case too poor, especially when unguided by aircraft, itself impossible after nightfall. No Man's Land was becoming ever more difficult to
negotiate with supports and supplies, and parts of the Australian protective barrage were falling harmlessly behind the foremost enemy troops. The
final point in the message was as important as any, for men can fight for
a period without food, but not without water.

On the Australian left Luther's 9/RIR 21 had foiled 32nd Battalion
attempts to extend their territory eastwards. The situation on this flank was
especially serious because the point where the Diggers' new communication
sap was destined to break in to the newly captured line (to be marked with
a signboard, which cost the life of Sergeant C. Garland who was carrying
it) was dangerously close to the boundary of the present incursion; if that
boundary was overrun, the scheme became instantly defunct. Parties from
the 30th Battalion and 8 Field Company working on it remained in extreme

jeopardy, at the mercy of shell and shot, and especially Bavarian sharp-shooters secreted in the battered breastworks of sector IIa. Because of an administrative blunder, work on a second sap inside the line of the first, which would have been so very valuable, had not yet commenced.

Hostile shelling on this eastern flank posed a persistent problem. Von Scanzoni's gunners played no role. Seven minutes after the assault began 50th Reserve Infantry Division guns assumed responsibility for No Man's Land and the original Australian trenches. It left four Bavarian field batteries to target the Diggers wherever they were observed. Two were firing from the ridge behind Fromelles, concentrating solely upon the area of the 1915 craters, Delangré Farm (*Tote Sau*) and the network of trenches where the *Kastengraben* met the front line—a scene of intense Australian troop concentration and activity, not least because it was also from this point that the communication sap was being driven in the opposite direction.

Failing light brought with it a slight breathing space. As runners became less visible to hostile eyes, messages were a little easier to deliver, which was just as well because direct communication by telephone had not yet been possible and pigeon supply was dwindling. On parts of the captured frontage—along the ditches—ground conditions now resembled those experienced by the British at the very birth of trench warfare in late autumn 1914. What the Diggers were effectively attempting to create was a brand-new front trench. As it became clear that the British 184th and the 15th Australian Brigades had failed for a second time to carry the Sugar Loaf, there were only a few precious hours to rectify matters—for both sides. If the Australians were to remain in situ and build on their partial success, a substantial nocturnal reinforcement was critical, not least to physically construct more durable defences.

By dusk the communication sap was well underway and Tivey's 8th Brigade had been joined by the reserve battalion, the 30th. Originally detailed as carrying parties, one group under Captain F. Krinks went straight into action, stiffening resistance near Delangré Farm. Finding it awkward to efficiently function from the trenches, the men took to sharp-shooting and bombing from shell-holes east of the *Kastengraben*—a most vulnerable position, not least because the farm was still untargeted by Allied artillery. Although it had been de-selected as an infantry objective before the assault, Australian gunners now believed the ruins were occupied by their own troops. Upon receiving news to the contrary McCay ordered a concentration shoot, which destroyed the light-signalling station and encouraged the enemy to show himself. Two Lewis guns plus crews, sourced by Krinks himself, helped bring an early Bavarian counter-attack to a standstill. Further attempts to infiltrate the Diggers were universally rebuffed.

As losses mounted, more reinforcements were despatched. Two companies of the 29th Battalion were brought forward to act as carrying parties, releasing the entire 30th for consolidation and defence. Digging and sandbagging continued along the ditch. Neither side was yet aware of the intentions of the other.

At this time von Braun's message log begins to reveal that although elements of RIR 20 had moved quickly to protect his regiment's flank and *Hintergelände*, the RIR 21 commander and his men were themselves eager to take the lead in reclaiming lost regimental territory—it was a matter of honour. It was quickly recognised that piecemeal Bavarian counter-attacks would achieve little of value; a coordinated effort was required. They must take time over the first key moves on the Fromelles chessboard.

By 9.30 p.m. von Scanzoni had completed the wider hermetic sealing of the break-in. Any attempt at deeper penetration would encounter an arc of machine guns and heavily garrisoned strongpoints. Behind, in the *II Stellung* on the ridge were arranged several companies of support troops, and in buildings, trees and the Fromelles church tower a ribbon of artillery observers surveyed the theatre unfolding below and beyond. Selection of targets and fine-tuning of trajectories and ranges in preparation for the hours of darkness, when fall of shot could not be guided by eye, was complete. There was an adequate stock of shells, and the situation appeared stable. All was well in the Bavarian camp.

On the Sugar Loaf flank of the incursion where circumstances had already become relatively clear, counter-attack orders were issued to I and II Battalions of RIR 16. Ninety minutes later the following ominous general order was issued to all Bavarian units in the Fromelles sector: '*Attack to be pressed home into our front line trenches!*'

The leaders of RIR 21 convened at their command post and agreed that the terrain demanded careful reconnaissance before counter-attacks could be launched. During the last few hours resistance had been noted in certain unexpected isolated locations, and because of the unremitting passage of *Engländer* and matériel across No Man's Land, the invader's true potency was still difficult to gauge. In von Braun's sector, at least twenty hostile machine guns had been distinguished, plus a few less-troublesome trench mortars. Small-arms fire was irritating and treacherous. Although hostile shelling was erratic, that too was locally perilous, posing a threat to movement anywhere in the *Hintergelände*; despite the onset of darkness it may well disrupt the concerted assaults now required.

Von Braun despatched two three-man scouting patrols. *Leutnant* Munck reported back that the English were still holding about 150 metres of front line to the east of the *Kastengraben*. The greater part of IIa was still in Bavarian hands but initial counter-attacks had made little progress against a fierce enemy defence supported by automatic weapons. The foremost trench from which Munck observed was in a poor state, but remained defensible should the enemy elect to expand his attacking front; the condition of the wire was fair, and the garrison adequate and well armed. Machine guns had been augmented and were sufficient. To his left, by the light of flares and star shells he could see No Man's Land enfiladed by RIR 20 machine guns; enemy troops going to and fro were clearly sustaining numerous casualties. The sighting problem caused by the mine crater lips had been largely overcome by careful placement of machine guns and good shooting by 50th Reserve Infantry Division artillery. Enemy progress on the sap continued, but it was clearly slow and costly and did not yet form a threat.

Along the ditch, meanwhile, the Diggers of three 8th Brigade battalions performed wonders in building breastworks and fire bays. Despite their efforts, however, ground conditions appeared to be getting worse. Charles Bean's *OHA* notes that some Diggers believed:

> . . . the enemy was putting into action some device for flooding them out. The troops were standing and working in water, and many men who were hit were in grave danger of drowning, unless mates were at hand to pull them out. Appeals were constantly sent back for 'dry rifles and Lewis guns'; some men kept beside them three or four rifles, collected from the dead and wounded, in case their own weapons became choked with mud.

The suspicion had no foundation: the ditch was merely a drain; perhaps shelling had released a flow from elsewhere.

The selection of this position at the planning stage as the foremost Australian line of defence was a costly error. Save for more and more digging and building, there was nothing anyone could do to arrest the steadily mounting casualty count, and those who were digging were not able to defend. Under such critical stress, physical strength was not limitless. The injured were helped to shelters in the old Bavarian front line where basic dressings were applied. Only walking wounded stood any hope of departing enemy territory, and that chance was slim. In 'home ground', across No Man's Land, the situation was little better. At every stage in the evacuation chain the medical services were overwhelmed, their messages anxious and pleading: 'Number of casualties exceeds capacity of medical staff and stretcher bearers . . . Our old front line is very full of wounded AAA Can you help with stretcher parties. Very Urgent AAA Every dug-out is reported full AAA Want 100 men to take 150 wounded men AAA All dressing stations full in addition AAA Can you assist?'

The greatest problem the Diggers were now about to face had its origin in a decision made by Colonel Fred Toll just seventy-five minutes into the action. Having vainly reconnoitred in search of the third enemy line, Toll left an advanced party under Major P. Eckersley in temporary cover along the roadside ditch facing the *Schmitzgraben,* and in various other isolated spots between the two battalions on either flank. He then instructed the majority of his men to fall back and consolidate the Bavarian *front* line. In a message to Brigade he explained the move thus: 'No works to hold so fell back to enemy first line. Send ammunition across urgently. Machine guns and crews required. Am strengthening parados. Will require entrenching tools, picks and shovels, sandbags. Many casualties but cannot estimate until first count after reorganising.'

Coghill's 32nd Battalion, scrapping and scraping in the ditch, were now some 175 metres in front of and to the left of Toll's main body of troops; to Toll's right Cass' 54th were in a yet more advanced position. What Toll had done by falling back was create a deep 'backward step' in the centre of the

Diggers' defences: across their newly captured ground, therefore, there was no continuous fortified protective line. At 10.20 p.m. Toll reported that although movement could occasionally be seen he still had no contact with the 32nd, and connection only by phone to Cass. Messages reveal uncertainty: he 'considered' his advanced troops to be 200 yards (180 metres) ahead, but 'in no formed earthworks'. Five minutes later he was unsure as to the area of terrain his battalion occupied, by which time Eckersley's party had also pulled back to occupy positions around 100 metres in front of the HQ dugout in the Bavarian breastworks. The 'balance of our Battalion were scattered and mixed up with other units', he later reported; there was 'a huge gap of hundreds of yards', and that the 'flank was a source of anxiety the whole of the night and it was evident that if attacked from this direction our position would be extremely difficult to hold'. As midnight approached, the Digger units were no closer to being drawn together. Tactically, the situation could hardly have been worse. The central step was to remain, later becoming more pronounced than ever and thus leaving the flanks of three different Australian units 'in the air'.

The Bavarians were as yet unaware of their enemy's predicament. For them, the overall situation still remained stable and with each passing minute they felt more in control. Machine-gunners were crouched over their sights awaiting the *Engländer* exodus that all were beginning to anticipate, probably before dawn. All of this was unknown to McCay, who remained seriously misinformed on all fronts. Just before midnight he notified brigades, artillery and engineers that the 61st Division held the apex of the Sugar Loaf and were attacking again in order to extend and link with the Diggers at Rouges Bancs. The 15th Brigade was required to assist, 'to take and hold the whole of the original objectives', but to 'avoid the error often committed in France of holding captured trenches too thickly, as unnecessary casualties occur and men cannot dig or consolidate trenches. Corps Commander and I congratulate you on splendid work done.' A nocturnal attack. Elliott was asked if he might succeed if his reserve battalion was made available. He was, he said, 'willing to try'.

Half an hour later McCay was only marginally better informed. It became clear that after the previous attack the 59th Battalion was still held up in front of the Sugar Loaf and were digging in. This, he said, was 'unsound'; the troops should either try to get in alongside the 61st Division or, if that was not possible, pull back to advanced trenches half-way across No Man's Land and endeavour to forge a connection with that portion of the enemy line now occupied by the 60th Battalion. Which route to follow was left to the discretion of officers on the spot.

Thirty minutes later McCay was made aware that neither option was feasible. Telephoning XI Corps he posed a gloomy question: '15th Brigade is of no further use for attack. Am I to hold on with the rest of the Division'. Corps required time to consider options, so the answer was affirmative.

At 1.10 a.m. Elliott received the order, 'Abandon attack and organize defence of our original line.' Next, the 14th Brigade was informed that assaults on the Sugar Loaf had been abandoned: 'The 15th Brigade is no longer on your right but back in original trenches. Please connect your right in German trenches with our original line digging in as much as possible. Have asked 15th Brigade to assist you in this.'

The situation had at last become clear enough for all to grasp. It was not pleasing. The Allied attack had failed catastrophically on most of both divisional fronts. Although some British troops were still holding out in RIR 17 trenches opposite Fauquissart, the enterprise there could already be accepted as having been roundly defeated. *Leutnant* Keller, commander of 1 Company RIR 17, described the mopping-up process:

When the English troops in the trench saw our men approaching, they withdrew behind the next traverse, throwing hand grenades as they went. Without hesitation Vizefeldwebel Herb advanced at the head of his section and bombed the English troops back from traverse to traverse while the men at the rear of his section kept up a steady supply of hand grenades. Eventually the enemy climbed out over the parapet and attempted to retire to their own lines in single file. Whilst part of the section shot down the fleeing enemy, the remainder of the section continued to bomb its way further to the left until it joined up with the OC 4/17 and men of his company and the 9th Company. The English troops trapped between them then surrendered.

As early as 9.15 p.m. there had already been twenty-five prisoners in Aubers, seventeen more en route, and four British machine guns in Bavarian hands. The events at Fauquissart were a miniature version of the fate that would befall the Diggers during the next ten hours.

Save for some desultory shell- and machine-gun fire, all had become quiet between Devil's Jump and the Sugar Loaf. Dawn, and all the agony that it would surely entail for the beleaguered Diggers, was fast approaching. The Australian right flank was entirely exposed and the western communication sap, pushing ahead famously, was vulnerable to surprise attack. Artillery and machine guns were ordered to deliver deterrent barrages and McCay requested heavy artillery support.

The Bavarian counter-attack instructions to all units stated that on no account should frontal attacks be launched but that once the boundaries had been fully secured, troops were to be concentrated on both flanks of the incursion. Reconnaissance suggested that neither was under serious hostile threat.

As the clock ticked into 20 July, British and Australian commanders were still considering how best to re-launch the offensive; original aspirations were still achievable, they felt. At the same moment in Haubourdin the staff of 6 BRD were coming to recognise that they might be on the verge of the most glorious triumph, albeit defensive, in the unit's history: maximum advantage *must* be extracted. News of general failure would probably by now have reached most *Engländer* within Bavarian territory. When the pressure was increased, morale would plummet and the men would become wearier by the minute, as much in recognition of the bleakness of their prospects as from the arduous work that consolidation and defence of enemy positions always involved. The Bavarians were on the most familiar terms with the terrain; the pinioned Diggers were not. Confusion and chaos should be expected.

Von Scanzoni ordered the vanquishment to be completed before dawn. The sooner it could be achieved the better, because sunrise might bring with it further hostility. Before turning the screw, he requested neighbouring units to secure their lines against surprise nocturnal attack, to enhance defensive weaponry and to react instantly to his requirements. In order to keep every available man on duty iron rations were issued from the reserve.

The problems created by Colonel Toll's 'step' in the Australian line have already been outlined. There is, however, another intriguing and important aspect to the action. It relates to where having entered enemy territory, the 14th Brigade Diggers dispersed. It will be remembered that all levels of command had received the strictest orders not to advance beyond their assigned objectives: the Bavarian *I Linie*. At 8.20 p.m. the following message arrived at 14th Brigade headquarters from the 54th Battalion:

> *Am holding a line 150 yards from German front line. Battalion on my left appears to have drawn back. Am consolidating but my line is very thin and have no supports. <u>Send if possible the two Companies of 55th</u>. Have put Lewis gun on my flanks also machine guns. My men went too far forward and our own artillery caused some losses so they came to present position.*

The phrase 'too far forward' fails to describe what actually took place. In his post-action report, Colonel W. Cass offered a little more detail:

> *The enemy's barrage was very heavy on the section allotted to the 14th Brigade and as soon as our men moved forward over the parapet they were met by machine-gun and rifle fire which caused heavy losses in No Man's Land. The Companies moved forward in perfect order losing the senior major and the remaining Company commander while doing so. The trenches were easily captured, and two machine-guns in addition. Our men followed the fleeing enemy for about 600 yards and then came under fire from our own artillery also. We retired to the German first system of trenches and at about 150 to 300 yards in rear of their first line set to work to dig a trench.*

There is no explanation as to why these troops were allowed to chase the enemy, nor how strong a force did so. In fact the men did not come 'under fire from our own artillery', but *advanced* into their own protective barrage. Bavarian records reveal that there is also no doubt that substantial numbers did not later retire to the 'German first system', but remained isolated far beyond the assigned objective. It was an action that not only caused confusion but dangerously diluted efforts to form defensible positions in the correct locations.

Elsewhere, Hughes and White (32nd) followed orders, drawing back men who strayed too far. Toll's initial venture towards *Schmitzhof* was a reconnaissance—some 360 metres beyond the objective. Von Braun's post-battle report mentions Eckersley's advance guard:

The patrols advancing on the Schmitzhof [31st Battalion patrols] *were repeatedly driven back by fire from the left side of the Türkenecke. The patrol to the west* [elements of the 54th or 55th Battalion moving towards Grashof], *however, in approximately company strength, succeeded in digging itself in well, but suffered heavy casualties from infantry and artillery firing on them from the Brandhof.*

The records of RIR 21 note the same hostile patrols being repeatedly driven back. In the *OHA* Charles Bean expressed doubt about Australian troops being here, in the region of the *Hofgarten*—the area through which 31st Battalion troops had to pass to reach the road where they dug in and resisted. In a letter of 22 May 1926 Bean questioned Toll as to whether 'any of our men were firing from or near the most advanced point reached by you? My reason for asking is that the Germans say we penetrated even farther. This may have been a story brought back by frightened German soldiers, but the German records are generally fairly accurate.' Four days later Toll replied in the affirmative: he 'moved his right flank up to the road, as before mentioned. On my return my men were still firing heavy, but at doubtful targets.'

Von Braun also refers to Eckersley's patrol coming under 'enemy barrage fire', by which he meant Allied shelling. After several desperate pleas from brigades, on McCay's orders the guns finally lifted from their own troops to more indistinct lines believed to be well in advance of the forward-most Diggers. But the original barrage line was in fact correct: it was the troops who were too far forward. Artillery Flight 201 reported thus:

Whilst the German barrage fire on the English front line trench system and rear area was very well distributed and registered and lay like a close-meshed net over the front line and the communication and approach trenches, the English artillery fire gave the impression of disorganised scatter-gunnery and uncertain targeting, with great gaps left untouched and shells falling on areas where there was nothing worth shooting at.

Although perhaps disorderly, the barrage was nevertheless effective in several times stalling the movement of Bavarian supports. Among this 'scatter-gunnery' lay the aforementioned Diggers in the region of *Grashof*—some 500 metres from their assigned positions. Their advance towards this spot is noted in 14th Bavarian Brigade records. At 7.00 p.m. a message arrived from two runners who had been awaiting orders in the rear of the sub-sector. It reported that 'the English had broken into our lines near the right flank of IIIa and were moving forward towards *Grashof*'. At 7.50 p.m. RIR 21 reported 'The English are at *Grashof*'. An hour later 12th Brigade observers warned RIR 16 that 'Enemy in IIb, c, d is now closing on *Grashof*'.

The patrol was estimated at 'approximately company strength'. Given the circumstances (and the orders) it represents a substantial number of men (200 or more) who *should* have been consolidating and defending positions half a kilometre to the rear. Charles Bean is guarded on the subject, saying that although 'a few Australians returned saying they had wandered this distance, the report is possibly true of some small party. It is certain that no large body penetrated half that distance'. Again, primary sources in Munich reveal rather more than Bean was able to glean. Several maps show the routes taken and positions occupied by the Diggers. From Rouges Bancs they followed the *Grashofbahn* tramway, stole through hedges in front of the *Zerchossen Hauser* and reached a point close to *Grashof*, at this time unfinished and unmanned, which is why they only came to be fired upon from *Brandhof*, a key Bavarian intermediate defensive strongpoint equipped with machine guns and a *Grabenkanone*. There, they appear to have been joined by 31st Battalion men moving forward past the *Wasserloch*, close to the furthest point of Toll's reconnaissance. The Diggers did not occupy *Grashof*, but created a south-west-facing defensive line in an adjacent field.

Despite numerous Bavarian patrols, there the men would remain for several hours. Their fate is described in a report by Weiss of 3/RIR 20, who noted that his company, 'having crossed the tramway track, stumbled unsuspectingly on a poorly fortified trench occupied by the enemy, which it cleared in short order. Some of the enemy garrison were killed by hand grenades, some were bayonetted, and the survivors who surrendered were taken prisoner and sent back to the Brandhof'.

This action took place around 2.00 a.m. on the morning of 20 July, which means that the Diggers remained for much of the battle several hundred metres beyond their comrades at Rouges Bancs. They may have had Lewis guns, for a machine-gun symbol appears on two Bavarian maps. Who gave the order for them to dig in there—for an order *must* have been issued—remains unknown. It cannot be said exactly what effect their solo action had upon the garrison defending the 'correct' positions, but any defensive influence they were able to exert was clearly minimal. Would later waves of Diggers have known that a 'hunting party' was still lurking in the pastures beyond the objective? Australian gunners would have been entirely unaware; indeed, to inform them would have revealed that corps and divisional orders had been disobeyed.

It has also become clear that some of the party may have evaded discovery, probably with the help of Flanders mist, when the trench was overrun by 3/RIR 20. The report of RIR 21's *Pionier* Company notes that at 5.00 p.m. on 20 July—the evening following the battle—a *Leutnant* Raab and three *Gruppen* (a *Gruppe* was eight men led by an NCO) were tasked to search for a party of enemy with a machine gun, believed to have dug themselves in between the *Zerschossene Haüser* and *Grashof*. They later reported:

> The ground up to Grashof was systematically searched and a Captain and four men were brought in. Spare parts were found, but the machine-gun itself was no longer there. Vizefeldwebel Weinzierl recorded the trenches there which had been occupied by the enemy, in which approximately 100 dead were counted.

One hundred dead. The identity of the captain is not noted, and Bean makes no mention of the event in the *OHA*. Who the officer might have been remains a mystery (he evidently survived). That Lieutenant-Colonel Cass remained aware of a 'discrepancy' in deployment is revealed by a message sent to neighbouring officers at 11.25 p.m. on the night of 19 July:

> *Keep touch with both flanks. It is said that two coys of 55th are in front of our line and I have a message asking that no more flares be sent up. Do you know anything of other troops being in front of us? If so please state where they are. Be careful of Germans in Australian uniform speaking English and getting amongst our men. Let each man be sure of his neighbours.*

Around 12.30 a.m. Lieutenants Lovejoy and Hirst (both of 54th) replied, respectively, 'Have no knowledge of any of our troops being out in front', and, 'I know nothing of companies in front of our lines'. Who then were these troops, what did they hope to achieve, from whom did the flare message emanate, and what did it imply? The final lines of a further Cass communication with the 5th Division at 1.15 a.m. shed a little more light: 'The line has a fair field of fire and if supported we could re-take Rouges Bancs N 15 b 65.65. We had to leave it because of our own artillery fire.' Here, Cass reveals that his men occupied advanced positions bordering the junction and bend in the *Tommy-Strasse* to the rear of the Bavarian first system. Although Rouges Bancs was not part of the objective, it was a tactically sound move to place parties of advanced guards to warn of and deter hostile approach. When they retired, however, it left the 'deeply' advanced group at *Grashof*. Was it this party that was wary of being seen beneath the light of Australian flares?

There exists further and most unusual documented evidence of this event. On a hand-drawn Bavarian map the locations of the bodies of individual Diggers are noted (with red crosses), not only near *Grashof* but also beyond Toll's aforementioned ditch bordering the *Buurmann-Strasse*. Equally remarkably, for it offers a fascinating indication of fall of shot, the map-maker has marked the locations of shell-holes made by heavy-calibre Allied ordnance across the entire area invaded by the Australians. More clues can be found in German panoramic photographs taken from the ridge in August and September 1916. One can discern a row of crosses near *Grashof* that are not present in images taken from the same location before battle. The graves are unlikely to be Bavarian for their dead were taken to cemeteries behind the line, where glittering funeral ceremonies were arranged.

The emergence of these events makes the battle somewhat more complex than for many decades we have been led to believe. Within two hours of the initial assaults and despite McCay forbidding his troops 'on any account whatsoever' to go beyond the stated objective, half of the captured front was seriously jagged, stepped and broken—in substantial part because explicit orders had not been adhered to.

As a result, the combined orientation of Australian defences on the right flank almost formed a right angle. An advanced party was strung out from *Grashof* towards Rouges Bancs; at Rouges Bancs lay a 'semi-detached' group occupying posts skirting the bends of the *Schmitz-Strasse*; behind them in the key complex of enemy workings west of the *Tommy-Strasse* the Diggers occupied, in varying strengths, three lines of trenches. A much-reduced and almost officerless 53rd Battalion held the extreme right flank with the help of three Lewis guns; at the head were parties of bombers under Captain Charles Arblaster. On his left, in well-built defences south of the point where the Diggers' western communication sap pierced the Bavarian line, lay a mix of 54th and 55th troops deployed in individual posts.

Long before Bavarian counter-attacks commenced in earnest, therefore, Australian dispositions were far from what Corps and Division required or could envisage in their tactical mind's eye. They were also practically undefendable.

For communication purposes (telephone and runner) the HQs of both 14th Brigade battalions were established in dugouts close to the head of the western communication sap: McConaghy to the west, Cass to the east. Although its digging was no less dangerous for 14 Field Company and their 'attached infantry', the sap was considerably shorter than its eastern counterpart, not least because the engineers had carefully incorporated the remains of the 1914 British trenches into the scheme, workings that were already 30 metres in front of their own line. In parts, the sappers also employed existing ditches 3 feet (90 centimetres) wide and 2 feet (60 centimetres) deep.

At around 1.30 a.m. 14th Brigade HQ finally received a comprehensive and optimistic situation report, with sketch, from McConaghy in 'Hunland', the first of its kind. Supplies were moving freely between the lines, he said, but communication was poor, by runner or pigeon only. Consolidation remained 'energetic', and the sap was progressing well, with completion, it was hoped, by daybreak. Casualties, especially among officers, were heavy; forty to fifty prisoners had been taken; Stokes mortars had 400 rounds left. Supplies of small-arms ammunition were ample, and arriving without notable hindrance. Machine guns too were plentiful, and included captured weapons with abundant ammunition. The thirteen-point message, however, concluded thus: 'At present, apart from a certain amount of artillery fire, matters on the captured line are comparatively quiet, but it is realised by all that a very strenuous time is probably ahead in holding what we have taken.'

Colonels Cass and McConaghy, who after the death of Colonel Norris (53rd) strove so hard to coordinate the sector, were not only ignorant of the true nature of their dispositions, but had just become aware that the 15th Brigade had failed to carry the Sugar Loaf. A succession of patrols sent out to find the 60th Battalion had either returned empty-handed or not at all: all now knew the reason why. They anxiously awaited notification of renewed assault.

After midnight McConaghy tried to coordinate news from all sides. He appeared satisfied with the situation on his right flank, as was Cass, but to the left towards the 32nd Battalion there were 'only small groups of men holding the line at irregular intervals'. At 1 a.m. the following message was despatched to the 14th Brigade:

My Battalion is very scattered. I am in touch with 31st, 32nd, 53rd and 54th. There is a serious gap between 14th and 15th Brigades. Have made two unsuccessful attempts to establish communication with 15th Brigade. Very few dead huns about. They retired before our artillery. Have four Lewis Guns in action. All working hard on trenches which are in a very bad state. Cannot give you my position on map but it is in N 15 B.

Cass's 54th had by this time constructed a substantial breastwork to protect their ditch. Happily, sandbags had arrived in 'good numbers', and in some places the structure was over 2 metres high. With Vickers and Lewis guns and the sizeable garrison now present, they felt able to defend their front. This was not, however, where the Bavarians elected to concentrate their efforts. By 9.00 p.m. RIR 16 had already been told several times that it should on no account launch a frontal attack, but instead concentrate upon a narrow area along the flank in such a way that by recapturing the front-line trench they would cut off the *Engländer* who were already known to have penetrated deeper into the trench complex west of the *Tommy-Strasse*. One company was given responsibility for attacking the front line, a second for the support trenches, and a third to form an oblique linear block across the Australian right flank. The *Hintergelände* still remained secure. In sector IIa RIR 21 and 20 were charged to produce the mirror image.

With supports and reserves deployed in strength throughout sector III, by 10.30 p.m. RIR 16 were comfortable in their capability both to hold the line and assist in the excision of the enemy in IId, and even IIc if required. At 11.00 p.m. 10 Company occupied IIIa, the east face of the Sugar Loaf, together with about 100 metres of neighbouring IId, in which one *Vizefeldwebel* and fifteen men of RIR 21 held the trench blocks beyond which lay the Australians. To ascertain enemy strength, bombers of 6 Company pressed forward against the blockaded section. They found the first 50 to 80 metres lightly defended; four men were extracted from shelters—possibly the very first Diggers of the action to be taken prisoner. Their captors, under the command of *Leutnant* Arnold, also appropriated the first Australian machine guns. Arnold's subsequent report dated 28 July provides a vivid account of events building towards climax:

> *Before the 1st Company arrived in sectors IIIa and IId, I had gone forward with a storming party of the 6th Company consisting of 1 NCO and 8 men into the barricaded trench occupied by the enemy. Men of the 3rd section of the 6th Company, who had just dug a flanking trench towards the rear at the site of the barricade, attached themselves to my party and garrisoned the recaptured trench whilst keeping up the*

supply of hand grenades. I went forward at the head of the party, first in the trench, then with three men along the parapet, while the others advanced along the lateral communication trench. At a point about 50 metres beyond the barricade, there was a shell hole in the breastwork on the side facing the enemy trenches, in which a wounded Englishman was lying with a machine gun beside him. Gefreiter Kernbichl and Infantryman Christof noticed the Englishman, who had evidently been wounded by a hand grenade while attempting to return to his own lines with the machine gun. Christof brought him down from the parapet and the men following behind him brought in the machine gun and took it to the deep dugout in IIIa.

Looking down from the parapet I saw a German machine gun lying about 70 metres beyond the barricade at the entrance to the front trench, beside a traverse. It had evidently been blown from the parapet by a hand grenade, or even earlier by an artillery shell. I alerted the men following on in the trench to its presence, and assume that it too was taken to Sector IIIa. I paid as little attention to the two machine guns as I did to the prisoners; my only concern was to go forward as quickly as possible.

Arnold's was the opening western assault. As his men moved into action a 14th Reserve Infantry Brigade order instructed the divisional *Pionier* company to prepare: 'The Company is assigned to RIR 21 for service as bombing parties. The Company is to report to Command Post Schneider. Speed is imperative.' The curtain was about to rise upon the second act.

Chapter 14

THE BEGINNING OF
THE END

It was 2.15 a.m. when the stormtroops (known as 'night-owls') of 1 Company RIR 16 under *Leutnant* Fuchs arrived in IId. There they joined forces with Arnold's 6th to drive forward towards the *Tommy-Strasse*. While Arnold reconnoitred along the top of the breastwork, Fuchs worked his way forward behind the parados. From these positions of relative safety (for the Diggers occupied the trench itself and in the dark could not see their approaching enemy), both parties fired flares and hurled showers of grenades down among their enemy. Bayonet-men moving through the trench itself followed up, stabbing and rifle-butting any who offered resistance. Weak in number, the Diggers took flight, flinging bombs to impede the enemy advance. At this same moment Major R.O. Cowey (55th), moving in the opposite direction with the intention of visiting the right of the Australian line, was confronted by their exodus. Hearing nearby explosions followed by raised German voices, he ordered the men to stand their ground and hurried back to McConaghy's HQ dugout, barely 200 metres away, to report.

By 2.30 a.m. Cass's earlier comfortable message tone had vanished. He now pleaded: 'Please organise some system to send forward all necessaries as I cannot spare men to go for them. Grenades, water, ammunition, sandbags, urgently needed.' He also described not only gunfire and flares 'behind' his right flank—the advance of Arnold and Fuchs—but a counterattack advancing up the road leading to Rouges Bancs. This was the 3/RIR 20, endeavouring to make further progress having cleared the advanced Diggers near *Grashof*; they were stopped by a Lewis gun fired by the 31st Battalion party commanded by Lieutenant Drayton, dug in at the head of a spur leading back from the apex of the sharp bend in the *Schmitz-Strasse*. Drayton's men then themselves withdrew, creeping back to rejoin Toll in the old German front line.

Unknown to the Bavarians, there were now no advanced *Engländer* guarding the deep 'step' in the Australian line. Ten minutes later, hearing renewed tumult, Cass despatched a note requesting 'any information as to position on my right. Enemy machine gun fire is coming from my right rear and taking me in reverse. Is the right of 53rd Battalion secure? I can get no information regarding my flank on that side.' Half an hour later, the Diggers were defending the heaviest assaults yet made; Cass' next message is one of near desperation:

> *3 a.m. It is reported to me that the 53rd on my right has given away slightly and that the Germans are coming in about N 15 a 90.95 [along the Bavarian front line west of the Tommy-Strasse]. The enemy is bombing his way up the trenches. Supports are necessary immediately to strengthen 53rd. Once again grenades are earnestly requested. Will you please send me a big supply. Please send them forthwith or it will be a costly process to drive out the enemy if he gets established. My men are worn out with hard work and are too busy to be spared to act as carriers. At what time may I expect cable communication . . .*

By the time this message reached McCay, much of RIR 21's sector IId to the west of the *Tommy-Strasse* had been reclaimed by the Bavarians, and 4/RIR 16 had joined the surge, relieving exhausted spearhead troops. The leading grenadiers had thrown grenades until they could throw no more.

At the very tip of the Australian right flank, under siege from two sides and at risk of being cut off, those now in most danger were the party led by Captain Charles Arblaster (53rd) and Lieutenant A. Gunter (55th). Gunter had been instructed to guard the *Tommy-Strasse* where it bisected the second enemy line (*Deckungsgraben*): he had no choice but to send some of his men to assist Arblaster, as did parties from a series of nearby 54th and 55th Battalion posts. But soon the Bavarians were heard to be approaching the road, threatening to cross the front line *to their rear*. With redoubled Australian effort, they were bombed back.

Cass and McConaghy had already sent men across No Man's Land for more grenades. Upon their return, a party under Lieutenant W. Denoon played the Bavarians at their own game, advancing and bombing from *outside* the front breastwork—moving along the glacis and in the borrow pits. The surprise regained some of the lost ground, and bought a little extra time. For a while advantageously placed and courageously handled Australian machine guns then stifled further Bavarian advances.

At 2.46 a.m. came the first Australian message assessing loss in the assaulting battalions: at least 50 per cent, 'with a large proportion being officers'. The time had also come for the Bavarians to close in for the kill: patrols sent out to probe the situation inland of the front line returned reporting no sign of *Engländer*. The *Teufelsgraben* trench was investigated; it too was empty. The Bavarian garrison there was strengthened. Just after 3.00 a.m. it was established that the roadside trenches at Rouges Bancs positions were only weakly manned; the news was distributed via the freshly repaired telephone system.

After several further explorations RIR 16 reached the conclusion that the terrain covering Rouges Bancs to the immediate south seemed not to be occupied by significant enemy forces. The open ground behind, however, although devoid of enemy troops, was still under heavy hostile artillery and machine-gun fire. This, combined with the fact that it was intersected by ditches that could not be crossed without bridging, convinced *Oberleutnant* Schmidt that, although tempting, assault from this quadrant was unwise. His overall assessment at this time was: 'A large part of the trench occupied by the enemy had already been won back. Reconnaissance carried out by myself and ordered by the Adjutant found that the units leading the struggle were growing very fatigued and in danger of running out of grenades.'

There were now fresh Bavarian troops waiting at all points of the compass around the Diggers. RIR 16's Command Post III was able to report a pitched grenade battle in progress and that 800 metres of line had been won back. Their supports, until now quiescent in the *Hintergelände*, moved forward into the complex of trenches behind the eastern flank of the Sugar Loaf: all available forces were required to restore and garrison the recaptured positions. Von Scanzoni put the staff and two companies of II RIR 17—surplus to requirements in their own sector—at the disposal of RIR 16 and ordered them to march to Fromelles Chateau as potential replacements. Twenty minutes later, another message reported 1000 metres of trench had been retaken. It was forwarded to Division with the caveat that in the confused conditions the figure should not be taken literally but simply as an indication that the counter-attack was making good progress.

———

It was at the same time that Fuchs, Arnold and others were making their first concerted moves that von Braun issued the order to his own troops to begin manoeuvres on the eastern flank in conjunction with RIR 20:

> *The Kastengraben must be re-taken using hand grenades. The men from various companies stretched out along the Kastengraben cannot stay there or they will be shot to pieces by the enemy artillery at daybreak. Pull them out of the Kastengraben back to Tote Sau and then make your attack in conjunction with the renewed bombing attack from IIa. The enemy strongpoint must be stormed before daybreak. The bombing attack through the Kastengraben must be launched at the same time as the bombing attack from IIa.*

Earlier orders to attack the Australians adjacent to *Tote Sau* had initially resulted in pushing the Diggers back a little along the *Kastengraben*, but further progress was thwarted by an impenetrable hail of bombs and machine-gun fire—the Diggers could not sit and wait to be attacked:

offensive defence was the only option. Bavarian 7/RIR 21 went forward with elements of 1 Company west of the *Kastengraben* and fought off probing counter-attacks by small parties of 31st and 32nd Battalion troops, but abreast of the *Hofgarten* they ran into heavy resistance from machine guns on the parados of their old front line, and rifle fire from the newly built positions along the ditch. The frontal approach offered little in the way of shelter: they were forced to retire and regroup in the *Kastengraben*; so too were a party of 8/RIR 21.

A second attempt was held up in the same way. The Diggers were fiercely resisting, and it did not please von Braun for the clock was ticking. Attention had to be distracted from the flanks by infiltrating parties across the Australian front, thus drawing fire from all parts of the captured positions. In this way the locations of the most troublesome weapons—the machine guns—might be established. Bavarian 5/RIR 21 stole forward from the *Türkenecke*, likewise 4/RIR 20; both were thrown back by the combined fire from the troublesome parapets. It was at this point that Allied artillery staged a valuable display of *Sperrfeuer*: defensive barrage fire.

For the moment the Diggers were resisting admirably. The question was how long they could continue. Every machine gun in Cass' 54th and McConaghy's 55th was firing into the maze of trenches to the west and south, and east into the open *Hintergelände*. The battleground was getting narrower, thinner and, most importantly, more congested. In the dark it was difficult to establish who was shooting at whom: the combination of anxiety and an intermittent Flanders mist is said to have caused some Diggers to fire at trees. The Bavarians employed an alarmingly simple means of determining friend from foe—they sang a recognition song: '*Deutschland, Deutschland Über Alles.*' If the refrain was spontaneously taken up, shooting and bombing ceased; if not, the shadowy figures could only be hostile.

At 2.15 a.m. 4/RIR 20 slipped down from *II Stellung* near the crest of the ridge and passed into the *Schützenwald* via the communication trench that would in two days time border the newly dug Pheasant Wood grave pits. One third of the party then bore to the left and moved towards the *Wasserloch* to create a diversion in front of the 31st Battalion; the others carried straight on towards the *Kastengraben* and *Tote Sau*. RIR 20's report described the situation:

The Company reached the Schützenwald without loss. At B II, the Company commander received the following order: 'The Company is to go forward into Sector IIc with its left flank resting on the Nürnbergerstrasse.' The Company set out, but very soon began to drift to the right, as it failed to find any route to either right or left, and the right flank of the Company eventually reached the Kastengraben and skirted along it towards Tote Sau. Nearing that strongpoint, the Company spread out further to the left and very soon encountered exceptionally heavy MG fire from both sides [the Vickers and Lewis guns on the Bavarian breastworks protecting the 31st and 32nd Battalions] *and an intense barrage of enemy artillery fire. The MG fire from the right came from the Kastengraben, that from the left from the direction of the ruined houses; from the front it came from a trench that the English had made between the Kastengraben and the Rödergraben* [the converted ditch]. *The Company rapidly resolved to attack but was obliged to hold back due to the large number of troops from other units falling back towards them. The Company commander exerted his personal influence and resolute leadership and soon succeeded in rallying this body of men and leading them, with his own company, in a renewed attack. In so doing the Company commander was severely wounded and at almost the same time two officers and two Vizefeldwebel of the Company were also wounded and unable to continue. The temporary commander judged that it was pointless to persist with the frontal assault in the face of heavy fire from three sides and therefore pulled the Company back to re-group at the Tote Sau strongpoint, where other displaced elements of RIR 21 were also congregating.*

The Bavarians, now more numerous than ever in the exposed *Hintergelände*, could find meagre cover. Many simply lay flat on the ground to escape the sweeping bullets. To stem the flow of enemy troops and supplies across No Man's Land, von Braun called for machine-gun barrage fire from the ridge and a cascade of high explosive from light artillery. German 50th Division guns reacted swiftly, but the flow continued. To counter the troublesome but vulnerable Digger machine guns on the parapets, he then requested targeted volleys of shrapnel. The fire still continued.

Bavarian attacks across the open ground west of the *Kastengraben* had initially been unsuccessful. Men were said to have been unnerved by the darkness and the smoke, but primarily by the sheer fury of the Diggers' resistance. Some lost their way among the fumes; others retired to the safety of intermediate trenches and had to be cajoled into further action, usually by officer or NCO example.

Bavarians of 4/RIR 20 and 5/RIR 21 vainly tried to creep forward in front of the 31st Battalion, whose open right flank (which formed part of Toll's 'step') was administered by Captain Charles Mills; his orders were to hold on until relief by the 29th Battalion. On the far left flank the Diggers were every moment becoming aware of lateral enemy encroachment. The officer in charge, Major A.R. White, had his troops—by word of mouth— make urgent contact with Mills, who slipped across to receive a request for covering fire while White's men dealt with the trouble by themselves counter-attacking. As Mills began the journey back to his post he was first wounded in the hand, and then captured with a number of other men of the 31st and 32nd Battalions in one of the first RIR 21 rushes. The flank was finally breaking, and in more than one place. The Bavarians had already made small infiltrations around *Tote Sau*, now they forced a breakthrough along the front line. *Leutnant* Schwarz of RIR 20 gave this account:

> *The enemy fought very bravely, defended himself extremely skilfully and held his ground with exceptional tenacity. Three times he was able to launch powerful attacks against us, as he was continuously receiving reinforcements who were coming over in columns in group strength from the Runder Sumpf [Horseshoe] towards the breach in the breastwork and to the west of it. A Vizefeldwebel from RIR 21 then came to our aid by rallying men from Sector IIa (8/RIR 21 having arrived in the meantime and established a very strong garrison in the firing line of that sector) and, with a machine gun from RIR 20, pinning down the oncoming enemy troops with a hail of fire.*

The Diggers were fighting for their lives. Under Schwarz's attack, the point where the eastern communication sap had been planned to break in to the Bavarian front line was consumed, bringing to an end the flow of support troops across No Man's Land. At appalling cost the sap had been driven to within 20 metres of its destination; it now lay obsolete and useless. The only route of escape for the 8th Brigade appeared to be back across a No Man's Land punished by lead and steel. This was not in fact the case.

From this point onwards Bavarian accounts do not concur with Charles Bean's description of the fighting that then took place. Perhaps because of the paucity of accurate eyewitness testimony, and the lack of topographical knowledge by those who were later able to contribute to his research, it was not possible to produce a cohesive account of how the Bavarians prevailed in this sector. The Diggers did not know what was going on, nor the locations of their enemy. The disintegration of 8th Brigade resistance is recorded thus by RIR 21:

Pioneers from the 6th Reserve Pioneer Company had brought up hand grenades to IIa and the Kastenweg. Leutnant Schwarz, RIR 20, Leutnant Reuter, 8/21st, Leutnant Schwarzer, 6/21st, Vizefeldwebel Hölzl, 9/21st and Leutnant Friderich of the Pioneers were then able to lead their units forward in a bombing attack on the enemy, throwing him back to the entry of the Kastenweg into the front line, and from there, at around 4.30, breaking into the Kastenweg. This success also made possible the advance of the forward units in the Kastenweg and the sections coming from both sides of the Tote Sau and from the Tote-Sau-Graben. The enemy was thrown back, with some men being forced to surrender.

Leutnant Friderich's troop approached the Diggers' left flank from the east along the front line. Upon arrival they found the Australians already cleared from IIb as far as the entry of the *Kastengraben*, but still holding out west of that point, in the *Kastengraben* itself adjacent to *Tote Sau* and in the *Wassergraben*—the fortified ditch. Friderich detached a bombing party with orders to clear the *Kastengraben* rearwards from the front line, working towards the second *Pionier* troop commanded by *Leutnant* Drescher, who were now south of *Tote Sau* advancing in the opposite direction. Drescher's orders were to excise the Diggers' advanced posts and trench blocks. When he arrived on the scene, Friderich's men had already overwhelmed most of the objectives—including Major White's left flank.

The job was completed by a party led by *Unteroffizier* Kistler, who commanded a small group working forward both outside and inside the *Kastengraben*, hurling showers of grenades before them. Then elements of 4/RIR 20 joined the fight. After a brief combat around twenty-five Diggers surrendered and were led away along the *Etappengraben*. The *Kastengraben* was now cleared, giving the Bavarians a useful protective platform for the next stage.

The Diggers were still holding their ditch—which it had now become possible to attack laterally from the vulnerable east flank. *Vizefeldwebel* Bisle and *Gefreiter* (Corporal) Obermüller moved from the cover of the *Kastengraben* and rushed forward with a platoon of 4/RIR 20 for support. They came instantly under fire but, having thrown fifteen to twenty grenades, the immediate Digger garrison surrendered and a further fifty prisoners were led away. One machine gun was captured: it was trained on the *Etappengraben* but had ceased firing. The key objectives were now the ditch and the old front line: a dual lateral attack.

Bisle and Obermüller hurried to the front to join the leading group of *Pioniers,* whose assault was organised in the following way. Friderich and two others led the bombing attack, served by a supporting group supplying primed grenades. In the same way that the *Kastengraben* had been reclaimed, three leading *Pioniers* bombed from behind the parados *outside* the trench while others fought within and along it; infantry followed up with bayonet and rifle butt. The party pressed forward to where the *Rodergraben* met the front line, in so doing surging behind the Diggers holding the ditch, who were now faced with an unseen enemy to the front and parties of Bavarians encroaching to the rear, while at the same time under lateral attack from the *Kastengraben*. Friderich was here seriously wounded, so Bisle took command until the arrival of *Leutnant* Drescher and his troop. Drescher carried the fight forward until he too was injured by a grenade. The Bavarians had reached the western boundary of 31st Battalion territory—almost on the doorstep of Toll's HQ. RIR 20's battle report notes that after the clearance of sector IIb, the company pressed forward under the command of two officers of regimental *Pionier* Company 6, into IIc. There, the Diggers put up a stiff resistance but were overwhelmed with hand grenades and small-arms fire; those who were unable to save themselves by flight were taken prisoner. Three more machine guns were captured in the engagement.

Toll and his men were now running short of bombs, and his solitary Vickers gun had fallen foul of one of von Braun's shrapnel volleys. In the ditch the Diggers of the 31st and 32nd Battalions were left with little choice. Going forward was out of the question, and to the east the enemy were approaching with bombs; to the west the situation was unknown, but undoubtedly perilous because of the *Rodergraben*—this route of escape was not seen as an option. The sole course of action was, at a coordinated signal, to make a collective break for freedom by skirmishing back to the Bavarian front line, scaling the parapet and taking flight to the far side of No Man's Land. A fighting retirement.

They encountered strong, determined and now irate enemy forces. Many failed to reach the breastworks. Those who managed to scramble out were caught in the wire or cut down in the killing zone beyond, for Bavarian machine guns and sharpshooters in sectors IIa and b had been long expecting this very opportunity; for many hours there had been nothing else to shoot at. Few Diggers arrived unscathed at the sanctuary they had left some ten hours earlier. For those who did, it was a shocking return, for they found their own trenches were as shambolic, devastated and indeed corpse-ridden as the charnel houses they had just fled. At 4.35 a.m. as the situation reached its awful crescendo, another ghastly irony occurred: 5th Australian Division HQ received a message from XI Corps HQ in Sailly: 'Corps Commander congratulates you all on your splendid work.'

Back in the Bavarian lines, 5/RIR 21 and 4/RIR 20, whose progress had been repeatedly baulked by hostile artillery and machine guns, now hustled forward from positions in the *Hofgarten* to mop up ensnared stragglers. Von Braun reported:

> *The enemy's resistance now crumbled and he was gradually driven back by our troops advancing along the fire trench and the rear trenches, at the same time taking heavy casualties from fire in his rear from IIb. The machine guns also inflicted heavy casualties on the English troops who were now fleeing back towards their own positions.*

To many Diggers, how the Bavarians managed to get behind them was a mystery; some believed that underground passages connected dugouts in the line with positions to the rear. This was not the case: the only tunnelled features present were the mine systems and isolated HQ dugouts beneath the breastworks. It was primarily the speed of the *Pioniers'* advance that brought the 8th Brigade endeavours to a dismal close, but there were other contributing factors.

In Charles Bean's account of the fighting that took place at this time, he describes a surrounding manoeuvre. At no point in the Bavarian narrative is such an event described, nor does it appear on maps relating the evolution of the battle. There was no Bavarian approach along the *Rodergraben* (the part-built communication trench that roughly bisected the boundary between the 31st and 32nd Battalions), so encirclement was not possible. Both 5/RIR 21 and 4/RIR 20 were at this time pinned down (they followed up later), and 1st and 2nd platoons of 3/RIR 20, weak after their earlier exploits, were in holding and sniping positions astride the *Grashofbahn* tramway, several hundred metres west of the *Rodergraben*. There they remained until 10.00 a.m. that day.

Had the Diggers of the 31st and 32nd Battalions been aware that part of Toll's 'step' was as devoid of enemy troops as it was of their own comrades, they may have been able to retire to the German front line and then to move laterally towards the more defensible positions occupied by the 14th Brigade, and of course nearer to the sole remaining route of evacuation, the western sap across No Man's Land. The noise, smoke and general circumstances of close-quarter fighting disallowed this. Understandably, the Diggers believed their enemies must be approaching from all three quadrants. It was certainly not yet so.

As day began to break von Scanzoni's mission was not yet completed. A battalion of the 104th Reserve Regiment (Saxon) moved into reserve positions on the ridge behind *Grashof*, ready to augment the defence of von Braun's sector II once the struggle was concluded. Apart from 134 Machine Gun Company, this was the only external unit employed by

6 BRD. If necessary, they could be made available to take part in the final sacking of the last Digger enclave at Rouges Bancs.

From the east, the Bavarians had now bombed and bayonetted their way across the entire 8th Brigade frontage and were approaching territory occupied by the 54th and 55th Battalions. With both *Pionier* officers *hors de combat*, *Vizefeldwebel* Bisle once more assumed command. Although many Australian prisoners were already cleared from the battleground, there were by now scores more to deal with, many of whom were injured. The dead of both sides from the last ten hours of fighting lay everywhere, and dugouts and shelters overflowed with anxious Australian wounded.

The *Pioniers* came up against the flank of Cass's 54th supported by a few severed elements of the 31st. Cass, already aware that the right flank was creaking ominously, could not fail to hear their explosive and insidious approach. Although presently unaware of the despairing flight of the 32nd and 31st, the Diggers' predicament was nevertheless apparent. Colonel Pope at the 14th Brigade had already been advised, 'Position almost desperate'. When news of withdrawal on his east flank reached Cass, there remained little doubt as to what the next move must be:

> *I at once drew my left in on the German first line and now held a semi-circle. I arranged with O.C. 55th (McConaghy) to build a firing line facing west towards Ferme Delaporte, and reported this and the position of the Germans to Brigade HQ, again asking for artillery help. At 6.30 I received word that the 8th Brigade had retired and that I was to hold on until ordered to withdraw. At the same time I was told to save the Lewis and Vickers guns.*

This was the sixth time Cass had requested artillery support. It was an absurd situation. Only an hour ago he and McConaghy had been expecting details of reinforcement, relief, and even renewed attacks upon the Sugar Loaf; now they were under siege. Away to his far right Arblaster's party were surrounded. Arblaster chose the only route left open if he and his men were to escape the net: attack. A furious bayonet charge out of the trench and across open ground left few survivors; it was later described by the Bavarians as a 'supreme effort'. Arblaster himself fell into enemy hands, gravely wounded.

Unaware of any of these developments, at 5.00 a.m. McCay was in Sailly for discussions with Haking, Sir Charles Monro and his chief of staff, General Sir George Barrow, and Mackenzie of the 61st Division. Mackenzie explained that clogged trenches and communication chaos after the exploits of the previous day meant that he had been unable to deploy fresh units for further assaults upon the Sugar Loaf. The impasse was being cleared, however, and renewed action should be possible later. Dawn had arrived. During the meeting McCay was called away to the telephone. He returned with news from 5th Division HQ: the situation was everywhere looking wretched. A swift debate revealed that none yet wished to abandon the venture; Colonel Pope was willing to push in half of the 56th Battalion.

Then, as the commanders were considering tactics and timings, came the news of the 8th Brigade retirement. There was practically no ground left to hold, and therefore no territorial foundation upon which to build. Haking and Monro recognised the only option was abandonment— extricate the 14th Brigade, they directed. As McCay ordered an immedi- ate box barrage to protect the beleaguered Diggers, the following message was sent to Pope:

> *5.18 a.m. 14th Brigade are ordered to withdraw to our own line. 8th and 15th Brigades will cooperate with fire from their respective flanks in the case of the Germans following up or counter-attacking.*

Australian guns started firing the box barrage pattern at 5.40 a.m.: Cass had finally received his long-awaited support. It had an instant effect. Had it come earlier . . . Five minutes later Toll and a few exhausted battalion stragglers slid into the sap and crept across No Man's Land to the ruins of Brompton Road. On the right flank things had now assumed a strange calm: resistance and shelling was so fierce that the Bavarians had decided to exploit the luxury of taking stock, just in case a fresh attack materialised— unlikely though it was.

At 6.15 a.m. Cass reported his position:

> ... *much easier and improved. Had driven enemy back by counter-*
> *attack and grenades well out of bombing distance. Captain Dunoon*
> *55th Battalion did good work in leading his men forward to attack until*
> *wounded. Can you get artillery to neutralise enemy guns as our tempor-*
> *ary trenches will not stand bombardment. Is 8th Brigade retiring as I*
> *have just seen a message to that effect but doubt it. Colonel McConaghy*
> *states that report is correct.*

At the very same moment 14th Bavarian Brigade observers noted the
firing of yet another white flare. It was a signal from RIR 16 indicating
the location of the head of the assault along the front line: they had entered
IIc. All was therefore well, but Australian resistance was not only baulking
Bavarian expectation, it was causing wearisome and costly delays. Von
Scanzoni wanted the affair done and dusted. RIR 16 alone had already
delivered 2500 grenades packed in sandbags, 35 000 cartridges, fifty boxes
of machine-gun ammunition, 200 mortar bombs and a huge quantity
of flares. The *Hintergelände* secreted further stockpiles. Circumstances
remained overwhelmingly in the Bavarians' favour. Von Scanzoni made
available ten *Granatenwerfers* (grenade launchers) and 1000 rounds to
pulverise the Digger enclave and blow the invader out; they would not
be required.

Across the rest of the battleground at this time a somewhat unnatural
quiet had descended. There were a few desultory shells and the odd sweep
of machine gun, but otherwise nothing to signify the fury of the previous
night except the cries of invisible wounded calling from the wastes of
No Man's Land. Sector II had become the sole focus of hostility.

<hr/>

McCay's box barrage was not quite everything that the Diggers anticipated.
Although it certainly made their enemy flinch and hesitate, friendly shells
again fell among his men, especially those ensnared in the pocket of the
eastern flank.

This did not go unnoticed by the men of II Battalion RIR 16, who knew the enterprise was now drawing to a successful conclusion:

At dawn it became possible to see that the enemy had occupied the old support trench to the rear of IIc, and also two communication trenches. The enemy troops in that position were first hit by their own artillery and then shortly afterwards came under heavy fire from ours. They surrendered by waving a white flag. At the entrance of the tramway into IIc [entrance into Memorial Park from road], *about 80 English soldiers left their positions and came across to our trenches one by one with their hands in the air. Those who remained were bombed and either killed or taken prisoner.*

Soon it became noticeable that as the advance crept towards the *Tommy-Strasse*, Australian bombing became markedly less intense. Now machine guns were the bugbear. As the Diggers fell back into Cass and McConaghy's semi-circular enclave around the entrance to the sap—which had to be kept open at all costs—concentrated fire made it difficult to advance. The Bavarian troops were so eager to finish the job that they now elected to cross open ground rather than fight their way through battered and collapsed breastworks. Losses were substantial.

But the Diggers' precious machine guns were now being one by one filtered back across No Man's Land. RIR 16's progress towards the road was held up by one of the few remaining Australian weapons. Sited just to the rear of the trench and commanding the area of Bavarian advance, it was eventually subdued by further working forward and bombing.

The report of *Oberleutnant* Schmidt of I Battalion RIR 16 reveals the final hour of combat to be one of confusion, shock, fury and bloodshed—warfare at its most brutal:

Under these conditions bringing in the very large number of prisoners also proved to be exceedingly hazardous, and costly for us in terms of casualties. The scale of our losses in carrying out that task was mainly due to the treacherous behaviour of the enemy, who on a number of occasions pretended to surrender, but then resumed hostilities at close

range. The fact that in such cases our men gave short shrift should not
be held against them. The bombing battle raged on unabated . . .

With men streaming back both through the sap and across No Man's
Land, the Diggers now made one final attempt to drive the enemy back.
It succeeded, but only for a few fleeting moments.

Two sections of 2 Company RIR 20 completed the victory by enclos-
ing the final elements of Pope's 14th Brigade. *Oberstleutnant* Bourier,
commanding neighbouring I Battalion RIR 20, later reported on the
concluding moments:

One platoon of the Company was detailed to press forward further into
IIc, but contrary to the earlier report, that sector was still occupied by
the enemy. A squad from RPK 16 and elements of the 4/RIR 16 was
engaged there in a bombing battle. The Company therefore committed
a second platoon and the two platoons garrisoned the part of the trench
that had been recaptured by the bombing parties. There was continued
fighting with those of the enemy who were cut off from retreat and were
endeavouring, some individually and others in groups, to close on our
trench from the rear. These were overwhelmed with hand grenades and
small-arms fire and the survivors gave themselves up and were taken to
the rear by the Company. Behind the left flank of IIc the second line was
still quite heavily occupied by the enemy, who was continuing to offer
stiff resistance. However, once the front line trench had been almost
completely cleared, these enemy troops also surrendered and about
90 prisoners were led away. The Company then distributed itself evenly
across the trenches in IIc.

The same tactic that had ensnared the 8th Brigade had been repeated
upon the 14th. Cass and McConaghy, however, both managed to evade
capture. Cass himself later reported on the dramatic closing moments of
the enterprise:

I directed Colonel McConaghy to hold the German front line as
a rear guard and to ensure that his men covered the retirement of the

rest of the force. He gave orders (I understand) to Captain Gibbins whose Company was on my left to form this rear guard party, then left. Captain Gibbins seems to have misunderstood this and withdrawn his Company at once. Consequently the Germans rushed in between my front and rear and my 54th had to charge through them killing many in doing so. At 7.50 the order to withdraw reached me and I started the men through the sap. Unfortunately some of the men were too demoralised to go in an orderly way and broke across No Man's Land where they were badly cut up by machine-guns on both flanks and by artillery. The sap saved hundreds of lives. By 9 a.m. the last of the troops had crossed, thoroughly exhausted, and then were again subjected to a heavy bombardment while in our own front line. The need for medical attention in our first trench was most pressing, for I saw scores of men badly wounded and no help at hand to bind them up. The casualties were mounting up—there was no communication except by runners with Brigade HQ and all seemed too dazed to send for help.

It was at 8.05 a.m. that *Leutnant* Bindseil approaching from the north, finally shook hands with a *Vizefeldwebel* (sergeant) of RIR 21 who had advanced with the southern prong. The noose was closed. Shortly afterwards RIR 16 battalion commander *Oberleutnant* Schmidt and his adjutant arrived with two officers from RIR 21 to explore the sector. Around them apprehensive Diggers were being winkle-picked from holes, dugouts, shelters and ditches. Although all three officers were intimately acquainted with every nook and cranny of their sector, so great was the devastation and chaos that Schmidt was unsure exactly where they were situated on the map. As they argued, one of the RIR 21 officers said that they were at the company commander's dugout in IIc, pointing out a sign that read 'Company Commander's dugout'.

Maps in the records of 6 *Pionier* Company and the report of *General-major* Weissmiller, commanding the 12th Reserve Infantry Brigade, allow us to pinpoint the exact spot where the bag was closed upon the Diggers' brief and tragic endeavour. The last of the Diggers in the old Bavarian front line surrendered within the boundaries of today's Australian Memorial

Park: the very spot where the British attack of 9 May 1915 was brought to an identical conclusion.

On receiving the good news, von Braun left his telephones at Command Post BII and set out for the front lines. He wrote:

> To judge from their casualties, the position of the bodies, the number of spent cartridges, and the losses inflicted on the enemy, the trench garrison put up a courageous defence, but was overwhelmed by superior numbers. Mounting the counter-attack was made especially difficult by the completely open terrain behind the front-line positions and the lack of a sufficient number of communication trenches leading to the rear.

Unsurprisingly, Bavarian tactical reorganisation of fieldworks recommenced at the same time as repairs: the instant the fighting ceased. Units were consolidated and distributed, and as work began on clearing the wounded, the last of the prisoners were led away. The time had also come to establish what exactly the *Engländer* had intended to achieve.

Chapter 15

THE ENEMY IS QUIET

———>◦◦◦<———

20.7.16. After heavy fighting during the night and early morning, the Divisional sector was cleared of the enemy by 9.30 a.m. Approximately 300 unwounded and 180 wounded English prisoners were brought in.

21.7.16. By the 21st conditions had returned, in the main, to normal. The enemy is quiet. Every effort is being concentrated on repairing the badly damaged positions and clearing up. Teams from the Medical Company and the Recruit Depot are being formed to recover the fallen.

Report by Dr Ott, Medical Officer, 6th Bavarian Reserve Infantry Division

On both sides of No Man's Land, the immediate post-battle period was one of intense and anxious activity. Relief was essential, and repairs urgent. The Diggers struggled to come to terms with the disaster and the aftermath, especially the recovery of the many injured within and before their breastworks. Evacuation of the wounded remained painfully slow.

Bearers were permanently exhausted, trenches obstructed by the bludgeoning they had received, and infantry assistance scarce. Thankfully, hostile shelling soon dwindled; saving their precious stocks after a busy seventy-two hours, Bavarian guns now elected to fire only in retaliation. The imbalance in artillery effectiveness was stark. To offer just one example, of a total of seventy-five shelters in the RIR 16 sector (incorporating the Sugar Loaf), sixty were undamaged, seven sustained slight damage, and only eight were destroyed. Although there had been plenty of collateral destruction, the Allied guns had failed in their primary purpose of neutralising the enemy garrisons and thus protecting their own infantry.

The lines of 6 BRD now swarmed with specialist *Pioniers*. Uncertain as to whether more attacks would follow or where they might take place, reserves remained dispersed throughout the sector. Reorganisation needed to be swift, and so it was. Keen to return to structured normality, on 20 July 14 BRB commander Danner issued the following order: 'All secondments and detached duties are to be cancelled and the NCOs and men distributed among the battalions of RIR 21 to make the companies as strong as possible for defence against further attacks, which, in current circumstances, must still be anticipated. All other considerations must be subordinated to this priority.' That evening, as front-line combat strength returned to the customary 150 rifles, the Saxons ended their brief sojourn at Rouges Bancs and departed the sector.

Most Australian prisoners, able-bodied and otherwise, had been cleared from the battleground by 9.30 a.m. on the morning of the 20th. Mending breaches in the breastwork was relatively straightforward: rather than spend time and effort filling thousands of sandbags, troops simply robbed matériel from elsewhere, for the sooner the principal defensive barrier was reinstated, the sooner the garrison would be secure from snipers. Repair of the *Förderbahn* trench tramway, essential for transportation of construction material, began immediately. Within three days the entire system was once again fully functional, and electric lighting had been restored to most dugouts. As the work progressed, so the dead were discovered among the debris. Leaving them in situ was not an option. All regiments were instructed that:

... bodies in the front lines are to be collected as soon as possible, deposited in places where they are protected from the sun, and separated between English and German. The trenches are to be cleaned up immediately. Booty, and equipment of the dead and wounded is to be stored separately and immediately sent to the Regiment in Fournes. I especially wish to draw your attention to the fact that nobody, without exception, has the right to remove from the dead any kind of souvenir whatever these may be. Equally, no one has the right to remove equipment from dead or wounded Germans.

The next day 6 BRD produced a preliminary set of casualty figures. The final tally, including artillery and other units, listed seventeen officers killed, twenty-six wounded and two missing; 452 NCOs and men killed, 952 wounded and 204 missing. 'Booty' included twenty-three machine guns (immediately despatched for repair and conversion for German use), 231 rifles and a hundred side arms, plus telephones, tool-kits and a mass of ammunition.

Allied casualty figures are rather more difficult to ascertain. For the 5th Australians the accepted total is 5553 killed, wounded, missing and captured; the number for the 61st South Midlanders is 1547. Collating the reports from individual battalions, XI Corps assumed German losses to be 'severe'. They were far from light but, as always, British estimates were wildly inaccurate. For example, the CO of the 2/7th Warwicks believed his troops killed at least 200 enemy; the adjutant of the same battalion suggested 400. The Bavarian unit concerned, RIR 17, registered sixty-four dead and forty-nine missing across their entire sector. Colonel Fred Toll of the 31st Australians, who spent almost the entire action within enemy lines, estimated that the troops of his unit alone killed 500 and captured another 120 enemy. RIR 21 reported losses across their entire regimental sector (which encompassed the attacks of *six* Australian battalions) of 230 dead and eleven missing. Given the ghastly circumstances, a mollifying 'enhancement' was to be expected; indeed, it was traditional.

Von Braun calculated the number of fallen *Engländer* lying within his lines to be approximately 400. Added to his own casualties and those of neighbouring and support units, the total number of sector II dead and wounded to be attended to was around 1735—a colossal task. Extra teams of stretcher-bearers were deployed to assist regimental medical personnel. Two such parties of twelve under an NCO were temporarily attached to RIR 21. They were joined by a further detachment of a hundred recruits, deployed specifically to clear corpses. Similar teams were sent to RIR 17 on the evening of the 21st, and to RIR 16 on the 22nd, by which time sprayers for the treatment of the already putrefying remains in front of the breast-works had been received; the Bavarians had experienced all this before. By the evening of 21 July the clear-up was therefore well under way. Earlier that same day *Oberst* von Braun had issued Order 5220 directing the *Fasanen-wald* pits to be dug for the burial of enemy dead. Its key elements were:

The Engländer bodies will be buried in mass graves immediately to the south of Fasanenwald [Pheasant Wood] The removal of effects and identity disks, in the same way as for the German bodies, is to be carried out by the h-company, supported by one medical NCO and 4 men of the regiment, under the orders of the Regimental Medical Officer.

In order to expedite the rapid removal of the bodies, the dead are to be separated by nationality and laid out at depots close to the light railway, Grashof and Christuskreuz.

The misappropriation of even the most insignificant item of property from a body (German or Engländer) constitutes robbery of the dead and will be severely punished. The collection of effects, as ordered above, may only be carried out by the sergeant-majors at Beaucamps or in the presence of a senior NCO of the h-Company at Pheasant Wood.

The IIIrd Bn is to provide one section, in rotation, to assist at Beaucamps. The assistance of stretcher bearer sections from RIR 20 is requested.

The Ortskommandatur [Town Major's Office] at Beaucamps is to have mass graves dug for approximately 300 [Bavarian] bodies, separated by unit, but alongside one another. The officers are to be laid out separately in the centre.

For the burial of the Engländer dead, the h-Company is to excavate mass graves for approximately 400 bodies.

There were several 'separating grounds' for the dead, each associated with the trench tramway. To these places the dead of all nationalities were carried from the battleground by stretcher (or pole and groundsheet) and 'stockpiled', before the separation of English and Australian from Bavarian was made. From *Grashof* onwards the tramway had suffered little damage; it was again fully serviceable within twelve hours of the end of the battle. Some 800 metres from *Grashof* the track cut through the western corner of *Fasanen-Wäldchen*, known at that time to the British as South Hayem Wood. The grave site along its eastern edge appears to have been selected because it was easily accessible by trench, track, road and rail, out of view of the front lines, and on the direct rail route to Beaucamps, to which German military cemetery many Bavarian casualties were taken—employing the same tramway—for interment.

Having been roughly loaded onto trucks, the *Engländer* were pushed to a point adjacent to the Pheasant Wood pits. Upon arrival but prior to burial, identifying and other personal items were removed, bagged and listed before being despatched to divisional HQ in Haubourdin.

How long it took to dig the graves is not recorded, but given the substantial detachment of troops made available for the purpose, they were probably completed within two or three days, and likely to be still under construction as burials were taking place; the sooner the process was completed, the better for all concerned.

In May 2007 a comprehensive metal-detector survey by a team associated with Glasgow University Archaeological Research Division (GUARD) revealed a concentration of 'personal' material, such as buttons, buckles, etc., lying just beneath the turf adjacent to the tramline. This suggested that the bodies had been dragged from the trucks prior to being searched, the action causing items to become detached. Being still clearly evident in the fields, the raised ballast bed of the *Turkenbahn* trench railway (composed largely of brick fragments, probably from the ruins of Fromelles village) was a useful visible physical clue, for it offered an indication of the most likely areas of archaeological interest. Aerial photographs from the Imperial War Museum (IWM) in London assisted the process, showing the ground to the east of the track to be heavily worn, presumably by Bavarian boots, while that on the western side was practically unmarked. It was therefore possible to calculate with some accuracy the short stretch of line, some 15 metres in length, where unloading took place, and also the routes that may have been taken when carrying the bodies to each pit.

By the same metal-detector survey, the two key finds, without which the Fromelles Project may never have advanced beyond May 2007, were recovered: a pair of small medallions each bearing Anzac inscriptions. The author dug them both from the ground. Their recovery did not shed any light upon whether or not the remains were still in situ in the graves, but simply that Australian troops had probably been present at the spot.

As we have seen, records reveal that on 19/20 July 1916 the deepest penetration of Allied troops in this sector was '200 metres from Brandhof', a position 1100 metres west of Pheasant Wood. Diggers were encountered and killed at *Grashof*, a kilometre to the north-west, and Colonel Toll's advanced parties ranged to the area of the *Buurmann-Strasse*, also a kilometre from the site. No Bavarian document chronicles any penetration reaching *Fasanen-Wäldchen*. The wood and its environs were under Allied control for just two periods during the war: before October 1914, and from 3 October 1918 onwards, when the British 47th Division advanced rapidly through the sector, liberating Fromelles. Diggers were not present at these times, so Australian troops, alive or dead, could only have been present at Pheasant Wood on 19 or 20 July 1916.

We now know that of the eight pits dug by the H Company, six were used for burial, which appears to have continued for five or six days. Munich records suggest that both the initial recovery period and the Pheasant Wood interments were completed on 27 July, while contemporary Allied aerial photographs confirm that five of the eight pits were already backfilled by the 29th. The last three remained open throughout the war.

The bodies of 61st Division troops were initially carried to village cemeteries; at Fournes, for example, from which many men were exhumed after the war for re-interment elsewhere. Again, Bavarian documents tell us that British burials behind the lines took place only until 24 July when a Brigade order was issued by *Generalmajor* Weissmiller, containing the following instruction: '*Engländer* dead still remaining in and behind the trenches are not to be taken to Fournes, but are to be buried in a suitable place between the support line [*II Linie*—the support trench] and the second line positions [*II Stellung*—the main defensive system on the ridge].'

No indication as to the location of 'suitable places' in the *Hintergelände* has yet been uncovered. Of the 330 South Midlanders with no known grave, a considerable number therefore remain to be found. Added to the dead from 1914 and 1915, the battleground still conceals a sizeable phantom army.

The Pheasant Wood graves not only contained the bodies of men who fell within the Bavarian lines, however, for each infantry company was also charged to search for enemy dead lying *in front* of their sector—in No Man's Land—for recovery and proper burial. Bavarian patrols of No Man's Land resumed as early as the evening of 20 July. In every regimental sector there were up to eight per night, the reports on each foray being accompanied by maps marking the locations of significant 'finds'. There were Allied corpses everywhere. Bavarian *daylight* patrols recommenced on 21 July.

Enemy dead lying close by the breastworks were simply dealt with, others were more problematic. Frequent hostile Australian action hindered the process for both sides, as did the wide overgrown expanse of fields and ditches before the Sugar Loaf. With a huge area to survey, many bodies lay hidden in ditches, hollows and long grass, making detection a complex and protracted process.

When a body was found by the Bavarians the man's effects were placed in a sandbag, labelled according to sub-sector, and sent each day along with the morning report to regimental command posts. Rewards were available for the meticulous recovery of these items for they were 'of exceptional importance in the evaluation of the enemy attack'. Companies were therefore asked to note the names of NCOs and men who had carried out the task most zealously, and report them at the end of their tour of duty.

Evidence in the form of extracts from captured letters and diaries of many Australian 8th Brigade troops, dead and alive, confirms these instructions were assiduously adhered to. A huge body of personal ephemera was collected. It subsequently landed upon the desk of Fritz Lübcke at AOK 6. Among the lists of *Beute*—booty—one also finds a category entitled, 'Maps, orders, papers'. These documents were of especial significance for they frequently provided answers to many an enquiry unanswerable by prisoners. Understandably, recoveries were best carried out after dark, but nocturnal activity in No Man's Land was by no means secure or unilateral. On 23 July the following order was issued to RIR 17: 'The 3rd Battalion reports that there are 800–1000 *Engländer* dead lying in front of our lines. The patrols sent out last night found no bodies [German]. I desire that No-Man's-Land be rigorously searched by patrols tonight, and that any *German* dead be recovered and equipment retrieved.' Both sides therefore had search teams working concurrently in No Man's land.

As a result of the hot summer weather, the dead were found to be decomposing at an alarming speed. There was a critical need to deal with the problem, not simply to ameliorate living conditions in the line but to urgently counteract the effect of flies, which freely moved from decaying human remains to food sources in the trenches and indeed far beyond. In positional warfare, dysentery was as great an adversary as the enemy himself, and a battlefield covered with rotting corpses was the perfect breeding environment for this dangerous affliction. If not tackled instantly, sickness could affect an entire division in a matter of days. The problem had long been appreciated, and Bavarian contingency plans were already in place.

———

The period of Bavarian collection of British and Australian dead falls into two categories and two periods. The first was the initial clearance by dedicated teams, followed by burial either on or near the battlefront and in recognised cemeteries behind the line. When this 'mass recovery' was complete, responsibility transferred to specialist squads who began the second and longer phase of retrieval of those who had fallen in less-accessible locations—in No Man's Land, where of course there lay many times more dead than within the trenches.

The deputy director of Bavarian Medical Services ordered the issue of the aforementioned 'sprayers' that allowed corpses to be showered with a solution of potassium permanganate. The apparatus—two per company—resembled a kind of lance which allowed management of bodies 'from the safety of the trenches', i.e. it could treat bodies within reach not only of the breastworks but of the great many saps and listening posts before the line. The treatment was not designed to assist or slow decomposition; it simply counteracted the stench and deterred flies. Reducing the odour made the process of subsequent recovery a little less disagreeable. The solution was the colour of red wine, making it possible to differentiate between treated and untreated remains. Those that could not be recovered were regularly sprayed until burial (and usually liming) nearby, or until natural decomposition had run its very short summer course (Bavarian 'experiments'—recorded photographically—reveal a record of eight days for a corpse to be stripped to the bone by fly action). Through descriptions such as this in 1914, 1915 and 1916, it is easy to understand how so many uniform-clad skeletons were found in No Man's Land at the end of the war. If not recovered within a month, there would be nothing left but bones and cloth.

At this time it was not possible to make an exact return regarding the number of dead within and in front of the Bavarian positions, but by 23 July clearance of the near battlefield was already so well advanced that von Scanzoni was advised that completion was expected within the next few days. AOK 6 and 6 BRD were keen not only to know exactly which enemy units had been involved in the action, but the orientation of the dead, i.e. the direction a man was facing as he fell. It might then be roughly ascertained how many enemy troops had been killed in assault (facing the Bavarian line), or in retreat or retirement, when they would be found facing their own positions. Bavarian patrols gradually became aware of the ghastly human scale of their extraordinarily effective defensive achievement in No Man's Land. On 21 July before the Sugar Loaf, an RIR 16 patrol reported 'mountains of dead and wounded in the Orchard and *Australierstellung* [Rhondda Sap]'. The next day their machine-gunners are noted as preventing Diggers from reaching and saving their wounded comrades, and recovering the fallen. The tactic was one of simple logic: the longer the enemy could be kept away from their own dead, the more intelligence might be gathered by Bavarian patrols.

On 25 July, having reconnoitred the ground in front of the salient on several occasions, *Patrouillefuhrer* (patrol commander) Leonhard Schroppel of 3/RIR 16 reported: 'Those [Australians] which are lying close to the enemy line are strewn with white powder, perhaps kalk [chalk/lime].

The smell in no man's land is very strong.' The 'liming' mentioned here was standard Allied practice.

On 2 August a fresh phenomenon was discerned by RIR 16: 'Company A is asking whether in front of IIIa [the Orchard—the area of the 15th Brigade attack] the enemy had burned their dead around midnight.' An experienced three-man patrol was sent to investigate. They confirmed that the *Engländer*—again Australians—were indeed trying to dispose of bodies by burning with benzine. (It is only on 27 July that we find specific mention of Australian as opposed to *Engländer* dead: they were 14th Brigade troops who had fallen west of the Rue Delvas—the *Tommy-Strasse*.) So too, added RIR 17 the same day, were the British in the Fauquissart sector.

To find that the Allies resorted to such drastic action may come as something of a surprise, for it suggests that the remains were able to be recovered, which would have been the more honourable and dignified option. By 2 August, however, decomposition would have been so advanced and recovery so difficult and hazardous that burning was probably seen as both the healthiest and safest option.

One of the more controversial aspects of Australian history involves efforts to realise a 'truce' at Rouges Bancs for the purpose of assisting the wounded and collecting and burying the dead. The narrative relating to this event has a direct bearing on Digger losses and missing. At 10.25 a.m. on Thursday 20 July 5th Australian Division HQ issued a message to all three brigades. It read: 'Working parties on enemy parapets today afford an excellent opportunity for practice in sniping.'

Of all the documents relating to Fromelles, this ranks as one of the most perplexing. There is no doubt that numerous enemy targets were likely to present themselves, but the order clearly represented a death sentence for many an injured Digger lying beyond the Australian parapet, for if the Bavarians were being sniped they were very unlikely to exhibit any benevolence when it came to organised ceasefires and recoveries. How closely the order was adhered to is not recorded. Curiously, Bavarian daily reports for this day perhaps offer a clue, for they note enemy sniping as being lively and troublesome only up to 10.00 a.m., when it 'practically ceased'.

Experience had long demonstrated that the Germans were recognised, even celebrated, for their readiness not only to agree to, but participate in battlefield truces. It had happened before on this same ground, and in recent weeks on the Somme numerous occurrences had been recorded, several on 1 July. Some Diggers had experienced truces at Gallipoli, and a few within the 5th Australian Division may have heard of the famous events of Christmas 1914 that took place in the self-same fields where now so many of their comrades lay in agonies of pain, thirst and fear, as well as expectation and hope, awaiting salvation.

The earliest attempt at a truce recorded in the war diaries of AOK 6 was on 19 November 1914, when during the storming of Wytschaete a German request for a ceasefire in order to bury the dead (the wind was blowing in their direction) was refused by both the British and the French. With the onset of positional warfare needs changed, and new unwritten contracts evolved.

The key to realising truces was, as always, the acknowledgement of recognised *enemy* procedures. The vanquished bowed to the wishes of the vanquisher. Being so often the subjugator of Allied assaults, it was the Germans who usually dictated the terms. All that was required was a request, a discussion and a mutual agreement based upon humanitarian motives and basic trust. Afterwards, the pattern of events was long-established: an imaginary line was drawn dividing No Man's Land in two, and neither side violated the space of the other. Leaving weapons behind, the Tommies collected the dead and wounded on their side of the boundary. The Germans delivered British dead to the half-way line, usually but not always retaining wounded enemy soldiers who lay within their 'territory'. The sole intention was to swiftly bring succour and treatment to the injured and at the same time clear the field of remains that would otherwise become a sad and disagreeable health hazard—for both sides. As long as a procedure had been pre-agreed, truces generally passed off without untoward incident.

RIR 21's diary for 21 July suggests that the Bavarians were expecting just such an approach by their enemy: 'It would have been a customary thing to arrange a truce after the battle, but it was not granted by the English so the German troops prevented the English [Australians], from burying their own dead', it noted. The obligation to negotiate was Australian, not Bavarian.

Sniping at those with whom one was required to negotiate was no incentive to mutual understanding or trust. Bavarian records suggest that much misery could have been avoided had it not been for stubbornness on the part of XI Corps command, whose orders to the two divisions were rigid: no fraternisation, no flags signifying a request to 'parlay', no armistice of any kind.

To date, only one German document has been uncovered that mentions an attempted truce. It was noted by the Saxons of the 104th Regiment, the troops brought up in the afternoon of 20 July to temporarily garrison RIR 21 positions in IIb—the narrowest area of No Man's Land. With the trenches only 70 metres apart, every movement in this sector was visible.

2/104 in IIb, 21 July, 4.45pm to III/104
1. The enemy has been quiet by night and by day. Desultory MG fire during the hours of darkness.

At 10.30 a.m. the enemy put out a sign-board with the Geneva Cross on it. Three medical orderlies then appeared in front of the enemy breastwork and began to attend to the English dead and wounded lying there. One of the orderlies was called closer and told to go back to his trenches and send out an officer to parlay, if they wanted something. After immediately informing Regiment by telephone, the English officer who showed himself was told that any requests would have to be brought across by an envoy under a flag of truce. This brought no response.

After about an hour we saw about eighteen men over the enemy breastwork opposite this sector. They were fired on and took cover. The English trench appeared, after the [illegible] of these men [illegible], to be strongly manned.

At 4.00 pm a small sign-board with an inscription that could not be made out appeared on the enemy breastwork in front of the left flank of the sector. Underneath the board there appeared to be a stretcher lying on the breastwork. Nothing further occurred.

The Saxons sought guidance from their temporary 'parent' unit, RIR 21. Although there are certain disparities, given the time and place it is possible that this report relates to a well-known incident in the Australian narrative where a Private William Miles (29th Battalion) is reported to have gone out into No Man's Land on 21 July in search of a missing officer, a Captain Mortimer of A Company. Although not fired upon, Miles is said to have been confronted by an English-speaking German officer, who asked what he was doing. He explained and the officer made a telephone call, returning with the request that the man should go back to his line and bring a superior to discuss formal arrangements for recovering the wounded.

Soon afterwards Private Miles re-crossed the field with Major A. Murdoch, also of the 29th Battalion. After another call the German officer informed the two men that a truce was possible, but that in this case Murdoch must enter the German trench and remain there blindfolded until the procedure was complete. Murdoch, apparently willing to comply, returned to his own line and reported the development to Brigadier-General Tivey at 8th Brigade HQ. The route that Tivey's request followed from this moment has never properly been established, but Charles Bean's post-war correspondence with James McCay suggests that it was he who issued a categorical 'No' to the plan.

Murdoch and Miles did not return for further discussion. Although in places the Bavarians behaved charitably towards the several brave souls who took their life in their hands and crept out over the parapet with water bottles and field dressings, the wounded were generally forced to wait until nightfall before relief finally arrived. By then many had died. Over the next five or six nights hundreds of men were brought in, and many more breathed their last.

Although following orders, McCay's reputation suffered irreparable damage as a result of this incident, primarily because he made no attempt to persuade his superiors to waive regulations. His biographer, Christopher Wray, notes:

Although McCay undoubtedly made mistakes in commanding the division, ultimate responsibility for the failed attack lay with the British high command. For many in the 5th Division, however, the blame lay squarely at McCay's door. Had he been a different man, one known to be solicitous in regard to the welfare of his men like Tivey and Elliott, then

their response may have been different. McCay, though, was regarded
by the troops under his command as a martinet, demanding efficiency
while coldly unsympathetic to their needs. He may have claimed to be
proud of them, and probably he was, but popular opinion in the trenches
and among families at home in Australia fixed on McCay as the villain.
To them he, too, became the 'Butcher of Fromelles'.

In view of the several reports relating to truces found in Munich,
a footnote on page 440 of Charles Bean's *OHA* again sheds more light
upon the nature of his post-war research in Potsdam: 'It is interesting to
note that no reference of this incident appears to have found its way into
the official records either of the Australian or of the German Division.
It may be inferred that both sides felt conscious of having indulged in nego-
tiations which might draw the frowns of their respective G.H.Q.'

The Saxon report was indeed present in 6 BRD records. Again, given
more access Bean might have recorded the incident in a different manner.
On the other hand, perhaps he *was* aware . . . Whatever the situation, there
appears little doubt that the Bavarians were open to negotiation.

Clearance of the dead was sustained beyond the end of the fateful month.
The 5th Division war diary records the days of late July and August passing
'quietly', 'very quietly' or 'remarkably quietly'. Those units not required to
hold the line continued to supply working parties and fatigues to repair
and rebuild, and as fresh drafts of replacements arrived all ranks continued
training, attending courses and lectures, practising bomb and gas procedures, and preparing for the next 'stunt'. Intimations made by McCay soon
after the battle persuaded many that it may be another crack at Fromelles.

Although Charles Bean's report published in the *Daily Mail* on 24 July
revealed the gravity of the event as seen through the eyes of an Australian
observer, information regarding precise losses suffered by the British and
Australians on 19 and 20 July was of course not available to the Bavarians. The capture of two Diggers on the night of 12 August finally offered
them additional data. Private Charles Vernon was seriously wounded in the
chest and could not be interviewed; he died the next day. The second man,

Private Wilfred Welch, presented Lübcke with a very useful overview of post-battle tactics, troop dispositions, day-to-day activities and an appreciation of the morale of the 5th Australian Division, even though he had only joined his new battalion on 22 July. The divisional casualty count had been, he said, around 4000; nocturnal patrols were still seeking remains.

The capture of Wilfred Welch had serious implications, for it resulted in another change of tactic by the Bavarians. On the evening of Welch's interrogation the following document was circulated:

Nr. 1a 4184
6th Bavarian Reserve Division. 12.8.16
To: 12, 14 Res. Infantry Brigades. 8.15pm
1. In front of sector IId this morning a badly wounded and an unwounded Australian were brought in. The prisoners belong to 57th Battalion, 15th Brigade, 5th Australian Division. They have declared that their battalion has been in the trenches since 20th July and have not yet been relieved. The 15th Brigade lost three-quarters of its men in the attack of 19th July, during which two battalions were repulsed. The 5th Australian Division is said to have lost close to 4000 men during the battle of Fromelles. The 3rd Australian Division is said to be in reserve and expected to relieve the 5th in the near future. According to the prisoners, during the night the English and Australians retrieve the identity tags from the dead lying in no man's land. Further attempts are expected to be undertaken in the near future.

2. It is best not to prevent such efforts by the enemy to remove identification from their dead; rather we should use them as an opportunity to take as many prisoners as possible on the entire divisional front. The practice must begin on the night of 12/13th.

3. For this same purpose Stormtroops will be deployed from today until 18th August to assist RIR 16 to hunt Australian and English troops in no man's land. Lt. Kuh will arrive this evening at RIR 16. The Stormtroops will as far as possible be left to their own devices; it will not be necessary for them to work under orders. They will be attached to and quartered by RIR 16 as soon as possible.

The 5th Division unit history for this period reveals that the Diggers took the fact that their patrols were allowed to roam freely over No Man's Land as a sign of growing Australian domination: 'No Man's Land became our No Man's Land', said the author, Captain A.D. Ellis (29th Battalion). In fact von Scanzoni was setting traps.

———◦———

Recovery of the dead continued well into August. Decomposition had now turned the bodies into jelly-like masses and flies were present in clouds. Nevertheless, manual scrutiny remained essential, and the Bavarians were fully prepared:

Reserve Pionier Company
10 August 1916
9.) Medical services
The following protective measures are to be taken in connection with the recovery of bodies in front of our positions:

Men with chaps or minor lesions on their hands are not to be assigned to recovery details. Recovery teams are to be outfitted with protective overalls and gloves. On completion of the work, these are to be wrapped in cloths soaked in cresol soap solution and sent to a disinfection station.

For protection against the odour of the bodies, recovery personnel are to wear a wadding pad soaked in aluminium acetate over the nose, or a respirator, a limited number of which are still available from the office of the Divisional Medical Officer.

Medical personnel manning dressing stations in dugouts in the front line area will provide 3% carbolic acid solution, as directed by unit medical officers, for the washing of hands by recovery teams on their return, and tincture of iodine for first aid treatment of any minor finger wounds they may have incurred.

Bodies that cannot be recovered are to be sprayed with 5% cresol soap solution by means of a spray pump, or sprinkled with chloride of lime, and, wherever possible, covered with earth.

A special bulletin will be issued when fly veils arrive for the use of recovery personnel and sentries. Cresol soap solution can be obtained from Reserve Field Hospital 10.

Signed: von Scanzoni

This is an important document for it shows that bodies are still being sought and recovered almost three weeks after the battle—and twelve days after the Pheasant Wood pits were closed. Australian burials were therefore still taking place, and not only behind the lines. An order issued by von Braun five days later is particularly eye-catching:

Res. Inf. Regiment Nr.21 15.8.16
To: the 3 Battalions and the Company
To be destroyed after reading
Concerning: Securing of the front line.

The enemy has dug out to craters 17, 18 and 19 in front of the right flank of b [Delangré Farm sub-sector]. *Our own crater no. 11 is also located in the same sector. These four craters are to be protected by a strong barbed wire entanglement to stop the enemy from taking them. In the coming nights they are to be strengthened in such a way that a continuous belt is created in front of our position which should only have exits that are guarded by listening posts. Listening posts are to be constructed in each crater.*

The result of these operations is to be recorded in daily reports.

Similarly we should work with total commitment to gradually backfill the trenches that are at present filled with many corpses; these are to be filled right up to the enemy defences [wire]. *Because of the advanced state of decomposition, any touching of the corpses must be avoided. Sprinkling with disinfectant: this should be requested from the Battalion Aid Post.*

The sap in front of c should also be filled in so as to restore the defences in all places.

The Bavarians are thus once more engaged in backfilling duty in No Man's Land. The 'trenches that are at present filled with many corpses' include workings abandoned after the battle of 9 May 1915 that now lay in front of the 1916 breastworks, plus the two communication saps dug at such great cost by the Australians during the night of 19/20 July. Bean's *OHA* tells us that the sap at Rouges Bancs, 'with the help of Captain Smythe's company of 56th and Captain Scott's of the 5th Pioneers', was dug 'from four to six feet deep and duck-boarded through to the old German front': it was perfect for the disposal of remains.

As requested by von Braun, his men recorded the daily backfilling progress. Unlike shell-holes, any remains deposited in the saps would lie well below the farmer's plough and thus be more difficult to discern after the war. The same can be said for the post-war search and exhumation parties. Although highly detailed, CWGC burial returns do not verify whether these 'linear communal graves' were ever cleared.

At 7 a.m. on 8 September 1916 a nocturnal RIR 16 patrol returned from the area of the Orchard. They reported: 'The bodies from the battle of 19/20 July have been removed.' This is the last mention in 6 BRD documents of the recovery of Fromelles-related casualties. In a few days the Bavarians were to permanently depart the sector.

Chapter 16

AFTER ACTION

———⟫◈⟪———

British and Australian losses had, it was plain to see, been grave. With the Anzac establishment and organisation known in detail via the earlier statements of prisoners, von Scanzoni rightly suspected the opportunity for counter-attack had probably passed. Any fears he may have harboured were quickly allayed, for full details of the Allies' aspirations were confirmed in secret documents taken across No Man's Land by Digger officers. Indeed, they may have been in Bavarian hands since before the fighting had actually ceased at Rouges Bancs.

The second defence of Fromelles was another famous victory for 6 BRD, and undoubtedly their finest performance of the campaign to date. Plaudits and decorations were liberally distributed, the Crown Prince Rupprecht of Bavaria, commander of AOK 6, personally visiting the front to bestow them. A grand burial ceremony took place at Beaucamps. As for the battle, von Scanzoni felt the event was worth documenting to the fullest.

Division requests the submission of as many photographs (prints) as possible relating to the action at Fromelles (photographs of positions, battery emplacements, transport of ammunition, transport of prisoners, medical services, etc). Such photographs are of <u>great</u> value for the Division's report on the battle. Costs will be reimbursed on application. Division requests that the photographs, accompanied by a brief description of the subject, the time of the photograph, and the name and unit of the photographer, be sent as soon as possible <u>direct</u> to Divisional Command.

This request may account for the large number of photographs of the post-battle period that exist today.

Allied tactical and strategic thinking, however, remained something of a puzzle to the Bavarians. The action was too big and atypical to be classed as a raid, but at the same time, territorially unambitious. It was a muddle. The answers could be supplied by only one source: *Engländer* prisoners.

Strict rules were in force about the holding and questioning of captives. Post-war statements by returned and repatriated prisoners do not reveal how many NCOs and other ranks (as opposed to officers) were interrogated after Fromelles, but the comprehensive nature of Bavarian post-battle reporting suggests it was a considerable percentage of those captured. It is clear, however, that AOK 6 intelligence officer Fritz Lübcke and his colleagues concentrated their attentions primarily upon those most likely and able to yield the most valuable and diverse information: officers and NCOs.

Diggers and Tommies with wounds received attention before being interviewed. Apart from unavoidable delays caused by the deluge of casualties, most prisoners seemed to accept the situation with equanimity. Surprisingly few, regardless of rank, later expressed any serious complaints about their treatment in the days following the action. The able-bodied (unwounded) were taken to the Lille Citadel as soon as feasible, their time of arrival being notified in advance, and each group being signed for. On 20 July there were four deliveries of *Engländer* by 6 BRD. *Unteroffizier* Brandmaier handed over five soldiers; *Leutnant* Rauchenberger brought an officer and seventy-six soldiers; an unnamed *Oberleutnant* delivered six officers and 256 other ranks, and finally *Gefreiter* Denhauser arrived with one further *Engländer*. The majority of these *Engländer* were of course Australian.

In general after interrogation, prisoners of particular interest to certain units could be made available for further questioning so that enquiries of a more localised nature might be made. It appears that this did not happen at Fromelles, possibly as a result of the sheer numbers involved, but more likely because the men were so forthcoming. Lübcke was informed of those whose injuries restricted them to dressing stations or field hospitals. The data included rank and unit, where the capture had taken place, the nature of wounds, whether interrogation was worthwhile, and when and where it might most profitably take place.

In Reserve Field Hospital No. 8 in Haubourdin, Major John Hughes (32nd Battalion) was treated for grenade splinters in the right thigh, while Lieutenant John Matthews (55th) had suffered wounds to his lower legs and head. In Reserve Field Hospital No. 6 Captain Charles Arblaster of the 53rd Battalion lay alongside Lieutenant Vivian Bernard (31st). On 21 July they were transferred to St Clothilde POW hospital in Douai where they found Captain Charles Mills (31st) and Captain F. Ranson (53rd). All but Arblaster, who three days later died of septicaemia, spoke with *Hauptmann* Lübcke.

Wounded non-commissioned prisoners considered as potentially useful candidates could expect to be transported to hospital in Valenciennes, where they were held for questioning while receiving treatment. At the end of the interrogation process summaries were sent to divisions alongside an evaluation of information derived from captured documents. The complete narrative was retained at AOK 6.

Scrutiny of the many tens of thousands of interrogation reports held in the Munich archives reveals only a small percentage of prisoners 'holding their tongue'. The majority, probably out of fear (although none later mention either feeling or actually being threatened), convey a deal of information, much of it highly sensitive and valuable. It is possible that men 'spilled the beans' in the belief that the misdemeanour was unlikely later to be discovered. For some, this had actually happened during the conflict. On 25 May 1916 Crown Prince Rupprecht had issued Order No. 4871 to all his commanders:

Re. Information disclosed by German prisoners
The statement reproduced overleaf, made by a German soldier belong-
ing to a regiment of the 6th Army who was captured by the enemy
during the night of 9–10 May 1916, was recently found in the possession
of a British prisoner. The German soldier unfortunately gave an exactly
correct account of the dispositions of the regiments holding the front in
his Corps sector and an approximately accurate account of the disposi-
tions of the reserves in the various villages behind the front.

The fact that this statement has come to light will make it possible,
after the war, to bring to account and punish this man who forgot his
duty. I would ask you, most urgently, to warn and inform your men
and all newly arriving replacements of the grave harm they would do
to their country and their comrades if they were to give the enemy even
the smallest insight into our order of battle, the dispositions of our front-
line troops, the location and dispositions of our reserves and artillery,
the locations of ammunition dumps, or the approach routes used by
our reliefs.

Rupprecht's entreaty was of course applicable to all soldiers, regardless of
nationality.

The final section of the same document provides clues as to why the
Bavarians adopted such benign interrogation methods:

Just as we do not use coercive measures ourselves to extract informa-
tion from enemy prisoners, the enemy is likewise constrained from
using coercion to obtain intelligence from German soldiers who rightly
regard it as their duty of honour not to divulge information. A prisoner
who does 'talk' does not thereby improve his fate in any way. He will
be treated no better or worse than the enemy first intended. On the
contrary, he can only gain the respect of the enemy by refusing to disclose
any information.

Our enemies have taken measures to ensure that their troops know
only as much about their order of battle as they actually need to
know. Enemy prisoners therefore know very little about the disposi-
tions of their troops. Both the French and the British are rigorous in

preventing all but those who have work to do there from entering their gun lines.

It was guile and benevolence, not brutality, that tended to unlock Allied jaws. So successful was this approach (later taken up by the British, who were not initially averse to coercion) that some prisoners clearly felt no qualms in recounting entire life stories. Hardships commenced only *after* the prisoner had been affably but effectively milked. In the case of the Fromelles prisoners, the approach was manifestly profitable. As a result we find that the Diggers not only divulge operational secrets, but philosophise about the war, its origins, the future, their opinions of comrades, private prejudices etc., imparting invaluable material to the German military . . . and the German military propaganda machine. The information received by the latter usually required no embroidery but could simply be distorted to suit the exigencies of the moment. It was of course pre-filtered.

Lübcke's task was assisted by a weapon of inestimable value: the copy of General Haking's XI Corps operation order. It was the version issued to the 5th Australian Division that confirmed to von Scanzoni that the Allied attacks were a feint. The value was a dual one, however, for the Bavarians were able to flourish the documents as if they had been in their possession since *before the battle*. Evidence of this can be found in several post-war prisoner statements, such as that of Captain R.A. Keay (C Company, 32nd Battalion):

The main reason for the failure of the attack I think, was that the Germans knew all about it before it came off. This statement is proved by the fact that, when at Lille immediately after capture, a German Staff Officer who interrogated us told us that if we would not answer questions because we were giving away anything, we were mistaken, that all he wanted was verification, and thereupon drew from a satchel a type-written copy of General Haking's order for the attack, this was actually signed by the General and was certainly the same order that we had received the day of the attack. This seemed to us rather peculiar and on being sent to Dulmen camp I got into communication with a Sergeant Major Rennie who was in touch with the War Office and told him this amongst other information.

Statement given on 7 December 1918 in Ripon, Yorkshire

Keay was taken in by the trick, as too were Lieutenant Harold Lovejoy (A Company, 54th Battalion), Captain G.D. Folkard (D Company, 55th Battalion) and Lieutenant Albert Bowman (D Company, 53rd Battalion), all of whom expressed surprise, shock and dismay. One of these men, however, may have been a purveyor! The presence of the order undermined everything that incarcerated and demoralised Diggers needed to believe.

Some wounded Allied prisoners were treated by Bavarian medical personnel while still in the trenches. The conduct of their captors clearly varied; numerous men report threats with gun or bayonet, receiving blows from rifle butts, and being stripped of badges and insignia. Instances of viciousness are not uncommon, but they always relate to the passage from the field of battle, never to their interrogation. Private Tom Bolton of D Company, 29th Battalion, notes his treatment in the dressing station as 'good', but mentions men being shot after surrender. The chaotic, fractured and extended nature of the end of the battle meant that prisoners were being apprehended and the wounded attended to while bombing and hand-to-hand fighting continued around them.

Like 9 May 1915 at the Sugar Loaf, the desperate Australian rearguard action created the environment for extreme brutality, a pattern that can be distinguished in every other action of the war—indeed any war. Examples of this can be found in the testimonies (prisoner statements) of more than one Digger. For instance, upon realising the hopelessness of the cause, Lieutenant Albert Bowman had himself ceased fighting and ordered his party to do so. Not all of those nearby were aware of the capitulation, however, for the two Bavarian guards escorting Bowman were shot down before circumstances could be made clear by him.

Under such conditions 'treacherous behaviour', as mentioned by *Oberleutnant* Schmidt in Chapter 14, was as readily imagined as it was perpetrated; reactions at such a time and after such an eventful few days were likely to be swift and brutal. In general, as the combat concluded the Diggers were extremely fortunate that the Bavarians were not only obliged and determined to take as many prisoners as possible, but in a position, from the point of view of infantry strength, to do so. Had this not been the case, that chill phrase, 'No prisoners were taken', which appears on more than one occasion within the 1915 chronicles, could easily have pertained again.

Because the tactical situation remained fluid and potentially dangerous, the majority of those who surrendered were led away as swiftly as conditions allowed. Testimonies reveal that wounded men who were clearly *hors de combat* were often ignored as the battle drew to a close; the Bavarians either took up positions around and among them or, having relieved them of their weapons, surged past. Although on 20 July some men were left all day without treatment and others roughly handled, it is clear that most received reasonable care and consideration. Many, as previously mentioned, were treated in the trenches before being taken to dressing stations and hospitals, and a number were carried several kilometres on stretchers or in groundsheet 'hammocks' by Bavarian bearers; Private T.H. Herket (53rd) noted that he was borne away on the back of an enemy soldier.

A few wounded Diggers had taken cover so well among the devastation that it was only two or three days later that they were recovered. Holing up was a hazardous option, for the chance of escaping death by infection diminished with every moment spent untreated. As early as 5.00 p.m. on the evening of 20 July Australian medics were reporting cases of men 'commencing putrefaction in their wounds'.

Having been evacuated by the enemy, the deluge of wounded from both sides meant that some British and Australian troops had to wait a day or more for treatment in German dressing stations. When their turn came, the care was noted as being remarkable and, of course, surprising. Injections and inoculations preceded dressing and surgery. Men with more-complex injuries were more than once operated upon.

When enemy troops were captured (or their bodies discovered), a report was immediately made by telegraph or telephone to corps headquarters, who conveyed the data to the intelligence officer. The message was required to indicate:

a) the number of prisoners and their unit (the company, where possible),
b) the time and place of capture and brief details of the circumstances,
c) the unit which took the prisoners.

All documents such as orders, letters, maps, newspapers, diaries and papers were seized immediately after capture and sent without delay to AOK 6. The most important elements, such as particularly significant orders issued by enemy high command, were communicated by phone or telegram, or in extract form by motorcycle despatch.

The first 'questioning' took place in the trenches themselves; the key question, posed particularly to officers, was whether fresh Allied assaults were planned. Most prisoners would have had no inkling of such plans but, by reason of natural defiance rather than knowledge, replied in the affirmative. Prisoners were allowed to retain their military identity document or paybook, and personal non-military papers, money, identity disk, regimental insignia and photographs of family members after initial scrutiny, and provided that nothing of potential significance was written on them. All papers removed from the dead were despatched for evaluation accompanied by a brief report indicating the location at which the body was discovered and approximately how long it had been there. If large quantities of military documents were captured, they were taken to a place of safety and placed under guard. Lübcke and his colleagues were then informed.

Enemy maps and other especially valuable charts and plans were to be handed over to the finder's superiors at the nearest command post, from where they were safely despatched to Division and Corps. No Bavarian soldier was allowed to keep any captured material unless it had been scrutinised and found to be of no value. If a soldier took an interest in a particular 'souvenir', he could declare it when handing it in, and the item might be returned after evaluation.

Captured weapons, equipment and munitions were also sent in without delay, but only if they were of a previously unknown type or allowed unit identification. The questioning of prisoners about military matters by unauthorised persons was strictly forbidden, and detailed interrogations before prisoners were brought to HQ was avoided. Any noteworthy observations such as whether or not a man spoke German were recorded in a brief report sent with the escort.

Unit identification was of course essential. *Engländer* troops were asked for battalion rather than regiment, plus brigade and division. Captured telegraphers, signallers and radio operators were interrogated in the presence of English-speaking Bavarian officers with similar training. Experience also showed that 'specialist troops' such as pilots and observers (in particular the English) were frequently more communicative when talking to German airmen.

As far as was possible, prisoners were prevented from talking among themselves prior to interrogation. This was held to be especially important in the case of officers as on a number of occasions it was found that they concocted 'group agreements' about what was to be divulged, making it difficult for intelligence officers to ascertain the true situation.

Until 20 July 1916, the only Australian officer to fall into enemy hands had been Lieutenant Norman Blanchard at Bois-Grenier in early May. Now Lübcke was presented with a host of considerably more experienced men—and all Australian. It was a splendid opportunity; the question was how much information could be extracted.

In the Australian section of the Bavarian battlefront at Rouges Bancs, prisoners, wounded and unwounded, were escorted back to collecting stations in houses and farms behind the line. Preliminary questioning took place there. Papers were confiscated and personal items examined. The prisoners were given cards, written in German, upon which each man was required to write his home address and state that he was in German hands. One of the officers present, Captain Charles Mills, had been wounded in the hand. In his prisoner-of-war statement given on 21 January 1918 while interned in Switzerland, Mills described his early custodial phase:

I was not molested during my passage through the German positions. On arrival at the farm I was treated courteously. A German surgeon dressed my wound. I handed over the contents of my pockets at the request of an Officer and received everything back except a photo of myself taken at a studio in Melbourne, which he said he would keep as an example of the Australian uniform. The men were not ill-treated here. I was watching closely. All the wounded were dressed and those who could not walk were removed in motor ambulances. I asked that a meal should be provided for the men, but was told that there was nothing for them. They were allowed to lie down on some straw in a barn. At about mid-day an officer brought me a sheet of foolscap on which he had marked with coloured pencils in diagrammatic form, the colours of the battalions of the 5th Division. He said: 'This is right, Captain?'. I said, 'I have nothing to say'. The list was correct. At about 2pm we were marched to Lille—a long and hard march of three hours. Only one five minutes' rest was allowed. On arrival, we got our first meal—meat stew and brown bread.

The initial Bavarian Interrogation Report B No. 6138 lists 219 Australian prisoners including six officers, of whom Charles Mills was one. At the collecting stations they were deliberately questioned within view of wounded comrades receiving medical attention: another shrewd psychological strategy to put nervous captives at their ease at this frightening time. The sight of the injured being properly cared for by 'the enemy' helped to instil trust and thus promote the inclination to talk. Fritz Lübcke had a great deal of work ahead. His first impressions of the Digger officers were as follows:

The officers are very circumspect in what they say. Three of them are regular soldiers with 20, 12 and 8 years' service respectively, one returned to the Army three years ago, and two, who were bank officials in civilian life, volunteered at the outbreak of war. Both in a military respect and personally, they make a much less favourable impression than the average English officer.

Almost all the men are volunteers who joined the Army at the beginning of the war. Although the majority of them are strapping young men, their demeanour is generally unsoldierly and they have little to say for themselves, partly because they have only been on the Western Front for a few weeks and partly because they have little or no interest in military dispositions.

A highly detailed description of the object of the attack plus the composition and dispositions of the 5th Division followed. Then Lübcke approached the question of how it was that the endeavour came to fail so miserably. The response was as follows:

*The attack should have taken place on Monday, 17 July, but was post-
poned until Wednesday, 19 July, due to unfavourable weather conditions
resulting in poor visibility for artillery observation. The officers attrib-
ute the failure of the attack to the incompetence of the Divisional
commander. The men all say that coherent leadership was lacking
from the outset. Thus, for example, after their Company commander
was killed as they were leaving their own trenches, some companies
charged blindly and leaderless into our positions and in some cases
then pushed on into the second and third line of trenches, where they
found themselves surrounded by German troops advancing along lateral
communication trenches.*

*There were no special offensive training exercises in preparation for
this operation. The prisoners all describe their own casualties during the
attack as very heavy; in particular, they say they suffered heavy losses
after they broke in to the German front line trenches. The artillery of
the 5th Australian Division was specially reinforced with English heavy
artillery for this attack, as it has no guns of its own over 12.5cm calibre
(5-inch).*

In short, the officers were blaming McCay for not making certain that
troops were adequately trained and briefed. Results of questions about
reserves and the locations of other Australian divisions were inconclusive,
not least because the prisoners were not yet in possession of such knowledge. Nevertheless, some useful data was gathered about the disposition of
various battalions and an insight was gained into far wider perspectives:

*According to the officers, it relieved English troops (Tommies), but the
men all say that they took over the sector from another Australian
division, probably the 2nd Australian Division (? : Intelligence Officer).
During the relief, the men claim to have seen the 13th, 22nd, 45th and
47th Battalions. <u>One man</u> professes to know that the 2nd Australian Division was withdrawn from this sector and that men from that
division were expecting to be deployed on the Somme . . .*

*Neither the officer prisoners nor the men make any secret of their
war weariness, and they are clearly pleased that the war is over for*

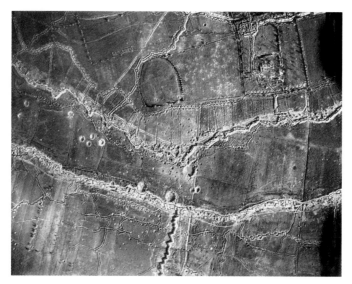

A German aerial photograph taken before 19 July showing the opposing lines in the Horseshoe (*Runder Sumpf*) sector with the Australian trenches above and the Bavarians below. The Cordonnerie Farm can be seen at top right. Numerous mine craters punctuate No Man's Land, with the two 9 May 1915 blows being clearly evident on the Bavarian front line to the left of the *Kastengraben* that can be seen at centre bottom. Note the ditches in No Man's Land. (BAM, Ingolstadt, G 1372-45)

A German aerial of Spring 1916 showing the Rouges Bancs/Sugar Loaf sector before advanced Allied jumping-off trenches were installed—Australians above, Bavarians below. The Orchard (*Obstgarten*) is clearly visible at the centre left of the image, with the Australian line running through its top left corner. The Layes Brook (*Layer-Bach*) and *Tommy-Brücke* are marked (in No Man's Land), and the area of the Memorial Park can be seen next to the road at centre right. Note the vestiges of the early (1914) British trenches close to the Bavarian line to the right of the *Rue Delvas (Tommy-Strasse)*. (BAM, Ingolstadt, G 1372-44)

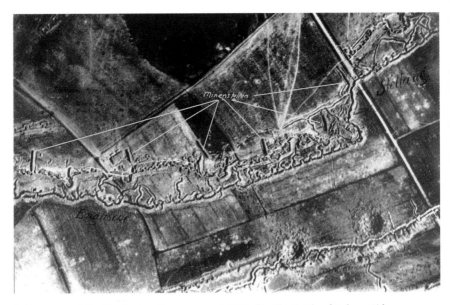

A German aerial taken during the summer of 1915 after the Battle of Aubers Ridge. Bavarian lines at bottom, with the two 9 May 1915 mine craters evident. Comparison with picture 1 shows how a far stronger Allied front line was reinstated behind the forward positions seen in this image. (Author's collection)

A scene behind the Bavarian front line. There are no trenches. The uneven ground levels in the foreground are evidence of earth being 'won' to fill a splendid variety of sandbags to build parapet, parados and shelters. (BAM, Ingolstadt, G 1395-68)

A view of the Rue Delvas taken from a point that would today be inside the Australian Memorial Park showing the beginnings of the 'barrier' constructed ahead of the Bavarian front line (see image 2). The picture clearly reveals the often useful Flanders mists. (BAM, Ingolstadt, G 1378-9)

A view along the Bavarian front line showing the firestep with riflemen at timber loopholes. Two curtained shelters are visible. Note the width of the trench. (BAM, Ingolstadt, G 1384-11)

A typical Bavarian machine-gun platform with a Maxim in action firing from the top of the breastwork. (BAM, Ingolstadt, G 1384-13)

The staff of 6th Bavarian Reserve Division at their Haubourdin headquarters. Gustav von Scanzoni is the genial-looking gentleman with a luxuriant white moustache standing at rear. (BAM, Ingolstadt, G 1395-59)

British dead in No Man's Land in front of the Bavarian trenches at Rouges Bancs after the battle of 9 May 1915. (BAM, Ingolstadt, G 1384-6)

Captain Fritz Lübcke (at centre, with goggles), Intelligence Officer for AOK 6, looking his habitual affable self with a variety of allied prisoners. (Author's collection)

The interior of a Bavarian dugout in the Fromelles sector. Several decorative items have been 'borrowed' from nearby abandoned houses. (BAM, Ingolstadt, G 3547a-257)

This photograph is believed to have been captured with the first Australian prisoners at Bois Grenier on 5 May 1916. One or both of the Diggers pictured may have fallen into German hands on this day. The sketch below was drawn and circulated to make the German Army aware of the appearance of a Digger. (BAM, Ingolstadt, 403-80-341)

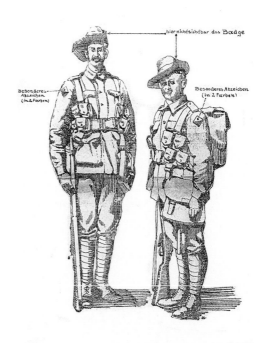

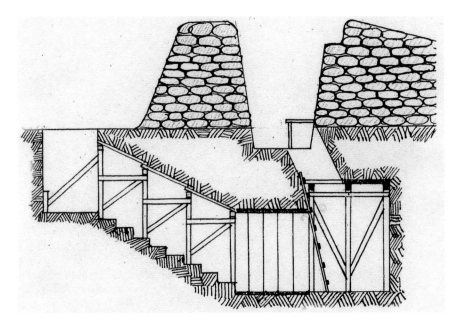

Bavarian double breastwork with fire-stepped trench and mined dugout below with two entrances. It does not need to be especially deep because the underground structure is protected from shells by the breastwork above. The entrance to the rear was typical German work. It was installed so that in the case of attack the occupants could quickly evacuate before themselves attacking from the cover of the rear breastwork. (*Kriegsarchiv* Munich, 6 BRD Bund 25)

A section of *Forderbahn* push-line near the crest of the ridge between Fromelles and Aubers. Once more, the personnel are protected by the Flanders mists. (BAM, Ingolstadt, G 1378-22)

A Bavarian battery of dummy guns and dummy gunners, with dummy trenches, breastworks and dugouts, all designed to deceive Allied air observers and attract hostile gunfire in order that the locations and calibre of Allied batteries could be identified. (BAM, Ingolstadt, G 1384-3)

An aerial of the Sugar Loaf and *Tommy-Brücke* sector from Summer 1916 showing the Orchard (centre left), advanced saps under construction, and the area of the Australian Memorial Park (above point 326). The Rhondda Sap is at far left. (Private collection)

Oberst Julius Ritter von Braun, commander of RIR 21, author of its regimental history and of course Burial Order 5220. (BAM, Ingolstadt, G 1380-42)

RIR 16 command post in the Hintergelände. Messages and orders were received and transmitted from positions such as this. (BAM, Ingolstadt, G 1373-26)

Nach den Angriffen am 19.7.16. bei Fromelles

Schlachtfeld bei Gravenstafel mit gefallenen Engländern.

Two versions of the same image. The top one is likely to be authentic. Research suggests it may show part of the Fromelles battlefield looking north-east from the Bavarian front line in the Wick Salient. The dead would therefore be British soldiers of the 2/6 Gloucesters. (Private collection) The bottom image, however, has simply been appropriated and cropped by RIR 247 for use in its regimental history. It purports to show the results of the action at Gravenstafel near Passchendaele in April 1915!

Vor der Bes...

Nach der Bes...

Comparative segments of two Bavarian panoramas taken before and after the Kulmbach raid on 15 July. The camera position is in the Bavarian front line where it is joined by the *Kastengraben* (see image 1). (*Kriegsarchiv*, Munich) _nng._

sung.

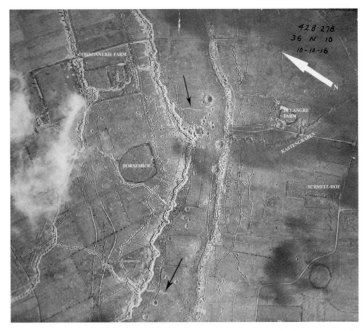

A British aerial photograph taken on 10 October 1916. The upper black arrow marks the eastern sap across No Man's Land, with the 19 July mine crater above it; the lower arrow indicates the sap used by many Diggers to withdraw from the enemy trenches on the morning of 20 July. (Private collection)

Allied dead on the Bavarian parapet at Fromelles. (BAM, Ingolstadt, 884-90-82)

A *Kastengraben*-style communication trench under construction. It was this kind of feature that the Australians had to double-lock and defend on 19 July 1916. (BAM, Ingolstadt, Germany, G 1378-13)

A communal grave dug by German troops. The geology, dimensions and depth, and the manner of burial, appear almost identical to the graves at Pheasant Wood. Beyond and to the left, other pits are being worked on. Location unknown. (Private collection)

An enlarged section of a British aerial photograph taken on 22 October 1916 showing the grave site along the southern edge of Pheasant Wood. The five closed pits and three open pits are clearly visible. The *Türken-Bahn* tramway can be seen cutting through the bottom left corner of the wood and diagonally traversing the fields. (Imperial War Museum, Box 199-359)

A well-tended *Einzelgräb* (individual burial) of a British soldier somewhere in the Fromelles sector. The Bavarian archives record considerable numbers of such graves. (BAM, Ingolstadt, Germany)

them. They are very worried about how they will be treated in German POW camps, as they have obviously been stuffed full of horror stories. When talking with the officers, the impression gained is that they are simply regurgitating the press agitation against Germany, which they all blame for breaching the peace. They do accept, however, that the violation of Belgian neutrality was a necessary act of self-defence on the part of Germany.

In their view, Germany has especially damaged its cause in the eyes of the neutral countries and the world at large with the shooting of Miss Cavell. In this respect too, they seem convinced of the truth of the sensational press reports. [At 6.00 a.m. on 12 October 1915 Edith Cavell, a British nurse working in Belgium, was executed by the Germans for aiding British and French soldiers to escape to neutral Holland. She instantly became an iconic figure for the Entente, her execution being widely used for propaganda purposes.]

The officers think that an early end to the war will only be possible if Germany capitulates. They believe that the ultimate victory of the Allies is inevitable, even if it takes a long time, because Germany will run out of reserves and cannot keep pace economically with England, supported by her colonies.

From these preliminary enquiries it can be seen that Lübcke gained a mass of useful material, both from the operational and propagandist viewpoint. More detailed individual questioning, particularly of the six officers, was to follow. NCOs too were interrogated. Platoon Sergeant J.R. Bonnett of A Company, 45th Battalion, recorded being held for a week in Douai, 'mainly that we might be rigorously questioned, but the Germans got very little information out of us'.

At the other end of the battlefield, interrogation of the forty-five men of the 2/7th Warwickshire Regiment, 182nd Brigade, was frustrating for no British officers had survived to be interviewed. The Tommies seemed to be entirely ignorant of the ground, the purpose of the attack, the dispositions and identity of neighbouring units, and even the scale of the enterprise. They were, noted Lübcke, 'less well informed about the purpose of the attack than the Australians. They had not at all been told about the extent of the action, nor the participation of the Australians.' There had been 'chaos from the start'.

If there was any later questioning of British troops, it may have been unprofitable for no further interrogation records relating to the 61st Division are present in the files of AOK 6 or 6 BRD. The lack of officer prisoners was particularly disappointing.

Lübcke's preliminary interrogation report was delivered on 21 July, within thirty-six hours of the start of the action. It offers evidence of the confusion felt by captured Diggers who had achieved and then lost objectives at such huge cost, while remaining oblivious as to how the rest of the battle unfolded around them. Perplexity is manifest, but their observations are immediate and 'unsullied' by hindsight and opinions of third parties.

The following day von Scanzoni circulated Report BR B No. Ia 3926 entitled 'Conversations with the captured Australian officers'. In it we are further enlightened as to how Haking's operation order may have fallen into Bavarian hands.

> The officers asked that they not be interrogated because, as officers, they were unable to divulge anything and were prepared to accept the consequences of their refusal, as German officers would do if captured by the British.
>
> Captain Mills, a regular officer with the 31st Battalion, 8th Brigade, 5th Australian Division, proved especially talkative. He did not reproach himself for being taken prisoner because he had done his duty and his men too had acquitted themselves bravely. He had, however, committed a serious error of judgement in allowing important documents to fall into our hands, which, of course, he should never have brought over to our positions with him. The attack had been abortive, in his opinion, owing to tactical failings. There were enough troops there, they had only to be committed. The attack should have taken place over a frontage of 2½ miles. He said that still more Australians were arriving here and that we would have to contend with them again in the future.

When asked whether more new Australian divisions were on their way, he had nothing to say on the matter.

Our machine guns had done excellent work, and we owed the successful defence of our positions to them and to the effectiveness of our artillery. They had been powerless against our grenadiers who headed the counter-attack. The most advanced Australian-held lines were in constant contact throughout the night with the rear, from where they received ammunition and hand grenades, but even so they had been unable to hold out any longer as the men were too badly fatigued and there was no longer any prospect of getting back to their own lines. They thought that we had brought up artillery reinforcements in the course of yesterday evening. He was very reluctant to accept that the defending Division had beaten off the attack entirely on its own, and thought that reserves must have been brought up from the Somme region. He complimented our marksmanship, but said that the Australians are also very good shots; they are born hunters and all of them shoot exceptionally well.

Lieutenant Cuminers [Captain G. Cummins, 55th Battalion], who with several of the other prisoners had fought at Gallipoli, said that they had frequently suffered similar defeats in that campaign. The men always went in spiritedly and often advanced great distances, right up to the gun line, but then the leadership usually broke down and the men were mown down or driven back again. He was amazed by Turkey's continued stubborn resistance; they had imagined that Turkey would be very easily defeated. This officer knew that three men from the 5th Division had fallen into our hands during our last raid. They were afraid that those men had given something away and that we had forewarning of the attack. They are in general astonished at the massive resistance that Germany is still able to put up. 'It's almost as if the Germans can bring the dead back to life again', he said.

All the officers were very concerned about the fate of their men. They said that the American envoy had found that British prisoners of war in Germany were going hungry. Questions had also been asked about this in Parliament. They regard the regular reports in the hostile newspapers of barbaric war-making and ill-treatment of prisoners by the Germans as foolish chatter; after all war is not a delicate trade. The officers were favourably impressed by our care of their wounded and treatment of the prisoners and repeatedly expressed their appreciation.

Lieutenant Cuminers believes that the majority of the men volunteered for the Expeditionary Force not out of a desire for adventure, but because they were well paid (5 Marks—sometimes 6 Marks—a day), and, for many of them, also out of patriotism. Australia feels itself part of the British Empire in the same way that the German states feel part of the German Reich. By taking part in this great endeavour they are demonstrating their loyalty to the Motherland.

The officers say that they are all weary of the war and do not believe that it can ever be settled on the battlefield; a way has to be found to bring the war to an end soon.

Captain Mills formed up the prisoners ready to march off and addressed a few words to them, wishing them all the best in the future and telling them that they had all done their duty. Rations would not be as plentiful now as they used to be—and here he jokingly remarked: don't laugh, you didn't get too much in Egypt either—and in this respect too they would have to learn to adapt to circumstances.

The operation order made it clear that the attack had been designed as a feint with strictly limited objectives so, unless the order itself was a shrewd British ruse, it could be assumed that no reserves were preparing to continue the action. There are no indications as to which 'important documents' Captain Charles Mills made a 'serious error of judgement' in bringing across No Man's Land; they may or may not have included this document.

Another Bavarian report, B No. 6132, reveals that a second order, that issued to the 31st Australian Battalion and signed by Lieutenant V.D. Bernard, was also 'captured' as the fighting came to a close. It commenced in similarly illuminating fashion:

1. With the object of preventing the enemy drawing troops from their front, offensive operations are to be carried out by troops of 11th Corps and 2 Anzac under the command of the G.O.C. 11th Corps.

Von Scanzoni and Lübcke were in possession of all thirty additional points. They explained in fine detail the Australian assault scheme, and included an appendix spelling out the entire artillery programme. On 24 July when Vivian Bernard was still being treated in hospital alongside Captain Charles Arblaster, translations of both orders were circulated throughout AOK 6—and beyond.

From time to time after the prisoners had been dispersed to their various camps, they were reminded by German intelligence personnel of their 'betrayal' by unnamed others, regularly accentuating the point that the operation orders had been in their possession since before battle was joined. It made painful listening, and post-war POW statements reveal how deeply the subtle instillation of anxiety and insecurity was made to permeate consciences and consciousness. Confidence in command was deeply undermined.

By the end of the month the interviews with other prisoners were complete, and a still more detailed document, B. No. 6179, was produced. Circulated on 30 July, it provided information about the attacks in both the British and Australian sectors, revealing how the intelligence jigsaw was built, and including information derived from a brigade order subsequently found on the body of a dead British officer. Thus the Bavarians had come into possession of operation orders issued to Division, Brigade and Battalion, and the complete artillery fireplan—almost the full set.

Lübcke's combined report is especially important because in its latter section it begins to delve into wider Australian issues as revealed by the Diggers:

> A 'Conscription Bill' on the British model has often been mooted, but none has yet been brought forward. The main reason for introducing conscription would be the same as in Britain—the unwillingness of married men to volunteer for military service as long as there is a sufficient supply of fit and able unmarried men who, without good reason, decline to enlist.

There is, however, no shortage of volunteers. In the early days men volunteered out of simple loyalty to the mother country, but as time went on that sentiment was joined, as the power of the German army became apparent, by fears for the security of their own country. Those fears are evidently being zealously stoked up by the press. Australians now almost always answer the question of what they are really fighting for with 'To stop Germany from taking over the world, and especially Australia'.

Although the Australian officers and men are in very good physical condition, they seem rather deficient in military qualities. The Australian officers are inferior in every respect to the British. As is to be expected in view of their educational background, they are completely lacking in judgment as to what is important militarily and what is not. The officers, for example, despite repeated protestations that their conscience as officers would not allow them to disclose military secrets, cheerfully dictated to us complete details of the planning and execution of the attack, and the dispositions of the units involved. The only information they seemed to regard as important was the identity of the units on their flanks and to the rear of their division; in that respect it was only with guile that we were able to extract a few incomplete fragments of information from them. Perhaps, though, given their deficient military training, they really did not know anything.

Several paragraphs then related to the formation of the 5th Australian Division in Egypt, and German speculation on the whereabouts of various Australian units. The document concludes with a remarkably prescient section by the captured officers about how the war would end and what might occur if German powers were not sufficiently curtailed after Allied victory:

Among the officers there is widespread feeling that events are moving towards a conclusion. The prospect of a third winter in the field does not appeal to anyone, except perhaps a few high-ranking officers in the rear. The Entente itself is certainly very eager to conclude this campaign in its own favour before winter. The Australians' confidence in victory is undiminished. They believe that the Allies must win because of their disproportionately greater manpower and capacity to manufacture munitions, their unrestricted trade with the whole world, and, above all, the fact that they have much more money.

They know nothing about the French; they look first and foremost to Britain and think she is so rich and powerful that she must inevitably triumph. Germany cannot withstand the unrelenting military and economic pressure indefinitely.

The condition for peace remains, however, that Germany must be subdued in a way that ensures she will not be able to launch another armed aggression against her neighbours in the future. Germany started this war with the aim of becoming a dominant imperial power in the world, and if she is not weakened by the peace terms, she will rise again within a few years, better armed than ever, and strike again.

To avert that danger, the Allies must carry on fighting, even if Germany makes attractive peace overtures to the Entente. Having learnt the lessons of this war, Germany would not make the same mistakes again in the next one. A Germany that is already capable of taking on half the world, if allowed to re-arm for a carefully prepared war of conquest, would pose an incalculable danger to the whole world.

As Germany is not yet even remotely close to being defeated militarily, there is very little prospect of an early end to the war. The main obstacle to an early peace is the absence of mutual trust. Open and trusting dialogue is something that has always been lacking in international diplomatic relations. With less distrust on all sides, the war could perhaps have been avoided, and peace might even now be hastened.

In Australia, antagonism against Germany has grown as the war has gone on. In the beginning there was no overt antipathy towards Germany. Australia simply felt obliged to support the threatened mother country, which most Australians still regard as 'home', and would have helped Britain in the same way against any other country with which she had become involved in a war.

It seems most unlikely that economic sanctions would continue for long after the conclusion of peace. Trading relations with Germany would soon be resumed. Japan and America pose a much greater competitive threat to Australia.

The Australians see first and foremost Japan as their natural enemy. As long as the Anglo–Japanese alliance continues, the danger is contained, but only temporarily, and Japan will surely threaten Australia one day. Fears of Japan harming the national interests of Australia were an unstated but substantial factor in the introduction of compulsory civil defence service in Australia on 1 July 1911. The captured officers are firm believers in the 'yellow peril' and think that the white races will one day have to stand together against the coloured races.

The prisoners have nothing but contempt for the United States of America. The American government allowed itself to be humiliated, by Japan and even by tiny Mexico. Worst of all, it stood by when hundreds of its citizens lost their lives at the hands of German U-boats [this refers to the sinking of the *Lusitania*] *and its only response has been words of protest. For that reason every self-respecting belligerent nation should despise the Americans, who only seem to be interested in making money.*

Hauptmann Fritz Lübcke's document is one of the most comprehensive and remarkable interrogation compilations in the Munich archive. What becomes abundantly clear through this resource and via post-war prisoner statements is that preparations for the 19 July attack had been inadequate in every department.

'Instructions for Infantry Brigadiers', the document issued by James McCay on 15 July 1916, outlined in twenty-four clear and concise points the required scope and mode of the attack. Nevertheless it was shabbily planned, the troops too new, too naïve, too inexperienced, and insufficiently prepared and protected. They were not acquainted with the objectives, either tactical or topographical. Some disobeyed orders. Above all, perhaps, Sir Richard Haking and his staff were guilty of the cardinal sin of anonymising the enemy. It is difficult to avoid the conclusion that even had the British and Australians captured and consolidated their objectives on 19 July, their residency would have been short-lived.

Through the Munich archive we are able to take the interrogations a step further. In his book on General Sir Richard Haking, Mike Senior notes that: 'The German press also played a part in establishing the Anzac legend and the *Berliner Tageblat* of 30 July 1916 described the Australian soldiers as, "unsophisticated sons of graziers and heirs to the land . . . What their fathers had brought to the wild colony lay in their bearing and eyes, and they were not to be taken lightly. Good shots, cruel fighters, steel-hard fellows."'

In employing this kind of language, the Germans are not praising their foe, but adding lustre to their own triumphs. Polish could be applied as much by omission as by exaggeration or alteration, and both the press pieces and the post-war unit histories are affected by this practice. In the knowledge that Allied intelligence, and indeed the Allied press, scrutinised every enemy newspaper article, such passages (there are many thousands of examples) were produced not only for the benefit of the peoples of Austria–Germany, *but equally for the foreign military and public*. Fascinating though they are, it is an error to take them at face value, however tempting that may be. To take one example: the 'hesitant' Digger assaults at the Sugar Loaf were best left unmentioned. Their inclusion, although fully illustrating the fear generated by the Bavarian defence, would serve to steal some of the lustre from the overall triumph. Far better that the international public perceived the Australians as great warriors—vanquished by fiercer and wiser Bavarian warriors. Which is also why the hesitance was not noted in regimental histories: we prefer to encourage and produce narratives that confirm our good opinions of ourselves—and foster it in others.

We now have to hand—for the first time—the documents that formed the very foundation of *all* reports on the battle of 19 July 1916. It is not difficult to see how headquarters in Berlin approached the selection, transformation and public dissemination of propaganda. By simply changing black to many a shade of grey, and very often to pure white, they needled, nurtured and misinformed, shrewdly buffing their own performance while at the same time pitting ally against ally.

Some of the most comprehensive pieces on Fromelles were written by official war correspondent Wilhelm Scheuermann. On 3 August the *North German Gazette* published a long piece entitled 'The Battle of Fromelles'.

In it we can see the conversion of *Hauptmann* Fritz Lübcke's interrogations into unalloyed propaganda. Naturally, Scheuermann concentrated his attentions on the Diggers; it was, after all, the first significant encounter with a substantial number of prisoners who had come halfway around the world to fight the German nation. Space does not allow reproduction of the entire article, but I have here selected some of the more illustrative comparative sections:

> *The English troops who took part in this action were Australians. For the most part they are war-volunteers and amongst them were many well-to-do farmers, strong, youthful men, who undoubtedly attacked with great bravery and proved themselves clever and tenacious in close fighting. The heavy losses which they suffered in the attack and the total failure of their terrible sacrifice, disheartened them very much. They had reckoned on certain victory and had counted on the superiority of their artillery of which they had been told so much.*
>
> *The officers made a good impression and showed themselves superior in education and bearing to the average English officer. The bravery of the men and their stamina is undoubted. They were nothing like so afraid of the horrors of hand-grenade fighting as the majority of newly recruited English soldiers. Against these men, who are no mean fighters, our heroic Bavarians fought magnificently. At the moment when the advance really began, great shouts of joy were raised. The men jumped on to the parapet, swung their helmets in the air and shouted 'Hurrah' before they fired the first salvo.*
>
> *As the English fled, the Bavarians shouted after them, 'Come on, come on, if you've got any pluck.' The men of the 11th Company (21st Bavarian Regiment) sang 'The Watch on the Rhine' as they cleared the enemy out of their trenches with hand-grenades. Even where the English temporarily forced their way through, the garrison fought splendidly, and machine guns continued firing until the last man had fallen . . .*
>
> *The English enterprise against Fromelles has caused headshaking everywhere amongst ourselves as well as in neutral countries, and perhaps even amongst the French and English themselves, for no one*

could imagine what the intentions of the English really were. Had it been merely a demonstration against the enormously strong German defences of Lille it would appear to have been undertaken with too large or too small a force so that the whole affair would have been a mystery had we not captured the English Operation Order. From this it appears that the English were of the opinion that we were taking the troops from this part of the front for employment on the Somme. They wanted to prevent this, to bind down our forces and, if possible, cause us to drain our reserves on the Somme.

This plan absolutely came to nothing, for the Bavarian Division which was attacked gained the ascendancy by themselves, without bringing up a single gun from any other position, and without need, even for a moment, of the reserves . . .

The spirit of the troops, the vast majority of whom have been fighting since the beginning of the war, and have fought in a number of bloody battles, was very much raised by this splendid success. Troops and commanders thoroughly agree that the English could do them no greater favour than often to repeat such enterprises as the Battle of Fromelles. Even during the fight a large number of an Australian Brigade which had been brought up later, could not be got out of their trenches.

This piece was followed by a second, which specifically related to the interrogations:

The British contingent defeated at Fromelles included two Australian divisions composed almost entirely of volunteers who had enlisted at the outbreak of war to come to the aid of the Mother Country. They were predominantly young, athletic men, but among them, by way of exception, was also a man of 68, who was brought in with a severe abdominal wound. Like most of the Australians, he professed to have joined the army out of enthusiasm for the British cause . . . and it was the duty of the colonies to demonstrate their gratitude to the Mother Country and come to Britain's aid . . .

Only a few of the prisoners averred that many of them—but not, of course, themselves—had only joined up for the high rates of pay.

Although the majority had been with the colours since the beginning of the war, and many of them had already fought in various theatres, they all conveyed a most unmilitary impression. One might well say that, almost without exception, they are not in the least interested in military matters and, indeed, that they perhaps quite deliberately make play of their indifference. Many of them, who might well otherwise be perfectly upstanding individuals, bear in their faces the typical convict features that were so recognisable to the gallant Bavarians. But there are also some among them who are evidently well-to-do, the sons of rich farmers, men who obviously set store by good clothes and personal grooming.

The officers made a good impression. Some of them were regular army officers, others were members of the reserve who worked in banking and similar occupations in civilian life. They have a certain amount of military training, which elevates them above the average of British officers, and they are better educated than the majority of their British counterparts.

The Australians approached the battle with great confidence. They believed that the German units manning the sectors opposite them were severely depleted as a result of the battle on the Somme and they had faith in the much-vaunted superiority of the British heavy artillery . . . But then, when virtually none of the first assault column returned alive, and when they saw that 'No Man's Land' was strewn with bodies, in places lying side by side and even on top of one another, a deep disillusion came over them. As a result, the troops in the following waves left their trenches only hesitantly and without offensive spirit, and some did not even 'go over' at all. The soldiers were shaken by the death of so many of their comrades and were both downcast by the failure of the attack and very angry. And their wrath was directed at the high command, which they condemned as incompetent . . .

Our artillery fire terrified them and they unanimously reported that some of their battalions had suffered casualties as high as 60%, moving between the assembly area and the trenches, most of them killed.

As is to be expected after so heavy a defeat, the prisoners, without exception, including their officers, had lost all stomach for the war. They said that their Australian comrades, on the whole, had had enough of this war, which kept them away from their proper occupations, and to which there was no end in sight. They were still convinced, however, that Britain would win the war, even if it were to go on for a very long time. No other outcome was possible because Britain was too powerful and had inexhaustible resources to call upon.

The Australians speak more openly and candidly about the causes of the war than the British . . .

It was apparent, incidentally, that even the educated and discerning Australians gave credence to the calumnies heaped on Germany by the British press. Virtually every accusation levelled against us is blindly believed, and so we cannot be surprised that many of the prisoners were initially astonished that the German soldiers treated them so chivalrously. Some of them were quite obviously under the impression that the Germans killed all British prisoners!

They were likewise astonished by the massive strength of Germany's resistance, since, by their reckoning, Germany must long since have exhausted the last of her reserves of manpower. A few of them who had already fought at Gallipoli conceded that they were from another hemisphere and were therefore in no position to pass judgement. There too they had experienced one setback after another and had always comforted themselves with the belief that Turkey was teetering on the verge of collapse—and yet now they were no longer there, and Turkey was clearly stronger and more vigorous than ever before.

One man's remarks on the strength of Germany's resistance spoke volumes about the attitude of these men from beyond Europe's shores. When they saw how ferociously the Bavarians fought them, the word went through the Australian ranks: 'It's as if the Germans can bring their dead back to life. How else is their insuperable resistance to be explained?'

The piece shows the designed metamorphosis of intelligence into propaganda, and illustrates the danger of taking such reports at face value. It was another ninety-five years before Munich's archives would finally offer a clearer window through which to view the *Gefecht bei Fromelles*, July 1916.

PART III

THE HEREAFTER

Chapter 17

A MUSEUM IN GENEVA

———————

The humanitarian camp has no homeland, and in war-time charity is not confined to the poor alone—it becomes universal.

The ICRC in World War One, ICRC booklet, Geneva, 2007

A fundamental aspect of the research relating to Pheasant Wood had been flagged in 2005 when studies began into the Red Cross Wounded and Missing files at the Australian War Memorial. The clue lay in the title. Most of the key information contained within the collection could clearly only have come from German sources. With diplomatic relations fractured, how and through whom was this done?

Throughout the conflict all the warring nations utilised the services of the International Committee of the Red Cross (ICRC), and it was through their efforts that the several governmental authorities and thus soldiers' families derived news of loved ones who had fallen into enemy hands, either

dead or alive. For news of men missing in action every household throughout Britain and her colonies (indeed all nations) relied upon the astounding
yet unsung labours of a team of volunteers working in a converted museum
in the Swiss city of Geneva.

The ICRC is today internationally recognised for its remarkable 150 years
in assisting prisoners of war, internees, refugees and the displaced. It formed
the vanguard of development in the formation of a structure for international humanitarian law when its gestation began in 1864. The diverse
nature of conflicts during the latter half of the 19th and early 20th centuries meant that the philosophical framework substantially expanded before
1914, manifested by agreements on human rights and the treatment of
prisoners at the Geneva Convention of 19 July 1906 and the Hague Convention of 18 October 1907. In August 1914, however, there was no satisfactory
humanitarian support structure for the kind of global conflagration that
was about to unfold. Such a framework had first to be constructed and then
constantly adapted as hostilities deepened and widened. During the First
World War the ICRC assumed more complex and diverse functions than
ever before.

Their skills, labours, determination and forbearance relate directly to
the several battles of Fromelles, the Pheasant Wood graves, and indeed
every action in every theatre between 1914 and 1918. Throughout the war
they received and processed information from Germany and the Entente,
and assumed the sole responsibility for its subsequent dissemination across
the globe. In the case of the Imperial and colonial nations, this meant the
supply of one copy of lists of dead, wounded, missing and prisoners to
the War Office in London, and three to the British Red Cross (BRC), who in
turn passed on relevant data to Red Cross Societies of the colonial nations,
including Australia. After the Gallipoli evacuation, the Australian Red
Cross Society, founded in August 1914 as a branch of the BRC, created the
Australian Red Cross Wounded and Missing Enquiry Bureau (RCWM),
their offices moving from Cairo to Victoria Street, London, and in late 1917
to larger premises in Grosvenor Place.

In early 2007 I contacted Geneva, explained the Fromelles case and
requested the archivists to search for references relating to soldiers of the
5th Australian Division during the period June to December 1916. Some

months later a response arrived: a list containing the names of not only prisoners of war but also those who died in battle. Research revealed that the majority were relevant to 19 July. A visit became necessary.

On arrival at the archive, I was presented with a set of *registres*—bound foolscap-size ledgers—covering part of the period in question—post-19 July 1916. Opening the first volume at random revealed a German death list (*Totenliste*). It contained not only personal details of both British and Australian dead, but much more, such as particulars of wounds, place of hospitalisation, treatment, time and cause of death, and location of burial. As further volumes were examined, the historical, genealogical, sociological and academic implications crystallised. More information was required. Had anyone ever studied the *registres*, and were there any articles, papers or reports which might assist my research? I asked. None. Why? The answer was unexpected: although the files had been open for decades, until that moment no historian or researcher had ever asked to see them.

It was an astonishing revelation. The lists represented vital missing links in not only the story of Fromelles, but the entire war. The lack of previous external analysis was an impediment, but the archive is so well organised that after two visits I had gleaned an understanding of how information gathered from the fields of battle in France and Flanders reached families across the British Empire. Here in Geneva, therefore, lay an interrelated but distinct database that complemented the RCWM files in the Australian War Memorial in Canberra; in fact, it was a primary element in their very existence.

The sequence relating to Pheasant Wood was as follows. The first 'transfer' of information regarding casualties was made after the battle by the divisional staff of 6 BRD when they passed lists of the dead to AOK 6; the second was by AOK 6 to the northern army *Gruppe*; the third from *Gruppe* to the Munich *Nachweisebüro*; the fourth from Munich to the Berlin *Zentralnachweisebüro*; the fifth was from Berlin to the ICRC in Geneva, where the material was quadruplicated. The sixth step was from Geneva to London, the seventh by the War Office and BRC to relevant offices in the UK and across the Empire. In Australia, the final vital step was completed by the RCWM, taking the news to the doorstep of every patiently waiting family.

Although in 2007 ICRC staff were aware that their 1914–18 antecedents had copied the *registres* several times for the benefit of other international agencies and societies, they were unaware that most of those copies were no longer extant. The historical significance of the resource which they daily employed to answer queries suddenly became monumental.

The *registres* comprise approximately 650 000 pages, each sheet holding from ten to thirty-five entries according to category. In addition there are seven million index cards and more than 350 linear metres of supplementary documentation, all relating directly to the lists. Associated documents explain the evolution of Red Cross work between 1914 and 1921 and the numerous problems faced by the committee in their pursuance of humanitarian goals. To put the holdings in a global context: although the First World War database is in itself colossal, it represents only approximately 1.5 per cent of the entire ICRC archive. Extrapolating further it can be seen that, despite running to tens of millions of entries, the entire 'British Empire-related' collection comprises only 7 per cent of the First World War archive.

Research in the ICRC archives leaves the visitor overwhelmed with admiration for the work of the Red Cross—not simply in relation to the events of 1914–19, but throughout every epoch of their existence. The archive reveals what the collective term 'World War' truly means, for there are no numbers, no statistics, only names—scores of millions of names, each one attached to a family, and each with an individual and unique narrative—and legacy. Study of the records is thus a profoundly sobering experience, and indispensable for that essential aspect of the historian's trade, the regular revision of perceptions.

It soon became clear that *Totenlisten* (deaths) and *Gräberlisten* (graves) relating to *Engländer* casualties were primarily generated as a result of failed allied offensive enterprises, or after actions where an attempted penetration of the German line had taken place and losses had been sustained within or near enemy territory: for example, small casualty-incurring enterprises like patrols and trench raids, abortive 'lesser' schemes such as the Aubers and Fromelles actions of 1915 and 1916, and fruitless 'major' enterprises such as the Battle of Cambrai in November 1917. To this index must be added grand and successful German offensives like the advances of spring

1918, when vast numbers of Allied troops, both dead and alive, became the property of the enemy. For particulars relating to the fate of British and Commonwealth soldiers, therefore, the ICRC lists can *only* offer information about men, living or dead, whose bodies or effects *fell into the hands of the forces of the Central Powers*. Conversely, information about German (or Austro–Hungarian) troops will be found in data provided to the ICRC by the Entente powers. For the purposes of my research, therefore, it was *German* files that held the greatest potential, and in Germany there was but one clearing-house—the *Zentralnachweisebüro* in Berlin.

Soon after the outbreak of war the Berlin Central Information Bureau (*Büro*) was established at various addresses in the city. In 1914 it was staffed by 900 personnel including retired officers, soldiers unfit for active service, women both young and middle-aged, and older gentlemen. Like the ICRC, all had volunteered their services for the common humanitarian cause. Although 'satellite' offices existed for other 'kingdoms' such as Bavaria, Saxony or Württemberg, all data relating to 'enemy' troops that required communication to Geneva and beyond was ultimately passed to and through the several departments of the *Büro*. From here family requests were accepted and forwarded relating to death certificates, 'missing' certificates, and statements of presumption of death. The public could either visit (the office opened at nine o'clock each morning, including Sundays and public holidays) or write to notify the authorities if a soldier reported as missing had written from a POW camp, or if information on a list was inaccurate or out of date. Whether it concerned arrangements for sending letters and packages, the repatriation of remains, pensions and allowances or matters regarding further hospital treatment or convalescence, any question relating to the war could be asked and would be answered.

The *Büro* was thus the sole central collection point for information relating to members of the German armed forces, be they dead, missing, wounded or captive. At the same time it dealt with citizens of the Entente, both military and civilian, who were prisoners or had died in Germany or in occupied territories. Information from regiments, field hospitals or from the enemy was sent to the relevant department—a *Referat*—which assessed each case and generated an index card in the name of the individual concerned. Cards from all sections relating to German soldiers were passed to *Referat I*, and those of enemy personnel despatched to *Referat III*—which in the case of Fromelles therefore became one of the key departments.

Every month prisoner-of-war camps sent in five copies of lists of inmates; hospital records were quadruplicated. Two were retained in Germany, one sent through diplomatic channels to the government of the relevant enemy country, and a further two to the German Red Cross in Berlin, of which one was forwarded to the ICRC in Geneva. Every list had a unique reference, and each page was individually numbered. They carried the date of despatch from the camp and the day on which the information was forwarded by the Ministry of War. The lists were then employed to create individual cards for every name, with a separate index for each country. These were arranged in alphabetical or phonetic order, the different classes—army, navy, air force—being thematically coloured and thus recognisable at a glance. Officers' cards were distinct from those of other ranks. Every record, even those relating to Serbs and Russians, was generated in the Latin alphabet with details written in German. They included all the presently available information about the individual and carried the unique number of the original list upon which the name first appeared. As the card index was produced solely for reference, there were no enquiry records and thus no database made of correspondence with enquirers. Unlike the ICRC's staggering throughput of enquiries, the *Büro* dealt with only 500 to 600 per day, the staff aiming to produce an answer within forty-eight hours.

Referat II assumed responsibility for all queries relating to the dead, and in particular the identification of unknowns. To that end, it sent every police station in Germany photographs of unidentifiable soldiers who had died in field hospitals, and occasionally personal effects found on the battlefields. The photographs were displayed, families coming to scrutinise the macabre images; a surprisingly large number of unknowns were identified by this means. The same approach was applied to soldiers whose trauma had led to memory loss: men who were no longer aware of their own identity. If no news about a missing man had arrived after a year, the military informed the relevant German authorities in the place where the man was last legally domiciled that he was now officially declared dead. Photographs of unidentifiable enemy dead were also taken and catalogued.

Referat II was also responsible for collecting information on the burial places (*Gräberabteilung*—graves department) of both German and enemy military personnel killed in action. It was a busy department, and in constant communication with staff members who had been specially posted to the front to take photographs and make plans of burial sites, which were subsequently catalogued by geographical area and accompanied by a list naming every identified soldier interred in the locality. The German database of post-war recovery and burials for the Western Front battlefields is kept in Kassel in central Germany. Maps and sketches associated with the collection not only show the locations at which bodies were found, but also where post-war recovery attempts had failed, and where men still lay. The burial places of these still-missing men—who are frequently named—are usually associated with trenches, dugouts or tunnels blown in by enemy action. They are numerous.

German regiments assumed responsibility for all graves in their sector, handing over the details upon relief. Graves were marked and lists updated monthly; recording on paper and in photographs was meticulous and of high quality. If a marker was erected by the Bavarians at the Pheasant Wood site—which appears likely—it would have received this treatment. In the Munich archive one may still find cemetery plans, paint swatches for memorials, cross and stone designs, font designs for various purposes and ranks, and the details of scores of burial ceremonies. Much documentation relating to reporting and treatment of graves still exists, and it was hoped that the diaries of German military padres and pastors would reveal important details. Of these 6 BRD had two, one Catholic, the other Protestant, and each kept an official journal; sadly, neither has survived beyond March 1916.

As we have heard, information on Entente troops was carefully recorded in a variety of lists, the communication of which to the 'hostile powers' was frequently suspended as a result of perceived failures in reciprocity. The hugely important grave lists, for example, were for some considerable time not passed on to either *Referat III* or to the Red Cross in Berlin. If not released by the Germans themselves, there was of course no way for Geneva to procure them. The ICRC invested huge diplomatic efforts in trying to obtain these documents, pleading, persuading, beseeching and begging for both sides to share their most critical of resources. It is probably because of wilful and persistent mutual obstinacy that so many families had to wait so long for news about their loved ones. For some—such as the relatives of the men in the Pheasant Wood graves—that news never arrived.

The personal effects of German *and* foreign dead were sent to *Referat VIII*, who sorted and forwarded them to the relevant department. Possessions of enemy casualties were returned to the respective countries by the diplomatic route, with an inventory accompanying every consignment; we cannot, however, know what was plundered or lost along the route.

The ICRC system shared several features with the *Büro*. It was divided into two main elements, the Entente and the Central Powers. By absolute necessity, work had to be centralised. The building selected was the *Musée* Rath in Geneva. In August 1914 there were less than a dozen personnel; by the end of the war almost 1500 men and women, mainly volunteers, came and went daily. As was outlined in the first chapter, documents from Berlin arrived as Prisoner Lists, Hospital Lists, Property Lists, Death Lists and of course, Grave Lists.

Bundles of these documents arrived daily in Geneva from Berlin, Paris and London. Some contained just a few names, others many thousands. In addition the ICRC dealt with an average of three thousand letters per day, most of which were enquiries from families. The largest single delivery was an extraordinary 18 000. Whereas the majority of enquiries were received by post, certain more fortunate families were able to visit the *Service de Réception* in person. Their cases received immediate attention, and over 120 000 such visits were made during the war.

The Berlin lists were simply collections of unbound sheets, some typed, others handwritten. After having been sorted into nationality, dated and individually numbered, packs containing a hundred to 150 were put together and handed to the relevant nation's section for registration. A green 'military' *fiche* (index card) was generated for *every* name on *every* page, and each was filed alphabetically. Family enquiries produced a white *fiche*. When fresh data was received it was added to the relevant card. When a match was made between a family enquiry and a soldier's *fiche,* be he dead or alive, it was called '*concordance*' and both green and white cards were combined in the same box. The family was immediately notified and both *fiche* and list were stamped with the date and the words '*communiqué famille*'.

Multiple copying by the *Service Dactylographique* was one of the major activities at the *musée*. Around a hundred typists were permanently employed in Geneva, each being assigned a specific role copying lists and *fiches*, or in producing correspondence, reports, letters, etc.

After copying, the 'new' lists were subject to a meticulous verification regime. In order to produce maximum accuracy copies were checked against the originals by three trained staff members. To prevent distraction that might result in error, they worked in an area screened from colleagues; for a family waiting for news the simplest spelling mistake could lead to months or even years of unnecessary distress. Once complete, the copies were despatched to ministries, associations and societies around the world. In the case of the 'Imperial' nations, as previously mentioned, this meant the supply of one set to the War Office, and three to the BRC.

Nothing could be done about spelling mistakes on original German lists, of course, and it will be appreciated that given the scale of the endeavour, errors were unavoidable. To ameliorate the problem special sheets listing the most frequent misspellings were printed for ICRC staff to study so that they might recognise and correct inaccuracies before a list was despatched to its final destination. By reason of there being so many 'Mc's and 'Mac's, the Scots tended to suffer more than other nationalities, for the traditional Gaelic prefix was frequently misread. A soldier named McClaren, for example, might become M.C. Laren, or perhaps Mr Laren.

The lists reveal that from time to time the Germans employed British prisoner 'clerks' to help compile their lists. Such documents are immediately recognisable by the handwriting, the style of notation and the 'instinctive accuracy' of spelling. It appears that some may also have been dictated, for one finds Young being spelled as Jonng or Joung, Sharp as Scharp, or Shaw as Schaw. The spelling of German names by British clerks probably suffered a far greater degree of error!

The first list received from Germany contained the names of twenty-nine wounded French soldiers. It appeared on 4 September 1914. But even at this very early stage of the conflict, reciprocity in the exchange of data regarding grave sites was a problem. The following British telegram was sent to Geneva on 18 September 1914—just six weeks after the outbreak of hostilities:

18.9.14

Hold back further enquiries pro tem. Detailed information will no longer be provided by us as hostile states do not reciprocate. Explanatory letter follows.

'Explanations' were never satisfactory. In France, whose army was to suffer far greater loss than any other Entente nation, groups such as the *Union des Familles des Disparus* (Union of the Families of the Missing) were formed to try to put collective pressure on governments to do more. Given that the war was between ostensibly 'civilised' nations, the union motto, *Dites-nous s'ils sont morts ou vivants* (Tell us if they are dead or alive) does not seem an unreasonable request; nevertheless, progress was painfully slow. The origin of the reciprocation problem lay partly in the absence of explicit agreements formulated prior to August 1914, and evidence of continuing discord appears on a regular basis well into 1917. Sadly, however, the bellicosity of some of the correspondence reveals that the siege war was in many respects fought both on the field of battle and in the offices of state by men with an almost breathtaking intractable obstinacy.

Ninety-five years later, this problem has somewhat complicated the research process because grave lists seldom accompanied corresponding death lists of the same era, usually arriving later and sometimes *much* later. For example, entries relating to 1914 deaths were still arriving in Geneva in 1918 and even 1919—leaving some families in a limbo of agonised ignorance for five years.

It becomes clear from the records that comprehensive grave lists were unlikely to have been present in the *registres* before April 1917. The Germans, however, do appear to have 'encouraged' their enemies by releasing small dribbles of information from time to time. Lists for 1916 are therefore extremely scarce: during that year information relating to only twenty-nine names is present in ICRC *registres*. It appears that these few soldiers were perhaps simply a rather insipid example of reciprocation.

Agreement of a kind was finally reached as a result of the discussions of spring 1917, and the first truly comprehensive grave list can be seen to arrive in Geneva on 18 June. Neatly arranged alphabetically and backdated to the earliest era of the war, it comprises fifty pages averaging twenty names per page. Critically, it revealed that individual names were sometimes also accorded a grave type: *E-Grab* referred to *Einzelgrab* (single grave), *M-Grab* to *Massengrab* (communal grave), while *S-Grab* is believed to mean *Sammelgrab*, a communal burial using coffins. There were also *Reihengraber*—communal graves with a single row of bodies. Sadly, no reference to graves at *Fasanen-Wäldchen* was present; the sole indicators therefore remained the names of the missing.

If no news was received about an individual for three months, the name was automatically placed upon a list of missing. As the first serious attempt to enquire into the fate of this ever-growing category of men, in July 1916 the ICRC introduced a new form of search tool. By painstakingly combing, cross-referencing and entirely rewriting the already immense alphabetical database of *fiches*, a completely new index was created, this time organised not by name but by regiment and battalion. It included the names of the living (prisoners of war), and also those of missing soldiers. Thus the POW comrades of missing men could be more easily and quickly located by checking an index of men belonging to the same unit. The ICRC could then directly contact potential witnesses where they were incarcerated, the POW camps—information which Berlin had of course already passed on through the Prisoner Lists. Lists of missing were therefore copied and sent to every camp where troops of the same unit were known to be held. They were accompanied by a standardised form upon which 'informants' were required to certify that they knew the individual, how they knew him, what his fate was, whether there had been a burial, etc. The forms were then returned pre-paid to Geneva.

This extraordinary endeavour brought either relief or closure to tens of thousands of powerless families; it could only have been contemplated and carried out by those who had access to the original German information. In 1917 yet another tracing method was devised by the ICRC in order to 'give greater accuracy of information concerning the whereabouts of soldiers presumed dead': a geographical index recording places of death and graves, complete with maps. This resource is now sadly absent and the curators are not able to shed any light upon its fate.

It is worthwhile here remarking upon the testimonies of French prisoner-of-war informants preserved in Geneva. These documents consist of no less than 90 000 reports filling two hundred and twenty-eight 400-page volumes. A British equivalent is believed to have been sent back to the UK but, like the four copies of the general lists, they too have sadly been lost or destroyed. What a precious resource they would have made.

At the same time and for the same action similar enquiries were undertaken by Red Cross personnel in Britain, France and Belgium, tracing and interviewing soldiers who had survived an action. Again, each was required to recount what he had seen, when, and who else had been present. When sufficiently recovered, the wounded too were questioned in this same way.

Many examples of these indispensable interviews can be seen in the Australian War Memorial's RCWM files. Among them are found small index cards written in German. These are believed to be the original cards generated by the *Zentralnachweisebüro* in Berlin. They were not passed to Geneva during the war, and did not originally form part of the archives of the Australian Red Cross or the ICRC. It now appears likely the cards were 'removed' from the *Büro* after the war by Captain Charles Mills, the Australian officer wounded and captured at Fromelles in July 1916.

As a result of his injury, in 1917 Mills was released from captivity and interned in Switzerland, there linking with the Australian Red Cross to assist with the welfare of Australian prisoners, a role for which he was later awarded an OBE. After the Armistice he was charged with scrutinising the Berlin files for information on the fate of missing Diggers; his signature can be found on many a letter. Generated from data supplied to the *Büro* from German units at the front, the cards formed the foundation for the Berlin indices and therefore the lists sent to Geneva. Among them can be found information relating to not only Fromelles but all other Australian actions during the war. Amalgamation and study of the documents in the Munich military archive, the ICRC and the AWM goes a long way to completing the story of how notification travelled from a trench or shell-hole in France to a doorstep in Sydney.

When fighting finally ceased with the Armistice of November 1918, the work of the ICRC was by no means complete. Listing continued as a further 400 000 German and Austrian prisoners fell into Entente hands;

indeed, the despatch of prisoners' relief parcels (the celebrated Red Cross parcel) was sustained after the declaration of peace in late June 1919. After this time the agency continued to receive a great many daily requests from released prisoners and internees, relatives of the missing, and fractured families. Scores of thousands of men were still unaccounted for. A new post-war body was therefore formed: the Tracing Service. It was to become a permanent ICRC facility.

The arrival and collation of lists from Berlin was to continue until the beginning of 1920. When work finally ceased in 1921, over seven million *fiches* had been generated at the *Musée* Rath.

Was a list of the men buried at Pheasant Wood produced at the time of the interments? Given the measure and robustness of *Oberst* Julius von Braun's recording and reporting revealed in the collections of the military archives, and of course his Order 5220, the answer is more likely to be affirmative than negative. How comprehensive it may have been is unanswerable.

Where might it be? We know from the ICRC *registres* that details were passed to Berlin. Logically, these could only have been gathered at the time of burial. The list may have been lost or destroyed—but it may equally be still lurking somewhere in Munich's files.

Given that no other contemporary lists of names relating to the Pheasant Wood graves had been uncovered before my first research visit to Geneva in 2008, the twin databases at the AWM and Commonwealth War Graves Commission (CWGC) were initially the sole sources of names for the men likely to be buried there. It was important to make the CWGC aware of the ICRC resource because once it was digitised, everything on their own database might be cross-referenced with the *registres*, opening up an extraordinary new world for genealogists and historians alike, and of course indicating many a site where missing soldiers may potentially still lie. The Fromelles case was once more acting as a catalyst for change.

Chapter 18

THE BITTER GRAVES

———⟫●⟪———

Before the Armistice had been signed refugees and evacuees began the migration back to the scene of their 1914 evictions. Mingling with soldiers, prisoners, and representatives of numerous international bodies, they were eager to rebuild homes, replace lost possessions and reconstitute the land—at German expense of course. Claims could literally be made for everything down to the last teaspoon—even new-laid eggs! At the same time the military authorities struggled to impose some form of order upon the pressing business of recovery, reburial and commemoration, not only for those soldiers with known and marked graves, but also the numberless men who still lay unfound along the old Western Front.

Returning the land to agriculture entailed the clearing and subsequent erasure of many hundreds of small burial grounds (of fewer than forty graves) established during the war, and the moving of contents to 'concentration' cemeteries. It was a colossal task. The work, continued by Major-General Sir Fabian Ware's Directorate of Graves Registration and Enquiries (DGRE), began barely a week after the Armistice.

The remarkable character of Sir Fabian Ware takes pride of place in the Great War hall of fame. Ware tried to enlist at the outbreak of war but was rejected on account of his advanced age of forty-five years. Through the influence of powerful friends he was able to engineer a non-combat role, acquiring command of an ambulance unit provided by the British Red Cross. Arriving on the Western Front in September 1914, he became concerned at the lack of official procedures for the recording of graves. He therefore devised and proposed an organisation to properly register identifications and burials. Having secured official backing, by October 1915 his Graves Registration Commission had logged more than 31 000 individuals.

The Somme Offensive of 1916 caused Ware profound anxiety. The losses of the first few days far exceeded anything the forces of the British Empire had ever suffered. A visit to Fourth Army headquarters to enquire about arrangements caused him to note, 'There was no organisation for the purpose of the time and I was satisfied after having discussed the matter with them that it was impossible to establish any proper organisation at that time in the middle of severe fighting.'

Ware's resolve led to the creation of corps and divisional burial officers, whose prime responsibility was to liaise with operational units and padres, ensure and supervise proper clearance of the battlefield, and record personal details and grave locations. As Director of Graves Registration and Enquiries he became well known to the ICRC. On 22 February 1917 he wrote to Geneva seeking clarification and action, and offering assistance in the delicate business of reciprocity.

In the issue of 'Nouvelles' dated 10.2.17 particulars are given of exhumations of French soldiers for the purposes of reburial by the Germans in central burial grounds in the occupied part of France. It is known that similar exhumations of British soldiers who have fallen in Belgium have taken place and I shall be most grateful if the Committee of the International Red Cross at Geneva could use its influence with the German Red Cross Societies to obtain any details as to such exhumations and when they take place.

The graves of a number of British soldiers who fell on the line of retreat in Belgium in the Autumn of 1914 have been unofficially reported to me but very few details as to the exact positions have been obtained. If the Berlin Red Cross Society has received any lists from military formations or other sources as to the locations of these graves I should be very grateful for any steps that could be taken to approach the German Government on this matter. If a measure of reciprocity is demanded, lists of registered German graves could be furnished and, later on, photographs of cemeteries where German soldiers have been buried. No exhumations of German soldiers have as yet been made in the areas at present in the occupation of the British Armies.

It may interest you to know that a further order has been issued, with particular reference to the Somme area as to the marking of enemy graves and the care of enemy burial grounds. This is in confirmation of previous orders that enemy graves are to be marked and cared for in the same way as graves of the Allies.

The ICRC passed Ware's letter to Berlin, but the response was negative; the Germans were awaiting the results of previous reciprocation agreements.

As the conflict on the Western Front dramatically deepened in 1917, claiming ever-greater numbers of lives, Ware began to consider the post-war situation. The grave was the elementary physical link between the living and the departed; because the decision not to repatriate bodies had been taken, the State's duty to make every effort to provide one was paramount, for there would surely be a demand for families to visit and walk upon the historic soil of the battlefields. The establishment of organised 'official' cemeteries for British dead had been sanctioned by the French State in December 1915, but when fighting finally ceased what would be the fate of the many hundreds of makeshift burial grounds and tens of thousands of isolated graves? Who would continue the essential job of recording, and how long might it take? The Imperial War Conference in London in April 1917 offered an opportunity for Ware to put his case. Knowing the gathering would be attended by representatives from all the Allied nations, and that they planned to discuss the 'Care of Soldiers' Graves', he submitted a draft charter.

The situation in France was actually the simplest to deal with. France had already agreed to allot territory for cemeteries in perpetuity. In fact, the

French government volunteered to *look after the graves and cemeteries*, but the offer was graciously refused. In addition, the graves of many soldiers, known and unknown, lay within Entente territories; for those that did not, a relatively satisfactory mutual recording and notification procedure had been agreed with the Central Powers. But, being entirely within enemy territory since its evacuation in early 1916, Gallipoli in particular required special consideration.

It was on 23 April, the eleventh day of conference, that members resolved that an Imperial War Graves Commission (IWGC) should be formed which should 'as soon as possible after their appointment and organisation prepare an estimate of the probable cost of carrying on the work entrusted to them and to submit same to Governments of the United Kingdom and Overseas Dominions with their recommendation as to the proportion that should be borne by each'. Ware (now a brigadier-general) assumed the office of vice-chairman of the newly created IWGC; it was a position he would occupy until his death in 1948. The work of post-war recovery thus took place beneath his gimlet gaze.

Despite there being an estimated 160 000 bodies to deal with, relocation of remains from cemetery to cemetery was relatively straightforward. Those in isolated but marked graves were usually easily identified, exhumed and re-interred, but the scores of thousands of 'invisible' dead posed a solemn challenge. There was a manpower shortage. Demobilisation had made it difficult to retain service personnel in France and Flanders—understandably, most soldiers were keen to escape scenes of suffering and loss, put the war behind them and return to family, hearth and home.

There was disorder and confusion, and an incentive was required. It was decided to recruit a labour corps in Britain to form the practical nucleus of the recovery effort in France and Belgium. An extra 2/6d (17 cents or 12.5 pence) per day in addition to the standard military pay had the desired effect. By mid-1919 the corps' establishment was almost 4500, and the task of clearing small battlefield cemeteries already advanced.

It was seen as fitting that the missing should, wherever possible, be traced and recovered by comrades of their own nationality. Thus the Canadians began work on the Somme around the symbolic sites at Courcellette, and at Vimy Ridge. For the same reason, the Australian Graves Services (AGS) commenced work alongside almost 1100 assisting personnel on the Villers-Brettoneux and Pozières battlegrounds.

Despite the scale of loss in July 1916, the Battles Nomenclature Committee had (like the Germans) continued to dignify the Fromelles attacks with the title 'action'. The term 'battle' would not appear in official publications for many years to come, simply because the units involved had not been accorded a 'battle honour'. The ground between Fauquissart and Delangré Farm was thus not classed as warranting special Australian treatment. The action of May 1915 *was* classed as a 'battle' so, although on 19 July 1916 the Diggers had suffered from its operational legacy, there was a bizarre ultimate 'benefit': the ground was to be carefully swept by the British simply because the earlier encounter was on the official list as the Battle of Aubers Ridge.

Battlefield clearance *during* the war was a grisly and unending task, usually carried out by men who were untrained or unfit for front-line duty. After fighting finally subsided on the Somme in November 1916, for example, there was a vast hinterland of debris and corruption to deal with: the ground gained by Allied troops since 1 July. Among and beneath it lay the bodies of thousands of troops of a dozen nations. Large numbers of soldiers were drafted into the area to carry out essential but profoundly distressing work. Private J. McCauley, 1st Border Regiment, later recalled:

> *I was attached to a company of about 150 men, and our task was to search for dead bodies and bury them. Two issues of raw rum were served out to us daily, to kill the dangerous germs which we might inhale. It was a ghastly job, and more than ever I learned what war meant . . . We worked in pairs, and our most important duty was to find the identity discs. After our morning's work was over, a pile of rifles and barbed-wire stakes would mark the place where we had buried our gruesome discoveries. There they lay, English, German, Australians, South Africans, Canadians, all mingled together in the last great sleep.*
>
> *Often have I picked up the remains of a fine brave man on a shovel. Just a little heap of bones and maggots to be carried to the common*

burial place. Numerous bodies were found lying submerged in the water in shell-holes and mine-craters; bodies that seemed quite whole, but which became like huge masses of white, slimy chalk when we handled them. The job had to be done; the identity disc had to be found. I shuddered as my hands, covered in soft flesh and slime, moved about in search of the disc, and I have had to pull bodies to pieces in order that they should not be buried unknown.

It was in August 1916, largely as a result of Fabian Ware's exhortations, that explicit instructions for burial and salvage were officially laid down. Pamphlet 'SS 456, Burial of Soldiers' required the removal of personal effects (the 'salvage') including money, rings, watches, photographs and letters, as well as paybooks and *one* identity disc. Special attention was paid to the pockets and the braces, and the neck and wrists—hence the necessary but ghastly fumbling endured by Private McCauley and his colleagues.

The dual identity disc system, whereby one disc was taken at the time of burial and the other left upon the body as a safeguard for future identification, was introduced only in September 1916. This is an important aspect of the Fromelles case because unless a soldier had privately purchased a pendant or bracelet inscribed with his details (far from uncommon), at the time of battle he would be wearing only one recognisably official form of identity. The private ID would hopefully have been removed, bagged, listed by the Germans, and returned to the family via the Berlin *Büro* and the Red Cross. The paucity of personal items found in the Pheasant Wood graves when they were cleared in 2010 indicates this was indeed the case: the Bavarians overlooked little. Had the two-disc regime been in operation in mid-1916, it would clearly have made identification in 2010 relatively simple, especially in conjunction with DNA testing.

Although the introduction of the two-disc policy was to make a tremendous difference to the identification process, the groups or isolated remains buried on the field of battle during or after an action were by no means safe from further disturbance. Stakes, crosses, rifles, and other indicators were often swept away by subsequent combat over the same territory. So too were the remains themselves.

In February 1919 the Secretary of State for War (or War Secretary) Winston Churchill reported to the British parliament that there were still about 64 800 men whose fate remained to be determined. It was in these horrific statistics that the greatest humanitarian challenge lay. The finding of long-lost fathers, sons, brothers, husbands, and the providing of a grave for each, was a debt owed not only to the dead, but to their families. In so many cases, the character of the Great War meant it could never be paid.

On 10 November 1921 the London *Times* published a small piece entitled 'Battlefield's Search Ended'. In early September of that same year the officer in charge of the search process, Colonel J.K. Dick-Cunyngham, colonel commandant of British troops in France and Flanders, certified that the old battlegrounds were now cleared of 'such isolated British and German graves as were marked in any way above ground which was accessible, or could have been found by reasonable search'. So ended three years of intense activity.

The initial prime focus had been isolated marked graves, for they were the easiest to identify. In the Fromelles sector there exist records of early war period British graves in No Man's Land still being in situ—with the original cross—in 1919. Next on the list had been the dissolution of small battlefield cemeteries, mentioned earlier. Substantial numbers of Allied troops were also exhumed from enemy burial grounds, the graves of these men being usually marked and recorded by the Germans. Finally, there were the invisible graves of the missing.

While relocation and concentration of known graves continued, the battlefields themselves were systematically scrutinised, in certain especially bloody places often many times over, by men trained to detect signs that might indicate the presence of human remains beneath the surface, a specialised skill.

Meanwhile, lacking soldiers and their housekeeping skills, sandbag parapets and breastworks soon rotted and slumped. Nevertheless the accessible residue of conflict was enormous, and formed a valuable source of raw material for the local people. Here was timber for building and burning, metal for roofing, pumps for drainage and tools by the thousand.

There were huge quantities of brass shell cases. The pure copper driving-bands on unfired and unexploded projectiles were especially prized—with five shells per square metre being discovered in some areas, they were far from uncommon. Great danger lay in their removal, however, and numbers of foragers—children included—were killed and injured.

Although it was illegal to gather and sell such 'booty', the capacity to earn extra money—often two or three times the daily wage for labouring on the land—ensured that it was surreptitiously harvested, hoarded and sold to merchants. Clearing all battlefield debris would have taken decades, so having salvaged the most useful material, the remaining 'junk' was pushed into the nearest and deepest trench or shell-hole—as long as it lay beneath the plough's blades, it posed no problem for cultivation.

Having cleared waterways, cleaned roadside ditches and re-installed hundreds of kilometres of land drains, ploughing began. To 'sweeten' the earth, lime was often harrowed in. Unless of practical agricultural use, the once essential but now sightless sentinels—pillboxes and observation posts—were either blown up with explosives or destroyed by hand. In this land of clay, the pulverised concrete provided an excellent and valuable base for roads and tracks.

Slowly the killing fields of Fromelles returned to production, but in regions that had suffered the greatest torture by the guns, such as the Somme and the Ypres Salient, the earth was sometimes unable to make the same response, and crop yields remained low. There were plagues of insects, copper worms and mice. A deep ploughing scheme was therefore instigated; it helped more than just the fertility of the soil, for not only was a fresh hoard of valuable booty lifted to the surface, but another swathe of human remains.

Exhumation was a year-round activity, so accommodation was required near the place of work; the now famous Nissen hut came even more into its own. An exhumation company comprised thirty-two men divided into squads, each issued with rubber gloves, picks and shovels, and wooden stakes to mark the location of each body found. A sheet of canvas and a length of rope were supplied to wrap and bind the remains, plus a stretcher to carry it from the field. As was the case for the Bavarians after the battle, cresol was a part of the kit—as was a pair of wire-cutters, because for some time after the Armistice the battlefields remained strewn with steel thickets (an estimated three million miles (4.8 million kilometres) of barbed wire was at one time present).

The 'British' segment of the Western Front—from the Belgian coast to south of the Somme River—was divided into three areas, the respective headquarters being at Lille, Douai and Péronne. The battlegrounds themselves were then subdivided into 500 × 500 yard (460 × 460 metre) squares corresponding to subdivisions on trench maps produced during the war. A survey officer marked out the area, and from available records drew the attention of the burial officer overseeing the sector to the number of remains believed to be present. Unsurprisingly, these estimates were frequently imprecise. Although a knack was quite quickly developed, familiarity and practice was essential in knowing where to dig. Less than a year into the process the IWGC remarked that, unless previously experienced men were engaged, '80% of the bodies which remain to be picked up would never be found'.

The average party required for an individual exhumation and reburial was at least five. Its excavation encompassed a certain area around the body so that any loose or fallen associated items might also be collected. Having been lifted from the ground, the remains were laid out on the cresol-impregnated canvas sheet (which later became the shroud) and a careful search for the disc and other identifying articles began. First the neck and wrists were examined; then, if the uniform was present, pockets were searched. Every item was noted, bagged, and delivered to HQ alongside the details of the recovery and reburial.

By 1920, 10 000 men had been employed in grave-associated work on the battlefields. Although a considerable number were volunteers, the cost of perpetuating the service for years into the future was considered prohibitive. A line had to be drawn, and the decision to terminate in the autumn of 1921 was made. As the closure date neared, the numbers of men likely to remain permanently missing began to be estimated and revealed; the results came as a ghastly shock, and not one that was easy to come to terms with.

Families still relied solely upon the State for news, hope and succour. The parliamentary statement by Sir Laming Worthington-Evans, the Secretary of State for War, that officially ended the search was published in the

London *Times* on 10 November 1921 and reminded everyone that: 'Since the Armistice the whole battlefield area in France and Flanders has been systematically searched at least six times. Some areas, in which the fighting had been particularly heavy, were searched as many as twenty times.' The statement was not strictly accurate.

Nevertheless, the work of the DGRE and affiliated organisations was over, which meant that the British Army was no longer responsible for the battlefields. In future, remains found during agricultural or rebuilding work would be dealt with according to a set of new and clear regulations. Exhumation, identification and reburial was to be overseen solely by the IWGC.

This decision, reached so soon after the conflict, caused profound distress to tens of thousands of families who still entertained—some since 1914—an anticipation of at least being able to visit a grave. With the new policy the sole avenue of optimism lay in a carefully worded exclusion clause provided by Sir Laming Worthington-Evans in his statement: 'In cases where relatives or friends can produce from their own knowledge evidence that the body of an officer or soldier may be found in a particular locality, special search will be made under the instructions of the Imperial War Graves Commission, if the Commission is satisfied that a good prima facie case has been made out.'

The possibility that families either possessed, or could gain access to, information of such a nature was slim. The surviving pals of a missing man might roughly remember time and place of burial, but producing the kind of definitive evidence required by the IWGC *Adjudicataire*, the sole arbiter of whether a search would or would not be sanctioned, was practically an unattainable aspiration. If a man had been buried by his own comrades or those of another unit, then perhaps a war diary or some other official document might contain useful information, but in the 1920s such records lay with those producing the official histories and were unavailable to the general public. They were also subject to formal closure until the 1960s. If a soldier had been buried by the enemy, and notification of the site had not reached the British authorities via the ICRC, producing adequate evidence was entirely beyond a family's reach.

Approved searches could only commence once a 'Request for Authority to Exhume' had been sanctioned, a scheme drawn up, costs estimated, a working team brought together, and after the harvest of any crops at the site. Even when an investigation involved a potential mass burial these same regulations were strictly adhered to. The CWGC say their archives contain only three such cases, all brought by the director of records in Ottawa. They involve parties of Canadians lost as a result of shell damage to a deep dugout in which they were sheltering, and their comrades' inability to subsequently effect rescue, i.e. the men had been buried alive. In each case a trench map reference and the names of the victims were supplied, plus a narrative of the event and sometimes the testimony of eyewitnesses.

That a number of searches for the remains of *individuals* were undertaken is also certain, but at present there is no record of a successful conclusion. Such special cases involved intense labour. In one instance in October 1927 the IWGC registrar notes that 'not only was it exceedingly difficult to pick up precise locations because of the similarity of the country (in many instances), but digging in almost all instances meant a series of trenches, because it was the only satisfactory method, and this means considerable work and a fair amount of cost'. Without the old trench systems as a reference, finding precise locations was more a matter of luck than judgement. The cost of one enquiry known as the 'Upton Case' was in the region of £20—at the time, a hefty sum. Such cases might involve a search for an especially 'worthy' individual, or be brought by a family of influence or wealth; in general, however, they were entirely beyond the pocket of most families.

Although the consequences of closure were foreseen by the IWGC, it nevertheless resulted almost immediately in crisis. At an IWGC meeting on 18 October 1921, fears were expressed that the public would require an explanation if they came to know that remains were still being uncovered at the rate of 200 per week. By the middle of this final year the erstwhile rural battlefield areas were fast being returned to agriculture, the work primarily being carried out by local civilians assisted by paid piece workers. In the hurly-burly of reconstitution and rebuilding it was not always convenient to follow the statutory reporting guidelines. On 9 September 1921, almost on the eve of closure, the situation was highlighted by H.F. Chettle, IWGC director of records:

The Belgian Government is employing gangs of about 250 men, each under a foreman, and working in pairs of gangs, to reclaim the devastated area. One gang levels the ground roughly, and the other digs it over. Each gang covers about 2.5 hectares a day, and is paid by piece-work. (The Belgian Graves Services employs much smaller gangs, who work only where the Belgians fought.)

These gangs are under orders, like all other Belgians, to report bodies discovered. In practice, however, they very often do not report British bodies because they would lose time and pay by doing so. The French and Belgian Governments pay them 2 francs for every French, Belgian or German body reported; we pay them nothing. D.G.R. & E. used to attach soldiers in pairs to the gangs; we have no personnel to use in watching them. M. de Groote [a Belgian foreman from Bruges], *who takes a keen personal interest in our dead and sacks his men if he finds them failing to report, is an unexpected exception to the general attitude of the 'reconstruction' personnel.*

The commission came close to recommending that searches in certain sectors of the Ypres Salient, Arras and Somme battlefields should be continued beyond the looming 'deadline'. It was also recognised that some especially bloody districts had never actually been searched at all. These included High Wood on the Somme, Saint Eloi near Ypres, and Bourlon Wood, part of the Cambrai battleground. But by October it was too late to make meaningful representations: the army had departed. In correspondence dated 19 September, referring to Belgium, a Major Williams anticipated 'that about 25 individual remains will be reported every week if we do not pay for reports, and about 70 every week if we do'.

The greatest problem lay in the fact that the known and relatively controllable army operatives, who ostensibly retained the 'symbolic and emotional' regard for the work, had now been replaced—at least for the reporting of finds—by farmers and reconstruction parties, occasionally overseen but more often than not visited from time to time by a commission employee. But the fact that the army had not always looked upon the grim and unchanging task with the expected 'reverence' had also previously become evident enough: there had been strikes, drunkenness, misuse of army equipment, and more serious allegations, some relating to the treatment of the remains themselves. There is also evidence of a macabre factional rivalry relating to who found—or rather who buried—the most remains. One Australian officer working in the Ypres Salient accused the British of hacking bodies in two in order to 'exaggerate' their count. It may well have been true: the activity was almost impossible to police. Ultimately, however, the very presence of experienced ex-military personnel made the chance of successful recovery that much greater. French and Belgian civilians, while acknowledging the sacrifice made in the liberation of their lands, were understandably keen to get back to normal life; for some this inevitably involved a certain 'expediency'. Could they be trusted to report findings? It was a serious concern.

The predicament was perceived to be less acute in France than Belgium; but, given the colossal scale of sacrifice along the 600 square miles (1500 square kilometres) of the key battle zones, the very fact that it existed at all was unacceptable. To terminate the army contribution at a time when so many bodies were still being recovered was seen as both precipitous and disrespectful. Were the public to hear of some of the practices reported to the IWGC, the results could be politically catastrophic; heads would certainly roll. Measures were therefore quickly put in place to ameliorate the crisis. The commission requested and received an exhumation officer, a clerk, additional personnel to assist with the identification and 'estate' of the dead, the use of specially selected local labour for exhumations and reburials, and a renewed contract for coffins. In important addition, the British finally elected to pay finders a 'bounty': a meagre 2 Francs per body was enough to ensure reported numbers rose instantly and dramatically.

By late 1926, most remains were being revealed during cultivation, and by 'metal-searchers'—official salvage parties with official contracts. Unofficial activity also continued: it was so widespread as to be practically impossible to manage. In effecting the extraction of millions of tons of timber, concrete and metal, much digging was required; it revealed many fresh finds. In early 1927 it was noted with sober concern that the numbers of remains being found was again increasing, but at the same time it was also clear that a great many were not being reported: men were effectively being re-sacrificed, this time in the interests of progress. It is true that in an era where telephones were rare, especially in rural areas, it often required considerable effort to convey information. Sometimes a passing commission vehicle might be seen and hailed, but more often than not reporting a discovery involved visiting the nearest town hall, the only building likely to be equipped with a telephone. On the one hand, there were farmers who would always happily walk several kilometres to do so; others were not inclined to halt work at all. Those farms which had been re-established on particularly bloody ground might receive regular visits from commission officials, but the majority did not. It had to be accepted, of course, that no one could be forced to comply, but if remains were not reported the chance of their being at a later date re-found and recovered was almost non-existent. On 9 March 1927 the IWGC chief registration officer produced an evaluation of what the future might hold:

> I estimate that we shall recover between 2500 and 3000 bodies during the financial year 1927/1928. There will probably be a sharp drop in the figures the following year. It is very difficult to estimate far ahead but I am of the opinion that during the five years 1927–1931 between 7500 and 10 000 bodies will be recovered . . .
>
> The numbers to be found during the five years following 1931 can only be a matter for conjecture. Bodies will certainly be found but probably in very small numbers. Surface indications, such as abnormal vegetation, colour or height of crops, scraps of clothing and equipment brought to the surface, will be so slight as to be overlooked or probably with the passing of sentiment, ignored.

Undoubtedly, the pragmatism of progress suggested there was likely to be a 'passing of sentiment' among French and Belgian civil populations, but this was not the case among the families of the missing. During the war the people of Britain and her Dominions had not expected to pay such an agonising price; there had been no precedent and thus no warning. Equally, they were unprepared for the fact that governments would decide not to repatriate the dead, leaving families with no grave in a local churchyard to visit and care for. These realisations took time to assimilate and accept;

in the meantime enquiries continued to flood in. It is equally important to appreciate that the Empire had only recently emerged from the Victorian age, an era in which the ritual of mourning had reached an extraordinary stature in society.

After the war, only upper- and middle-class British families could afford to visit graves in Belgium and France 'under their own steam'. Farther flung theatres, such as Turkey or Palestine, were beyond the resources of most, although by 1926 special cruises to the Peninsula were being offered (from London) for 70 guineas. The majority of British working-class bereaved were unable to afford any kind of holiday, even a domestic one, so the prospect of visiting Europe was far beyond their pocket.

There were numerous survivors who had lost fathers, brothers, sons, nephews, uncles, but who had no interest in revisiting scenes of suffering, preferring instead to invest their energy in starting life afresh. For those keen to go, governments were frequently encouraged by MPs to try to find funds to provide at least one opportunity for this crucial symbolic and healing gesture. However, the sheer scale of the war, the monumental loss, and thus the numbers of bereaved made the cost prohibitive. It seemed to many that their nation could afford to fight, but not to deal with the legacy. Demands that the very poorest should surely be assisted also fell by the wayside because this would involve people being forced to obtain letters of reference from a local worthy or churchman, or enduring a humiliating means test in order to prove eligibility, i.e. that they were poor enough to warrant State help.

For most Australians, a visit to Flanders was almost unthinkable; photographs of graves, supplied free upon request, were the best most could hope for. If requested, the original timber grave marker—after replacement by a Portland headstone—could be sent through the post in a cross-shaped canvas bag.

Travel to the former battlefields was nonetheless significant. A host of guidebooks appeared as tour companies seized upon the potential. Most volumes concerned themselves with the accessible and symbolic Western Front—the place where greatest profits were to be made. A guide was produced for Gallipoli; but none for other theatres, such as Salonica, Palestine or Italy. The most famous company of the day, Thomas Cook, enjoyed bumper profits throughout the 1920s, tailoring trips to the pockets of the various classes of traveller—whether pilgrims, the bereaved, or merely the inquisitive—and linking with Belgian and French regional authorities who had spotted the same commercial potential. Organisations such as the Ypres League arranged package tours, primarily for parties of ex-servicemen, but also for the wider public. Time constraints (the trips were organised for weekends and bank holidays) meant that tours did not stray beyond the boundaries of the salient. The Western Front was open for business. After the Wall Street Crash of 1929, the Great Depression took away for several years the travel hopes of many a family. Nevertheless, a steady stream continued to arrive to watch the landscape of Flanders become ever less recognisable as a battlefield.

Throughout this period the Fromelles battleground remained a backwater, overshadowed by the majestic scenes of loss on both its flanks at Loos, Arras, Somme and Ypres. Almost a hundred years later, the reaction of the relatives of the soldiers occupying the Pheasant Wood pits suggests that regardless of the passage of time, a graveless death still represents a great deal more to grieving families than a man simply ceasing to exist.

Chapter 19

RECOVERIES, RESOLUTIONS
AND REVELATIONS

—➤●◄—

*Peasants everywhere are scything weeds and burning them in smoking heaps.
But the trenches beyond Sailly are still shaggy-topped with teazle crowns and
woolly nettle heads. One wonders how many different units at what different
times occupied those 1914 trenches. Here still, one picks up old blue water-
bottles and faded green straps and pouches of British uniforms. They are poor
trenches—the mere staves that lined them to keep up the mud are all warped
and good dug-outs are few. The Germans of course swept o'er all this in 1918.
Witness the 'busted' concrete telegraph posts growing dozens of rusty iron
wires from their stumps, witness the lumpy solid cement-bags by the side of
the road. But between 1914 and 1918 what a history! A little way beyond the
British line is a cemetery called 'V.C. Corner.' There are two hundred and
thirty crosses and on every cross is exactly the same legend—'G.R.U. Unknown
Australian soldier.' There is no name in the whole of the cemetery. Some time
some band of Australians charged here and did not come back and were not
taken prisoner. Old rifles with broken rusty bayonets have been placed against
the white-washed cross-surmounted entrance. Not many paces on one comes to*

the German line wrought in impregnable concrete, a line of snug beds in which
it seems one might comfortably await the Last Day.

Stephen Graham, *The Challenge of the Dead*, 1921

The earliest post-war reincarnation of Fromelles village grew from the ashes of the old. Bricks are hardy survivors; they were cleaned and recycled, which is why some villages once practically erased often now look as if war has never passed through. Steel girders that once fortified pillboxes served for lintels, timber baulks as door frames, duckboards as paths. Furniture and household goods, 'borrowed' by the troops for the duration, were reclaimed from dugout and blockhouse, and from unscathed areas beyond the battlegrounds came trucks carrying more of life's necessities: seeds, machinery, doors, glass, beer and wine.

Landscape repairs had to wait until repairers had homes—or at least hovels—in which to live. The first were built from war waste: timber-framed shacks walled and roofed with corrugated iron. When in 1920 the 9 × 6-metre prefabs donated by the Canadian nation appeared, the return to 'normal' life took another step closer. A surprising number of these attractive timber cabins still survive.

For some time many of the old front-line fortifications remained in place, the rusted barbed wire still guarding vacant trenches against departed enemies. Men long since missing and missed were discovered still enmeshed in the iron thorns, sad and ragged bundles of bone and cloth. As late as April 1920, remains were still being found here *on the surface*. Along this graveyard of so many causes, no sentries challenged the few visitors. Trench signs rotted and fell. Strange to say, some of the earliest notices to reappear did not mark sites for the benefit of pilgrims, but warned them off: *Chasse Reservée*—and occasionally 'Trespassers Will Be Shot'.

Today that ribbon of steel, wire, timber and concrete has long been erased, and in its place a carpet of fertile earth now conceals and protects the archaeology of this fragment of the First World War stage. It is a cultured soil, full of meaning and memory and, to the practised eye, still littered with bullets, shrapnel, steel splinters and fragments. Yet inches beneath the plough the old melancholic world remains. And it is still inhabited. In countless lost graves lie buried the numberless missing of half a dozen nations: the accepted potential destiny of all who served.

Recovery was simultaneously undertaken by French, British and German teams. The units that exhumed and reburied Allied dead in the Fromelles sector were British: the 6th, 8th, 48th and 84th Labour Companies working alongside Nos. 27 and 33 Graves Registration Units. At first bodies were carried to nearby burial grounds, but these sites were limited in area, and at some point appeared the inevitable sign, 'Cemetery Closed'. Remains were then taken further and further afield, beyond Flanders into Artois, then Picardy, and even across the border into Belgium.

In the case of the symbolic but somewhat anachronistic VC Corner Australian Cemetery, the recovery of remains was carried out by No. 27 Graves Registration Unit and the 48th and 84th Labour Companies. Interments took place here in the spring of 1920, between 6 March and 20 May.

The individual crosses noted by Stephen Graham in the epigraph for this chapter were not replaced with Portland headstones. Instead, they were removed and the ground turfed to leave two crucifix-shaped central rose-beds. It gives the visitor the false impression that there are two large communal graves and much 'spare' space in the cemetery.

So extraordinarily concentrated were the losses in the Rouges Bancs–Sugar Loaf area that one constantly finds the remains of Diggers and Tommies being recovered from one and the same map reference. On 2 November 1921, for example, at 36 N 10 b 15.05 were found the remains of Major R. Harrison (54th Battalion AIF), Privates Peach and Johnson of the 13th Kensingtons, a further Digger and a Tommy, both unidentified, and a nameless man of the Rifle Brigade: a mix of 1915 and 1916 casualties. On this one battlefield, intermingled with Australians, were found men of the Royal Hampshire Regiment, Buckinghamshires, Northamptonshires, Berkshires, Gloucesters, Black Watch, Dorsetshire Regiment, Grenadier Guards, West Yorkshire Regiment, the Rifle Corps, Kings' Liverpool Regiment, Scots Guards, East Lancashires, Royal Irish Rifles, Welch Fusiliers, Worcesters, Devons, Sherwood Foresters, Scottish Rifles and Lincolnshires. Plus Portuguese troops. Close to Pompey Elliott's Brigade HQ at Le Trou Post, a cross was found 'In Memory of 13 British

Soldiers'; only three bodies were present. Some 200 metres away was another: 'To the Memory of 49 Australian Soldiers.' At the same reference another Digger grave is noted: it contained 115 bodies.

There is evidence too of Australians being originally buried in or near the 'filthy ditches' occupied on the night of 19 July. In mid-March 1924, with the 'assistance of GB List No. 609/1 and GB Plan', a trench grave containing twenty-two British dead from 9 May 1915 was located close to the place where Charles Arblaster and his comrades made their final desperate sortie on the morning of 20 July 1916. No Man's Land, especially astride the *Tommy-Strasse*/Rue Delvas at Rouges Bancs, was a blanket of human mortality. Only occasionally were remains identifiable. If clothing was not present, footwear could be a good indicator, for not only were British and Australian boots often of a different style and make, but soldiers were accustomed to inscribing name and number within. Likewise, personal items such as groundsheets and cutlery were often marked. If there was no indication of nationality, the man—regardless of where on the battlefield his body was recovered—was reburied as a UBS: Unknown British Soldier. There are therefore many cases where the label 'British' should almost certainly be 'Australian', and vice versa.

Upon the closure of official searches in September 1921, it was stated that the Western Front had been searched on at least six occasions, with certain especially bloody areas receiving yet greater attention. In one way, of course, Pheasant Wood cannot be accurately described as a battlefield, for it only twice hosted brief infantry action: in the autumn of 1914, and as the conflict drew to a close in late 1918. Nevertheless, like everywhere else, in September 1921 recovery work in the wider sector did not cease. There were still scores of cemeteries to clear and graves to concentrate, but as the nature of discovery shifted from deliberate to adventitious, the scale of the enterprise dwindled to a fraction of what it once had been.

In 2004, in expectation that a search of the site must sooner or later be sanctioned, and to gain an insight into potential working practices, Lambis Englezos set about contacting battlefield archaeologists in Europe.

All expressed interest, but none could offer useful advice without further supporting data. Geophysics might offer insights, they suggested.

In Australia, renewed media coverage and the consequent re-burgeoning of public interest and pressure, combined with persistent harrying of politicians and bureaucrats to sanction a physical examination of the site, kept the Fromelles file on the desks of the government and its advisers. It was clear to them that, despite the available facts falling short of the required official evidentiary guidelines, Englezos and his colleagues were unlikely to let the matter drop no matter how resistant the government line. Likewise, mounting a counter-argument would probably not help achieve resolution; indeed, it might even aggravate the situation, inflaming certain hot-heads and thus providing further ammunition to the media. The government and the Australian Army were slipping between a rock and a hard place.

A 'speculative search' was discussed, but that raised the spectre of setting a precedent: not only would it probably be publicly funded and potentially costly, but if successful, it might encourage other campaigning groups to follow the same course. The cheapest and indeed wisest route was the one that was eventually selected: to bring together a panel to hear the evidence and produce an independent evaluation that would hopefully satisfy the public, at least temporarily. It was approved in March 2005.

On 10 June that year, Englezos, Selby and Fielding were at last able to present their case in person. The meeting was convened by the Australian Army and chaired by Roger Lee, head of the Army History Unit. A central character in the Fromelles story, Lee was effectively Englezos' sounding board, and since the earliest days had played the admirable but delicate role of non-judgemental and impartial adviser, helping to steer the crusade in a direction that would not only keep it legitimate, but most importantly, dignified. As a military historian himself, Lee was well aware that there was often more to a narrative than that which appears in print; he was therefore not prepared to make any judgement before further research and consultation had been carried out. He was also aware that the campaign was influencing military sensitivities and indeed sympathies, and that the chief of the army was of the opinion that, should the evidence become compelling, he himself was of a mind to proceed with action that would properly honour Australian dead. That statement contained a barely hidden implication: honouring an unknown number of nameless men would be awkward—in order to name them they must first be found. The estimated number, now being calculated by several different and disparate groups, still hovered around 165.

Other agencies suggested cutting costs by accepting the Englezos theory and simply erecting a memorial at or near the gravesite. This same proposition was later discussed by myself with the Commonwealth War Graves Commission; but who were the men to be commemorated, what was their nationality, and how many lay there? What, exactly, might one inscribe upon such a memorial? It was not a viable option.

Armed with the findings of Dr Fuchs, plus the Bowden file, an AWM aerial photograph and an estimate of the potential number of missing Australians (now adjusted to 163), Englezos and his colleagues did enough to convince Roger Lee's panel. They decided that while sufficient evidence existed to 'warrant further investigation of records pertaining to Pheasant Wood', a physical exploration was unwise until further data had been uncovered to confirm that the site had indeed been used as a burial ground. This would be done by researching German, British, Australian and French records.

As a result, panel member Dr John Williams of the Department of Germanic Studies at the University of Sydney and author of the recently published *Corporal Hitler and the Great War 1914–1918*, suggested that as he was about to embark upon a European trip, he would willingly do some research on behalf of the Army History Unit. Such an offer held potential, for Adolf Hitler himself had not only served with the 16th Bavarian Reserve Infantry Regiment, but been present at both the Battle of Aubers Ridge in 1915 and Fromelles in July 1916. Dr Williams would be aware of the relevant archives and their collections.

Here, therefore, lay a source of potential new evidence—evidence from which the Englezos theory might possibly be proved . . . or disproved.

The substance of the Williams Report, delivered to Roger Lee on 7 February 2006, came as a surprise to many on the panel. Its references universally related to post-war publications: secondary sources. It soon transpired that Dr Williams had neither visited the Munich archive, nor spoken with the curators there.

On the other hand, he did visit Fromelles, in late November 2005 touring the battlefield and the vicinity of Pheasant Wood with Martial Delebarre, amateur historian and president of the local historical association (FWTM— *Fromelles Weppes Terre de Mémoire* 1914–1918). M. Delebarre introduced Dr Williams to his vice-president, M. Jean-Marie Bailleul, who according to the report was working on a history of all the German regiments who fought in the Armentières-La Bassée sector, and had almost reached the point of knowing not only the place of burial, but the war record of every German soldier buried on the plain of Weppes between 1914 and 1918—a truly remarkable undertaking. M. Bailleul's observations could therefore be taken as 'informed'. They were also emphatic and persuasive. He advised Dr Williams that the alleged grave pits visible in aerial photographs were possibly 'mortar positions'. This was a curious analysis, for the features lay in open ground in plain view of Allied aircraft—entirely contrary to normal Bavarian working practices. M. Bailleul showed Dr Williams a map indicating the exact locations of 'all graves dug by the Germans in this sector between 1914 and 1918'. There was, M. Bailleul pointed out, 'no record of graves being dug near Pheasant Wood'. His own belief was that 'the constructions by Pheasant Wood were military and defensive in nature'. Dr Williams was persuaded, and strongly concurred in print.

Among several curious and unexpected interpretations, the report was sceptical that mass graves would have been dug *before* 19/20 July 1916 in preparation for the coming attacks, i.e. the understanding being that the Bavarians might have established burial pits in *anticipation* of hostile action; it was suggested that the word *grab* (grave) may have been confused with *graben* (trench); the pre-war civilian narrow gauge railway (the *Ligne Michon*, that served the villages along the crest of the ridge) was confused with the German military *Forderbahn* system; if human remains were ever present at the site, they were more likely to be Portuguese soldiers killed at the beginning of the 1918 offensive. The report also commented on the relative unreliability of regimental histories, making reference to both Charles Bean's and James Edmonds' mistrust of them.

Finally, it was suggested that in his post-war history of RIR 21, Julius Ritter von Braun's declaration that there were graves at Pheasant Wood was itself incorrect. The statement was, said the report, 'not borne out by

German official records', and further evidence would be difficult to find because German maps and documents had been 'lost in flames' during the Second World War, and holdings of Bavarian First World War material were unlikely to help because, the report stated, they were 'minor and limited'. How von Braun had made his error was 'immaterial', but he may have committed it because he was, 'possibly trying to interpret scrappy documents written in haste'.

The primary source records (upon which the Bavarian unit histories were based), including an immense collection of supremely relevant maps, plans, drawings and photographs, did indeed exist, and on a grand scale— in Munich. A telephone call, letter or email at this time enquiring whether the documents were extant would have revealed their colossal magnitude, and opened an Aladdin's cave of enlightenment and possibilities—and indeed eliminated this writer from the Fromelles Project. The report's conclusion was that there was no indication of graves near Pheasant Wood, 'only evidence that refuted it'. For any expert panel, such a statement from a respected authority would have come as a 'book-closing' declaration. As we are already aware, however, Dr Fuchs had said no such thing. His reply to Mr Walter Dumps actually stated:

All four of the regiments mentioned in your letter, which together formed the Bavarian 6th Reserve Division, published regimental histories. But only the history of RIR 21 mentions the burial of the Australian dead. A search of the archives of the regiment and the Division found nothing. I can therefore only cite the few sentences from the regimental history, which do however confirm what you know already. Since June, regimental headquarters had been at Seehaus (Carnoy Farm). The entry for 20.7 states ' . . . The enemy's losses were much greater. In this Regiment's sector alone there were 399 enemy dead, with several hundred more lying in no-man's land, where they fouled the air for weeks until, despite being fired on by the enemy, our patrols were gradually able to sprinkle them with chloride of lime and cover them with earth . . . For the enemy dead, mass graves were dug behind Pheasant Wood. Work also had to be begun on filling in two saps that had been dug by the enemy from his lines to ours during the night of 19/20 July and were now full of enemy dead . . .'

Although the notes, references and acknowledgements in *Corporal Hitler* reveal that during his research for the book Dr Williams had not visited Munich to scrutinise the original war diaries of Hitler's regiment, division, corps or army group, it may still appear unusual for a researcher, having travelled halfway around the world, to disregard the very resource where key material was most likely to reside, and instead choose to visit a location (Fromelles) where no useful local information had previously been brought to light, and there to rely upon unreferenced opinions.

Conspiracy theorists, of which there were (and apparently still are) many cite as evidence the previously mentioned article in *The Australian* newspaper of 18 July 2003 entitled 'Lest We Overlook 250 of our Fallen'. In it Jonathan King reported Dr Williams as saying: 'We know there are remains of many Australian soldiers buried in mass graves near Fromelles and it would be good to recognise this site. If the Government doubt Mr Englezos they could commission an official search to prove or disprove his hypothesis once and for all.' In the same piece Martial Delebarre is quoted as saying he had 'always known Australians were lying in this farmer's field, but nobody has ever believed us'; in each case, no corroborating evidence was offered. The situation was both confusing and confused . . . and destined to become considerably more perplexing.

The Williams Report was delivered to Roger Lee on 6 March 2006. Despite the numerous anomalies, it naturally served to form a disincentive to the panel of experts. The commissioning of further research appeared unlikely. For the Englezos camp, it was a heavy blow to their hopes. Yet there were those whose natural inclination was not to blithely accept everything. The fact that Dr Williams had said one thing in 2003 and had now changed his mind despite having failed to visit Munich meant that the door of the archives there remained open.

Time passed. In September 2006 an important event occurred in Belgium, when the remains of five Australian soldiers killed in 1917 during the Third Battle of Ypres were found near Zonnebeke. The discovery, although not uncommon and therefore not especially noteworthy, was nevertheless to have a profound effect upon the Fromelles case, for exactly one year later three of the five were identified, not through identity discs or personal possessions, but by DNA analysis (a fourth has since been named). That viable DNA samples could be extracted from remains interred in similar geological and hydrological conditions to those at Fromelles would later add weight to the arguments of those demanding full exhumation, DNA testing and reburial of the Pheasant Wood remains. It was another seminal event.

In early October 2006 Englezos and Selby sent me the sum total of latest evidence. It comprised a copy of Second Lieutenant John Bowden's death voucher, a copy of a letter from the ICRC regarding his case, von Braun's piece from the regimental history of RIR 21, the latest calculations for the number of missing, five British aerial photographs showing the grave pits, and a map with the site indicated. For over a year it had not been possible to add anything more. Indeed, as a result of the Williams Report it appeared that hopes for official recognition had actually taken several backward steps.

But the key tipping point in the saga was just a few days away. In Munich, Dr Fuchs had by this time been succeeded as director by Dr Lothar Saupe. At the request of Roger Lee, earlier in the year the deputy chief of the (Australian) army had contacted the German defence attaché, Commander Franz Josef Birkel, to appeal for a search of German archives for evidence relating to the Pheasant Wood case. At first Commander Birkel's colleagues advised that all potentially relevant documents would reside in the military archive in Potsdam; it took several months to organise a search in the correct resource: the Munich *Kriegsarchiv*.

On 11 October Lambis Englezos received a letter from Roger Lee containing photocopies of two German documents, both unearthed by Dr Saupe. One was yet another copy of sections of Julius Ritter von Braun's history of RIR 21; the other, however, was a text no one had yet seen, for it came from the original *war diary* of RIR 21. This was Regimental Order 5220: the original command issued on 21 July 1916 to prepare graves at *Fasanen-Wäldchen* for dead *Engländer*. Englezos emailed the copies to me. The momentous connotations were instantly apparent: the two pages of typewritten text would be overwhelmingly influential in changing attitudes and setting political wheels in irreversible motion. Ironically, they came from the pen of the 'mistaken' *Oberst* Julius Ritter von Braun. Twenty-three copies had been circulated within 6BRD. If in 2005 Dr Williams had visited Munich instead of Fromelles, he would have been almost certain to find this critical and historic document.

The burial order supported other material that was now coming to light in Australia. In 2004 Englezos and Selby had entered into correspondence with a Mr John Guest, a descendant of Lieutenant Eric Chinner of the 32nd Battalion AIF, who had been killed during the battle. The family had compiled an archive, which had since found its way into the State Library of Victoria and other repositories. By 2006 it had been established that the papers included correspondence from November 1916 to January 1928 between C.E.W. Bean and Mr Mervyn Chinner, brother of Eric, relating to the family's quest for the grave. In one of several communications, Charles Bean refers to eliciting the assistance of a Major G.L. Phillips, Australian representative of the Imperial War Graves Commission. On behalf of the Chinner family, he had written to him on 21 September 1927:

Dear Phillips

The German regimental histories say that the dead bodies of our men who fell in the trenches about Delangre Farm on 19–20 July 1916 were buried in a common grave behind what they called 'Pheasant Copse'. I don't know whether this place has been identified, but I expect you know it. If its position is known, would you be so good as to let me know the location, and also whether the remains there have been removed to V.C. Corner or elsewhere. If you happen to know where an officer named E.H. Chinner, of the 32 Battalion, A.I.F., who died in German hands on 20 July 1916 is buried either there or (by the Germans) at Beaucamps cemetery, I should be grateful for the information.

The letter makes it plain that Pheasant Wood was at that time considered, at least by Bean himself, as a 'certified' burial place of Australian soldiers. On the same day Bean wrote a letter to Mervyn Chinner, in which he said:

I am inclined to think that your belief is correct, and that he was buried in a common grave by the Germans at Fromelles.

As to obtaining any trace from the German side, the only course that I could suggest would be to search the cemeteries on the spot. There is little likelihood, however, of your brother having been placed in a separate grave unless he reached hospital. The history of the

21st Bavarian Infantry Regiment, which was opposed to him, says: 'For the fallen enemy, mass graves behind Fasanen Wood were arranged.' This means Pheasant Wood or 'Pheasant Copse' (for the German word means 'little wood'). The German dead were buried in the cemetery at Beaucamps. I think your brother would probably have been buried behind Pheasant Copse; whether this grave has been discovered by the British graves authorities, I do not know, but if so the remains have probably been removed to V.C. Corner.

Major Phillips' reply to Bean's enquiry arrived a few weeks later and quoted the following extract from an official British report he had received on 18 November 1927:

'Delangre Farm and Pheasant Copse are in the area which was covered by the Australian Graves Department in their search for isolated graves. They re-buried the Unknowns in V.C. CORNER AUSTRALIAN CEMETERY. [This is correct as this work was carried out under my personal instructions, (GLP)]

'Lieut. CHINNER is recorded by the Germans as having been buried by them in the vicinity of Fromelles in a trench grave. And his name is included among those commemorated in V.C. CORNER CEMETERY. The Remains of this Officer have not since been found, identified or re-buried by the British Authorities, and his actual grave is unknown.'

In replying to Mervyn Chinner, it today seems ironic that Bean quotes parts of the self-same passage from von Braun's RIR 21 regimental history that was sent almost eighty years later by Dr Fuchs to Walter Dumps, for Lambis Englezos, Ward Selby and John Fielding had embarked upon the self-same quest as the Chinner family. But what Bean could have done for Mervyn Chinner, yet did not, was to request his colleagues in the German archives to search Bavarian war diaries or burial records for references to graves in the immediate post-battle period. Had the document uncovered in 2006 by Dr Saupe been produced in 1927, it is more than likely that its fine detail would have fully fitted the criteria for a 'special' IWGC search of the area—for the VDK records would almost certainly also have been brought to light. Given the data to hand and especially the number of remains involved, it is more than likely that the graves would then have been discovered.

Having received Phillips' response, Charles Bean replied to Mervyn Chinner on 17 January 1928:

> *Dear Chinner*
>
> *I have heard from Major Phillips of the Graves Commission concern-*
> *ing my enquiries about your brother's grave. He says that your brother*
> *was stated by the Germans to have been buried by them in the vicinity*
> *of Fromelles in a trench grave—that is, presumably a common grave.*
> *It is therefore almost certain that he would be buried in the common*
> *grave dug by them on 20 July 1916 at Delangré Farm. Under instruc-*
> *tions from Major Phillips himself, those who were buried at Delangré*
> *Farm were disinterred and reburied in V.C. Corner, and your brother's*
> *name is included among those commemorated there. A few from a*
> *different part of the field were reburied in Rue David military cemetery,*
> *but it is not at all likely he was one of these.*

This is a perplexing communication. Having earlier stated his belief that Eric Chinner was 'probably' in the Pheasant Wood graves, and having received no confirmation from Phillips that the bodies there had been found and recovered, Bean now drops references to Pheasant Wood in favour of Delangré Farm; he also does not copy Phillips' reply for Chinner. Had he done so, it is unlikely he could have avoided further questions from the family. At this point Pheasant Wood falls by the wayside for a second time.

On 12 December 2006 I presented the Fromelles case to Lord Faulkner of Worcester's All-Party Parliamentary War Graves and Battlefield Heritage Group in the House of Lords. They requested a close watching brief. The reason behind this action lay in what one might term the 'extrapolated politi-cal arithmetic' of the graves. Julius Ritter von Braun's writings contained figures with highly potent implications. His regimental history spoke of 399 enemy dead to be cleared from the battleground; Order 5220 of 21 July 1916 commanded the digging of graves to accommodate 400 bodies. The numeric correlation was not only persuasive but potentially useful, for the figures contained both the opportunity Englezos and his colleagues sought, plus a political firecracker.

From the beginning of the quest it had persistently been asserted that approximately 165 missing Australians lay at Pheasant Wood. As a result of Englezos' persistence, a number of other agencies, some of them official, had also been encouraged to examine the records. They arrived at similar totals. If von Braun's figures were taken at the face value of 399/400—which they had to be, because of the absence of conflicting data—and the various estimates of the number of Diggers missing was even in the 'ballpark' category, then the balance of dead in the pits must logically be British soldiers. They were almost certainly not Bavarians, for Order 5220 was explicit about German dead being transported elsewhere. This meant that 235 of the 316 missing of the 61st (2nd South Midland) Division may also have been interred at Pheasant Wood—and were lying there still.

By now I had traced in the Imperial War Museum photograph archive an assemblage of British aerial images of the Pheasant Wood area. They offered a time-lapse sequence from June 1916 until September 1918. Apart from the wood, the communication trench and the tramway line, no features of especial note were visible in June, but on 29 July four pairs of rectangular pit-like features were evident along the southern edge of Pheasant Wood; five appeared to have been backfilled. They were still clearly discernible in images taken in August and October 1916, and even in April and September 1918. British trench maps sourced from the IWM and the National Archives in Kew, London, were also found to be marked with symbols showing a grouping of German fieldworks at the location.

In most cases the features are un-annotated, suggesting that as the Germans clearly made no attempt at concealment, they were not seen as carrying any military importance. Had they been significant or suspect, an annotation would certainly have been appended; indeed, a description and suggested purpose may well have appeared in British intelligence summaries. In almost conclusive addition, however, the aerials clearly showed that throughout the war the location drew almost no Allied artillery fire, i.e. the site was never looked upon as worth shelling. It was reasonable to assume, therefore, that the objects—whatever they actually were—had always been regarded as benign.

Despite three pits apparently being 'unused', no one could yet know the physical character of the 'occupied' graves, and therefore how many men had been buried in each. All future discussions and plans, therefore, had to be formulated around a potential figure of 400 dead, the majority of which might now be British, not Australian. The complexion of the entire project was altered by this arithmetic.

At 9.48 a.m. on 15 December 2006, just three days after the Parliamentary Group meeting in London, the second meeting of the Fromelles expert panel opened in Canberra. This time Selby, Englezos and Fielding were not invited to attend. Roger Lee introduced a new member, Nigel Steel, senior historian of the Imperial War Museum in London, at that time working on exchange with the Australian War Memorial. Before leaving for Australia, Steel had been my co-secretary in the All-Party Parliamentary Group. He and I had often discussed the Fromelles case and remained in regular correspondence. Steel explained to the panel his knowledge of the saga. He outlined the nature of Glasgow University's Centre for Battlefield Archaeology (CBA), citing recent ground-breaking geophysics work on the Western Front related to a memorial for the Tunnelling Corps which I had instigated, and also their connection with the Parliamentary Group. Both parties, he suggested, might assist the Australian cause, one politically, the other practically. To his knowledge, the CBA was the only faculty on earth who actually *taught* battlefield archaeology. The originators and principals of the Centre, Dr Iain Banks and Dr Tony Pollard, had also founded the *Journal of Conflict Archaeology*.

With this in mind, the panel members discussed the new evidence in detail. Most of those present were unable to accept that the IWGC and other organisations could have failed to undertake the most meticulous post-war search of the ground, especially if they had already been made aware of the presence of recorded graves. This, however, was an instinctive reaction rather than a conclusion based upon historical data, which was now becoming available. The panel was told that documentary evidence existed that on more than one occasion in the early 1920s an Australian official had been requested to search the area but reported finding nothing.

Discussions were lengthy and intense, sometimes ardent. Finally, although some members still remained unconvinced, the majority agreed that mass graves *had* once existed at Pheasant Wood and at present no evidence existed to say they had been cleared. Practical action would therefore have to be considered.

The new data was now beginning to dramatically alter perceptions and sensitivities in both Australia and Britain. The possible Anglo–Australian content of the graves possessed great potential, because it had the power to shift the project into a new political sphere—from national to international. Whereas for several years the 'Missing of Fromelles' had been looked upon as a solely Australian matter, it was now more than likely that any further official action would have to involve two nations. Dialogue also needed to be opened with the relevant French *bureaux*.

In Australia the issue remained an emotive one. The authorities were acutely aware that Englezos' belief that the men were still there was almost obsessional, and that he possessed a natural talent to use the media to generate support and sympathy. A swift decision would be wise.

Having received the von Braun documents, I put together a dossier and arranged an appointment with David Parker, Peter Holton and Peter Francis at their CWGC headquarters in Maidenhead in order to present the commission with the fresh evidence. As a result of a four-year exchange of emails with Englezos, the commission was already aware of his views, objectives and tireless persistence. Now it seemed that his gut feeling might have substance. It was again confirmed that their own archives contained no indication that bodies had been recovered in or near to Pheasant Wood. The outcome was plain: the time had arrived to reflect upon a task last undertaken by their IWGC antecedents almost ninety years before: the construction of a new cemetery for First World War casualties.

The next discussions to take place in the United Kingdom were with Derek Twigg MP, British Minister for Veterans. After the All-Party Parliamentary Group meeting in December 2006, I had drafted a report and a letter from Lord Faulkner to the minister outlining the situation posed by the possible division of nationalities in the graves. It stressed the need for discussion about potential British governmental participation in funding an archaeological mission to Pheasant Wood, an eventuality that was becoming daily more credible, and also intimating that failure to participate might be damaging. Dr Tony Pollard attended, advising on the likely archaeological schedules and relevant techniques.

Inter-governmental correspondence then commenced. Senator Bruce Billson, the Australian Minister for Veterans Affairs, wrote to his British and French counterparts to warn them of a possible upcoming request for an investigation. The Australian authorities were keen not only to act fast, but to do so without being perceived as reacting in a knee-jerk fashion to public pressure. In the interests of expediency they therefore undertook to pay for the initial practical investigations themselves. The stated parameters were as follows:

Evidence suggests that some Australian casualties from the battle were probably buried in mass graves near Pheasant Wood.

There is no clear evidence as to whether the bodies were recovered after the war. Evidence exists that the graves were known to be there, but there is no documentation indicating the area was or was not cleared, and the probability of finding such documentation now is low.

CWGC documents for cemeteries in the area do not record any remains being brought from Pheasant Wood, but not all the cemeteries have collection records and not all relevant cemetery records may have been examined.

The only way to obtain evidence as to whether the graves were cleared would be to conduct investigations at the site.

The responsibility for the remains of Australian service personnel is a Government responsibility. Therefore, whatever investigations are conducted should be done under Government auspices.

Any investigation should be the minimum required to obtain the evidence as to whether the sites were cleared.

On 6 February 2007 Senator Billson officially announced that a team from GUARD had been selected to undertake a non-invasive study of the site. They were not to try to find the remains, but by using modern techniques simply attempt to establish the *likelihood* that the ground, i.e. the graves, might not have been disturbed. After discussion, it was agreed that the methods employed were to be topographic survey, geophysics and metal-detection. The study would be complemented by a dedicated research trip to the Munich military archives to be carried out by myself. The Englezos hare had finally been loosed.

———————

It is important at this point to leap several years into the future, for in late 2012 the recent history of the project was suddenly catapulted into the realm of absurdity. It was alleged by M. Jean-Marie Bailleul that since 1991 he himself had been in possession of copies of German documents that proved the presence of graves at Pheasant Wood. The evidence he produced derived from the archives of the VDK: the *Volksbund Deutsche Kriegsgräberfürsorge* (the German equivalent of the CWGC). Until 2011 the VDK operated an office and archive in Pérenchies, not far from Fromelles, and it was here that M. Bailleul first began his research in the 1990s. An entry on a page in the *Zentral-Nachweise-Amt für Kriegerverluste und Kriegergräber Nr V 19731/ 20B* (Central Office for Missing Soldiers and Soldiers' Graves) not only listed five communal burials at *Fasanen-Wäldchen*, but the dates of interment (21 to 26 July) and the number of *Engländer* present: 248.

It was during discussions about the introductory panel text for the new Fromelles museum that this revelation came to light. M. Bailleul let it be known that he wished to be credited as the first to have established the presence of the Pheasant Wood graves. No one, however, had ever seen or heard of his documents. For thirteen years, throughout the period of research, geophysics, test excavations, exhumations and reburials, he appears to have assumed private ownership of the information. He had, he said, tried to tell people of his knowledge, but no one would listen. The long-suffering Lambis Englezos—an ostensibly close colleague of M. Bailleul—had not been informed, nor had the mayor of Fromelles, M. Huchette, nor the owners or farmers of the land upon which the burial site lay. Likewise, none of the French, Australian and British authorities were enlightened, nor the archaeological and forensic teams who carried out the work, the researchers, the Anglo–Australian enthusiasts, and above all, the families of the men who potentially lay in the pits. Indeed, based upon the most recent formulations, on 8 June 2007 Englezos was contending that the Pheasant Wood graves contained 60 of an estimated 171 missing Diggers, and as many as 220 of the 316 (missing) English.

When asked to whom he *had* confided the VDK information, *M.* Bailleul named two persons. The first was Martial Delebarre, who had assisted both GUARD and Oxford Archaeology throughout the finding and recovery process. The second was Dr John Williams who, having largely based his report upon *M.* Bailleul's negative judgements, unsurprisingly firmly denied having ever seen any such evidence.

In May 2009, I had myself made enquiries with the VDK in Pérenchies, asking whether any allied burials were listed among their records. The answer was negative. In March 2013 the documents scrutinised by *M.* Bailleul were photographed in the VDK archive at Kassel, Germany, by my researcher and interpreter, Dr Claudia Condry, and the images sent to me. There were two files relating to Fromelles. The *original* German documents (*Hauptgräberliste, Zentralnachweisebüro* reference number W 10 VII) from which *M.* Bailleul's information had been taken and copied, revealed a very large number of German, French and British remains requiring clearance after the war. The file was split into three sections: a list of remains in military cemeteries (*Soldatenfriedhof*), another noting those in field-graves (*Feldgräben*), and a register of men (all German) whose burial places were unknown (*Gräbstatte unbekannt*). There were also hand-annotated maps that revealed the locations from which remains had (and evidently had not) been recovered, the sites being marked with a handwritten red symbol resembling a Maltese cross. Next to each cross was a unique number which was exclusively associated with the four-digit German trench map square in which it lay. Each of the locations corresponded to its own entry on the lists. These offered the most critical detail: the contents of the graves. The maps and lists covered the area of the German front line, the all-important *Hintergelände,* and the rear areas behind the *II Stellung.* On page 10 of the *Feldgräben* list was an entry for *Fasanen-Wäldchen*: site number eight, map square 3305. Here were registered 248 *Engländer* buried in five pits, with the dates of death between 21 and 26 July 1916. Added annotations in French replicated every phrase of the German data. The graves were recorded as being 'at the southern edge' of the wood. These words, so tightly focussing the topographical spotlight, were present in two hands and two languages, German and French: the precise position was thus known by both the French and German authorities *during* the period of British and Australian post-war searches. There were no English annotations. Had these documents been produced in 2005 or before, it need hardly be said how they might have influenced the perceptions of Roger Lee's panel of experts and thus the evolution of the project. They were not disclosed until early 2013.

The non-disclosure saga was still not over, for among the documents in Kassel was a letter from M. Bailleul to the VDK at Pérenchies dated 16 August 2006. In it M. Bailleul noted that three years earlier (presumably in 2003) when the topic of the potential existence of the graves came to wider public notice, he had been in touch with various parties interested in the First World War history of Fromelles. The circumstances, he said, had caused some people in the area to develop a sudden interest in Pheasant Wood because until that time no one had heard anything about such burials, not even the *Fromellois*.

At about this time, the letter continued, an Australian (evidently Lambis Englezos) appeared who was convinced that he had made a sensational discovery. The man made superhuman efforts to find evidence to support his theory that mass graves were still in existence at Pheasant Wood, pursuing this belief despite the well-known fact that all remains had been exhumed in the 1920s when they were handed over to their respective national representatives for reburial in their own military cemeteries. Given that remains have always been regularly uncovered in the region, and indeed had been found during M. Bailleul's tenure as vice-president, this was a perplexing declaration. It was then stated that the systematic removal of the dead by the German authorities began on 10 August 1921, and that all the graves—including mass graves—in Fromelles were gradually cleared, including those at Pheasant Wood, so it was highly unlikely that mass graves with hastily buried remains of Australian soldiers were in existence anywhere in Fromelles today, and rumours to that effect should not be given any credit.

The letter concluded with M. Bailleul saying that he thought the contents might be communicated to the German Embassy in Australia to help stop any attempt by any individual who wished to uselessly disturb Fromelles soil.

Alongside this epistle was an associated letter from the VDK office in Pérenchies to their headquarters in Kassel. Dated 18 August 2006, it quoted everything M. Bailleul had said, but sagely added that it could not be ruled out with absolute certainty that remains which had not yet been found—including Australians—might still be buried in the Fromelles area; those who were interested in the matter were advised to contact the CWGC.

The appearance of the letters rendered irrelevant the date that M. Bailleul might originally have seen the records. From the point of view of the research and recovery effort, the information was of course too late for useful employment—and yet it was clearly one of the most fundamental elements in the history of the Pheasant Wood project. There remained one question to be answered: what was the motivation for keeping the detailed records secret for so long. In 2006 M. Bailleul had employed the documents as definitive evidence that the *Fasanen-Wäldchen* graves had been found and cleared after the war, which dovetailed with what he had so persuasively said to Dr John Williams in November 2005, influencing the character of the report to Roger Lee and his specialist panel. The motivation at this time seems to have been to preclude further research. In 2012, however, M. Bailleul appears to have presented the self-same documents as equally definitive evidence that he himself had known since 1999 that the remains were still in situ. The motive remains an enigma.

Had the burial data been revealed during the period of Anglo–Australian research and deliberations, and before GUARD's verifying test dig, the documents would have transmitted a set of most commanding indicators: that the graves existed, that they were known to exist by the officials of four nations, and that there was still *no evidence to suggest that they had ever been cleared*. Page 10 of the VDK Fromelles list would probably have become then and there the foundation for the wider research effort, with every subsequent piece of data supporting it. Indeed, the new CWGC cemetery may well have been planned around 250 instead of 400 graves. But by the time the project was launched in 2007 it was already too late.

It is little wonder that in historical research the truth is frequently so difficult to establish. M. Bailleul's history of the German regiments is yet to appear.

Chapter 20

THE GRAVES BEFORE
THE WOOD

It is now clear that the Pheasant Wood graves had been carefully documented by the Bavarians at the time of burial, further reported on several
occasions by the Berlin *Nachweisebüro,* and by the Red Cross in Germany
and Geneva, noted by the VDK and the French authorities during the
early post-war recovery period, recorded in a Bavarian regimental history,
repeatedly mentioned in official correspondence throughout the 1920s, and
mentioned by Charles Bean to a number of enquiring families. One of the
most intriguing aspects of the Fromelles Project is why Pheasant Wood's
250 soldiers were not located and recovered after the war.

The burials had been reported and re-reported every step of the way:
not the actions of a contemptuous or unfeeling military force. That 6 BRD
put serious thought into the treatment of both their own dead and those
of the enemy is revealed by an abundance of contemporary documents.
In a report dated 20 March 1916, for example, von Scanzoni's divisional
and brigade staff had discussed the exhumation of isolated and small
group burials into larger formal cemeteries, both existing and new. The

prime reason for this considerable undertaking was the perceived danger that when peace returned and the fields were reinstated, graves might go unnoticed, ploughed over and lost. There were also, of course, international agreements to adhere to. Despite the manpower situation, von Scanzoni had acted swiftly, and just four days later instructed the process to begin. Records were deposited at Haubourdin, and included details of British and French soldiers killed *before* 6 BRD arrived in March 1915, noting rank, name, number, unit, date and occasionally cause of death, place of burial and, where relevant, grave number. That both sides were aware that detailed records were being produced by their enemy is made clear in an important letter from the ICRC vice-president to the Berlin Red Cross dated 28 February 1917, in which it is stated:

We previously had occasion, in 1916, to ask you to communicate to us, wherever possible, the grave plans and lists that are prepared with such care in the offices of the German Ministry of War (Gräberabteilung), and you replied to us in your letter no. VII 134034 of 2 February 1916:

'We are informed by the Prussian Ministry of War, to which we conveyed the import of your esteemed letter of 4 January, that, based on the Gräberlisten sent to it, the Zentral-Nachweisburo creates a reference card for every fallen soldier, i.e. including members of the foreign armies. On the back of each card there is a sketch, which clearly indicates the place of burial. These cards form a separate index. An exchange of grave registration cards with the hostile governments would be welcomed.'

In that correspondence, the only condition that you posed was complete reciprocity on the part of the hostile governments. On the basis of that declaration, the International Committee entered into discussions which, happily, have now borne fruit, as is evidenced by the enclosed letter. We therefore consider that the principle has now been agreed, and we have today sent a letter to the British Government, asking it to send us details and photographs of the graves of German soldiers from the battlefield of the Somme. We ask you, for your part, to send us the documents in your possession relating to the places of burial of members of the British forces who have fallen behind German lines during the present war.

Although the Australian War Memorial holds the cards acquired from Berlin by Captain Charles Mills, none with sketches as described above have yet come to light. Some appear on the VDK maps. Although the majority are German, there were also numerous French and British graves, for clearly no party could exclusively discover the remains of their own countrymen. But why so many? With Verdun, the Somme, and then the 19 July battle, it appears there may have been insufficient time and resources to complete von Scanzoni's March 1916 directive. After 19 July, the situation became yet more complicated for the Germans: their Verdun offensive had dissolved, but the Somme was destined to grind on and on. Meanwhile, orders were received not only to multiply many-fold the fieldworks in the forward zone, but to put in place the vast pillbox-based defence-in-depth scheme throughout the *Hintergelände*, onto the ridge and across the plateau beyond. It was work that required a far greater investment in men and matériel than anything that had passed before. Although the plan to concentrate field graves may have been abandoned, recording was carefully maintained.

The answer as to why the Pheasant Wood men were not physically located during the official search period can clearly only lie within the thirty-six months following the Armistice and before clearances were brought to a close in September 1921.

The Australian Graves Services (AGS), composed of AIF officers and other ranks, was formed especially to deal with matters connected with the collection and re-interment of Australian dead, the erection of headstones, the construction of war memorials, etc. Created in January 1919, the unit commenced duty that same month with an establishment of seventy-five staff in France and Belgium, and nine at Australia House, their London headquarters in the Strand. The Service worked in association with the IWGC, the army labour companies, the Directorate of Graves Registration and Enquiries, the Graves Registration Unit, German war-graves officials and local people.

It appears not to have been a very happy ship. Poor leadership and the resulting disorganisation allowed the various officers of the Service too much autonomy, and this quickly led to indiscipline and poor working practices and results. Numerous references in CWGC and AWM archives suggest that things seldom ran smoothly. Both officers and men were described as a 'rough lot', and strikes were not uncommon. As well as the issues with indiscipline, there were persistent reports of inefficiency. The situation first came to a head in March 1920 when reports were received by the Commandant of the AIF in London concerning irregularities in behaviour. The following month a court of enquiry resulted in the following statement:

GENERAL REMARKS—30th April 1920

The Australian Graves Services were primarily instituted by the Australian Government for the purpose of honouring the memory of those members of the A.I.F. whose lives had been sacrificed in the Great War.

It is the undoubted wish of the Australian Government that this work be carried out. The fields of operation covered by the Australian Forces are very extensive and cemeteries must necessarily be scattered over a large area.

That the work may be properly accomplished requires detached parties detailed to great distances.

Supervision of these parties is difficult and no definite record of the work is readily obtained beyond the report of the party itself.

Opportunity for abuse is great and unless the most rigid discipline is maintained this work intended to sanctify and hallow the memory of the dead must develop into a serious scandal bringing humiliation and disgrace upon the Australian Forces.

Up to the date of investigation by this Court of Enquiry no reasonable or definite plan of carrying out the work seems to have been formed, and many of the officers and men selected did not realise the dignity and importance of their position.

The appalling condition apparent in March 1920 must come as a warning for the future generations of those in charge, that unless immediate and drastic action is taken for proper control, this effort to honour the dead shall only be the means of bringing shame and disgrace upon the good name, fame and reputation of Australia.

Signed, W. Meikle, Capt.

P. Fenelly, Capt. Chairman

Among the court's thirty-five 'findings of fact' were 'common and frequent drunkenness', staff routinely sharing their quarters with 'women of ill-repute', drunken discharge of weapons to the imminent danger of others, improper use of military vehicles, a comprehensive lack of record-keeping, carelessness resulting in fire, idleness, attempted sale of an ambulance, and sundry misdemeanours involving tyres, fuel, military equipment, etc. There were also complaints from mayors and local residents. As a consequence, for 'scandalous behaviour' and 'conduct unbecoming' several officers were relieved of their duties and returned to Australia.

It was not the end of the matter. Later that same year it was found necessary to convene another enquiry. Among the 790 pages of the reports relating to the two hearings lie several possible indications as to why the Pheasant Wood graves may not have been found by physical search.

The AGS was originally divided into three geographical sections, each with responsibility for certain sectors of the battlefields. The 'Northern Section', based at Poperinghe near Ypres, looked after French and Belgian Flanders, including the Fromelles and Aubers sectors. It was commanded by a Major Alfred Allen.

Alfred Allen, an architect by profession, had during the war worked with the Australian Red Cross Society in London, firstly with wounded soldiers, then in organising transportation back to Australia, and finally as a sort of night-time warden, keeping troops awaiting repatriation out of trouble on the streets of London. On 1 December 1918 the rank of honorary captain had been conferred upon him, 'without pay and allowances'. On 22 July 1919 he was again promoted, this time to the rank of major in order to serve in Europe as an inspector of the AIF Graves Detachment.

In one vitally important respect, the selection and posting appears to have been somewhat ill considered. It was not a question of lack of knowledge, capability or sense of duty on the major's part, but a more basic human reaction by his new colleagues: Allen's subordinates had all seen active service either in the Dardanelles, on the Western Front or both. He had not. To have 'done one's bit' was not only a source of fierce pride but was looked upon as a prerequisite if a man was to have the correct 'feel' for the grim task of recovery, and indeed the necessary authority over one's staff. The new Inspector was looked upon by many of the section as a 'camouflaged civilian' who had *not* 'done his bit'. Nor, it was later ascertained, could he, before arrival in France, read a military map.

It appears, however, that Alfred Allen may have drifted into his position as a 'grave-finder' as much by accident as design, for in 1918 he had put his name forward to join the IWGC as an architect representing Australia. In the summer of 1919 that application was approved. Having been vetted and accepted by every agency up to ministerial level, he was given responsibility for all matters of construction in France and Belgium. His title—Chief Inspector of the Australian Graves Services—meant that he outranked Captain Q.S. Spedding, the OC (officer commanding) then leading the service. Until his arrival, no one was in overall control of the Service, each area being run independently Once there, Allen began to take stock of the wider environment, which being inextricably connected to burial and memorialisation, quite naturally included the *recovery* of the fallen. It was a difficult time for Allen.

'The want of organisation', as he was to report on 30 March 1920, was immediately revealed when he was forced to establish his HQ in wooden huts at Bird Cage Camp in Poperinghe instead of the official and more comfortable location of Saint-Omer, a bustling, attractive and undamaged market town with comforts and facilities outstripping anything that battered 'Pops' could offer. Allen appears to have felt slighted, but nevertheless got on with the job. But there was to be internecine antagonism from the start.

'Now that my office and staff were settled I then began to feel it was time my duties as supreme authority in France were put into power', he said. Allen's colleagues did not recognise any such authority, for it seems that no one had informed them that an Inspector had been appointed. The combination of circumstances seriously abridged his influence.

Reports of continuing enmity and poor performance led to the second court of enquiry. Convened at Australia House in December 1920, it resulted in a wholesale reorganisation of the AGS. Although more officers were 'moved on', Allen himself nevertheless retained both the confidence of his peers and his position. He was obliged to participate in the enquiry, and it is during his testimony relating to a 19 July 1916 casualty that clues pertaining to the Pheasant Wood graves appear.

On 12 March 1919, before the posting of Alfred Allen, the then Lieutenant Spedding received an order from London headquarters to carry out a search for the remains of a Lieutenant Robert David Burns of 14 Machine Gun Company, registered as missing since the battle of 19 July 1916. The order contained the following passage:

A communication from Germany states that there are five large British graves before PHEASANTS WOOD near FROMELLES and another (no. 1.M.4.3) in the Military Cemetery in FOURNES. Burials were effected in these graves by the Germans after the FROMELLES action and it is thought that probably Lt. Burns' body may have been interred in one of these graves.

The request originated from the Burns family, who after lengthy efforts had finally received information as to the potential location of the remains of their loved one through the Australian Red Cross. It appears that Lieutenant Spedding took no action, so on 8 September 1919 the order was re-issued, this time by the commanding officer of the AGS at Australia House. It was marked, 'For your information and necessary action please', and concluded with the request, 'May a search be made when you are operating in this area, please, and this Office advised result.'

By this time Alfred Allen had taken up his post. Still no action was taken. On 16 January 1920 there arrived a further demand from the same source which terminated with a terse, 'I shall be glad if you can now advise me in this matter.'

Allen replied six days later, saying that he hoped to investigate the sites the following week. On 21 February he was able to report:

Lieut. R.D. Burns, 14 M.G. Coy.
With reference to A.G.S. 12/M of 16–1–20, up to the present we cannot get a satisfactory statement from G.R.U. or D.G.R.[E] etc. re. the removal of collective graves before Pheasant Wood. Called at G.R.U. Beaucamps (O.C. in charge of this area) and left all particulars which are being investigated. Will call next week and do all that is possible. There must be some records here. Will report when complete. A collective grave

was found at Fournes with the following inscription: 'Massengrab der
am Getechtv 19/20 Juli 1916 ber Fromelles. Gestallenen Englander'—
but up to the present no information can be given as to who is buried
there. [Although the above transcription of the German inscription
contains mistakes, it translates as 'Collective grave from the action at
Fromelles, 19/20 July. Dead English.']

The OC at Beaucamps then wrote to Allen stating, 'I regret I have been
unable to locate these graves. There seems a probability these officers may
be buried in Fournes German Cemetery, as there are crosses to unknown
soldiers about this date'. Presently, Allen received notification from the
Australian Red Cross that it was their belief that Lieutenant Burns was
buried at either Pheasant Wood or Fournes. He therefore returned to the
Fromelles sector to carry out a further search, and on 4 March wrote:

Lieut. R.D. Burns, 14 M.G. Coy.
In regard to my report N.12/1/4 of 21.2.20 re. above, I desire to say that
after another search and investigation the cross referred to in my former
letter as being in a German cemetery at Fournes is in my opinion the
cross and grave asked for, as the cross and grave were originally placed
by the Germans at a spot near Fromelles and Pheasant Wood and since
collected by them and replaced in this cemetery.
*   The G.R.U. and G.R. and M. [unknown acronym] have no records*
and state that they would not owing to the Germans doing the removal
etc. Upon this and other reports and observation I would advise the
acceptance that Lieut. Burns is buried with others in this grave.

How Major Allen came to the conclusion that the cross in Fournes had
been moved from Pheasant Wood along with the remains is not explained.
On 15 March, however, the words 'Yes accept' were appended to this
document by Major G.L. Phillips, CO of the AGS in London, and a corre-
spondent and colleague of Charles Bean. It here becomes evident that the
German burial documents stating the precise location of the five pits at
Fasanen-Wäldchen were not known to the British authorities at this time.
Alfred Allen's brief note to Phillips may well have settled the closure of

searches at Pheasant Wood. The next task was to open the Fournes grave at the earliest possible moment and establish whether remains were present.

On 20 May 1920, assisted by Imperial Labour Corps staff, the exhumation of the Fournes grave took place. Staff Sergeant Thomas Rowe of the AGS witnessed the event in the absence of Major Allen, who was then suffering from a bout of typhus. The working party excavated to a depth of 8½ feet (2.6 metres) without result, and then began to prospect laterally. Five bodies were soon revealed and exhumed: one officer and four other ranks—but all were British. Having recovered from his illness, in December 1920 Major Allen was able to make his own statement to the second court of enquiry. The Burns case had been included in the hearing because, strictly against regulations, a relative had apparently been given permission to attend the expected exhumation. Major Allen claimed: 'Before any question of the exhumation of Lieutenant Burns' body arose I made an exhaustive search all round Fromelles, Pheasant Wood and a portion of Fournes.'

Allen then confirmed that he had already examined considerable sections of the 'non-battlefield' area of Fromelles; but where he searched, when, for how long, and with whom, has never been established. There was no mention of three large open pits in the area he had been called upon to search, i.e. 'before Pheasant Wood'. Given that German mass graves were largely of standard dimensions, had he actually seen them his curiosity would surely have been aroused.

Upon later being recalled to the stand, however, he was asked, 'Was a cross erected by the Australian Graves Services over the supposed Burns grave, with his name on it?' He responded: 'No. It was largely due to reports by the local people that the Germans had removed the bodies and the cross bearing the inscription from Fromelles to Fournes that it was assumed that one of them might contain the body of Lieutenant Burns.'

The response is difficult to comprehend. Who could the 'local people' have been, and how could they have known? Fromelles—and its battered sister communities of Aubers, Le Maisnil and Neuve Chapelle— were devoid of civilians from mid-1915 until the end of the war. On 15 November 1918 the inspector of the *Zone Rouge* noted just one inhabitant in Fromelles. Perhaps it was people from Fournes or Beaucamps, the nearest occupied conurbations, who passed on the information, although this too sounds unlikely.

Today, with access to the original wartime aerial photographs, the three open graves at Pheasant Wood are plain to see, but only because they have become a focal point. If one could select the most *unremarkable* features of any post-war Western Front battleground, it would be holes, cavities, pits, hollows, scrapings and other sundry diggings. With several thousand miles of trenches, countless millions of shell-holes, thousands of mine craters, dugouts, gun- and mortar-pits, and all manner of other military delvings, holes were simply ubiquitous. Indeed, the act of digging was not only the very essence of the Great War but, as we have seen, for many years it also formed the major element of post-war activity. But Major Allen, and others, had been told where the holes—the graves—were located.

Had he understood? There is the question of the often repeated but perhaps mildly ambiguous words, 'five large British collective graves *before* the *Fasanen-Wäldchen*'. Might there have been confusion about the meaning of the word 'before'? Did it mean in front of the wood from the viewpoint of the British and Australians, i.e. on the side adjacent to the front lines? Or behind it, on the village side? We shall perhaps never know, but it seems probable that had the graves been evident Major Allen's 'many miles' of perambulations in the area would have traced the site. Even for an inexperienced 'grave-finder' the directions appear adequate; at most, there were only two relevant 'sides' to choose from.

The key question in the Burns/Allen narrative relates to the potential exhumation and reburial of the contents of the pits. For what reason might the Germans have either wished or needed to go to the immense (and profoundly disagreeable) trouble of opening, clearing and relocating large numbers of *Engländer* from graves that had deliberately been positioned in a place with no practical or tactical military value? The site had been selected because it was perfect for the purpose: between two trench systems, invisible to the enemy, unmolested by their guns, and creating no obstruction to manoeuvres. It was unlikely to be disturbed.

No evidence of mass exhumation and relocation of enemy dead has yet been found in German records. It certainly occurred in the case of individuals and small groups hastily buried (usually near the trenches) after an action: bodies that were, for want of a better term, 'in the way', and that may have been subsequently 'encountered' either during fieldworks or as a result of hostile action. Given its central location between the two main *Stellungen*, and the limited nature of the actions that followed 19 July 1916, it seems most unlikely that Pheasant Wood would have been classed as such. Furthermore, the VDK records reveal considerable numbers of remains that were not relocated from field grave to cemeteries.

Aerial photographs reveal that in September 1918 three of the eight grave pits were still fully open and starkly visible in the landscape. Because the heavy clay ground was of little agricultural value (and according to local knowledge has remained so ever since), it is possible that they stayed open for some time after the Armistice. In 2006 and 2007 I myself made enquiries with the *Fromellois*, especially farming families, seeking anecdotal evidence that might help to ascertain when the pits might have been backfilled and by whom. None was forthcoming. Nobody—not even members and officers of the local historical society—were able (or in the case of *M*. Bailleul, inclined) to offer any evidence, anecdotal or otherwise, that graves had ever been recorded or suspected at the site.

This is the critical question: were the three empty pits still open when Major Allen carried out his searches? It is possible, perhaps even likely. If so, might he have believed them to be graves that had already been emptied and left vacant, or some other form of fieldworks? Had this been the case the major would almost certainly have mentioned it as an extenuating circumstance in his reports and during the enquiry. He did not. This leaves us with five eventualities: a) he made no exploration of the ground at all; b) the exploration was incomplete; c) it was carried out in the wrong place; d) the graves were overlooked; and e) the graves were deliberately ignored.

To an experienced man, the nature of the surrounding terrain or vegetation might have offered clues. Employing 'normal' practices such as probing visually suspect ground with a thin rod and smelling the hollow tip for aromas of corruption—a standard technique employed across all battlegrounds to find shallow burials—was of minimal use, for being 'designed interments' the Pheasant Wood remains lay too deep for probes to reach. The ground itself appears to have divulged no clues. Ironically, had the authorities requested a search of Royal Flying Corps aerial photographs, the site would have been instantly self-evident. Although aerials would almost certainly have been made available upon request, no evidence has yet been uncovered to suggest they were put to such a use.

It remains unclear how well acquainted Major Allen was with the Fromelles area. His duties were by necessity primarily associated with Belgian Flanders—a huge responsibility and grim undertaking that created stress and tension between nationalities. Indeed, it was Major Allen who had during the enquiries pointed the finger at British recovery teams for 'chopping men in halves in order to double their body returns'. We know from the records that Fromelles—a narrowly contained battle-field where combats, although bloody, had been relatively brief—was, by reason of the colossal, lengthy and costly engagements elsewhere, not looked upon or treated in the same way as the priority sites of the Ypres and Messines Salients, Pozières or Villers-Brettoneux. French Flanders was almost certainly not a regular destination for Major Allen; indeed he may never have had cause to visit the sector until called there by the Burns case.

What of the VDK documents held at Kassel? Might they have had a bearing on Allied post-war searches? CWGC files show that recover-ies at Fromelles were on a number of occasions successfully assisted by 'enemy' documentation, for the phrase 'located through German records' is frequently encountered in the burial returns. The files were undoubt-edly available for Allied scrutiny, for German searches were called to a halt in August 1921, just three weeks earlier than the British. The *Fasanen-Wäldchen* entries did not state that the remains had been recovered, and the entry and its French annotations revealed that both the German *and* the French authorities were aware of the existence of the graves at the same time that British and Australian recoveries were underway in the sector. The French clearly had access, but Major Allen and his colleagues appear to have been entirely unaware of the lists: lists that definitively placed the graves' location 'on the southern edge' of the wood. There were two associ-ated German 'grave' maps; one was comprehensive and relevant, the other not. Curiously, if employed on its own, the relevant example would simply have confused the situation. The reason is a little surprising: the marked location of site number 8 in map square 3305 does not correspond with the place described by the lists, but shows it as being some 150 metres to the east . . . evidently a cartographer's error.

Neither the German lists nor maps are mentioned as being consulted by the British authorities at the time of Major Allen's search, and no direct reference to them has yet been discovered in other archives. It may simply have been a recurrent symptom of that old wartime malady, poor communication. Perhaps, like the Red Cross *registres*, no one thought to ask.

Major Allen's court of enquiry statements relating to the Burns case appear to have closed the chapter on Pheasant Wood as a burial site, for although intensive exhumation work was undertaken along and between the old front lines from the autumn of 1919 into the spring of 1921, records suggest it is unlikely that any further attention was paid to the backwater of *Fasanen-Wäldchen*. There was also no fresh external impetus to continue official probing, for it appears that no more enquiries from Australian families were received and followed up before mid-September 1921, when battlefield searches of the kind the AGS had been charged to undertake ceased for good. From that date, with very few exceptions, the missing would be found by luck rather than experience and judgement. There were many.

Although the recovery situation improved as a result of the two enquiries, General Fabian Ware was clearly anxious to see AGS personnel boarding ships bound for Australian shores. In a November 1921 letter to the IWGC land and legal adviser, Major A.L. Ingpen, he pleads, 'Am most anxious you should convince Shepherd of our ability to carry on satisfactorily without Australian officers who should be withdrawn immediately as confusing records and otherwise causing much mischief.' One curious aspect of the courts of enquiry papers is that although they can be found on the AWM website, the CWGC documents recording the same events are still firmly closed, unavailable for public scrutiny even after ninety years. A request for access was denied, which makes one wonder what evidence might still lurk in the CWGC vaults . . .

Despite widespread public criticism, Britain and Canada grudgingly but quietly accepted the termination of battlefield searches. Australia did not. Prime Minister Billy Hughes stated that he would not let the matter drop, saying that his men—meaning Major Allen and his colleagues—should continue their quest. But that was not to be.

The Allen story is not yet quite complete. The major's prowess as a body-finder or 'discoverer of missing men' was to become almost legendary. Several newspaper articles appeared suggesting that if Allen 'could not find our boys, no one could'. Indeed, his skills appear to have occasionally verged upon the mystical, so much so that a sense of propaganda and puffery permeates this aspect of the case.

The most extreme example comes from the pen of John Oxenham (real name William Arthur Dunkerley, 1852–1941). Oxenham was the era's most popular novelist and poet, selling more than a million volumes of poetry during the war; his hymn, 'For the Men at the Front', is alone believed to have sold eight million copies. His support for the war was founded upon Christian idealism and an absolute faith in divine purpose and divine love. Clearly a close friend of Alfred Allen, it is possible he tried to 'come to the rescue' by writing an article based upon his capabilities as a body-finder. This extraordinary document was entitled 'A Discoverer of Missing Men—Major Allen of the A.W.G.S.', and can be seen in full on the AWM website. Excerpts are worthwhile reproducing, for they explain his extraordinary charisma:

> Abraham Lincoln is said to have had in his office one drawer marked 'If you can't find it anywhere else, LOOK HERE!' And the word in Northern France and Belgium is 'If you can't find any trace of a missing A.I.F. man, ask Major Allen!'
>
> When all hope of discovery has been absolutely given up by everyone else, as a final resort such information that has been obtainable has been sent by Australia House to Major Allen, and in eight cases out of ten he solves the mystery and sets the seal of certainty on lingering hopes and doubts at home. For lack of knowledge is more agonising than assurance of death.
>
> A Quaker, a non-drinker, non-smoker, non-swearer, a born leader of men, with a most remarkable memory, an intuitive perception of possibilities, and a mind trained to minute observation and deduction, no finer man could have been chosen for the arduous post he fills. Not

many could do his work as he does it. Nothing less than the loftiest sense
of duty and a keenly sympathetic understanding of the urgency of what
he is doing could carry him through with it.

But he is in every respect a big man—bodily, mentally, and spiritu-
ally, and he does his grim and gruesome work in a spirit of reverence and
devotion to his fellows, alive and dead, which is a tonic to his own soul
and to the souls of those he meets . . .

His parish, as he calls it, is everywhere north of a line drawn from
St Valery on the French coast through Arras to the German frontier.
It includes, of course, all the battlefields round Ypres, Passchendaele,
Poelcapelle, and Messines, Wytschaete, Dixmude etc. etc. But on
occasion, when necessity calls, he ranges far beyond his own borders
and discovers missing men no matter where they may lie. If they are
his men, he wants them, and he will go miles, away out into strange
territory, to find them.

Even without the 'spin'—as dangerous in peace as it is in war—
Oxenham's piece is indicative of the skills which Major Allen is said by
some to have possessed. Nevertheless, the Imperial War Graves Commission was by no means entirely content with the performance of any of
the exhumation companies, protesting that the units were 'obsessed with the
idea that their reputation depended on their concentrating [burying]
the highest possible number of bodies in the shortest possible time', and
thus allotted insufficient time and regard to identification. Despite identification being paramount to families, it was at times made a low priority to
the simple duty of dignified recovery and reburial.

In May 1921 the senior IWGC agent in France, Lieutenant-Colonel
E.A.S. Gell, noted in his journal that dedicated attempts at identification
were being made only when time allowed. At that time approximately
600 bodies per week were being uncovered, of which 20 per cent were
identifiable. What Lieutenant-Colonel Gell meant was that unless the disc
was evident, further identification efforts—such as the careful scrutiny of
clothing or accoutrements, the sifting of personal items, or the scrutiny
of ground in the immediate vicinity—was not always carried out to the
standards that had hitherto pertained.

There can be no doubt that substantial efforts were invested in searching and clearing the Aubers and Fromelles battlegrounds and at least a part of the old German *Hintergelände*. Evidence of other collective graves, several of considerable scale, appear in both CWGC and German records. Some are behind Allied lines, and there are many in No Man's Land; others lie within 'enemy' positions. Shell-hole interments are also noted; in such cases the remains are often impossible to separate into distinct individuals. And there were, of course, many recoveries from German cemeteries, each grave usually being marked, numbered and listed. The huge numbers still missing from the 9 May 1915 engagement, however, suggest that it was perhaps only the key battlefield areas that received close attention. The VDK records reveal evidence of potentially unrecovered communal graves from this era.

Although rapid, the Pheasant Wood burial was a substantial undertaking. The site was large, apparent and, at the end of the war, undamaged by shellfire; the trench tramway offered a giant topographical clue; there were existing German and International Red Cross notifications directly relating to the graves; and three pits probably remained open when Major Allen conducted his searches—if not, they could only have been backfilled recently and may thus have been evident in the landscape. Von Braun's regimental history of RIR 21 which, as we know, included details, was published *before* official searches terminated. Local enquiry at this time would certainly have offered useful information.

The more one examines how and why the graves might have been overlooked, the more baffling the situation appears. Major Allen's examination was carried out in the early European spring, when vegetation was only just re-awakening. Undergrowth was low: it was a fine moment for a visual search.

But Pheasant Wood was not alone—there were a number of key sites that were explored either perfunctorily or even not at all. In May 1921, some four months before searches were brought to an end, the IWGC suggested several areas where the quest 'might usefully be continued'. These included large parts of the battlefields of Ypres, Arras and Somme—a vast expanse of territory. Woodland—frequently the scene of bloody and prolonged combat—returned quickly and inconveniently to nature, becoming a jungle of shattered trunks, branches and impenetrable thorn. In mid-December 1921, after the search period had been terminated, Lieutenant-Colonel E.A.S. Gell had cause to visit the Cambrai sector. He noted:

> To Bourlon Wood to see the condition of it, as report goes that large numbers of bodies are still missing there. We worked our way through part of the wood, but soon the tangled undergrowth became so thick that progress was impossible. Brambles grew in such profusion that I give it as my opinion that no systematic search is possible. I do not believe that wood has ever been searched properly, let alone re-searched.

A similar situation pertained at High Wood on the Somme, and a number of other sites. Pheasant Wood, however, had only twice been briefly fought over—and almost bloodlessly on both occasions. It occupied a place at the very opposite end of the spectrum of difficulty, and indeed significance. Ironically, Charles Bean, who visited and photographed the Fromelles sector on 11 November 1918, could during his perambulations have easily stumbled across the three open pits adjacent to the hidden remains of up to 250 of his countrymen.

Chapter 21

A TOLERATING OF MYSTERIES

One often detects a sense of outrage that such great loss of life was allowed to take place at Fromelles. This is largely affectation: men go to war not to die but to kill, and since time immemorial the human race—always led by the most 'developed' nations on earth—has perpetually striven to perfect engines of destruction specifically designed to ever more effectively take life. During the First World War both the speed at which such inventions were devised and produced, and their efficiency, reached an historical zenith. Britain was at the forefront. As for the troops, they were fully aware of the meaning of the word 'duty'. As George Birmingham (Father James Hannay) candidly suggested in *A Padre in France*, 'The soldier's business is to kill the enemy, and he only tries to avoid being killed for the sake of being efficient.'

In civilian life we expect things occasionally to go wrong, but are often still surprised at certain failures, for time and effort has usually been invested in forethought in order to minimise the risk of malfunction. History, however, shows us that in war the chance of malfunction is multiplied many-fold. Tragic scenes must be expected because tragedy is what is deliberately being engineered, with both sides determined to inflict tragedy upon the other. These actions have consequences that can subsequently be re-engineered to suit the exigencies of the moment. When, after the 'tragedy' of Kulmbach on 15 July, for example, General James McCay presented his Diggers a few days later with what he called a 'chance of getting more than even', he was simply exhorting them to compound one tragedy with another. It is an unchanging facet of human conflict.

One of the many legacies of the First World War was the duty recognised by its several belligerent nations to provide both the participants and those who waited for word of success or failure, life or death, with an authoritative written context by which the events and final outcomes might be adequately understood. That context—which we call history—was also integral to grieving, remembering, healing and commemorating. But its creation required careful selection and construction. The primary vehicle was the 'official history', a necessarily summarised version of events. The OH was supplemented by a second influence: the slightly more personal and frequently more detailed but also abridged unit histories.

With a deal of military and political management, the catastrophe of Fromelles was played both up and down by the third and, from the public's point of view, most important agency, the press. Charles Bean, first as a working journalist and then as the author of the *OHA*, perhaps did his best to portray the truth by injecting as much accuracy as the censors allowed, or indeed that he permitted himself, for he was already inextricably absorbed in the development of a concept that he and others had begun in Gallipoli: the Anzac legend. Giving birth to such a legend complicated his task because, once begun, myths under construction require not only continual supplementation, but protection. It was far from easy, for in the final analysis history and legend do not make comfortable bedfellows.

On 24 July 1916, in a piece for the London *Times* and the *Daily Mail*, Bean labelled Fromelles as an 'attack' that had resulted in 'severe' casualties. The powers that be were not pleased, for the British official *communiqué* described it as, 'some important raids on a front of two miles in which Australian troops took part'. Raids . . . not attacks. The Germans translated and circulated both *communiqué* and article, themselves noting the contrast. To Digger and Tommy, this was a distinction of considerable significance: their 'battle' had been downgraded, and yet all the participants looked upon the clash as something far greater than the word 'raid' could ever articulate.

Almost within hours of the final capitulation at Rouges Bancs on the morning of 20 July, everyone's attentions instantly refocussed upon the Somme and the ensuing twenty-eight months of bitter struggle. It was not a question of choice: there were further battles to fight. Overshadowed by Gallipoli, Bullecourt, Pozières and numerous other bloody actions, Fromelles slipped from the collective Australian memory. After the Armistice, awareness of the 19 July action only slowly resurfaced.

Its early resurfacing in post-war Australian newspapers make fascinating reading. In *The Sydney Morning Herald*, for example, there appeared on 26 July 1919 a substantial article entitled 'Fleurbaix' in which with dazzling hindsight Lieutenant-Colonel Charles MacLaurin laid the blame for the disaster primarily on spies:

> The attack was to be made on 17 July, but it was put off to the 19th owing to a hazy light; meantime we knew exactly the number of men who were to go over the top, the exact number of guns behind them, the exact sector to be attacked by each division, and the exact hour of zero. And if we, non-combatants [MacLaurin was a medical officer], knew these things did others know them also? At that time Flanders was reeling with spies; half the Flemings were in the pay of both sides, and ready to sell all France for five francs.

Colonel MacLaurin may have been surprised to hear that some of the key information handed to the Germans was an Anzac endowment—offered by prisoners on several occasions before the action, and afterwards through the operation orders captured on 20 July. It is clear that Charles Bean was aware of these and other things, but in the *OHA* he skates somewhat casually around the subject, saying, 'The prisoners' answers to their questions read much like those of German prisoners captured by the British;

but the process was hardly necessary, for either on a prisoner or one of the dead, the Germans found a copy of Haking's order, which told them all they desired to know'.

The statement told the reader but a fraction of the story. Because Bean, as he here appears to confirm, had seen the prisoners' responses to Lübcke's questions, he would know full well their extent and value to the enemy. With the Somme making grisly progress for the Allies, the 'process' of which he speaks was absolutely essential to the Germans. Like their predecessors, the prisoners were expected to sing. They sang. In chorus. Bean would also have been aware that two of the operation orders and the artillery scheme had been found on Australian officers, probably Captain Charles Mills and Lieutenant Vivian Bernard, who on absolutely no account should have taken them across No Man's Land. This information could not be revealed in the *OHA* because if it were linked with revelations provided by Diggers and Kiwis captured in May 1916, it might have cast a somewhat different light on the narrative of the first three months of Australian presence on the Western Front, their first battle, and thus the work in progress on the Anzac myth. Omission or obfuscation was the prudent path. Better to explicate and celebrate the disaster than reveal potentially unpleasant truths.

In his *Sydney Morning Herald* article Colonel MacLaurin goes on to make several assumptions that seem to be based upon those seeds of doubt carefully planted and nurtured after the battle by AOK 6 intelligence services. Others are less easy to find a provenance for. He describes the Germans as having 'hundreds of machine-guns'; we know the 6 BRD figure was a maximum of forty. The Allies, he says, benefited from a gigantic force of artillery, 'probably the mightiest ever concentrated up to then in the world'; far from the truth. The Sugar Loaf he describes as 'a sinister and terrible place, crowded with concrete emplacements in which a great force of heavy artillery was to be concentrated, under British command'. This reveals how in the imagination of readers the Sugar Loaf soon became the unconquerable fortress bastion that many still imagine it to have been. The British heavies, it is then stated, 'never actually landed a single shell' on it, a statement refuted by numerous reports on both sides of the line. And when the assault began, 'there was no sign of an attack on our right, and similar messages kept coming back, more and more agonised.

What had happened was that by some awful feat of blundering the 61st had not cut their own wire, and had made no sally-ports to let their men out. As these fresh young English lads jumped out of their trenches they could do nothing but run up and down the line like rabbits seeking a way through'. Although we are now aware of a more accurate narrative, nonsense such as this is all too easily repeated, exaggerated and embellished, and thus transformed into 'fact'.

The 2nd Australian Division trench raids in June and July were described thus by MacLaurin:

> *Every night they were over, killing, plundering, and taking prisoners, but with trifling loss to themselves; but as a result that division became extraordinarily competent, and brother Boche became peevish in the extreme, and at last most infuriated. To attack such men came the Fifth Division, composed of half-trained and half-disciplined soldiers.*

The latter sentence brought the writer some criticism, and yet it probably spoke more truth than the rest of the article. Like the 61st Division, McCay's men were prepared for a lengthy period of acclimatisation and a gradual introduction to combat, no more. To throw both into action appears to have been more than ill advised, but the decision to do so was based upon confidence instilled, as was so often the case, by the gunners. If the enemy had been brought to their knees before the assault, then the attacking troops need not be either experienced or of high quality. Sir Richard Haking had promised there would be no resistance, and made certain his subordinates broadcast that conviction.

In closing, MacLaurin called for the official report of the battle to be published. This would have produced minimal benefit. Even if every Allied document had at that time been made available to the public, it would have helped no one to fully understand the sequence of events that led to the catastrophe, for most of the key answers lay not in Canberra or London, but in Potsdam. And in any case, official commentators—like MacLaurin himself, ignorant of the wider truth and possessed of a perhaps forgivable jingoism—had already settled upon his approach. It was propaganda re-propagandised, considered and composed to influence the beliefs of a nation.

The following year on Saturday 10 April 1920, *The Argus* published an anonymous article entitled 'FROMELLES, 1916! A Glorious Failure. WHAT REALLY HAPPENED'. The piece is more considered than MacLaurin's, but simply summarises in text and style Captain A.D. Ellis' *Story of the Fifth Australian Division*, published the same month (it may indeed have been written by Ellis). The initial assault is related thus: 'It terminated, as all such hand-to-hand fighting terminated throughout the war, in the absolute triumph of the Australians and the extinction or capitulation of the Germans.' Twenty-four hours after that assault, German propagandists were composing similar sentences about the self-same termination, but with the nationalities transposed.

Ellis's bulky history suffers from the same lack of balanced detailed knowledge, and thus context, as the products of other journalists and authors of the epoch. As a result, in both the article and the book, readers do not come within a country mile of finding out 'what really happened' on 19 July 1916. Later, when McCay, Ellis, Elliott, Haking, Haig, Birdwood and other men of influence (indeed, one could list every officer and man in the AIF and British Expeditionary Force) came to write or speak of Fromelles, not one knew the wider realities. The assiduous Bean knew more than most, and more than he could say.

The Anzac legend that he himself had helped to create made Charles Bean's task of writing the *OHA* exceptionally difficult. The challenge was to find a suitable manner to report Fromelles that would reassure the readership that the vision he had created in Gallipoli pertained on the Western Front, and grew ever stronger throughout the war. There was no choice but to omit or distort. Readers should not make the mistake of thinking this is in any way unusual: it is universal to all wars and to all nations: it can today be discerned (or at the very least suspected) on an almost daily basis. Sometimes the public are deemed to require protection from unpalatable facts, but more often than not it is the perpetrators of the errors and their peers who seek the safeguards to cover their own vulnerable rear ends. This is partly why official records are officially 'closed', the period of closure varying according to the sensitivity of the content. They are 'opened' when the risk of culpability is considered sufficiently diminished. In especially delicate cases, destruction was common; that too is a practice that continues.

Charles Bean had all this to take into consideration—particularly when writing his 'official' wartime commentaries. What one might call 'strategic rhetoric' was thus unavoidable. It will perhaps come as no surprise to the reader to hear that research into other Australian actions indicates that Fromelles is by no means the only instance where diversions from the actuality were seen by the official historian as not just prudent but obligatory.

Bean knew he need not fear whatever came to be published in German official and regimental histories, for few Australians (or British) would take any interest in them, not least because, to quote Charles MacLaurin, they were written by 'filthy Boche', who 'slaughtered our own clean-living and beloved Australians'. Given the circumstances and the epoch, this was an entirely conventional view, shared by the peoples of all the Entente nations who had been subjected to years of conflict, misery, misinformation and unremitting propaganda—because Germany chose to go to war. Equally conventionally, it has left historical equilibrium languishing in the shadows of those conforming and tolerant custodians, disinterest and indifference. I have myself met 'historians' who refuse to consider German primary sources when they do not dovetail with long-favoured allied secondary sources. Sometimes, however, it is only the recognition of flawed foundations that stimulates fresh research. Such was the genesis of this volume.

By the time the *OHA* was published in 1929, the Anzac myth was set in granite and tempered steel; to have revealed then what Bean knew would have exposed him to the displeasure and disapproval of not just his peers, but an already convinced and conditioned Australian nation and, indeed, empire. For Australia, Bean's history became the only required history—and after all, did it not contain an impressive throng of German references? For such an august and respected chronicler to make any later allusion to alternative appreciations might have set a hare running that some inquisitive and dogged researcher might have chased—to Bean's cost.

It causes one to wonder how often he fought the impulse to confide in others what he knew to exist in Potsdam. Possession of known material, and knowledge of the certain existence of a great deal more key data that was likely to contradict the Anzac legend, must have frequently served to regulate his thoughts and words. The savagery of conflict and the rhetoric involved in its tribute and remembrance are intertwined. What Bean finally elected to publish was written, as politicians would say, 'for the best of reasons'. In all its component parts, war is a treacherous business, and the Fromelles story exemplifies how it clearly remains treacherous to those who study it, even a century after the event.

By the time of Charles Bean's death in 1968, no one had looked beyond his work. He had been practically beatified. The *OHA* was the Digger's Rosetta Stone, and most subsequent publications served to sustain its pre-eminence. Herbertson's collection of German unit histories still slumbered upon the shelves; the primary sources lay in Munich gathering dust

In Australia, the legacies of Gallipoli, Fromelles, Pozières, Bullecourt and other actions carry with them a sanctity fashioned by Charles Bean and others that can be hazardous to tamper with. Challenging the myth is often akin to throwing down the mediaeval gauntlet or proposing a duel. This is not the purpose of this book; the object is dispassionate debate to help reveal a better truth.

The curiosity of future generations will not so easily be suppressed. With enhanced access through digital technology, in the coming decades we should be prepared to adjust many a perception and sensitivity. It is essential that we do.

It is now becoming clear that Fromelles was not fought against the long-accepted backcloth, and nor did it unfold in the way we have for so long been encouraged to believe. The narrative of the legacy in relation to the Pheasant Wood burials is also far from straightforward. The same can probably be said of a host of other actions. Time and further research may tell. With Fromelles, we have on the one hand the search for the truth about the battle, and on the other a battle for the truth about the search process itself.

It is seldom profitable to enter into the realm of seeking and assigning cul-pability, for that usually implies subjectivity. When scrutinising the evidence it must first be accepted that there are often things we cannot know because the knowledge died with the bearers, and that some document-based sources of wisdom may have—deliberately or otherwise—been lost, concealed or destroyed.

The perceived villain of the Fromelles piece has always been Lieutenant-General Sir Richard Haking, a soldier who was neither unfamiliar nor unpractised at defending the commander's role after a defeated enterprise: it had been necessary on two important occasions and a number of lesser instances before Fromelles 1916. For almost ten years, at every step of his career Haking had been subordinate to Sir Douglas Haig. Having met Haig in 1896 at Staff College, he served with him in South Africa, and under him before the war at Aldershot. The two men shared an offensive philosophy; in the parlance of the time, they were 'thrusters'. Haking had spent nineteen of his twenty-one months on the Western Front observing, considering, and in ventures great and small, from time-to-time assaulting the Aubers Ridge and its neighbouring sectors. Whether he was fixated upon its capture we cannot say; what may be said with some confidence is that he felt he 'knew' the region, robustly promoted it as a strategic gateway, and frequently sought authority for offensive action there.

Knowing the region, however, is not the same as knowing the enemy, and it seems clear from all Haking's schemes that neither he nor his staff were ever in possession of the knowledge or indeed the weaponry to allow the development of tactics that would bring about the fall of the ridge and the great prize in its lee, the city of Lille. The costly undertakings to do just that brought him widespread condemnation among the ranks and the worst reputation a commander could have: an assumed disdain for the wellbeing and lives of his troops. Fromelles 1916 placed the blackest of seals upon his character—he was henceforth regarded as a 'butcher'.

Few of influence had the courage to make such comment at the time, however, and when criticism does appear it is *sotto voce* in private diaries, never as a public statement. That was the *modus operandi* of the era. A few eyewitness commentators spoke up years later. They mention the difficult nature of the ground, muddled planning, tactical misconceptions, inadequate artillery and infantry, but none speak of the quality of enemy forces or their meticulous measures to repeatedly baulk Allied assaults of precisely the kind Haking elected to employ. Why? Because none of Haking's critics knew the enemy either, and it did not do to praise the Germans when one's vanquishment had been on each occasion so utterly comprehensive. Curiously, it is the 'British Official History' that comes closest to (dangerously condensed) truth: 'To have delivered battle at all betrayed a great under-estimate of the enemy's power of resistance', said Wilfrid Miles—but yet again, in hindsight. There may have been dissenting voices before and after 19 July, but almost to a man they remained mute at the most important moment. Charles Bean veers away from mention of German aptitude by closing his chapters on Fromelles with the following passage:

> A particularly unfortunate but almost inevitable result of the fight was that, having been unwisely combined with a British division whose value for offence, in spite of the devoted gallantry of many of its members, was recognised as doubtful, the Australian soldiers tended to accept the judgment—often unjust, but already deeply impressed by the occurrences at the Suvla landing—that the 'Tommies' could not be relied upon to uphold a flank in a stiff fight.

These words have had lasting impact. After eighty-four years perhaps their significance may now be somewhat tempered by Munich's contribution to the narrative.

Sir Richard Haking's post-action report to First Army was succinct. It began: 'Briefly speaking, the Artillery preparation was adequate, there were sufficient guns and sufficient ammunition. The wire was properly cut and the assaulting Battalions had a clear run into the enemy's trenches.' The passage is written with such fabulous self-confidence because the readership for whom it was produced—men from the same military stable and lineage as Haking—were expected to accept his synopsis without question. And accept it they did.

With equal poise he evaluated the performance of the South Midlanders and Australians. The latter were 'not sufficiently trained to consolidate the ground gained'; the former were, 'insufficiently imbued with the offensive spirit to go in like one man at the appointed time'. The Diggers had, however, 'attacked in the most gallant manner'. Again, the Germans remain anonymous.

The South Midlanders had trained in Britain for eighteen months. They had been in theatre for seven weeks, during which period they carried out several small raids. This was their preparation for major combat. The 5th Australians had less than seven days trench experience in France: no time for training or raids, and indeed too short a tenure for even the most meagre initiation into the ways of warfare in Flanders. They had themselves been raided, however, and during Operation Kulmbach on 15 July were subjected to a short but shattering demonstration of enemy capability.

Given both units' lack of familiarity with active service, one might judge that the primary failure was one of command: Haking's decision to throw such inexperienced men into action. The German positions, said his report, would have been 'a gift' had two trained divisions been employed. Given the Bavarians' preparations, this assertion is more than doubtful—but for someone of Haking's station, such words came effortlessly and accompanied by little anxiety: there was meagre prospect of his being held accountable, for the action was, after all, merely diversional—and everyone subsequently broadcast that it had indeed achieved its strategic aims, even if tactically it was catastrophic.

It had been, Haking said, essential to use the selected divisions because time did not allow other more suitable units to be deployed. The remark for which he received the greatest condemnation was, 'I think the attack, although it failed, has done both divisions a great deal of good': a typical and often-employed perspective derived from British military tradition.

One cannot make an assault without placing one's troops in positions from which they are able to successfully operate; by definition, all are hazardous. If the enemy's defensive resources have neither been recognised nor neutralised, no amount of experience ever helped a man trapped immobile in a crowded trench to evade hostile (and in this case, friendly) shellfire. Likewise, no amount of grit, hardness or training assists in the negotiation of a shell-, mortar-, grenade-, and bullet-swept No Man's Land such as that which the troops encountered at Fromelles. Courage, gallantry or valour of even the highest quality carries no armour.

Much has been written about the lack of experience within Australian ranks, especially in relation to officers. It is also said that a shortage of troops 'hardened' in Gallipoli was felt. Because serious damage to the Diggers' prospects and morale was suffered long before 6.00 p.m., both observations are unsound. Hundreds, many with the requisite experience, were removed from the combat equation before the whistles blew. Numerous Diggers later said it was as if the enemy were aware of what was about to take place. They were indeed aware, but suspicion only became conviction when activity within and outside their own trenches betrayed Allied intentions in the hours prior to the attack. The Bavarians were trained, prepared and, quite understandably, particularly watchful.

Of far greater importance than has hitherto been considered, however, is the question of unsubdued German artillery. Sir Douglas Haig drew attention to this aspect on three separate occasions, requesting assurance not only of the destruction of the German wire and fieldworks, but hostile guns and gunners. The demand was unequivocal, and was made as a result of almost three weeks of bitter struggle on the Somme, and the mass of wretched Anglo–French evidence provided during the previous bloody year.

In his post-battle analysis, at no time does Sir Richard Haking mention the failure to suppress Bavarian guns, guns that many Australian prisoners later referred to as 'devastatingly effective'. In a post-battle note to General Sir Herbert Plumer, GOC Second Army, Haking said he felt, 'the artillery work turned out even better than I expected though many of the Batteries had very little experience'. We cannot know what expectations he had entertained nor, more pertinently, upon what intelligence the remark was based, but it does tend to make his analysis of the infantry performance yet more defamatory.

At the time, no high-ranking officer, British or Australian, challenged him—except Sir Douglas Haig. Despite almost two years of failed offensives, great and small, employing almost identical tactics, on 19 July there remained an across-the-board undervaluation of German capabilities.

On 20 July Haig noted in his diary:

GOC First Army reports that Haking's attack only partially successful, and after visiting the Corps HQ at dawn, he (Monro) decided to

THE LOST LEGIONS OF FROMELLES

withdraw the units which had got into the Enemy's trenches. The troops
seem to have somewhat become disorganised. The reality of the fighting
and the shelling seems to have been greater than many had expected!
So the experience must have been of value to all, and the enterprise has
certainly had the effect of obliging the Enemy to retain reserves in that
area. Besides, by merely bombarding the Enemy's front on similar lines
again, we will compel him to mass troops to oppose a possible attack . . .

Later in the same entry we are offered more clues as to Haig's attitude at this
time, showing he is fully aware of the limitations of inexperienced units
and the need for their careful introduction to conflict:

I also saw General Gough at Toutencourt. The Australians went in
[to the line] last night opposite Pozières . . . He proposes to attack
Pozières with them on 22 early, 1.30am. I told him to go into all details
carefully, as 1st Australian Division had not been engaged before, and
possibly overlooked the difficulties of this kind of fighting.

On 22 July the C-in-C again visited Gough to check that the neophyte
Diggers had 'only been given a simple task' at Pozières. It once more reminds
us that Haig was not in a position to disbelieve or dismiss assurances force-
fully and confidently tendered by his commanders, which is what happened
at Fromelles with Monro, Haking, Plumer, Mackenzie and McCay.

On 30 July 1916 Lieutenant-General Sir Henry Wilson (GOC IV Corps)
referred (privately, in his diary) to the recent action as 'a botch job'. In his
book *Fromelles 1916*, Paul Cobb writes:

In 1937, when the British Official History was being compiled, a number
of officers who had served at Fromelles were invited to comment on the
draft chapter covering that attack. Their remarks were overwhelmingly
negative. Capt. Wilfred Greene, for example, a staff officer attached
to the 61st Division HQ wrote: 'The operation was bound to be
a costly failure. Those responsible for planning it showed complete
ignorance of the ground . . . no amount of preparation or training
would have enabled a success to have been made of an attack which

was (a) tactically misconceived and (b) made with inadequate forces, inadequately supported by artillery over ground where it was not possible to consolidate the position captured, dominated as it was.' Lt. Col. M. M. Parry-Jones, of the British 183rd Brigade, summarised his comments on the draft chapter: 'What could be expected of such an attack but failure.'

What we do not learn from these individuals is what was said *at the time*, by them, by their superiors, or by their subordinates. How many officers (and indeed other ranks) felt the venture, restricted as it was to the most minimal objectives, to be doomed, but elected to say nothing? After the battle Brigadier-General Pompey Elliott is reported as being beside himself with emotion, looking, according to Charles Bean who was on the spot, like 'a man who had just lost his wife'. Elliott's grief was undoubtedly genuine, for his brigade had just been flayed alive, visiting distress, disappointment and no doubt fear of the future upon him. The emotional brew, however, might also have included a sense of guilt regarding his self-confessed 'loyalty and deference'—the failure to make his opinion known to his superiors at those moments when more might have been done to ameliorate the carnage which he himself plainly foresaw.

Elliott was an experienced soldier who had served with distinction in the Boer War and at Gallipoli. In this most serious of situations, where the lives of many hundreds of men lay in his hands, loyalty and deference might appear to be frail reasons for keeping one's own counsel, particularly when that counsel had been supported by a staff officer with a direct line to Olympus and the commander-in-chief. We cannot know what psychological agonies Elliott may have experienced, but a terrible lesson appears to have been learned, for on at least two occasions after Fromelles he is known to have argued vehemently against planned 5th Division actions— and prevailed. For years after 1918 he regularly corresponded with Bean, Monash, McCay and others about a range of war-related grievances. Pompey Elliott died by his own hand in March 1931 at the age of fifty-two.

As a result of Fromelles, James McCay became a member of Haking's Butchers Guild. It has been said that his decision to transfer Vickers machine guns, Stokes mortars and Lewis guns to 'Hunland' with the tail of the infantry assault was a terminal fault. But Haking had already given everyone assurances—which other key figures championed—that when the troops arrived on the far side of No Man's Land there would hardly be a living German to be found. There was therefore no need for McCay to put key weapons at risk. It is for Haking's plainly controvertible assurances of universal German annihilation that he may be held culpable, for not a single previous British action on the Western Front had given those assurances adequate foundation. Finally, of course, what we can never know is how the attacks might have unfolded had the divisional frontages been exchanged, British for Australian.

After Fromelles, every commander—from Haig to Haking—made the claim that the sequence of summer actions in French Flanders had achieved the aim of holding German divisions in place. The statements were obligatory. Whether they were true, even in part, remains unclear, given that they were presented in the form of unsupported statement and unassailable claim. There are 'general understandings', 'rumours', extracts from prisoners' statements and assurances, none of which stand up to scrutiny. Indeed, verification can come only from the Germans themselves, and no supporting evidence has yet been found in the papers of AOK 6.

The ultimate war diary extract in this book—a chilling but vitally important one—must go once more to the Bavarians. The following passage formed the summation of 6 BRD Report No. 106 (1) to *Armee-Oberkommando 6*:

> *The action at Fromelles is a feather in the cap of this Division. All arms contributed to the victory, but once again the laurels must go to the infantry.*
>
> *From the perspective of higher command, this action is in itself of very little importance. Taking advantage of the surprise occasioned by the mine explosions, and having destroyed our breastworks and wire with exceptionally heavy artillery fire, several hundred British troops broke into our lines on a frontage approximately two company sectors wide and captured ground beyond our front trench. Deployment of the Divisional Reserve was hardly necessary, and the troops in the front*

line were able to muster sufficient strength to remedy the situation and take back the captured positions.

The significance of the action lies rather in the importance that the enemy attached to <u>his</u> enterprise. The notebooks, orders and plans found on dead enemy officers (147 of whom fell within and in front of our positions) revealed that this was not just a small-scale demonstration; the enemy had serious aspirations of achieving a major breakthrough. He hoped to capture the Fromelles-Aubers line and then turn to the south and attempt to join up with the Indian Corps attacking our VII Corps. To that end he had dug and mined for weeks and months, meticulously planned and prepared the lines and objectives of his attack, the composition of the assault formations, their actions before, during and after the attack, and their route of advance on Fromelles, and finally he had drawn up his 7th and 8th Divisions and powerful artillery forces in front of Laventie.

Considering all these preparations and this concentration of forces, however, the attack ended in dismal failure. The offensive broke down not because the troops failed—they fought bravely—but because the British command, intimidated by the German artillery fire, lacked the resolve to fully commit their reserves and—just as General Buller did at Tugela—thus threw into jeopardy the success they had already achieved and shamefully abandoned those of their comrades who had broken into our lines to a not uncertain fate.

Because of the groundwater conditions, this Division's defensive positions consist not of deep trenches but of breastworks which, being high and, in spite of all reinforcement, unsolid, present an attractive target to the enemy's artillery. If he brings up sufficient heavy artillery with enough ammunition, the enemy could therefore succeed again in the future in achieving similar lesser or greater incursions in this sector— but they will never be more than local successes. On the evidence of its conduct of the action at Fromelles, the British command will never be capable of achieving a major breakthrough. Just as it was a hundred years ago at Waterloo, the British army of today is a defensive army. It may succeed in denying victory to its adversary, but it can never be victorious itself.

Readers will by now recognise this action as the Battle of Aubers Ridge. The author, writing on 29 May 1915, was a certain *Generalleutnant* Gustav von Scanzoni. His troops—primarily of RIR 16—had just sustained 579 casualties around Rouges Bancs. What XI Corps elected to do the following summer was what von Scanzoni and his staff had suspected, expected and planned for: it was thus that Fromelles became an extra-ordinarily faithful replica of Aubers. The 1915 battle is seldom assigned more than a page or two in histories of Fromelles, and indeed remains shamefully un-commemorated at the place where it was fought, yet it played a monumental role in leaving the bodies of thousands of Diggers and Tommies so intermingled in death on the battlefield, that when fighting ceased in 1918 it was frequently impossible to distinguish one from the other. The attacks of 1914, 1915 and 1917 are as inseparable as were those dead. It is also worth bearing in mind that many who *survived* both actions were to die long after the events as a direct result of the wounds they had sustained.

First and Second World War military history is perhaps unique in commonly reporting the weightiest of matters without the automatic provision of a corroborative 'enemy' narrative, a context that can only add validity and accuracy. In analogous professions, such as police or legal work, both closely related to historical research, we rely upon the fullest range of balanced impartial testimony to provide an informed evaluation, opinion and ultimately judgement.

What the Fromelles chronicle vividly states and restates is that man is fallible not only when declaring and waging war, but in its contemporane-ous reporting, and subsequent analysis and retelling. The kind of results produced by research into the several actions at Rouges Bancs may be extrapolated to any chosen event throughout the span of the Great War: in every case where German records exist, one finds alternative and frequently unexpected interpretations. This work exposes how much more there is to know and learn, and how contrast and corroboration is essential if we are not to form flawed perceptions, accept them as unchallengeable truths, and pass them on, retaining and frequently augmenting imprecision.

So where are we? The numerous fiery debates generated by the centenary suggests that we will probably never agree on the causes of the conflict, those responsible for its outbreak, whether it was right for the British Empire to join the fray, what might have happened had Britain stayed on the sidelines, if, when and how the fighting could have been brought to a swifter close, the qualities of political and military leaderships, or the long-term corollaries. Indeed, we cannot even concur on how the centenary should be commemorated. But this is hardly surprising. It is a complex issue, and we each base our perceptions and beliefs upon wisdom derived from an influential journey that incorporates nationality, education, family history, politics, class, journalism, the pulpit, and the depth of one's personal interest. The principal ingredient is probably the era into which one was born, for personal interaction with those who directly experienced the conflict surely controls how deeply one's own life and consciousness was permeated and thus affected. With that generation of men and women now vanished, it becomes more and more difficult to perceive their war—and their era of youth. Here were societies living under conditions and influenced by controls that are almost beyond our modern comprehension. In 1914 Britain, for example, only twenty per cent of the adult population were enfranchised: a formidable issue to dissect. Sadly, there are many millions in the erstwhile belligerent nations who are unaware a Great War was ever waged—and thus how the history of the 20th century unfolded and today's world assumed its form.

History, especially military history, has always been and always will be commandeered by agendas. During the Great War and for many years afterwards, the public was told what the powers-that-be wished them to know. It is the traditional approach, and continues to this day. It generally takes the form of soothing statements frequently repeated that build into a positive narrative that both justifies actions and protects individuals. But when dusty files finally emerge from murky vaults, opportunities generally arise to filter the finer reality. Combining the results of all archival sources, however, does not produce the truth: that remains forever beyond the reach of the military historian, because every man and woman who bore witness to the war experienced an individual and differing daily reality, and thus often recall and recount diverging impressions of the self-same event. As some of the evidence in this book illustrates, there cannot be a trustworthy 'common view'. Indeed, it is perhaps prudent to mistrust those who declare themselves certain, for we can neither study nor know it all.

Each fresh historical scrutiny simply provides a step along an eternal route towards better *forms* of truth. Ultimately, this is all that historians are able to produce. What readers elect to accept or decline has never been in the author's gift; their belief, approval—even tolerance—is optional. Yet the past remains and will remain the only thing from which we may learn; it survives everyone. It is primarily historians' offerings that help us understand former times and—most important of all—provide platforms upon which the teaching of subsequent generations may be based. Will those generations thank us for fingering the nettle at this exceptional moment of opportunity for historical liberation and commemoration? I think not. Some revelations may not sit comfortably, but that is of no consequence, for historians do not exist to produce work that enhances people's good opinions of themselves; history is not there to be 'liked', it is there to be learned from.

Whilst authors carry a responsibility to those who created the history of which they write, so too do curators of museums, visitor centres, and historic sites. To be successful, their task demands the same impartial and balanced approach. Let us therefore take the inheritance uniquely bestowed by the *Fasanen-Wäldchen* graves and employ it in the creation of something worthy of all those who lived, served and died during the interlaced international narrative of Fromelles 1914–1918. The village may today have its own museum and of course the Pheasant Wood Military Cemetery, but by far the most eloquent, effective and beneficial act would be a de-polarisation of the most symbolic ground of all—the site known as the Australian Memorial Park—and its conversion into a fully-interpreted Franco/Anglo/Australian/German facility that summarises the opening actions of 1914, the establishment and evolution of positional warfare in the region, the Christmas Truce, the Battle of Aubers 1915, the engagement of 1916, the Georgette Offensive of spring 1918, the liberation of the village, and the myriad small actions that were so instrumental in creating the unique character, ambience and history of the sector, and of course in forging the delicate and diverse legacies that human loss and injury eternally yields.

ACKNOWLEDGEMENTS

The author is indebted to many people of several nations for their assistance with this book. In particular I would like to thank the staff of the Hauptstaatsarchiv Kriegsarchiv in Munich: Dr Lothar Saupe, Claus Mannsbart, Christa Georgi, Gabrielle Von Guillaume, Adam Hutek, Brigitte Jakobi, Sandra Karmann, Reinhard Kirner, Hans-Joachim Döring and Renate Spiess; and the staff of the Bavarian Army Museum in Ingolstadt: Dr Ernst Aichner, Maria Simonds, Dr Christian Stoye.

My work in both these archives would have been impossible without the assistance of interpreter and translator Dr Claudia Condry, whose faculties neatly dovetailed with those of specialist translator, Mick Forsyth. My gratitude to you both.

At the archives of the International Committee of the Red Cross in Geneva, I am indebted to the director Fabrizio Bensi, and to his colleagues Daniel Palmieri, Marie Meriaux, Claire Bonnelie, Anne Cespedes and Isabelle Kronegg.

I thank Craig Tibbitts, Aaron Pegram and Anne-Marie Conde of the Australian War Memorial, and the Memorial itself for permission to use extracts from the Bean papers and other documents.

I am grateful to Roger Lee, head of the Australian Army History Unit, for his generous assistance, and to historians Nigel Steel and Jeremy Banning. I am grateful to Tim Whitford for sharing his own very personal story and observations, and to psychotherapist Maggie Lindsay Roxburgh for her invaluable assistance, insights and advice relating to the Fromelles Project.

I owe a special vote of gratitude to Victoria Burbidge, British representative for the Association Fromelles-Weppes Terre de Mémoire 1914–1918, for sharing her remarkable archival and historical knowledge of the Aubers/Fromelles sector, and for her scrutiny, analysis and collation of the mountain of data I acquired from the International Committee of the Red Cross in Geneva. And to Glen Phillips for his splendid genealogical work—a 'digger' if ever there was one.

I thank Dr Iain Banks and Dr Tony Pollard of Glasgow University's Centre for Battlefield Archaeology, with whom I have shared many a remarkable experience and from whom I have learned so much.

I am grateful to Roy Hemington and Peter Holton of the Commonwealth War Graves Commission, and indebted to the staff of its German counterpart, the *Volksbund Kriegsgräberfürsorge*. I am grateful to Richard Walsh and Rebecca Kaiser of Allen & Unwin, and to copy editor Clare James for her exhaustive attention to detail and erudite suggestions. Thanks, too, to designer Paul Hewitt for the redrawing of the Bavarian maps.

Finally, my thanks to Ward Selby whose meticulous chronicling of the frequently explosive saga of Pheasant Wood has been so helpful during the writing of this book, and of course to the detonator himself, Lambis Englezos.

The provenance of the images in this book are noted within their respective captions. My grateful thanks to all the relevant archives for granting authorisation for reproduction.

ARCHIVAL SOURCES AND SELECT BIBLIOGRAPHY

—————◆—————

Space does not allow the individual listing of every file, book or document scrutinised in British, German or Australian archives. As this volume concentrates upon the Bavarian story, I have emphasised the Munich collection. A full set of notes, plus a complete source list, Roll of Honour, and bibliography will appear later on a dedicated website along with the unedited version of the text, which will include the unabridged German reports.

HAUPSTAATSARCHIV KRIEGSARCHIV, MUNICH

Armee Oberkommando 6 (AOK 6)
Bund Ia 11a—*Nachrichtendienst* (intelligence reports)
Bund 44—Intelligence from the British front, newspaper reports, civilian material, enemy trench warfare tactics
Bunde 45–48—Secret Police
Bund 66—Enemy tactics
Bund 100—Military and civilian law and punishments, fines, populations of towns and villages, work
Bund 158—AOK 6 Quartermaster
Bund 260—Post and correspondence
Bund 261—Daily reports

Bunde 283–288—Artillery intelligence

Bunde 317–325—Aerial intelligence

(M126) 384 (96)—Actions, 1916, letters and correspondence; 16 to 31 July 1916

(M127) 385 (97)—As above, 1 to 15 August 1916

(M173) 431 (374)—Intelligence services 1a, 1 July to 31 December 1916

6th Bavarian Reserve Infantry Division (6 BRD)

Abteilung I

Bund 1—War Diary (HQ)

Bund 8—Selected reports regarding the battles of Aubers and Fromelles, plus special orders for Fromelles defences, March 1916

Bund 9 Akt 6—Kulmbach raid

Bund 10—Daily reports 1915

Bund 11—Daily reports 1916

Bund 12—Register of daily reports

Bund 13—Maps, Aubers sector

Bunde 14 to 16—Maps of the Aubers/Fromelles sectors to February 1916

Bund 17—Army and Corps orders

Bund 18—Divisional orders

Bund 19—Maps and sketches relating to patrols, plus reports, 4 April to 31 July 1916

Bund 20—Stellungsbau: Construction of defences (for the period prior to battle)

Bund 21—Battle reports, Fromelles

Bund 22—Translations of prisoners statements, Aubers era

Bund 23—Translations of prisoner statements, Fromelles era

Bund 24—Intelligence summaries, includes helpful information from entire Western Front plus relevant data from other theatres. Translations of pieces from British newspapers.

Bund 25—Construction of positions (Fromelles area) including development and design of practice grounds

Bund 26—*Pionier* material

Bund 27—Communication: light and sound signalling, dogs, pigeons

Bund 28—Aerial reconnaissance

Bund 30—Maps

Bund 31—Construction of third line of defences, plus gas warfare and railways

Bund 32—Artillery: construction and location of positions, weather, patrols, general news and enemy intelligence

Bund 72a—*Briefbuch*: letters and short correspondence, 23.3.15 to 15.1.17

Bund 72—*Briefbuch*: letters etc., 1917–19

Abteilung Ib

Bund 74—Billeting details

Bund 76—Special orders

Abteilung II

Bund 79—Secret journal

Bund 81—Exchange of letters book

Bund 89—Daily orders for divisions

Bund 94—Daily notebook

Bund 96—Cemeteries, graves and burials (German troops only)

Bund 98—Priests notes and diary, Akt 12: interpreters within the division including languages spoken

Bund 100—Civilian related material: supply of material, civilian labour, etc.

Bund 104—Losses, German only

Bund 110—Crimes against humanity and the rules of war

Bund 117—Receipts

Bund 125—Spoils (booty): captured equipment

Bund 124—General papers, telegrams

Abteilung IId

Bund 126—Enemy dispositions 1.1.16–31.7.16

Bund 128—*Wirtschaft*: accounts

Bund 138—Miscellaneous letters

Bund 139—*Stabsquartier* (HQ) report books

Bund 140—*Stabsquartier* war diaries

Bund 141—*Divisionsartz* (Medical) diary

Bund 143—Medical formations for 16, 17, 20 B.R.I.R's

Bund 144—Medical sections by area

Bund 146—Medical, including priests and dogs
Bund 147—Diseases, mental illnesses, self-mutilation, water treatment
Bund 153—Blood tests and post-mortems

Gruppenstaffelstab (part of Army Train)

Bayerisches Gruppenstaffelstab 6, Gefechtbezeichen

IV3 E/1, Bunde 8, 12 and 13—War diary, includes material on cemeteries, graves, grave markings (German only) and sawmills, etc.

IV3 F/2, Bunde 9 and 10—Letter, books, doctors reports, secret documents

IV4 B/12—Sanitation

IV4 C/14—Telephone messages and telegrams

IV4 D/16—*Ortskommandanteuren*

TITEL II

Bund 1—*Feld Intendantur*, war diary

Bund 20—*Feld Intendantur*, prisoners

AKTEN IId

Bunde 8 a and b—Messages to and from AOK 6 and Army News Office, mainly intelligence reports and general propaganda from all fronts

6th Bayerisches Reserve Infantry Division Lazarett and Sanitats Kompagnies (hospitals and stretcher-bearers)

Bund 10—*Feld Lazarett* 8 diary, menus

Bund 11—*Feld Lazarett* 9 diary, menus

Bund 12—*Feld Lazarett* 10 diary, menus

Bund 24—*Sanitats Kompagnie* 17 (all German material)

Reserve Pionier Kompagnie 6

Bund 1—War diary (entire war)

Bund 2—Appendices to war diary

Bund 7—*Forderbahnen*: trench tramways and railways

Bund 8—Maps and sketches

Bund 10—Divisional orders, January to November 1916

Bund 16—Mining (14 Infantry Brigade)

Reserve Pionier Kompagnie 7
Bund 1—*Kriegstagebucher* (war diaries, for entire war) with maps and plans
Bund 4—*Forderbahns*, including sketches, plans and drawings
Bund 6—Report books by N.C.O.'s of the day
Bund 7—Losses and graves (German)
Bund 27—Graves: designs and sketches of cemeteries and memorials (all German)

Feld Rekruten Depot—6 BRID
Bund 12—Diary

Ersatz Bataillons
Five Ersatz units were ultimately employed by 6BRIR, the 21st, 14th, 3rd and 1st. Seven large files were examined but none of these units were found to be in theatre at the time of the battle.

12th Bavarian Reserve Infantry Brigade (12th BRB), incorporating 16 and 17 Res. Inf. Regiments)
1c Bund 17/7-11—Maps, news of enemy forces, 1916/17
2ab Bund 24/3—Brigade Orders March 1916–August 1916 inclusive
2ab Bund 11—Letterbooks 15.5.16 to 12.8.16
Bund 2 Akt 4—Weekly intelligence and reports from observation posts, and report on the action of 19/20 July 1916
1c Bund 17/7-11—Maps
1aa Bund 2/4—*Beilage* (appendices) 1.7.16 to 30.9.16 (July missing)
1aa Bunds 7 and 8—*Gefechtsakten*
1b Bund 15/1a-2a—Patrols
1b Bund 18—Special orders
2ab Bund 22/3—Army orders
2ab Bund 24/3—Brigade orders 9.3.16 to 31.12.16

BRR 16
Bund 4—*Gefechtsberichte* 9.5.15
Bund 7—*Kriegstagebuch* (war diary), reports on operations (including Kulmbach and Fromelles)
Bund 8—*Anlagen* (appendices) to war diary

Bund 9—Appendices, sketches, accounts, reports

Bund 12—I Battalion war diary

Bund 14—II Battalion war diary

Bund 18—III Battalion war diary

Bund 20—Tactics, maps, orders for various battalions

BRR 17

Bund 1—*Kriegstagebuch* (war diary)

Bund 3—Appendices to 30.4.16

Bund 5—Appendices 1916

Bund 13—Plans and sketches to March 1916

Bund 14—Plans and sketches for April 1916

Bund 15—Plans and sketches for May 1916

Bund 16—June 1916

Bund 17—July 1916

Bund 18—August 1916

Bund 37—Tactics, orders, messages 1916/17

Bund 39—Patrols, etc.

Bund 40—Mining including patrols

Bunde 43, 44 and 45—Maps, sketches and aerials 1914–18

Bunde 47 and 48—Regimental orders

Bund 50—I Battalion war diary (23 books)

Bund 51—I Battalion war diary appendices

Bund 52—I Battalion orders

Bund 54—II Battalion war diary

Bund 55—II Battalion orders

Bund 56—III Battalion war diary

Bund 57—III Battalion orders

14th Reserve Infantry Brigade (14 BRB) incorporating 20 and 21 Res. Inf. Regiments

1aa Bund 1—*Kriegstagebucher* 1916 (war diaries)

1aa Bund 3—*Tagesberichter* (daily orders)

1aa Bund 4—*Gefechtsberichte* for 19/20 July 1916

Bund 11 Akt 3—*Kraftverteilung*: dispositions, garrisons and weaponry

BRR 20
Bund 1—War diary (4 books)
Bund 3—War diary appendices including trench designs
Bund 5—Tactical material, *Pionier* records, enemy patrols etc. Akt. 1: behaviour of trench garrison under heavy artillery fire; behaviour in the case of gas attack. Artillery action including concentration and number of hostile shells fired.
Bund 9—Maps, sketches and aerials
Bund 10—I Battalion, war diary
Bund 11—I Battalion, tactics and trench warfare intelligence including material from other theatres
Bund 12—II Battalion, war diary with appendices
Bund 13—II Battalion, tactics
Bund 14—III Battalion, war diary and appendices
Bund 15—III Battalion, tactics and operations
Bund 16—III Battalion, Regimental orders

BRR 21
Bund 1—War diary (3 books)
Bunde 5 and 6—Appendices for pre-July 1916 era
Bund 7—Appendices for July 1916
Bund 8—Appendices for August to December 1916, including lessons learned
Bund 11—Tactics, war experience, intelligence
Bund 12—Patrol reports, daily reports by battalion
Bund 13—Maps and sketches
Bund 14—Tactical, maps and sketches
Bund 15—Patrols, late 1916 and 1917 only
Bund 16—Operations, mainly 1917
Bund 18—Operations, 1917
Bund 22—I Battalion, war diary and appendices
Bund 23—II Battalion, war diary and appendices
Bund 24—II Battalion, appendices (1917)
Bund 26—III Battalion, war diary to 30 June 1916
Bund 27—III Battalion, war diary and appendices for July 1916 onwards
Bund 28—III Battalion, Regimental orders, all war (10 books)

Bund 29—I Battalion, orders, all war
Bunde 30 and 31—II Battalion, orders, all war

ARCHIVES OF THE AUSTRALIAN WAR MEMORIAL, CANBERRA

AWM 1DRL 0428: Red Cross wounded and missing and POW files
AWM 4: Australian Imperial Force unit war diaries, war of 1914–18
AWM 25: written records, war of 1914–18
AWM 26: Operations files, war of 1914–18
AWM 30: Prisoner-of-war statements, War of 1914–18
AWM 38: 3DRL606, Records of C.E.W. Bean: diaries, folders and notebooks
AWM 44: Official History, manuscripts, war of 1914–18
AWM 95/1316, Australian Red Cross Society: POW Department and
    Wounded and Missing Inquiry Section files, war of 1914–18
AWM 229/2 Court of Enquiry Proceedings

THE NATIONAL ARCHIVES, KEW, LONDON

WO 95 series: War diaries of British units (diaries of Australian units are
    also accessible at Kew)
Cab 45/171: List of questions upon which answers from the German point
    of view are required by the Commonwealth Historian in connection
    with the writing of the Australian Official History of the War

COMMONWEALTH WAR GRAVES COMMISSION, MAIDENHEAD

Concentration of graves (exhumation and reburials). Burial returns for the
    following cemeteries:
VC Corner
Rue-Petillon
Rue-du-Bacquerot
Rue-David
Royal Irish Rifles
Pont-du-Hem
Lille Southern

Le Trou Aid Post
Laventie
Estaires
Croix-du-Bac
Cabaret Rouge
Aubers Ridge
Tyne Cot
London Cemetery Extension (High Wood, Somme)
Terlincthun
WG 1294/3/2, Exhumation—France & Belgium general—army
exhumation staff
WG 1294 Parts 1 and 2, exhumation by IWGC—general file
WGR1—938
WGR1—500 Request for authority to exhume 15 Canadian soldiers
WGR1—558 Request for authority to exhume 16 Canadian soldiers
WGR1—938 Request for authority to exhume 7 Canadian soldiers

INTERNATIONAL COMMITTEE OF THE RED CROSS, GENEVA

Registres of lists supplied by Berlin *Zentralnachweisebüro* throughout
the war.
Associated correspondence between belligerents in CG1A document series,
including newspaper cuttings.

VOLKSBUND DEUTSCHE KRIEGSGRABERFURSORGE (VDK), KASSEL, GERMANY

Files relating to casualties, burials, recoveries, re-burials and lost graves in
the Fromelles and Aubers sectors, plus associated correspondence.

SELECT BIBLIOGRAPHY

Anon., *Fieldworks Designs, Fieldworks Plates, German Fieldworks, Mining
Notes,* unpublished Royal Engineer reference material
Anon., *Report on the Survey of the Western Front 1914–18, Appendix VIII,*
HMSO, London, 1924

Anon., *The Work of the Royal Engineers in the European War, 1914–1919*, RE Institute, Chatham, 1922 (variously titled *Military Mining, Geological Work on the Western Front, Water Supply, Supply of Engineer Stores, Experimental Work, Work under the Director of Works, Bridging, The Signal Service, Miscellaneous*, etc.)

Barnes, A.F., *The Story of 2/5 Gloucestershire Regiment, 1914–1918*, Crypt House Press, Gloucester, 1930

Barton, Peter, *The Battlefields of the First World War*, Constable and Robinson, London, 2005

Barton, Peter, *The Somme: A new panoramic perspective*, Constable and Robinson, London, 2006

Barton, Peter, *Passchendaele: Unseen panoramas of the Third Battle of Ypres*, Constable and Robinson, London, 2007

Barton, Peter, *Arras: The Spring 1917 offensive in Panoramas including Vimy Ridge and Bullecourt*, Constable and Robinson, London, 2010

Barton, Peter, Doyle, Peter and Vandewalle, Johan, *Beneath Flanders Fields*, Spellmount, Staplehurst, 2004

Bean, C.E.W., *The Official History of Australia in the War of 1914–1918*, Angus and Robertson, Sydney, various volumes, 1920–42 (Fromelles is covered in Volume III, published in 1929)

Beaverbrook, Lord, *Politicians and the War*, Butterworth, 1928

Blake, Robert (ed.), *The Private Papers of Douglas Haig, 1914–1919*, Eyre and Spottiswoode, London, 1952

Boullier, John A., *Jottings by a Gunner and Chaplain*, Charles H. Kelly, London, 1917

Bristow, Adrian, *A Serious Disappointment: The Battle of Aubers Ridge 1915 and the munitions scandal*, Leo Cooper, London, 1995

Butler, Colonel A.G., *Official History of the Australian Army Medical Services, Volume 2: Western Front 1914–1918*, Australian War Memorial, Canberra, 1940

Chidgey, H.T., *Black Square Memories: An account of the 2/8th Battalion the Royal Warwickshire Regiment 1914–1918*, Blackwell, Oxford, 1924

Cobb, Paul, *Fromelles 1916*, The History Press, Stroud, 2010

Corfield, Robin, *Don't Forget Me, Cobber: The Battle of Fromelles*, Miegunyah Press (Melbourne University Publishing Limited) 2009

Cron, Hermann, *Imperial German Army 1914–18: Organisation, structure, orders-of-battle*, Helion and Co., Solihull, 2001

Domelier, Henri, *Behind the Scenes at German Headquarters*, Hurst and Blackett, London, 1919

Downing, W.H., *To the Last Ridge*: *The World War One experiences of W.H.Downing*, Grub Street, London, 2002

Duffy, Christopher, *Through German Eyes: The British and the Somme in 1916*, Weidenfeld and Nicholson, London, 2006

Edmonds, Brigadier-General James E., *Official History of the Great War: Military operations France and Belgium 1915*, Imperial War Museum/Battery Press, London 1995

Ellis, Captain A.D., *The Story of the Fifth Australian Division*, Naval and Military Press, Uckfield, 2002

Feldman, Gerald D., *Army, Industry and Labor in Germany, 1914–1918*, Berg, Oxford, 1992

Finlayson, Damien, *Crumps and Camouflets: Australian tunnelling companies on the Western Front*, Big Sky Publishing, Newport (Australia), 2010

Graham, Stephen, *The Challenge of the Dead: A vision of the war and the life of the common soldier in France, seen two years afterwards between August and November, 1920*, Cassell and Company, Ltd., London, New York, Toronto and Melbourne, 1921

Gregory, Adrian, *The Last Great War: British society and the First World War*, Cambridge University Press, 2008

HMSO (His Majesty's Stationery Office), *Manual of Field Engineering*, 1913

HMSO (His Majesty's Stationery Office), *Manual of Field Works (All Arms)*, 1925

HMSO (His Majesty's Stationery Office), *Manual of Military Engineering*, 1905

Hancock, Edward, *Aubers Ridge*, Pen and Sword Military (Battleground Europe), Barnsley, 2005

de Halsalle, Henry, *Degenerate Germany*, T Werner Laurie Ltd, London (undated)

von Hindenburg, Field Marshal Paul, *Out Of My Life*, Cassell, London, 1920

Hirschfeld, Gerhard, Krumeich, Gerd and Renz, Irina, *Scorched Earth: The Germans on the Somme, 1914–1918*, Pen and Sword, Barnsley, 2009

Housman, Laurence, *War Letters of Fallen Englishmen*, Pine Street Books (University of Pennsylvania Press), 2002

Hulse, Captain Sir Edward Hamilton Westrow Bt., *Letters Written from the English Front in France between September 1914 and March 1915*, privately printed, 1916

Keneally, Thomas, *Australians: From Eureka to the Diggers*, Allen & Unwin, Sydney, 2011

Knyvett, Captain R. Hugh, *Over There with the Australians*, Hodder and Stoughton, London, 1918

Kronprinz Rupprecht vom Bayern, *Mein Kriegstagebuch*, Mittler, Berlin, 1929

Lee, Roger, *The Battle of Fromelles 1916*, Australian Army History Unit, Canberra, 2010

Liddell Hart, Basil, *The War in Outline*, Faber 1936

Lindsay, Patrick, *Fromelles*, Hardie Grant Books, Prahran, 2008

Lloyd George, David, *War Memoirs of David Lloyd George*, Ivor Nicholson and Watson, London, 1933–36

Longworth, Philip, *The Unending Vigil: A history of the Commonwealth War Graves Commission*, Leo Cooper, Barnsley, 2003

Ludendorff, Erich, *My War Memories 1914–18, vol.II*, Hutchinson, 1919

McMullen, Ross, *Pompey Elliot*, Scribe, Carlton North, 2002

Miles, Captain Wilfrid, *Official History of the Great War: Military operations, France and Belgium, 1916*, IWM/Battery Press, London, 1992 (two volumes)

Pedersen, Peter, *Fromelles*, Battleground Europe series, Leo Cooper, Barnsley, 2004

Prior, Robin and Wilson, Trevor, *Command on the Western Front: The military career of Sir Henry Rawlinson 1914–1918*, Pen and Sword Military Classics, Barnsley, 2004

Pritchard, Major-General H.R., *History of the Corps of Royal Engineers*, volume v, Institution of Royal Engineers, Chatham, 1952

Richards, Frank, *Old Soldiers Never Die*, Naval and Military Press, Uckfield, 2010

Robbins, Simon, *British Generalship on the Western Front 1914–18: Defeat into Victory*, Frank Cass, London, 2005

Rose, Captain G.K., *The Story of the 2/4 Oxfordshire and Buckinghamshire Light Infantry*, Blackwell, Oxford, 1920

Senior, Michael, *No Finer Courage: A village in the Great War*, Sutton Publishing, Stroud, 2004

Senior, Michael, *Haking: A dutiful soldier, Lieutenant General Sir Richard Haking, XI Corps Commander 1915–18, a study in corps command*, Pen and Sword Military, Barnsley, 2012

Sheffield, Gary, and Bourne, John (eds.), *Douglas Haig: War diaries and letters, 1914–1918*, Weidenfeld and Nicholson, London 2005

Sheldon, Jack, *The German Army on the Western Front 1915*, Pen and Sword Military, Barnsley, 2012

Sheldon, Jack, *The German Army on the Somme 1914–1916*, Pen and Sword Military, Barnsley, 2005

Smith, Leonard, Audoin-Rouzeau, Stéphane, Becker, Annette, *France and the Great War 1914–1918*, Cambridge University Press, Cambridge, 2003

Terraine, John, *The First World War, 1914–18*, Hutchinson, London, 1965

War Graves of the Empire, special edition of *The Times*, London, 1928

Ware, Sir Fabian, *The Immortal Heritage: An account of the work and policy of the Imperial War Graves Commission during twenty years, 1917–1937, with an introduction by Edmund Blunden*, The University Press, Cambridge, 1937

Whitehead, Ralph J., *The Other Side of the Wire Volume 1: With the German XIV Reserve Corps on the Somme, September 1914–June 1916*, Helion and Company Ltd., Solihull, 2010

Whitehead, Ralph J., *The Other Side of the Wire Volume 2: The Battle of the Somme. With the German XIV Reserve Corps, 1 July 1916*, Helion and Company Ltd., Solihull, 2013

Williams, John F., *Corporal Hitler and the Great War 1914–1918: The List Regiment*, Frank Cass, Abingdon, 2005

Wilson, Brevet-Major B.T., *Studies of German Defences Near Lille*, Chatham, Kent, 1919

Winter, Denis, *Haig's Command: A reassessment*, Pen and Sword Military Classics, Barnsley, 2004

Woodward, David R (ed.), *The Military Correspondence of Field-Marshal Sir William Robertson, Chief Imperial General Staff December 1915–February 1918*, Bodley Head for ARS, 1989

Wray, Christopher, *Sir James Whiteside McCay: A turbulent life*, Oxford University Press, 2002

Wynne, Captain G.C., *If Germany Attacks*, Tom Donovan Editions, Brighton, 2008

INDEX